THE PHYSICAL
PHENOMENA
OF MYSTICISM

THE PHYSICAL PHENOMENA OF MYSTICISM

by

HERBERT THURSTON

www.whitecrowbooks.com

The Physical Phenomena of Mysticism
By Herbert Thurston. First published 1952.
This Copyright © 2013 by White Crow Books. All rights reserved.

Published and printed in the United Kingdom by White Crow Books;
an imprint of White Crow Productions Ltd.

No part of this book may be reproduced, copied or used in any form
or manner whatsoever without written permission, except in the
case of brief quotations in reviews and critical articles.

For information, contact White Crow Books
at 3 Merrow Grange, Guildford, GU1 2QW United Kingdom,
or e-mail to info@whitecrowbooks.com.

Cover Designed by Butterflyeffect
Interior design by Velin@Perseus-Design.com

Paperback ISBN 978-1-908733-57-3
eBook   ISBN 978-1-908733-58-0

Non Fiction / Body, Mind & Spirit / Catholicism

www.whitecrowbooks.com

Disclaimer: White Crow Productions Ltd. and its directors, employees, distributors,
retailers, wholesalers and assignees disclaim any liability or responsibility for
the author's statements, words, ideas, criticisms or observations. White Crow
Productions Ltd. assumes no responsibility for errors, inaccuracies, or omissions.

CONTENTS

CHAPTER I: LEVITATION 1

CHAPTER II: STIGMATA 31
    Stigmata before St. Francis 31
    Were St. Francis' Stigmata Unique? 42
    The Genesis of Stigmata 54
    Stigmata and Sanctity 66
    A Stigmatization Imposture? 78
    The Case of Padre Pio 90
    Hysteria and Dual Personality 104
    Some Conclusions About Stigmata 113

CHAPTER III: TOKENS OF ESPOUSAL 123

CHAPTER IV: TELEKINESIS 135

CHAPTER V: THE LUMINOUS PHENOMENA OF MYSTICISM 155

CHAPTER VI: HUMAN SALAMANDERS 163

CHAPTER VII: BODILY ELONGATION 183

CHAPTER VIII: *INCENDIUM AMORIS* 199

CHAPTER IX: THE ODOUR OF SANCTITY 211

CHAPTER X: INCORRUPTION 221

CHAPTER XI: THE ABSENCE OF CADAVERIC RIGIDITY 257

CHAPTER XII: BLOOD PRODIGIES 269

CHAPTER XIII: THE CASE OF MOLLIE FANCHER 279

CHAPTER XIV: MORE SEEING WITHOUT EYES 309

CHAPTER XV: THE MYSTIC AS HUNGER-STRIKER 323

CHAPTER XVI: LIVING WITHOUT EATING 345

CHAPTER XVII: MULTIPLICATION OF FOOD 365

CHAPTER I
LEVITATION

1

At a time when much attention is being directed by popular writers to the manifestations of spiritualistic mediums, it does not seem out of place to recall the fact that, if we are in search of marvels, no class of materials is so worthy of study as the records of Catholic mysticism. Throughout Holy Writ, from the days of Pharao to those of Simon Magus, the position seems to be taken up that while true believers do not possess any monopoly of signs and wonders, the mighty works which they perform by the power of the Most High are in every way more stupendous than the prodigies of natural or diabolical magic with which they are placed as it were in competition. We may fairly assume that the same principle holds good in post-biblical times.

Nevertheless those engaged in psychical research, and even Catholics themselves, have so far paid but little attention to the physical phenomena of asceticism. A prejudice against the literature of the supernatural seems to have been created by the uncritical methods of hagiographers. Living themselves in an atmosphere of unquestioning faith, they have accepted and repeated without discrimination all the marvels of which they found any record, and it has rarely occurred to them that the statements of virtuous and well-meaning people are sometimes as untrustworthy as those of unscrupulous romancers.

Readers of Mr. Wilfrid Ward's biography of Cardinal Newman will recall the trouble caused in the early days of his conversion by the publication of the Oratorian series of *Lives of the Saints*. Whatever view be taken of the episode, and of the action of those concerned, it is plain beyond question that the general tone of the works translated provoked criticism, and was unacceptable to a considerable body of the Catholic clergy and laity. Apart from their inadequate literary presentment, the matter of these volumes gave offence by "the abundance of *imperfectly proved* miracles" which jarred upon English taste and seemed to smack of extravagance and sensationalism. I have ventured to italicise two words in the phrase used by Mr. Ward, for the hitch undoubtedly lay there. The English Catholic of early Victorian days made no difficulty about accepting the miraculous in the abstract, but he did not believe that miracles were things of daily occurrence, and if great demands were to be made upon his credulity he not unnaturally considered that proportionate evidence should be fortheoming. Now, taking the average Saint's Life of Italian origin, even when it is based, as is often the case, upon the depositions of the witnesses in the process of Beatification, no exact references are supplied, and no indication is afforded of the value of these sources, or of the nature of the testimony, or of the circumstances under which it was given. The marvellous event deposed to by a single witness in extreme old age who had heard the story in his youth from some third person unnamed, is set down as a fact with the same trustful confidence with which the biographer records the details attested independently by a dozen different contemporaries who had lived in daily intercourse with the Saint and had been the spectators of all his actions. In the one case as in the other the reader is left in the dark, he has to take the narrator's word for it, and if he detects, as he often may, an underlying tendency to strain every point that can be made use of for purposes of edification, it is hardly to be wondered at if the multiplication of astounding marvels leaves him unimpressed. The result is certainly unfortunate, for the evidence accumulated and relatively easy of access in the processes of beatification and canonization, printed with the sanction of the Congregation of Rites, is often more remarkable, and notably better attested, than any to be found in the Proceedings of the Society for Psychical Research.

Now, as a physical marvel, of frequent occurrence in hagiographical records, which is peculiarly suitable for investigation, I propose to take in the first instance the question of the levitation of the human body. Is it a fact that Saints, when in a state of ecstatic trance, have been lifted from the ground and have remained suspended for a notable time in mid air, without the interference of any human agency? I say that this is a matter peculiarly suitable for investigation, because the fact, if it is a fact, requires no expert evidence to attest it. The cure of a blind man, or of a cancerous growth, or even in many cases the apparent raising of the dead to life, are always apt to leave behind a certain element of uncertainty. How do we know that the man was really dead? Was the growth correctly diagnosed as malignant? What was the cause and nature of the blindness? Was the inability to see organic or merely functional? To determine these questions there is often need of the best expert evidence, and even then physicians and surgeons of the highest eminence will be the first to confess their liability to error. But given sufficient day-light and fairly normal conditions the most uneducated witness is competent to declare whether a particular person was standing upon the ground or elevated in the air, the more so because, owing to the state of trance in which the subject of the inquiry is found, it is quite possible for the witness to approach and satisfy himself by the sense of touch that the spectacle presented to his eyes is no illusion. Of course it is well known that from the days of Iamblichus, or earlier still, to those of D. D. Home the number of persons without any claim to saintship who are said to have been levitated, either by the agency of spirits or by forces magical or psychic, has been considerable. One particular instance is especially famous, as it was attested by three witnesses, Lord Lindsay (afterwards the Earl of Crawford), Lord Adare (afterwards the Earl of Dunraven), and Captain Wynne, who affirmed their absolute conviction of the genuineness of the occurrence before a committee of the Dialectical Society and at other times. On this occasion, December 13, 1868, Mr. Home is alleged to have floated out of one window on the third floor at No. 5, Buckingham Gate and in again at the furthermost window of the adjoining room. The three gentlemen mentioned were all present, but the lights were very low; one of them afterwards said that he saw what happened by the light of the moon, but as there was a new moon on December 13th, this is impossible if the date is correct. There seems no doubt, from all the accounts preserved, that the witnesses had been worked up to a high pitch of nervous excitement by Home's announcement of what he intended to do, and it must also be admitted that there are many discrepancies among the witnesses as to minor details. The late Mr. F. Podmore, who had twice discussed the evidence at some length, delivered himself on the second occasion of the following general pronouncement:

Personally I find no difficulty whatever in explaining the whole of the recorded feats of levitation, whether of Home, Gordon, Eusapia (Palladino), or Stainton Moses, as simple instances of rather crude sense deception in which the sensory data played an extremely small part. All the favouring conditions are present— a dim light, subtle suggestion on the part of the medium and a considerable degree of emotional exaltation.

Mr. Podmore was a resolute sceptic, and it seems to me that there is much more difficulty about explaining the allegations made in the case of Home's many feats of this kind than the reader would infer from the words just quoted. Nevertheless the points which Podmore makes are all good points. These feats were all performed in a subdued and uncertain light. They were all in some sense "staged "and led up to by suggestions of a rather dramatic kind. Hence the witnesses were in a state of expectant attention, and if we admit the possibility of any hypnotic influence being exerted by Home the conditions were in every way favourable.

Now what more directly concerns us here is the fact that in the levitations of the mystical order, such as we read of in the lives of the Saints, all Mr. Patmore's objections fall to the ground. Except on rare occasions these manifestations took place in full daylight.

Secondly, there was no desire on the part of the mystic to produce an impression or to attract attention to what was happening. On the contrary we have overwhelming evidence in case after case that those who were liable to these ecstasies and raptures did their very best to hide them from the eyes of men. Their humility was outraged by the notice they excited and by the veneration which was paid them in consequence. What is more, these levitations occurred, as a rule, without any warning and without the least predisposition on the part of the witnesses to expect such phenomena. If only the facts are attested by witnesses for whose good faith we can answer there seems no possible ground for resisting the conclusion that the most universal and familiar of all the physical laws which govern our material existence in this world has over and over again been suspended by some agency external to the person affected and wholly spiritual in its nature.

But before appealing to what seems to me to be the mass of good and satisfactory evidence available in this matter, let me call attention to one or two examples of a type which might easily produce a bad impression upon the inquirer and lead perhaps to the rash inference that these alleged aerial raptures of the Saints are no more than picturesque fragments of Christian mythology. Let us begin with Francis of Assisi, the most popular of Saints, and one whose type of holiness is held in veneration by hundreds of thousands of those who profess no allegiance to the Catholic Church. In the Stigmata section of the *Little Flowers of St. Francis* we read as follows concerning the happenings when the Saint allowed Brother Leo to visit him in the remoter solitude of Mount Algeria:

> And from that hour the said Friar Leo commenced to scrutinise and to consider the life of St. Francis with great purity and goodwill; and by reason of his purity, he merited to behold how many a time and oft St. Francis was rapt in God and uplifted from the ground sometimes for the space of three cubits, sometimes of four, and sometimes even to the height of the beech-tree; and sometimes he beheld him raised so high in the air and surrounded with such radiance, that scarcely could he see him. And what did this simple friar do when St. Francis was so little raised above the ground that he could reach him? He went softly and embraced his feet and kissed them with tears, saying: "My God have mercy upon me a sinner; and for the merits of this holy man, grant me to find Thy grace."

Of course this story is relatively late, and St. Francis' modern biographers—Father Cuthbert for instance—have exercised a judicious discretion in excising its more extravagant features.

Father Cuthbert tells us nothing about his being raised to the height of the beech-tree or his soaring almost out of sight, though these things are found in the Latin *Actus B. Francisco et sociorum eius*. He confines himself to the statement that "oftentimes Brother Leo ... would find him in ecstasy lifted above the earth . . . and drawing nigh timidly he would kiss the feet of Francis." But is there any real evidence that the Saint was raised from the ground at all? Certainly if such a favour was conferred upon any of God's friends we should expect the first recipient of the stigmata to have been among the privileged ones. Still presumptions cannot take the place of evidence in an inquiry like this. St. Bonaventure, writing about 1261, undoubtedly mentions that the Saint was found praying at night radiant with light and completely lifted from the ground (*toto corpora sublevatus a terra*) But St. Bonaventure, though he had been appointed to write the official biography of the founder of his Order, had never known him personally; he depended for his evidence on others, and in so much of that evidence as has been preserved to us there is no mention of levitation. The difficulty is a serious one, for such early materials are by no means scanty. We seem to be between the horns of a dilemma. Either the lifting from earth was a common feature of St. Francis' prayer or it was a supernatural favour witnessed only on rare occasions. In the former case, no doubt, we can understand better how it may have been passed over in I Celano, or in the documents represented by Sabatier's *Speculum, Perfectionis*, simply because the writers had grown familiar with this characteristic and had ceased to think of it as a wonderful miracle such as they evidently considered the Stigmata to be.

But upon this supposition how are we to explain the fact that when Gelano about 1245 set about writing a second legend, after diligent inquiry had been made in order to bring together all available material, he should still have nothing to say about the Saint's levitations in all the long chapter *De Studio Orations S. Francisci* which goes into so much minute detail? He tells us how the Saint sought out retired places for prayer or made a screen of his cloak, how in the wilds he groaned aloud and bedewed the ground with his tears, how he beat his breast with a stone, how his spirit seethed with the ardour of his love and his whole being became transformed, but no word is said which hints at his being physically raised from the ground. It is even implied that Celano knew of only one instance in which the fact that he was in ecstasy was betrayed to others. We are forced, then, to the alternative of believing that any external revelation of God's miraculous dealings with his soul was of rare occurrence, and that if Brother Leo really beheld him raised from the earth he was therein wonderfully privileged. In this case how can we suppose that he would have preserved silence when expressly appealed to, as we know he was, to supply new details for the Life of their beloved Father, or how could the information thus collected by Crescentius have failed to find a place in Celano's second *Legenda*, or in the *Book of Miracles*, or in the work of the Three Companions as far as that is traceable? The plain facts from which we cannot escape seem to be these: first, that down to 1260, thirty-four years after the Saint's death, we hear no word about any sort of physical levitation; secondly, that St. Bonaventure before 1266 states very simply that in prayer St. Francis was often radiant with light and raised from the ground; thirdly, that a later generation, certainly before 1320, declared that he soared to the tree tops and almost disappeared from view.

It is possible, even, that the story may have no better foundation than the accidental use by the early biographers of the word *suspendebatur* in a figurative sense, meaning that he was entranced. What remains clear is that we cannot demand credence for so stupendous a miracle as interference with the law of gravitation without better evidence than has so far been furnished by the surviving records of the life of St. Francis.

Curiously enough, if we turn to the history of St. Francis' great contemporary St. Dominic the case is very similar. In common with most of his modern biographers Mother Francis Raphael tells us: "Often, in rapture, he was seen raised above the ground; his hands then moved to and fro as though receiving something from God, and he was heard exclaiming, "Hear, O Lord, the voice of my prayer when I cry unto Thee, and when I hold out my hands to Thy holy temple.'" Again the same writer in relating the wonderful resuscitation of young Napoleon, the nephew of Cardinal Orsini, uses the words of Sister Caecilia, said to have been an eyewitness of the marvel: "But when he came to the elevation of our Lord's Body and held It on high between his hands, as is the custom, he himself was raised a palm above the ground, all beholding the same, and being filled with great wonder at the sight." This no doubt will appear to many a sufficiently positive and plain statement, but it stands without independent confirmation, it was not written down by Sister Caecilia herself but imparted to her amanuensis some sixty years after the event, and, as M. Jean Guiraud points out, "the document requires some modifying; there is a tendency towards exaggeration and the marvellous." On the other hand we have to take account of the sober, convincing and infinitely precious depositions made by the intimate friends and fellow religious of the Saint as early as 1233, twelve years after his death. They are not chary of details regarding his wonderful devotion in prayer. More than one of them had watched him by stealth when he spent the best part of the night in the church. They tell us about his groans and sighs, his intense fervour and his penitential exercises, but there is no word which suggests that he was ever seen by any of them raised from the ground, or that there was any tradition among his first companions that this was known to have happened. The same silence is maintained by all the early biographers. It was only some fifty or sixty years later in Thierry d'Apoldia, Sister Caecilia and Stephen of Salhanac that we first find an account of these marvellous upliftings.

Much the same difficulty occurs in the case of a third great ascetic and founder of a religious Order, St. Ignatius Loyola. Bartoli beyond doubt narrates how at Barcelona in 1524 the Saint was seen more than once raised four or five palms from the ground while he breathed forth the most burning aspirations of love, and the whole room was filled with a dazzling light. Moreover this statement rests upon the deposition of Juan Pascual in the process of Canonization, and other testimony was given by the Jeromite nuns of Barcelona concerning similar raptures before the altar of St. Matthew. Still here again the evidence cannot be called satisfactory, for Pascual was then a very old man deposing to events which happened in his early youth, while the nuns could only testify to the facts at second hand. In the case of St. Francis Xavier, who is said to have shared the same privilege as his master Ignatius, the evidence is in some ways rather better, but once more it is noteworthy that we find nothing about these raisings from the ground in the affidavits of the sixty witnesses or so who gave evidence at Goa, Cochin, Bacaim, and Malaca in 1556, four years after Xavier's death. They had all known him personally and had repeatedly assisted at his Mass, but no startling levitations, it would seem, had ever taken place in their presence. But in the later inquiries which were held in 1616 there was a good deal of evidence of this kind, though it is only fair to say that other scenes of the great Missionary's labours were now for the first time introduced into the cause. From these various examples we must, it seems to me, draw the conclusion that the evidence for levitation in the case of some very eminent Saints is far from satisfactory.

No doubt the absence of adequate proof does not by any means imply that this mark of the divine favour was never enjoyed by them, but we cannot appeal to such cases if we wish to convince a sceptical opponent of the truth of the phenomenon. But, to my thinking, the most satisfactory example of this phenomenon is to be found in the case of St. Teresa, the great reformer of the Carmelite Order, in whose life we shall, I think, meet with evidence of a very different character. To begin with we have St. Teresa's own testimony in the matter. It is contained primarily in Chapter xx. of the Life written by herself. Speaking of the difference between Union and Rapture, the Saint tells us that rapture is absolutely irresistible. "It comes, in general, as a shock, quick and sharp, before you can collect your thoughts, or help yourself in any way, and you see and feel it as a cloud, or a strong eagle rising upwards and carrying you away on its wings." That the Saint is speaking not merely of the fact that the spirit is torn away violently from its sense perceptions and is overpowered by the trance, but also of the physical elevation of the body into the air, is made plain by what follows:

LEVITATION

I repeat it; you feel and see yourself carried away you know not whither. For though we feel how delicious it is, yet the weakness of our nature makes us afraid at first... so trying is it that I would very often resist and exert all my strength, particularly at those times when the rapture was coming on me in public. I did so, too, very often when I was alone, because I was afraid of delusions.

Occasionally I was able, by great efforts, to make a slight resistance, but afterwards I was worn out, like a person who had been contending with a strong giant; at other times it was impossible to resist at all; my soul was carried away, and almost always my head with it—I had no power over it—*and now and then the whole body as well, so that it was lifted up from the ground.*

The meaning of the words I have italicized cannot possibly be mistaken. After this St. Teresa goes on to make reference to an incident which is probably the same as one mentioned by her biographer Yepes. Bishop Alvaro de Mendoza was giving Communion to the nuns at their *comulgatorio* (i.e. the aperture in the wall of the choir through which they received Communion) when the Saint was suddenly rapt in ecstasy and, being irresistibly lifted up from the ground above the height of the aperture, she was in consequence unable to communicate. At any rate she herself tells us:

This (the being lifted up into the air) has not happened to me often: once, however, it took place when we were all together in choir, and I, on my knees, on the point of communicating. It was a very sore distress to me; for I thought it a most extraordinary thing and was afraid it would occasion much talk; so I commanded the nuns—for it happened after I was made Prioress— never to speak of it. But at other times, the moment I felt that our Lord was about to do the same thing again, and once in particular during a sermon—it was the feast of our house, some great ladies being present—I threw myself on the ground; then the nuns came round to hold me; but still the rapture was observed.

I made many supplications to our Lord, that He would be pleased to give me no more of those graces which were outwardly visible; for it was a grievous affliction to me that people should make so much of me, and because His Majesty could honour me with His favours without their becoming known. It seems that, of His goodness, He had been pleased to hear my prayer; for I have never been enraptured since. It is true that it was not long ago.

In the same chapter the Saint speaks of the efforts she had made to resist these ecstasies, and especially their physical effects. The whole is too long to quote, but I may call attention to such detached sentences as the following:

> It seemed to me, when I tried to make some resistance, as if a great force beneath my feet lifted me up ... I confess that it threw me into great fear, very great indeed at first; for in seeing one's body thus lifted up from the earth, though the spirit draws it upwards after itself (and that with great sweetness, if unresisted), the senses are not lost; at least I was so much myself as to be able to see that I was being lifted up.... After the rapture was over, I have to say that my body seemed frequently to be buoyant, as if all weight had departed from it, so much so that now and then I scarcely knew that my feet touched the ground.

One thing remains quite clear from this description and from the whole chapter, and that is that St. Teresa, being perfectly conscious of the physical effect of levitation produced on many occasions by these raptures, persistently fought against all such exterior manifestations which betrayed her privileged condition as a friend of God and made her appear singular. The same attitude of mind, as we shall see, was conspicuous in many of the other great mystics who enjoyed similar favours. Secondly, it is to be noted that there can be no possible doubt that we have here the actual words and thoughts of St. Teresa herself. I have before me, as I write, the facsimile edition of the Saint's own autograph copy; the same, in fact, as was submitted to the censors of the Inquisition during her life-time. We find reproduced in this volume her own characteristic handwriting extending over four hundred pages, together with a facsimile of the *censura*, a highly favourable judgment, of Father Domingo Banes, the inquisitor who in 1575 examined the volume and subscribed his name. Thirdly, it is well to bear in mind that after 1566, when this autobiography was completed, the Saint's raptures, as she on more than one occasion stated, became notably less frequent, though they did not entirely cease. But in any case after that date the external manifestations which betrayed these ecstatic conditions to others were few and far between. This will help to explain the comparatively small number of witnesses who in the episcopal inquiries, antecedent to the process of beatification and canonization, were able to depose that they had with their own eyes beheld the Saint raised from the ground in ecstasy. The taking of these *informationes* was only begun in 1595 or 1596, thirteen years after the death of Teresa and thirty years after the writing of the book from which we have been making extracts. If, as she implies, her raptures in public had at no time been frequent, it could hardly be expected that many of the actual eye-witnesses would then be surviving to give their testimony. None the less, evidence of a reliable kind was not lacking, and I may conclude this present article by quoting one or two specimens. For example, Sister Anne of the Incarnation at Segovia in her deposition, made like the rest under oath, states:

> On another occasion between one and two o'clock in the daytime I was in the choir waiting for the bell to ring when our holy Mother entered and knelt down for perhaps the half of a quarter of an hour. As I was looking on, she was raised about half a yard from the ground without her feet touching it. At this I was terrified and she, for her part, was trembling all over. So I moved to where she was and I put my hands under her feet, over which I remained weeping for something like half an hour while the ecstasy lasted. Then suddenly she sank down and rested on her feet and turning her head round to me she asked me who I was and whether I had been there all the while. I said yes, and then she ordered me under obedience to say nothing of what I had seen, and I have in fact said nothing until the present moment.

This is a perfectly simple and straightforward piece of evidence. The incident happened in broad daylight, there could have been no anticipation of any supernatural manifestation of the sort, no subtle suggestion. The Bollandists, giving references, declare that several witnesses deposed to similar instances. Bishop Yepes, who knew her well, recalls in his *Vida de Santa Teresa* another occasion when the Saint, struggling against an ecstasy which came on just after she had received Communion, made a desperate clutch at the bars of the grille as she was rising in the air and in great distress of mind cried to God, "Lord, for a thing of so little consequence as is my being bereft of this favour of Thine, do not permit a creature so vile as I am to be taken for a holy woman." On another occasion, he goes on, when a rapture suddenly came upon her in choir, she clutched at the mats (*esteras*) on the floor and was raised up into the air with them still in her hands. Marie de San Jose, another contemporary and friend of the Saint, declares in certain manuscript notes, still unprinted, which Mir has examined, that Mother Maria Baptista had on two different occasions seen her beloved superior raised from the ground. But the whole case is very much strengthened by the large number of other holy ascetics besides St. Teresa of whom similar and much more wonderful levitations are recorded upon quite trustworthy evidence.

2

The importance of her case lies in the fact that not only was she seen by others raised in the air, but that she herself bore witness to the reality of these levitations. At the same time no one who has studied her life and writings will be disposed to question either her good faith or her excellent common sense. It is equally clear that all self-advertisement was remote from her thoughts. If she wrote any account of her raptures, this was only to help others and in entire submission to the judgment of her spiritual directors. St. Teresa's mystical experience and intellectual gifts were so exceptional as to lend special weight to her utterances, but it is worth while pointing out that she is not the only one who has left a description of these physical upliftings written from the point of view of the subject who experienced them. Here, for example, is an extract from a letter of Suor Maria Villani, a famous Dominican nun in the seventeenth century, herself a candidate for beatification:

> On one occasion [she informs her director] when I was in my cell I was conscious of a new experience. I felt myself seized and ravished out of my senses, and that so powerfully that I found myself lifted up completely by the very soles of my feet, just as the magnet draws up a fragment of iron, but with a gentleness that was marvellous and most delightful. At first I felt much fear, but afterwards I remained in the greatest possible contentment and joy of spirit. Though I was quite beside myself (*benche stavo fuora di me*), still, in spite of that, I knew that I was raised some distance above the earth, my whole body being suspended for a considerable space of time. Down to last Christmas eve (1618) this happened to me on five different occasions.

As Suor Maria went on to inform her confessor that she had obtained the grace from heaven that these favours should not become known to others, and as satisfactory evidence is lacking that she was ever seen uplifted from the ground, we are bound to receive this statement with a certain amount of caution. Even so illustrious a Saint as Mary Magdalen de'Pazzi had curious illusions as to her physical remoteness from earth when in the trance state. She shouted at the top of her voice when a question was addressed to her by a bystander, and then was heard saying to herself "they can't hear me down there; it is too far off." On the other hand this great mystic was beyond doubt in some way exempt from ordinary physical laws.

> She went [writes her confessor, Father Cepari] with incredible swiftness from one place to another, mounting and descending the stairs with such agility that she seemed rather to fly than to touch the earth with her feet. She sprang securely on to the most dangerous places, as when, on the feast of the Invention of the Cross, May 3, 1592, she ran into the choir and without human help or any sort of ladder leapt on to the cornice . . . the height of which from the floor is about fifteen *brachia* (i.e., about 30 feet) whilst in breadth it is not more than the third of a *braccio*. From this, she with perfect safety took down the crucifix and having unfastened the figure from the cross she placed it in her bosom, clasped it to her and then brought it to the nuns to kiss, and taking off her veil, wiped it as though it had been covered with sweat, actions which in such a situation would have made anyone else's brain reel.

St. Mary Magdalen de'Pazzi has left no description of her feelings or degree of consciousness in the state of ecstasy. But another Saint, St. Philip Neri, who was her contemporary, and who undoubtedly on many occasions was seen raised from the ground at Mass and at other times, seems to have given some measure of confidence to his beloved disciple Father Gallon. At any rate this Father, writing only five years after Philip's death, states that "he (Philip) afterwards explained on one of these occasions that it seemed to him as if he had been caught hold of by someone and in some strange way had been lifted by force high above the ground." The accounts given by Gallon, Baca and the other biographers leave the impression that, like St. Teresa, Philip resisted these raptures to the utmost of his power, but was not always successful in foreseeing and forestalling them.

So far as regards the law of gravitation in itself, it does not greatly matter whether an ecstatic is raised above the ground three inches or thirty feet, and we have as much reason to be impressed if such an incident happens once as if it happened fifty times. Still it is very natural that a flight to the tree tops or to a distance of many yards, especially if the experience be several times repeated, should be more widely bruited abroad than the manifestations we read of in the lives of St. Philip or St. Teresa. Hence when Mr. Andrew Lang and other students of psychic phenomena discuss the subject of mystical levitations it is nearly always St. Joseph of Copertino to whom they make appeal in this connection. Certainly, if we may trust the published narratives of his Life, his is by far the most astounding case of levitation of which we have any record. It would be impossible to give a detailed account of his elevations and flights, which seem to have been observed on more than a hundred different occasions. It is possible, however, that there may be considerable exaggeration in what the witnesses tell us of an incident at the Rosella friary near Copertino, thus related by his biographer Pastrovicchi. It occurred when a Calvary was being erected there by the friars.

> Two crosses were already placed, but ten persons with united effort could not raise the third which was 54 palms high (about 36 feet) and very heavy. On seeing this, Joseph, full of ardour, flew about eighty paces (70 yards) from the door of the friary to the cross, lifted it as easily as if it were a straw, and placed it in the hole prepared for it. These crosses were the object of his special devotion, and from a distance of ten or twelve paces, he, drawn by his crucified Saviour, would rise to one of the arms on the top of the cross.

I think that there may well be a good deal of exaggeration here, not only from the astounding nature of the incident in itself, but also from the fact that, though reference is made to the depositions taken at Nard in the process of beatification, the witnesses do not seem to have been eye-witnesses. Moreover, as the Saint left Copertino in 1638, never to return, the Calvary must have been erected some thirty years—probably more—before this evidence was given. Such an interval leaves plenty of time for all sorts of legends to grow up, which soon become, in a quite uncritical atmosphere, a matter of implicit faith. More credence may be given to the stories related of the Saint during his sojourn at Assisi (1639-53).

When, in 1645, the Spanish Ambassador to the Papal Court, the High Admiral of Castile, passed through that town he visited Joseph of Copertino in his cell. After conversing with him he returned to the church and told his wife "I have seen and spoken with another St. Francis." As his wife then expressed a great desire to enjoy the same privilege, the Father Guardian gave Joseph an order to go down to the church and speak with Her Excellency.

To this he made answer "I will obey, but I do not know whether I shall be able to speak with her." In point of fact no sooner had he entered the church than his eyes rested on a statue of Mary Immaculate which stood over the altar, and he at once flew about a dozen paces over the heads of those present to the foot of the statue. Then after paying homage there for some short space and uttering his customary shrill cry he flew back again and straightway returned to his cell, leaving the Admiral, his wife and the large retinue which attended them speechless with astonishment.

Now this story is accompanied in the biographies both of Pastrovicchi and of Bernini with a great array of references to the depositions in the process, and it is expressly stated that these were made by witnesses "de visu" who had been actual spectators of the scene. Still more trustworthy is the evidence given of the Saint's levitations at Osimo, where he spent the last six years of his life. There his fellow-religious saw him fly up seven or eight feet into the air to kiss the statue of the Infant Jesus which stood over the altar, and they told how he carried off this wax image in his arms and floated about with it in his cell in every conceivable attitude. On one occasion during these last years of his life he caught up another friar in his flight and carried him some distance round the room, and this indeed he is stated to have done on several previous occasions. In the very last Mass which he celebrated, on the festival of the Assumption, 1663, a month before his death, he was lifted up in a longer rapture than usual.

For these facts we have the evidence of several eye-witnesses who made their depositions, as usual under oath, only four or five years later.

It is very difficult to believe that they could have been deceived as to the broad fact that the Saint did float in the air, as they were convinced they had seen him do, under every possible variety of conditions and in many different surroundings.

It is much to be regretted in the case of St. Joseph of Copertino that the printed record of the process of canonization, or at any rate that portion of it known as the *Positio super dubio de Virtutibus* with its *Summarium*, is a book of extraordinary rarity. It has recently been stated that only two copies are known to survive, still there can be no doubt that the record exists, and what lends it a quite remarkable importance is the fact that Prosper Lambertini, afterwards Pope Benedict XIV, who is the supreme authority on evidence and procedure in canonization causes, had personally studied all the details of the case. When the cause came up for discussion before the Congregation of Rites, he was *Promotor Fidei* (popularly known as the Devil's Advocate), and his "animadversions" upon the evidence submitted are said to have been of a most searching character. None the less we must believe that these criticisms were answered to his own complete satisfaction, for not only was it he himself who, when Pope, published in 1753 the decree of Beatification, but in his great work *De Servorum Dei Beatifications, etc.*, he speaks as follows:

> Whilst I discharged the office of Promotor of the Faith the cause of the venerable Servant of God, Joseph of Copertino came up for discussion in the Congregation of Sacred Rites, which after my retirement was brought to a favourable conclusion, and in this eye-witnesses of unchallengeable integrity gave evidence of the famous upliftings from the ground and prolonged flights of the aforesaid Servant of God when rapt in ecstasy.

There can be no doubt that Benedict XIV, a critically minded man, who knew the value of evidence and who had studied the original depositions as probably no one else had studied them, believed that the witnesses of St. Joseph's levitations had really seen what they professed to have seen. It is also certain, as Mr. Lang points out that these witnesses made their depositions upon oath at Osimo, Assisi and other places in 1665-6, that is to say only two years after the Saint's death.

For another great ecstatic, St. Peter de Alcantara, of whom marvellous flights are recounted by his biographers, it must be frankly admitted that no very satisfactory evidence is at present producible. Brother John of Santa Maria, the author of the earliest detailed history of his life and work, printed his book in 1615, whereas the Saint had died in 1562, fifty-three years earlier.

St. Teresa had seen him once rapt in ecstasy, but though her words imply something more than an ordinary trance, she does not explicitly say that he was lifted from the ground. Still it is to my thinking incredible that in the atmosphere of austerity and truth which surrounded the early years of St. Peter of Alcantara's reform, a quite baseless legend can have grown up regarding his flights through the air. It is stated by all his biographers that in choir he was sometimes seen raised fifteen feet or more above the floor until his head touched the roof. On other occasions he soared like a bird to the top of the trees, or was projected through narrow doorways like an arrow from a bow, or again flew up with arms outspread to embrace a crucifix on a high eminence. The very details given (for example, of the startling cry, creating terror rather than devotion in those present, with which, as in the case of St. Joseph of Copertino, these extraordinary flights began) do not seem likely to have been invented for purposes of edification.

St. Peter of Alcantara in Spain died a whole century before St. Joseph of Copertino died in Italy, and yet in many features, though not in all, their aerial raptures show a close correspondence.

Undoubtedly the best confirmation of such marvellous incidents as those just spoken of lies in the fact that trustworthy evidence of other elevations, the same in character though possibly less in degree, is available in the Beatification processes of numerous other Saints of more recent date. The printed volumes containing these records are not very readily met with here in England, but I may illustrate from one or two processes which are accessible to me the kind of testimony which they supply.

A rather striking illustration, which we have lately come across, of the necessity for caution in dealing with these marvels calls for notice here. It occurs in the published Life of the Venerable Anthony Margil, a holy Franciscan missionary in Mexico and Guatemala, who died in 1726. The Life professes to be founded entirely on the depositions taken in the process of beatification and it was compiled at Rome by the official Postulator of the Cause who must, of necessity, have been intimately acquainted with the available evidence. One would, therefore, be disposed to regard the statements of fact contained in it as exceptionally trustworthy, and almost as though they were covered by the papal decree printed at the end of the volume which declares Father Anthony Margil to have practised all Christian virtues in a heroic degree. In an engraving prefixed to the Life a portrait of Father Margil may be found in which he is represented floating in the air together with a devout client, and although a closer inspection reveals that this picture has reference to an alleged miraculous escape from the Indians which took place after the holy man's death, the casual reader can hardly fail to find in it some connection with the many levitations attributed to him in his life-time. Of these the biographer speaks in the following passage:—

> A soul which was so inflamed with the love of God could not fail to be constantly absorbed by celestial delights and ravished out of itself in the ecstasies which are the ordinary privilege of Christ's holy servants. Of these happy transports he had familiar experience, and very often it happened that his soul in the vehemence of its flight towards God carried with it heavenwards the dead weight of the body, so that he was actually raised from the ground. Father Simon de Hierro, who was long his companion, deposed to having seen him many times in great raptures while he prayed.
>
> Maria Treio watched him praying at Adaes five or six inches above the earth, and John de Armiso saw him in the same district raised nearly a foot in the air while he was saying Mass. In Mexico on one occasion, having been admitted into the convent of the Poor Clares to hear a sick nun's confession, he was lifted a couple of feet from the floor as he exhorted his penitent to practise conformity with the divine will. Rose de Rivera in the same city related that more than once the good Father, on passing through her garden and meditating on the perfections of God who had created such beautiful flowers, began to cry out: "Wonderful! wonderful!" and as he said this his whole body was raised from the ground. Further it was there also, in the great priory dedicated to St. Francis, that Brother Jerome Garzia, early one morning, when he was calling the religious to rise for Matins, felt a violent draught blowing through the choir and apparently coming from the direction of the church tower. Looking to discover the cause, he found the servant of God raised in the air with arms extended in the form of a cross, gyrating round and round with incredible velocity. In Guatemala Father Joseph Paniagua saw him radiant with celestial glory, while John of Jesus Surraine Birriesa, having had occasion one night to look for him in the church, found him there suspended so high above the ground that the skirts of his habit brushed the intruder's head. Moreover, the same witness, on another occasion, whilst serving his Mass, having noticed that the whole altar was shaking after the consecration, raised his eyes to the celebrant and saw that he was lifted a foot and a half from the predella. He was so dazed by what he had witnessed that the holy priest when he came out of his ecstasy

had to bang his hand against the altar to rouse his server to attend to his duties.

Now it happens that by an unusual chance the British Museum possesses a copy of the three volumes of the Positio super Virtutibus for the beatification of Father Margil, containing the Summarium and the argumentation based thereupon; in other words, we have in these volumes so much of the depositions of the original witnesses as is ever printed for the use of the consultors of the Congregation of Rites. A comparison of the biography with the sources upon which it is based thus becomes possible and proves to be curiously instructive. To begin with, the Father Simon de Hierro, referred to in the above extract as long the companion of Margil, gave evidence himself at Mexico in 1757, thirty-one years after the death of the holy missionary. He spoke in the most enthusiastic terms of the Father's spirit of prayer, of his untiring zeal, of the austerity of his life, of his deprivation of sleep, etc., but not one word in this deposition suggests that Father Margil ever had ecstasies or was seen raised from the ground. What we do find, however, is that before the "Apostolic" Commission some years later when Father Hierro himself was dead, two witnesses declared that they had heard Father Simon Hierro say that Father Margil had frequent ecstasies and was sometimes lifted up into the air. In other words, this intimate friend and companion of the holy man is represented as bearing witness to things which, when he was himself being examined and upon his oath, he never ventured to affirm. And the whole evidence for the levitations proves to be of this character; it is either mere hearsay or, on the face of it, untrustworthy. For example, it is true that Maria Treio and John de Armiso are stated to have witnessed these upliftings in the air, but they never made any such deposition themselves. They had apparently died before the inquiry took place. All we know is that one Marcus Martinez, a witness who was nearly eighty years of age, deposed in 1778 that he had heard them say so; he did not remember when or where. But perhaps the most surprising testimony is that of John of Jesus Surraine Birriesa, who is so complacently cited at the close of the extract translated above. It is true that he professed to report facts of which he had himself been an eye-witness, but he gave his evidence at Guatemala in 1771, forty-five years after Father Margil's death, and, as the *Summarium* expressly informs us, Birriesa was at that date *ninety-five years old*. Neither was the old man content with declaring that in serving Father Margil's Mass he had beheld him raised in the air, he stated in his deposition that while thus elevated he saw upon his head a crown of thorns with blood trickling from it, all which disappeared when the Father came to himself and continued the Mass. Though there were some forty witnesses examined in the first "ordinary " process held at Guadalasara and Guatemala within twenty years of the missionary's death, not one of them suggested at that time that any levitation phenomena had been seen or heard of in connection with Father Margil.

The only hint of anything of the sort appears in the statement of a Father, who had acted as his confessor, to the effect that after the consecration of the Mass he flushed deeply and trembled so violently that he seemed to be struggling to prevent himself from rising in the air. Obviously this evidence proves nothing. The same convulsive movements after the elevation were noted in a holy and well-known religious priest who died in London very recently. Unquestionably Father Anthony Margil, though apparently he has not yet been beatified, was a man of most saintly life and of apostolic zeal, and it is quite possible that he may sometimes have been raised from the ground. At the same time, after a very careful study of the depositions, we must point out that there is nothing in the testimonies adduced which justifies such a conclusion. With the single exception of the statement of the nonagenarian Birriesa, every one of the incidents recounted in the above extract depends upon hearsay evidence given long after the event.

St. Bernardino Realino, S.J., died at Lecce in Southern Italy in 1616. In the inquiry held at Naples in 1621, Signor Tobias da Ponte, a gentleman of rank and high character, deposed upon oath that in the year 1608 or thereabouts he came to Lecce to ask the spiritual help of this venerable and holy priest. It was, said the witness, a Saturday in April after Easter. The Father's door seemed to be closed to visitors, and accordingly Signor Tobias took a seat in a lobby which was just outside his room. As he sat with his eyes on the room door, he noticed that the door was not completely shut and that through the aperture a certain glow or radiance of light was streaming. This appearance puzzled him and he began to wonder whether there could be a fire within.

Accordingly he drew near and pushed the door a little further open in order to peep into the room. Thereupon he perceived Father Bernardino in a kneeling attitude before his *prie-dieu*, his face turned towards heaven, his eyes closed and his whole body lifted a good two and a half feet above the floor (sin aria *sollevato da quattro buoni palmi sopra*), while, rapt in ecstasy as he was, he kept repeating these words:

Gesu Maria state in mia compagnia. The witness then described the feelings of reverence mingled with fear which led him, after gazing for a while at this spectacle, to slink away home like a culprit, though he had time to notice again the radiance which streamed from the room through the partly opened doorway.

So far I have summarized the report, but now I translate textually:

> Being asked to take good heed and bethink himself whether all that he had described was not rather an hallucination or fancy of his brain and whether the radiance and light he had seen was not a reflexion of the sun's rays or an ocular deception or some other natural effect, he answered: "The thing was so clear, unmistakable and real, that not only do I seem to see it still but I am as certain of it as I am of speaking now, or of seeing the things around me. ... I noticed the light coming through the doorway not only once, but twice, thrice and four times, before the shadow of any such idea occurred to me. And so I began to debate with myself how there could be any fire in the room, since the rays which issued from it could only be caused by a great fire, just as when the blacksmiths at their forge are hammering the red-hot iron on the anvil, and so I stood up on purpose and pushing open the door I saw with my own Eyes Father Bernardino raised from the ground as unmistakably as I now see your Illustrious Lordship. . . ." And being again admonished and bidden to be careful not to be led by any mistaken sense of devotion to exaggerate or to represent the facts otherwise than as they really were, because the saints had no need of such perverse championship, but on the contrary are displeased thereby, and being asked again whether any part of his statement needed modification, he replied: "What I have deposed is the whole, pure and unvarnished truth, without fiction or exaggeration, and it seems to me a small matter in comparison with the sanctity, virtue and miracles of Father Bernardino."

The witness was further questioned as to the situation of Father Bernardino's room, and he seems in reply to have given precise and satisfactory details.

Now I am unable to say how far this account is representative of the usual handling of witnesses in the episcopal process of inquiry—the proceedings are not generally reproduced in the summaries so fully as this is—but even one such specimen may be sufficient to show that these investigations were entered upon with a serious purpose of arriving at the actual facts. In the case, therefore, of biographies which are founded upon the beatification processes of the last three centuries, it seems to me that the statements made are not lightly to be set aside, even when precise references to the printed page are not given. It is impossible to discuss the subject adequately in a few words, but I may mention as a personal impression that in looking through the score or two of such printed processes as are accessible to me I have found very little trace on the part of witnesses or commissioners of a desire to manufacture evidence of marvels. If such a tendency occasionally betrays itself, the Promotor of the Faith in his *Animadversiones* is not afraid to draw attention to it in the frankest terms. This restraint is especially noteworthy in the witnesses de visu who gave evidence in the "Ordinary" processes held within a few years of the Saint's death. The witnesses in the "Apostolic" processes of later date who could testify to nothing at first hand, but only related the stories they had heard from others, or the traditions prevalent in the locality, are in some instances obviously inclined to exaggerate.

So far as the fact of levitation is concerned, the case of St. Bernardino Realino is not exactly a strong one. As the *Promotor Fidei* pointed out in his animadversions, the Signor Tobias da Ponte, whose evidence I have quoted, was the only witness who claimed to have actually seen him raised in the air. Still the *Postulator Causa*, replying to this criticism, showed that there was good confirmation in other directions. Father Anthony Beatillo, who gave evidence in a different place and on a different occasion, told the whole story independently, having heard it several years before from the same Signor Tobias, a fellow-countryman and friend of his, to whose character he paid a very high tribute. His report accurately tallied with da Ponte's first-hand account.

Moreover a number of witnesses deposed to the brilliant and supernatural light which had many times been seen to radiate from Father Bernardino's countenance while in prayer, though on these occasions he had not been raised from the ground.

It is disappointing not to have access to the processes of those ascetics who like St. John Joseph of the Cross, O.S.F., St. Gerard Majella C.SS.R., St. Martin Porres, O.P., or Blessed Dominic of Jesu Maria, O.C.D., have been specially conspicuous for their aerial raptures. One would like, for example, to see the terms of the depositions upon which rests the story of St. John Joseph's experience in Naples Cathedral. A few years before his death (1734), when the old man could only get about with the aid of a stick, he ventured to mingle in the dense crowd which came there to venerate the blood of St. Januarius. In returning from the altar rails his stick was knocked out of his hand, and without this he was helpless. Accordingly he turned to his dear San Gennaro and begged him to come to his aid. On this he found himself lifted up in the crowd and without touching the ground he was carried right out of the door of the cathedral. There he sat down on the levitation steps, and when a friend of his, the Duke of Lauriano, asked him what was the matter, he replied merrily: "Nothing, only I have lost my steed." The Duke offered him his carriage, but the old man answered, "No, no; it will come, the stick will come." Pushing his way into the building the Duke soon after perceived that there was immense excitement among the crowd, who were shouting, *Miracolo, miracolo*, and looking up he saw the Saint's stick moving through the air a foot and a half above the heads of the people. Then the stick floated out of the church and bumped against its owner, who clutched it and set off home to rescue himself from the over zealous veneration of those who surrounded him.

One would be inclined to dismiss such a tale as pure fable from beginning to end, if it were not that there seems to be good evidence that St. John Joseph was himself on very many occasions seen raised in the air, sometimes a few inches, sometimes five or six feet, and once to the roof of the church, while in 1728 he took part in a procession, making believe to walk, but in fact, we are assured, carried through the air in ecstasy a distance of two miles, half a foot or more above the ground.

It would be impossible to call attention here to even a tithe of the stories, more or less similar in character, which meet us in our hagiographical records. Dominic of Jesus Maria, whose name was mentioned above, is said to have been raised above the ground in the presence of King Philip II of Spain and his Queen, and in that state of ecstasy to have complied with the mental commands of His Majesty, to whom the Saint's superior temporarily committed his own authority. On another occasion the same holy Carmelite when rising in the air was caught hold of by a sceptical witness who believed these ecstasies to be a trick. The critic was carried up along with the Saint, and becoming afraid, loosed his hold, so that he fell to the ground and was severely injured. Blessed Tommaso da Cori, O.S.F., falling into an ecstasy when he was giving Communion in the church at Civitella, rose to the roof so swiftly that the congregation thought he must have broken his head against the rafters, but after a short interval he sank gently back to earth, holding the ciborium safely in one hand and a particle between the thumb and forefinger of the other. He also on one occasion was raised up horizontally from his bed into the air during his last sickness. In the case of Blessed John Massias, a Dominican lay-Brother, who used to pray in the church at night rapt in ecstasy, a novice entering in the dark was frightened to death by coming into contact with the Brother's legs and feet as he hung suspended in the air. But of similar incidents there is literally no end. In the imperfect and limited inquiry which I have had time to make, I have taken note of the names of something over two hundred persons alleged to have been physically lifted from the ground in ecstasy. In about one-third of these cases there seems to me to be evidence which, if not conclusive, is to say the least respectable. This, however, does not at all mean that the other two-thirds are to be rejected as mythical, but only that no adequate testimony to the fact is at present within reach. Many are mediaeval cases recorded by writers long posterior in date.

They may have had good evidence before them, or they may have repeated or invented a quite baseless story. St. Dunstan may have been, as his legend reports, lifted up, chair and all, as he was delivering an address from his episcopal throne, but we cannot ignore the fact that in the earliest of our biographies the incident seems only to occur as an interpolation. On the other hand there can be little doubt that St. Richard of Chichester did actually discover his friend St. Edmund, Archbishop of Canterbury, raised from the ground in ecstasy as he was praying in his chapel, while the evidence for St. Catherine of Siena's levitations seems quite overwhelming. A large proportion of the reputed cases of aerial rapture only occur as brief entries in the menologies of the religious Orders. Data are in most cases wanting which would enable us to criticise or control the facts, but occasionally some scrap of evidence comes to light which proves that the claim thus made fully deserves to be treated seriously. I may quote in illustration the case of the great theologian Father Francis Suarez, a man of very holy life, but not of such saintliness as calls for recognition on the altars of the Church. With regard to Father Suarez a paper still exists couched in the following terms:

> I, Brother Jerome da Silva, S.J., hereby certify that I have written this document by order of my confessor, Fr. Anthony de Morales, and that the same Father has commanded me to give it to no one, nor to let it be read, but to keep it closed in an envelope with an endorsement absolutely forbidding anyone to open it until after the death of Father Francis Suarez.

The writer then goes on to explain that he has adopted this course because his confessor directed it, and because he himself, being in feeble health, is not likely to live long. The document gives an account of two occasions when the Brother found Father Suarez in ecstasy. It will be sufficient to transcribe the second incident.

Another day at the same hour—it was about two in the afternoon—Don Pedro de Aragon (the Rector of the University of Salamanca) asked me to request Fr. Suarez to be good enough to go with him to the monastery of Santa Cruz. As the Father had bidden me summon him whenever this gentleman called, I went up at once. Across the door of his room I found the stick which the Father usually placed there when he did not wish to be interrupted. Owing, however, to the order I had received I removed the stick and entered. The outer room was in darkness.1 I called the Father but he made no answer. As the curtain which shut off his working room was drawn, J saw through the space left between the curtain and the jambs of the door a very great brightness. I pushed aside the curtain and entered the inner apartment. Then I noticed that a blinding light was coming from the crucifix, so intense that it was like the reflexion of the sun from glass windows, and I felt that I could not have remained looking at it without being completely dazzled. This light streamed from the crucifix upon the face and breast of Father Suarez and in this brightness I saw him in a kneeling position in front of the crucifix, his head uncovered, his hands joined, and his body in the air lifted three feet above the floor on a level with the table on which the crucifix stood. On seeing this I withdrew, but before quitting the room I stopped bewildered, and as it were beside myself, leaning against the doorpost for the space of three Credos. Then I went out, my hair standing on end like the bristles on a brush, and I waited, hardly knowing what I did, beside the doorway of the outer room. A good quarter of an hour later I heard a movement within, and the Father, coming to take the stick away, saw me standing there.

I then told him that the gentleman was waiting. He asked me why I had not let him know. I answered that I had come to the inner room and called him but that he had not replied. When the Father heard that I had entered the inner room, he seized me by the arm, made me come right inside again, and then, clasping his hands and with his eyes full of tears, he implored me to say nothing of what I had seen, at any rate as long as he lived. On my part I asked permission to consult my confessor. To this he readily consented, for my confessor was also his. My confessor advised me to write this account in the form above explained, and I have signed it with my name, because all that it contains is the simple truth. And if it should please God that I die before Father Francis Suarez, those who read this may believe it as if they had seen everything with their own eyes. Otherwise if our Lord should will that Father Suarez die first, I shall be able to confirm the whole on oath so far as may be necessary.

—Jerome da Silva.

No one, I think, will be disposed to regard this piece of evidence as contemptible, but it is obviously a mere chance that any such record has been preserved to us. Without it, it would have been natural to assume that any talk of aerial transports in Suarez's case was just a pious fable unworthy of serious attention. As a matter of fact, from the point of view of the student of psychic phenomena, not a few of the most interesting cases of alleged levitation are to be found in the lives of mystics who have never actually been beatified. I have no room to go into detail, but by way of illustration I may draw attention to the curious experiences of Maria Agreda and of Passitea Crogi. In the former case we are told that the famous author of the *Mystica Ciudad de Dios* made such efforts to resist her ecstatic levitations that she vomited blood.

When she discovered that she had been made a show of by her nuns when in the trance state, and that her veil had been removed in order that curious strangers might be able to see the expression and radiance of her face, she declared she would rather have sat in the pillory. Bishop Samaniego, who knew her intimately, gives the following account of her ecstasies:

> The raptures of the servant of God were of this nature. The body was entirely bereft of the use of the senses, as if it were dead, and it was without feeling if violence was done to it; it was raised a little above the ground and as light as if it had no weight of its own, so much so that like a feather it could be moved by a puff of breath even from a distance. The face was more beautiful than it normally appeared; a certain pallor replaced the naturally swarthy hue. The whole attitude was so modest and so devout that she seemed a Seraph in human form. She frequently remained in this state of ecstasy for two or even for three hours.

Of Passitea Crogi, a Sienese Capuchin nun who died in 1615, her biographer, a learned professor of Arabic, who manifests a quite unusual sense of the value of evidence, writes as follows:

> According to the violence of the ecstasy she was lifted more or less from the ground. Sister Felice deposed that she had seen her raised three braccia. Sister Maria Francesca more than four braccia and at the same time that she was completely surrounded with an immense effulgence of light. This lasted for two or three hours. On one occasion at Santa Fiora in the house of the Duchess Sforza, when she was present with a crowd of other people, Passitea was surprised by a rapture, under the influence of which she remained raised from the ground at the height of a man. The Duchess, who was a witness of the occurrence, caused an attestation of the fact to be drawn up, which was signed by all present.
>
> We are also told that she was often transported from place to place without moving her feet and without touching the ground. Thus in an expedition she undertook with Suor Diodata on a muddy day, when the latter was covered with mire Passitea reached her journey's end without a speck.

Lastly I may note in concluding that these alleged levitations are not merely experiences of past and remote ages. They may be somewhat less frequent among the mystics of modern times but they still go on. The Carmelite nun of Pau, a Syrian by birth, Sister Mary of Jesus Crucified, who died in 1878, is stated by her biographer to have soared up in the air to the top of a lime tree, and when she was bidden by her Superior to come down she left in her hasty descent one of her sandals in its topmost bough, where on search being made it was espied the next day. Gemma Galgani, who being born in 1878 died in the odour of sanctity in 1903, was also lifted above the ground in ecstasy, so at least her confessor, who was also her biographer, declares. Finally I may note the curious experience of a still more recent ecstatic who died in 1912. One of her fellow-religious, Suor Maria Prassede, delle Crocifisse Adoratrici, in a letter of June 3, 1913, writes:

> I was still a novice and on those last occasions when Suor Maria della Passione was able to come down to the choir to receive Holy Communion, the Rev. Mother Superior bade me take her back to

her cell, because, as she was so ill, she had to return to bed almost immediately after Communion was given her. Well, no sooner had we left the choir together than I noticed that the servant of God, though she was in a most suffering state, mounted the stairs in an instant, as if she flew on wings, while I, though I was in perfect health, could not keep pace with her; so much so that it seemed to me that she never touched the ground but that she really flew up the flight of stairs which led to her cell.

Assuming, then, that we have reasonable ground for crediting the fact of levitation, there remains the question of its possible explanation. Theologians for the most part offer the rough and ready solution that in the case of holy people it is a manifestation of divine power, effected perhaps through the ministry of angels; but that in such cases as those of Simon Magus, sorcerers, and spiritualistic mediums, it is the work of the devil. Without venturing to reject this explanation outright, I find certain difficulties, too complex to summarize here, which suggest that it would be wise to suspend our judgment. I may confess that as regards the levitation of material objects (e.g., heavy dining-room tables) without contact, the spiritualistic evidence seems to me quite convincing, and if a table can be suspended in the air, it is hard to see why a man cannot. Sir Oliver Lodge adumbrated a spiritistic theory to explain these phenomena, Professor Charles Richet a materialistic one. They attribute strange activities to the ether, to teleplasm, to cryptaesthesia, etc., but it seems to me that in the present state of our knowledge we cannot even decide whether the effects observed do or do not transcend the possible range of what may be called the psycho-physical forces of nature. Perhaps it would be well to explain that levitation cannot be put forward as one of the miracles required either for beatification or canonization. That is to say, such a phenomenon, if well attested, would be accepted as corroborative evidence for the existence of an heroic degree of virtue in the subject, but the decree declaring that the Servant of God practised virtue in an heroic degree is not sufficient for beatification. It is necessary that, in addition, miracles worked after death should be satisfactorily proved in attestation of his sanctity.

Further, although it is commonly held that the Bull of Canonization imposes upon the faithful the duty of believing that the Servant of God so honoured is in the enjoyment of eternal bliss, no immunity from error attaches to the historical statements occurring in the Bull regarding the facts of his life or his alleged miracles.

In the *Quarterly Journal of Science* for Jan. 1875, and in Imbert-Gourbeyre *La Stigmatisation* (1894) II., p. 239, a list is given of levitated Saints, but in neither case is any attempt made to distinguish between well-attested and unsatisfactory examples. I set down here the names of twenty such ecstatics not mentioned in the text, choosing by preference those that are less widely known. It would be easy to make a list of treble the length. The date added to each is the year of death. I have also given a reference in each case to sources where further particulars may be found. "AA.SS." stands for the Bollandist collection of the *Acta Sanctorum*; "Process, *Summario*" for the summary of evidence found in the official *Positio super Virtutibus* submitted to the Congregation of Sacred Rites. Mediaeval examples, and such famous modem Saints as St. Alphonsus Liguori, etc., have been passed over.

Bd. Nicholas Factor, 1583 (Moreno, Vida, pp. 128-9).

Bd. Andrew Ibernon, 1602 (Process, *Summario*, pp. 319, 324-5, 331)

Bd. Gaspar de Bono, 1604 (P. A. Miloni, *Vita*, pp. 76-7).

Bd. Juan di Ribera, 1612 (V. Castrillo, Vita, p. 92).

St. Alphonsus Rodriguez, 1617 (AA.SS. Oct. Vol. xiii, p. 622).

Bd. Lorenzo da Brindisi, 1619 (B. da Coccaglia, *Ristretto*, pp. 136, 196).

Veronica Laparelli, 1620 (Process, *Summario*, pp. 138, 141).

St. Michael de Santis, 1625 (N. della Vergine, Vita, pp. 45-9, 56).

St. Peter Glaver, 1654 (J. M. Sol&, *Vida*, pp. 323, 389, 390).

Bd. Bernard da Corleone, 1667 (B. Sanbenedetti, Vita, pp. 63, 72).

Maria Minima Strozzi, 1672 (Vita, p. 19).

Juana de la Encamacion, 1705 (L. J. Zevallos, *Passion de Christo*, pp. 23-4).

Bd. Bonaventura Potentini, 1711 (AA.SS. Oct. Vol. xii, p. 154).

Bd. Francisco de Posadas, 1713 (V. Sopena, *Vita*, pp. 43-4).

Angiolo Paoli, 1720 (T. Cacciari, *Vita*, p. 147).

St. Pacifieus di San Severino, 1721 (Melchiorri, Vita, p. 73).

Bd. Angelo di Acri, 1739 (AA.SS. Oct. Vol. xiii. pp. 661, 673).

Clara Isabella de Fumariis, 1744 (Process, *Summario*, p. 103).

Gertrude Salandri, 1748 (Vita, an anonymous but admirable biography, pp. 220-4).

St. Maria Francesca delle Cinque Piaghe, 1791 (B. Laviosa, Vila, p. 52).

Andrd Hubert Fournet, 1821 (Process, *Summario*, pp. 376, 395, 396, etc.).

J. B. Cottolengo, 1842 (Process, *Summario*, pp. 411, 412, 416).

CHAPTER II
STIGMATA

1

STIGMATA BEFORE ST. FRANCIS

In turning to the most familiar and most widely debated of the physico-psychic manifestations here under discussion, we are met at the threshold of our inquiry by a question of fact to which it seems desirable to devote the whole of the present chapter.

Was St. Francis of Assisi the first ascetic who bore impressed upon his body the wound marks of our Lord's sacred passion? Until within recent years the answer returned by writers of all schools would have been unhesitatingly in the affirmative, but lately a difficulty has been raised on this point, and it seems to me that the doubt deserves a somewhat more patient and sympathetic treatment than has been accorded to it by such writers as Father Michael Bihl or A. M. Koniger.

The occasion for these later developments in the discussion was furnished by the publication in 1910 of a monograph by Dr. J.Merkt of Tubingen University which may still be regarded as the most serious attempt to explain from a rationalist standpoint the problem of St. Francis' stigmata. That such marks were borne by the Saint in the last days of his life and were observed in his dead body our critic does not dispute. He affirms, however, that the wounds did not date back, as the biographers of Francis commonly allege, to the vision of the Seraph in September 1224, but appeared only a few weeks before his death (October 3, 1226); also that they were little more than discolorations or abrasions of the skin, not fissures penetrating the flesh of the hands or feet; and further that scars or ecchymotic spots of this nature might easily be produced, and probably were, in fact, produced, by purely pathological conditions, given a subject whose thoughts were almost uninterruptedly concentrated upon the marks of our Saviour's passion.

All this, however, had equivalently been said by earlier writers like Karl Hampe, Georges Dumas, Paul Sabatier, and others. That which specially distinguished Dr. Merkt's treatment of the problem was the stress laid by him upon the fact that already before the date of the vision of the Seraph certain Christian mystics in the west were familiar with the idea of a physical reproduction of the wounds of Christ in their own flesh. St. Paul, of course, had written of himself (Galat. vi. 17) "I bear the marks (stigmata) of the Lord Jesus in my body," and there is some evidence that a rather literal interpretation of the words had begun to prevail among commentators in the twelfth century. But be this as it may, we cannot ignore the fact that two and a half years before the earliest date assigned for St. Francis' stigmatization, attention was drawn to the case of a religious enthusiast who showed the marks of Christ's wounds in hands, feet and side. Whether he was a fanatic, or even an impostor, does not greatly matter to our present inquiry. The noteworthy point is that the first notion of a "stigmatic" (*i.e.*, a person marked with the *stigmata*) was not derived from what is recorded of St. Francis himself. Moreover, there are two other slightly different but more or less contemporary cases, which cannot be so accurately dated. It is, to say the least, highly probable that these also originated independently of the Franciscan tradition. However we look at it, these are facts, or at any rate allegations, which cannot be ignored in any discussion of the phenomenon of stigmatization, and it is curious that on both sides so little attempt has hitherto been made to investigate the historical evidence involved.

The first and best authenticated example of a pre-Franciscan stigmatic is cited by Dr. Merkt from the Chronica Major a of Matthew Paris, who, under the year 1222, makes an entry in the following terms:

> In this same year, a few days before the Council held at Canterbury [this is apparently a slip of the pen for Oxford] by Stephen (Langton), Archbishop of Canterbury, a man was taken up who had in his body

and in his limbs, that is to say in his side, his hands and his feet, the five wounds of the Crucifixion. Together with him in the same Council there was presented a person of double sex, viz., an Hermaphrodite, who was under the same delusion as the first (*eiusdem erroris quo prior fuit obcaecatus*) along with an accomplice of his own. Being convicted of this error and confessing their guilt they, were punished according to the sentence of the Church. Similarly, also, a certain apostate, a deacon, who from a Christian had become a Jew, was likewise penanced in due legal form. Whereupon Falco (Fawkes de Breaute) at once had him arrested and hanged.

Although this account is not very clear, there can be no doubt that it is fairly correct in the main, and the date in particular is beyond dispute. The strange thing is that neither Dr. Merkt nor his numerous critics have apparently thought of seeking further information regarding this interesting case from the pages of the other English chroniclers. Several of these mention the incident, and there are good reasons for believing, as we shall see, that they are likely to be more trustworthy than the lively but by no means too accurate historian of St. Albans.

Let us begin with the *Dunstable Annals*, the compiler of which, Prior Richard de Morins, seems to have written up his narrative year by year from 1210 to 1241. He had assisted at the Council of the Lateran in 1214, and it seems highly probable that in some capacity he would have been present at the Provincial Council of Oxford. He does not tell us much of the stigmatic who was sentenced, but what he says is to the point. After speaking of the apostate deacon, who, it appears, was burnt to death, not hanged, the Dunstable Annals continue:

> Another deacon, on account of theft, underwent degradation. Furthermore, a certain woman who made herself out to be the Blessed Virgin, and a certain young man who made himself out to be Christ, and had perforated his hands and side and feet, were immured at Banbury (*immurati sunt apud Bannebirre*).

This record, entered upon the page in which we now read it in the same year in which the incident happened, must be regarded as evidence of a very high order. With this also agrees the brief note in the *Waverley Annals*, also a contemporaneous entry, to the effect that "a certain rustic who used to crucify himself (*qui se crucifigebat*) was imprisoned for life." More detail is vouchsafed us by Thomas Wykes, who, though not exactly a contemporary, wrote in that very monastery of Osney in which the Oxford Council held its sittings. Moreover, Thomas Wykes, as his editor tells us, "must always be looked on as one of the most interesting and most trustworthy historians of his time." His account of the apostate deacon who was burnt is more detailed than that of any other chronicler, after which he goes on:

> There was presented in the same Council a certain countryman, a layman, whose madness was such that he caused himself to be crucified, to the dishonour of the Crucified One, declaring that he was the Son of God and the redeemer of the world. By the sentence of the Council he was incarcerated, and being shut up for the rest of his life and fed only on hard bread and water, he ended his days in confinement.

The fullest account of our supposed stigmatic is, however, that supplied by Ralph, Abbot of Coggeshall in Essex, who was an undoubted contemporary and whose authority as a chronicler stands high. As his narrative breaks off abruptly in 1224, and as he is believed to have resigned his office as Abbot in 1218 through infirm health, there is every reason to suppose that his account of the year 1222 was committed to writing shortly after the events described. In accord with the other more reliable annalists he tells us that the apostate deacon was burnt, and then he continues:

> There was also a misbelieving young man brought up before the Council, together with two women, who were all charged by the archdeacon of that district with the grievous crime of infidelity. The young man was arraigned because he refused to enter a church or to be a participator in the sacred rites (*nec divinis interesse sacramentis*), or to pay heed to the admonitions of his Catholic father, and because he allowed himself to be crucified, bearing five wounds on his body which still could be plainly seen, and also because he encouraged these women to call him Jesus. One of the women, who was elderly, was accused of having for a long time been given up to evil incantations and of having by her magic arte brought the young man aforesaid to this atrocious pitch of madness. These two, in consequence, being found guilty of this grave offence, were ordered to be confined within two walls until they died. But the other woman, who was the young man's sister, was set at liberty because she made known their impious procedure.

The later historians add little except obvious errors—I may mention in illustration the statement in Ralph Higden that the young man after sentence of death passed by Holy Church was nailed to a cross at Abirbury—but one other contemporary chronicle, that of Barnwell near Cambridge, supplies a few more details which are not without interest. After stating that the young man's hands, feet and side were perforated, the writer adds that there were wounds also "upon the head," corresponding no doubt to the punctures of our Saviour's crown of thorns. Then he goes on:

> There was also taken up with him a woman who induced people to call her Mary, mother of Christ, changing her own proper name. This person gave out that she was able to celebrate Mass, and the fact was confirmed by certain evidence they discovered in the shape of a chalice and paten of wax, which she fabricated for such a purpose. On these two offenders the Council inflicted punishment according to their deserts, ordering that they should be immured within stone walls until death released them.

In the light of the details thus collected from various sources, all of them seemingly independent, we are forced to conclude that the youth was either a lunatic or a cunning rogue, but most probably a mixture of the two. The refusal to have anything to do with Church or Sacraments proves him to have been fundamentally in conflict with the whole religious system of the age in which he lived. We hear nothing from contemporaries of his setting up as a moral reformer, but the wish to have veneration paid him as Jesus, while his elderly companion figured as Mary, his mother, could never be regarded as otherwise than blasphemous by an educated Christian of the Middle Ages. Without some strain of madness, no one, least of all an illiterate rustic, could have persuaded himself in good faith that he was giving honour to God by persisting in such a role. Dr. Merkt's supposition of an intensely devout mystic hounded to death by a tribunal of worldly ecclesiastics whose vices he rebuked is thus effectually excluded. On the other hand there can apparently be no doubt as to the existence of the wounds, or scars, in hands, feet and side. The curious phrase, used more than once, that "he permitted himself to be crucified," seems rather to suggest that he had by some expedient made perforations in his feet and hands, that he kept these open, and that on occasion he allowed nails to be passed through them and driven into the wood of a rough-hewn cross. We are not told whether there was any foot-rest to the cross he used, but if there were, and he simply stood upright upon his pierced feet, there seems no physical impossibility that such a position, even with outstretched or upraised arms, should be maintained for some hours. On the whole, then, the evidence in this English case points to some sort of contortionist's or mountebank's trick which took a religious colour chiefly because the ideas and interests of that age centred round religious themes. On this supposition we cannot greatly blame Stephen Langton and his fellow bishops if they regarded the whole performance as an irreverent, not to say blasphemous, mockery of all that Christians deemed most sacred.

If this explanation of the Oxford incident be accepted as probable, we have clearly to do with something very different from the stigmata of St. Francis of Assisi. None the less the case does prove that men's thoughts were at this period much occupied with the wounds of our Saviour and with the possibility of a literal imitation in a living body of this aspect of His Passion. The two other cases of apparent stigmatization to which Dr. Merkt directs attention are vaguer and notably less well attested than that just cited. The first is known to us only through a passage in Stephen de Bourbon's *Tractatus*, a collection of edifying stories for preachers. Stephen, an eminent Dominican, who wrote about 1246, tells us of a certain Robert, Dauphin of Auvergne, whom he calls Marquis de Montferrand. After explaining that Robert had been unjustly suspected of heretical leanings on account of his collection of Albigensian books, he adds:

> This man many years before his death had borne upon his body the marks (stigmata) of the Lord Jesus as a reminder of His Passion and of the fidelity due to Him. Along with other penances which he performed in memory of our Lord's Passion he pierced his flesh every Friday with certain nails so far even as to draw blood (*cum quibusdam clavis carnem suam singulis sextis feriis usque ad sanguinis effusionem configebat*).

As Robert died in 1234, Dr. Merkt seems justified in his contention that the phrase "many years before his death" would naturally take us back to a period earlier than the stigmata of St. Francis. And this is the more likely because Robert is represented as being phenomenally old (antiquissimm atatis). No man, however holy, is likely to take up such a practice of mortification as a septuagenarian or octogenarian, and

Robert's virtue, at any rate in his early life, was not without its flaws. His collection of books seems to have been largely acquired by pillaging the neighbouring religious houses, so much so that Pope Celestine III. in 1193 wrote to the Archbishop of Bourges directing him to excommunicate Robert if he did not mend his ways. On the other hand it is not quite clear that the word stigmata means anything more than the scars of bodily penances in general, e.g., disciplines, spiked girdles and such like, but certainly the use of nails is suggestive. If the scars, however, were stigmata in the modern sense, they must in Robert's case beyond doubt have been self-inflicted.

The third example appealed to by Dr. Merkt is that of Blessed Dodo, a Praemonstratensian monk, of Hascha in Frisia. The account is to be found in the short Latin biography we possess of him, but the author of this is unknown, neither is there any quite satisfactory evidence that he was a contemporary. The passage with which we are concerned runs as follows:

> In the year 1231, on the Sunday after our Lady's Annunciation, Brother Dodo, a man of blameless life and conduct, was killed under the wall of an old ruin which fell upon him. For five years previously he had led a monastic and solitary life in this spot serving God and our Lady by day and night amid grievous bodily macerations, and so he ended his life as a sort of martyr by God's act and in union with God. Now when he had been crushed to death under the stones of this old sanctuary, they discovered that there were open wounds in his hands and in his feet and in his right side after the fashion of the five wounds of our Saviour. These, perchance out of sympathy with his crucified Lord, he carried for many years so that he could truly say with Paul, "I bear the marks of the Lord Jesus in my body." But down to the day of his death this was hidden from everyone, save from God alone, who knoweth all things.

Here again we have no certainty about the date, but I must own that if we accept the statements of our only authorities as reliable, Dr. Merkt seems justified in regarding this case of stigmatization as earlier than that of St. Francis. Thomas of Cantimpré describes the hermit Dodo as a very old man (*valde longava Mate provectus*). Now if he merited this description when he died in 1231, he must already have been old in 1224, and the experience of later centuries shows that in nearly all the recorded cases the stigmata have manifested themselves for the first time either in youth or in middle life. St. Francis himself was not quite forty-two at the time of the apparition of the Seraph. With regard to the nature of the phenomenon in Dodo's case we have, of course, nothing to guide us, and consequently the question whether the wounds were self-inflicted, or due to pathological causes, or were miraculous in origin, must be left unanswered.

As we are not here concerned to defend any thesis, but simply to sift the evidence, we must recognize candidly the possibility that in a good many instances the wounds were consciously or unconsciously produced by the subject himself. However little we may be disposed to admit that the physical phenomena of mysticism can be reduced to hysteria, still it cannot be disputed that the ecstasy of the mystic and the trance of the hysterical patient are very closely allied and cannot always be readily distinguished. The mimetic tendencies of the hysterical diathesis are the commonplace of all writers on the subject. On the other hand there is nothing more extraordinary in the accounts which have been preserved to us at all periods of the contemplatives who in a state of rapture follow the successive stages of our Lord's sacred Passion, than the dramatic instinct with which each scene is portrayed in their own persons. And in many cases it is not merely the part of our suffering Redeemer which is enacted, but, in some sense simultaneously, the cruelty and violence of those who tormented Him as well as the horror and the compassion of His friends. Let me illustrate the point from the account preserved to us of two ecstatics who lived in the latter half of St. Francis' own century.

About the year 1275 Philip, Abbot of Clairvaux, wrote a description of the marvellous things observed in the ecstasies of Elizabeth, a Cistercian nun of Herkenrode near Liège. She was marked with the stigmata, lived, it seems, in an almost continual state of trance, but, what was most remarkable of all, she used to enact in the course of each twenty-four hours the whole history of Christ's Passion, beginning at Matins in the middle of the night with the arrest of our Lord, and ending at Compline with His deposition in the tomb. Abbot Philip, who was sceptical about these occurrences until he came and saw for himself, lays stress upon the fact that the nun "at one and the same time represented the person of our Lord who was suffering and of the persecutor or executioner who was tormenting, the person of our Lord while He submits Himself, and of the persecutor while he pushes, drags, smites or threatens." Thus he tells us how, when Elizabeth was contemplating some stage of our Lord's ignominious progress from one tribunal to another, catching hold of the bosom of her own dress with her right hand she would pull herself to the right and then with the left hand she would drag herself in the opposite direction. At another time, stretching out her arm and raising her fist threateningly, she would strike herself a violent blow on the jaw so that her whole body seemed to reel and totter under the impact; or again, while her feet remained planted and motionless, she would pull herself fiercely by the hair until her head struck the ground. Similarly bending back all her fingers except an outstretched forefinger she would aim it at her eyes as if she meant to gouge them out, while at other stages writhing, as it seemed, in agony upon the floor, she beat her head against the ground over and over again. But the most frequently recurring feature in this ill usage of herself was the shower of blows which, when lying on her back in the trance state, she rained upon her breast with extraordinary force and violence. The spectacle greatly impressed the onlookers, but it is not easy to explain or to fit in with the rest of the representation of the Passion. Abbot Philip was able, it seems, to make a close examination of the stigmata in Elizabeth's hands, feet and side. He, with other abbots and monks who were in his company, saw the blood several times spurting from these open wounds, and also from her eyes and from beneath her nails, which last manifestation he explains by supposing that our Saviour's wrists may have been so tightly bound as to cause a similar haemorrhage. But now let us turn to the even more curious case of the nun Lukardis of Oberweimar, who was apparently born about 1276 and who died in 1309. An unusually full account of her mystical experiences is preserved to us in a Life composed by some anonymous religious who knew her well and who apparently wrote shortly after her death. Like Elizabeth of Herkenrode, Lukardis was subject to constant ecstasies and received the stigmata at an early age. But long before the stigmata manifested themselves she had adopted certain practices which must inevitably have helped, one may think, to facilitate their development. Thus her biographer tells us:

> Also with regard to the hammering in of the nails of Christ's cross, as she carried the memory of it inwardly in her heart so she represented it outwardly in action. For again and again with her middle finger she would strike violently the place of the wounds in each palm; and then at once drawing back her hand a couple of feet (*ad distantiam unius cubiti*) she delivered another fierce blow in the same spot, the tip of her finger seeming somehow to be pointed like a nail. Indeed,

though it appeared a finger to sight and touch, neither flesh nor bone could be felt in it and those who had handled it declared that it had the hardness of a piece of metal. When she struck herself in that way there was a sound (*tinniebat*) like the ring of a hammer falling on the head of a nail or on an anvil. On one occasion a person in authority thinking this kind of blow was a sham or a mere trick, in order to find out the truth put his hand in the way. But when she had struck but once he hastily drew back his hand, declaring that if he had waited for a second blow he would have lost the use of it forever. With the same finger, at the hour of sext and again at none, the servant of God used to strike herself violently on the breast where the wound came. The noise that she made was so great that it echoed through the whole convent, and so exactly did she keep to the hour of sext and none in this practice that the nuns found the sound more trustworthy than the clock.... Furthermore, it should be noted that the Servant of God, before the stigmata appeared, endeavoured, out of her great longing, to open the places of the wounds in her feet by boring them, as it were, with her big toe (*sua majori pedica quasi fodiendo*).

No doubt all this sounds very extravagant, and we may suspect the writer of a good deal of exaggeration, but the account abounds with psychological touches which are borne out by what we know of other similar ecstatics. Moreover, it is plain that the last thing the biographer dreamed of was to cast any doubt upon the supernatural character of her mystical experiences. He tells us quite plainly that these practices had been persisted in for two years before the stigmata showed themselves, but he nevertheless narrates how the wounds eventually developed as the result of a nocturnal vision. A most beautiful and delicate youth, who was himself marked with the stigmata, appeared to her and pressed her right hand against his right hand saying, "I wish thee to suffer along with me." To this she gave consent, and on the instant in her own right hand a wound was formed. About ten days later the left hand was similarly marked, and in course of time the feet and side. We are further told that at first Lukardis, "fearful of vain glory and the adulation of men," hid the wounds by wearing something in the nature of gloves, but afterwards she was supernaturally admonished to allow the marks to be seen "for the glory of God and the devotion of the faithful." The wounds, as in the case of so many other stigmatics of later times, bled regularly on Fridays, but not seemingly on other days. On the Friday in Easter week they hardly showed at all (*vix apparebant eius vulnera*), but on the Friday which followed they began to be conspicuous again "because she of her own accord had been solicitous to revive them" (*quia ea per se studuerat renovare*).

It will not, I trust, for a moment be supposed that the conclusion to be drawn from these facts is that in all cases of stigmata the wounds must be held to have been consciously or unconsciously self-inflicted. Such an inference, in my opinion, would be very rash, and, as I hope to show, quite unjustified by the evidence available. But whilst we may vigorously dissent from the arguments of such writers as Merkt and Hampe when applied to the stigmatization of a St. Francis, it must also be admitted in fairness that cases of self-infliction are not a *priori* impossible, and that consequently each example requires to be scrutinized narrowly and judged upon its own merits. As the example of Elizabeth of Herkenrode shows, the very vividness of the dramatic realizations of the trance state may lead the ascetic quite unconsciously to maltreat himself, and there is no reason in the nature of things why the boring of the hands or feet should not occur as spontaneously as the buffeting of the face or the beating of the body. Perhaps some of the incidents which so often recur in the lives of the Saints, when after a night of prayer the limbs of the man of God are found almost dislocated and his shoulders black and blue, should not be too confidently attributed to the agency of demons, but may possibly be explained as an intensely dramatic realization of the outrages endured by our Saviour at the hands of the executioners who so cruelly beat and tortured Him.

2

Were St. Francis' Stigmata Unique?

Whether St. Francis was or was not the first in time to bear upon his body the marks of our Saviour's wounds, there can be no possible dispute as to the immense impression which this marvel produced upon the minds of contemporaries. The keynote is struck in the letter which Brother Elias sent to the Provincial of France, and probably to other Provincials, immediately after the death of the Saint.

> And this said [so Elias wrote] I announce to you great joy, even a new miracle. From the beginning of ages there has not been heard so great a wonder, save only in the Son of God, who is Christ our God. For, a long while before his death, our Father and Brother appeared crucified, bearing in his body the five wounds which are verily the Stigmata of the Christ; for his hands and feet had as it were piercings made by nails fixed in from above and below, which laid open the scars and had the black appearance of nails; while his side appeared to have been lanced, and blood often trickled therefrom.

Thomas de Celano, or whoever was the author of the *Book of Miracles*, equally describes this portentous event as something unheard of since the world began, and the fame of it was not long in reaching all parts of Christendom, when it was enshrined in such popular chronicles as those of Vincent of Beauvais and Matthew Paris (i.e., Wendover). Of course one of the earliest references to St. Francis' stigmata now preserved to us is that contained in the following note written by the hand of Brother Leo beside the blessing which his beloved Father Francis traced for him over his own name:

> The Blessed Francis, two years before his death, kept a Lent in the hermitage of the Alverna in honour of the Blessed Virgin Mary, Mother of God, and Blessed Michael the Archangel, from the feast of the Assumption of St. Mary the Virgin to the feast of St. Michael in September. And the hand of the Lord was laid upon him. After the vision and speech he had of a seraph, and the impression in his body of the Stigmata of Christ, he made these Praises which are written on the other side of the sheet, and with his own hand he wrote them

out, giving thanks to God for the favour that had been conferred on him.

The authenticity of this priceless memorial of the Saint is now, practically speaking, uncontested, and we cannot too strongly emphasize the fact that Brother Leo himself in this autograph note not only vouches for the reality of the stigmata, without, however, describing them in detail, but also expressly assigns their appearance to the forty days' retreat on Mount Alverna "two years before his death." With regard to the nature of the stigmata our main source of information is Thomas of Celano, especially in his first Life of the Saint. This, which was written at earliest two years, and at latest four years, after the death of Francis, had been undertaken by the express command of Pope Gregory IX. The importance which Celano attached to the stigmata is apparent from the concluding sentences of the Life, in which he relinquishes the plural of authorship and recurs to the first person singular used in his prologue. "For the love of the Poor Man who died upon the cross and by His sacred wound-marks which blessed Francis bore in his body, I beseech all who read or hear this story to be mindful before God of me the sinner who wrote it." In this *Vita Prima* the description of the stigmata runs as follows:

> And while he (Francis) continued without any clear perception of its meaning (i.e., the vision of the seraph), and the strangeness of the vision was perplexing his breast, marks of nails began to appear in his hands and feet, such as he had seen a little while before in the Man crucified who had stood over him. His hands and feet seemed pierced in the midst by nails, the heads of the nails appearing in the inner part of the hands and in the upper part of the feet and their points over against them. Now these marks were round on the inner side of the hands and elongated on the outer side, and certain small pieces of flesh were seen like the ends of nails bent and driven back, projecting from the rest of the flesh. So also the marks of nails were imprinted in his feet, and raised above the rest of the flesh. Moreover his right side, as it had been pierced by a lance, was overlaid with a scar, and often shed forth blood so that his tunic and drawers were many times sprinkled with the sacred blood.

Again in his description of the dead body of Francis, Celano says:

His sinews were not contracted as those of the dead are wont to be, his skin was not hardened, his limbs were not stiffened, but turned this way and that as they were placed. And while he shone with such wondrous beauty in the sight of all, and his flesh had become still more radiant, it was wonderful to see amid his hands and feet, not the prints of the nails but the nails themselves formed out of his flesh and retaining the blackness of iron, and his right side reddened with blood.

All that I have just quoted in the text was unquestionably written, as already stated, within four years of St. Francis' death. The first notable development of this primitive account (which pace M. Sabatier and Dr. Merkt is in no way inconsistent with the letter of Brother Elias) consists in the statement of the *Book of Miracles* that the nails in the stigmata were in some sense rigid, and that if pushed in on one side they protruded more on the other. To be precise the author says, speaking of the crowds who came to look upon the Saint's body at Assisi:

They beheld the blessed body adorned with Christ's wound marks, that is to say they saw in the hands and feet not the fissures of the nails but the nails themselves marvellously wrought by the power of God, indeed implanted (*innatos*) in the flesh itself, in such wise that if they were pressed in on either side they straightway, as if they were one piece of sinew, projected on the other. They also saw his side reddened with blood. We who recount these things ourselves witnessed them, we felt them with the same hands with which we now write, with tear-filled eyes we traced what we confess with our lips, and that which we have once sworn in touching the holy Gospels we proclaim aloud for all time.

There seems little room for doubt that the author of the *Book of Miracles* was Thomas of Celano himself, though mediaeval notions of literary responsibility are so strange that I should not venture to affirm too positively that by these words Celano pledges his own credit personally as distinct from that of the eye-witnesses whom he here takes into a sort of literary partnership. We cannot date the treatise very exactly, but it must have been produced during the generalship of John of Parma, i.e., between 1247 and 1257, in any case more than twenty years after the death of St. Francis. Still this testimony of one who, with an unmistakable reference to the controversy which had arisen regarding the reality of the stigmata, so loudly proclaims himself an eyewitness, is of the highest importance. On the other hand one further addition found in the *Fioretti* but wanting in the earliest accounts, the *Legenda Major* of St. Bonaventure not excepted, leaves an uncomfortable impression that the very strangeness of the miracle opened the door to the acceptance of mythical developments. At any rate we read in the *Fioretti* that after the vision of the Seraph—

> Anon in the hands and in the feet of St. Francis the marks of nails began to appear after the same fashion as he had just seen in the body of Jesus Christ crucified, . . . and even so were his hands and his feet pierced through the midst with nails, the heads whereof were in the palms of the hands and in the soles (sic) of the feet, outside the flesh, and the points came out through the back of the hands and of the feet, where they showed bent back and clinched on such wise that under the clinching and the bend, which all stood out above the flesh, it would have been easy to put a finger of the hand, as in a ring; and the heads of the nails were round and black.

I may confess that, in spite of the endorsement of such a writer as J. Jorgensen, I was at first inclined to look upon the story of these widely curving nail-points, under which a finger could be thrust, as a late accretion. But the description seems beyond question to date back to the *Legenda Minor* of St. Bonaventure, and consequently must be older than 1274. The words used by St. Bonaventure are precise, and the passage is the more remarkable because this detail does not appear in the *Legenda Major* of which the *Legenda Minor* is professedly only a compendium. In any case this testimony is of the first importance in a study of St. Francis' stigmata.

> The heads of the nails in the hands and feet [says St. Bonaventure] were round and black, and the points, which were somewhat long, clinched and bent back, rose up from the flesh itself and stood out clear of the surface. Indeed the clinched portion of the nails beneath the feet was so prominent, and projected so far, that not only did it prevent the soles from being set down freely upon the ground, but a finger of one's hand could easily be inserted in the bend under their curved extremities—so, at least, *I myself heard from those who had seen them with their own eyes.*

This is a very astonishing piece of evidence and one hardly knows what to make of it. If it be in literal conformity with the truth, then we must perforce say that St. Francis' stigmata were absolutely unique in the history of such phenomena. In no one, so far as I am aware, of the fifty or sixty well-attested examples of visible stigmata which have been recorded during the past seven centuries, is anything to be met with which can be put in comparison with these rigid protruding nails. If one hesitates to put faith in the accuracy of the description it is not, of course, because there can be any wish to set limits to the Divine Omnipotence. No Christian would question in the abstract God's power, if it pleased Him, to make a new leg or arm grow in the place of one that had been amputated, but in the concrete we might reasonably demand the production of very unexceptionable evidence before a miracle so unexampled in all recorded history could expect to gain credence. The marvel described in St. Bonaventure's *Legenda Minor* and in the *Fioretti* is almost startling, and it seems to me that there is much excuse for those who find it easier to explain away the language of Bonaventure, and even of Celano, than to accept their statements at their face value. If we confine ourselves to what was written within the first three or four years after the Saint's death we have nothing which cannot easily be paralleled in the descriptions given of the wounds of modern stigmatics. There was, Celano says, an appearance in the palms of the hands of nail-heads black and round. Speaking of the *addolorata* Domenica Lazzari as seen on a Thursday in August, 1834, Dr. Dei Cloche says:

> About the centre of the exterior of her hands, that is to say between the metacarp of the centre finger and the fourth, there rose a black spot resembling the head of a large nail, the diameter of which was nine lines (a little more than an English inch) and the form perfectly round. It was more elevated in the centre and declined towards the edge; when closely observed, it had the appearance of clotted and dried blood.. ... About the centre of the instep of the right foot was a wound similar to that on the hands....
>
> I could not see the instep of the left foot, because it was firmly pressed, if not entirely covered by the sole of the right foot.

Similarly one of the witnesses in the beatification process of the stigmatic Giovanna Maria Bonomi (1670) explains how "the flesh of her hands stood out like the head of a nail " (*la carne delle mam se gli era levata in forma della testa d'un chiodo*). It is true that we are told in this case that the swelling was red (vermiglia), but if there was any incrustation of blood from the wound a darkening of colour must at times have been inevitable. Of similar round "nail-heads" in such cases many other examples could be cited from the description of stigmata at all periods. With regard to the appearance of clinching on the other side, Celano's language in the Vita Prima when attentively considered amounts to very little. He tells of marks that were long rather than round, and of a *caruncula quae camera reliquam excedebat*, in other words of a sort of little fleshy ridge which was raised above the surface. Mr. T. W. Allies, who visited Domenica Lazzari in July, 1847, some few years before he entered the Catholic Church, wrote immediately afterwards to a friend:

> On the outside of both hands, as they lie clasped together, in a line with the second finger, about an inch from the knuckle, is a hard scar, of dark colour, rising above the flesh, half an inch in length by about three-eighths of an inch in width; round these the skin slightly reddened, but quite free from blood. From the position of the hands it is not possible to see well inside, but stooping down on the right of her bed I could almost see an incision answering to the outward one and apparently deeper.

Let it be noted in passing that in Domenica Lazzari's case no doubt can exist regarding the wounds in the palms of the hands. They were seen again and again by several witnesses, many of whom declared that the wound went right through. The main point, however, is that in some modern stigmatics the wounds have exhibited at normal times (*i.e.*, apart from the periodical bleeding on Fridays) the appearance of a dark raised cicatrice. This may also well have been the case with St. Francis, with the peculiarity that the scar in the palms and insteps was circular, while that on the back of the hand and the soles of the feet was narrower and more oblong. A slight difference of shape between back and front would probably have sufficed to persuade mediaeval observers, awe-stricken in the presence of this unheard-of marvel, that what they saw were nails formed out of the substance of the victim's flesh. Moreover in twenty years' time such an idea, once suggested, would have taken firm root and developed new details until the witnesses who actually had beheld the marvel of the wound-marks were ready in perfect good faith to pledge their solemn word that there were not only scars but counterfeit nails protruding at the back, under the curve of which it was possible to insert a whole finger. I hope I am not taking too unflattering a view of the treacherous quality of human memory if I affirm, as the result of some years study of historical evidence, that in every considerable body of men there are not a few individuals who, without conscious insincerity, are capable of similar self-deception.

Unfortunately, when it is a question of doing honour to the dead or of advocating a cause, it is the more wonderful story which is the more acceptable. The man who mistrusts his memory or who expresses doubts goes unheeded, but the bold and picturesque assertion is welcomed, remembered, quoted, and not infrequently improved upon.

What lends in my opinion very considerable support to this view of St. Francis' stigmata is the character of the early representations of them in art. The venerable and distinguished artist Mr. N. H. J. Westlake, F.S.A., a convert to Catholicism now of sixty-two years' standing, published some time ago a monograph on *The Authentic Portraiture of St. Francis of Assisi.* In this he also includes admirable reproductions of the five earliest portraits of the Saint. One of these is believed to date from before 1220 and consequently shows no stigmata, but the other four give prominence to this feature, and in each case the wounds are represented simply as circular, without, so far as I can see, the slightest suggestion of nails clinched at the back. Now the picture by Giunta Pisano is ascribed to about the year 1230, four years after the Saint's death. It shows the backs of the hands quite clearly, but the wounds are simply round spots. Again, the panel at Pescia, by Bonaventura Berlingheri, is clearly dated 1235. It exhibits the inside of one hand and the outside of the other, but to my eyes the spot in both is circular, that on the palm seeming slightly larger than that on the back. Strange to say, Mr. Westlake remarks:

> This plate represents the picture now at Pescia, which is singular from the circumstance that one hand has been turned so as to show the inside and the formation of the point of the nail turned down, which form, it is asserted, the flesh assumed. It is so described in the Bull of Alexander IV (1255), which says that "in his hands and in his feet he had most certainly nails, well-formed, of his own flesh, or of a substance newly produced." It is difficult to recognize this in the photograph, but to show this formation was undoubtedly the object of the reversion of the hand: and it is still evident in the picture itself, as one gathers from eyewitnesses. In his other hand the Saint holds a book.

But if there is any suggestion of the clinching of the nail points, this is seen in the palm of the hand, not the back, and consequently on the wrong side. The photograph of Berlingheri's picture, so far as I can detect, shows nothing of this clinching, neither does the engraving of the same panel in the sumptuously illustrated work *St. Francois d'Assisi*. Similarly the two enamels in the Louvre, which M. H. Matrod assigns to an even earlier date (1228-30), exhibit the stigmata indeed, but simply as round marks in the hands and feet. It seems to me, then, that we cannot safely take our stand, as does for example Father Michael Bihl, upon the alleged unique character of St. Francis' stigmata, holding them to have been not merely wounds but an actual fleshy growth which imitated the nails of the crucifixion. Father Bihl maintains, no doubt rightly enough, that his understanding of the facts is fatal to any naturalistic interpretation. No power of auto-suggestion, no abnormal pathological conditions, could enable a contemplative to evolve from the flesh of his hands and feet four horny excrescences in the form of nails, piercing his extremities and clinched at the back. Such a manifestation, if it occurs, must surely be held miraculous. The question, however, is whether the evidence allows us to affirm the existence of these excrescences. There are numerous examples among the stigmatics of later date of the occurrence of raised scars, and there seems no reason why these should not so differ in form, front and back, as to suggest to eyes already overwhelmed by the marvel, the head of a nail in one case and the point in another. Let us take an illustration from one of the most recent of modern stigmatics, Gemma Galgani, who was born in 1878 and died in 1903. The following account, which is that given by her confessor and biographer, Padre Germano di S. Stanislao, C.P., will be of interest in spite of its length, for it illustrates strikingly the phenomenon of stigmatization in general, apart from its special bearing upon the point with which we are for the moment concerned.

From this day forward the phenomenon continued to repeat itself on the same day every week, namely on Thursday evening about eight o'clock and continued until three o'clock on Friday afternoon.

No preparation preceded it; no sense of pain or impression in those parts of the body affected by it; nothing announced its approach except the recollection of spirit that preceded the ecstasy.

Scarcely had this come as a forerunner than red marks showed themselves on the backs and palms of both hands; and under the epidermis a rent in the flesh was seen to open by degrees; *this was oblong on the backs of the hands and irregularly round in the palms.* After a little the membrane burst and on those innocent hands were seen marks of flesh wounds. *The diameter of these in the palms was about half an inch, and on the backs of the hands the wound was about five-eighths of an inch long by one-eighth wide.*

Sometimes the laceration appeared to be only on the surface; at other times it was scarcely perceptible with the naked eye; but as a rule it was very deep, and seemed to pass through the hand— the openings on both sides reaching each other. I say seemed to pass, because those cavities were full of blood, partly flowing and partly congealed, and when the blood ceased to flow they closed immediately, so that it was not easy to sound them without a probe. Now this instrument was never used; both because of the reverential delicacy inspired by the Ecstatic in her mysterious state, and because the violence of the pain made her keep her hands convulsively closed, also because the wounds in the palms of her hands were covered by a swelling that at first looked like clotted blood, whereas it was found to be fleshy, hard and like the head of a nail raised and detached and about an inch in diameter. In her feet, besides the wounds being large and livid around the edges, their size in an inverse sense differed from those of her hands; that is, there was a larger diameter on the instep and a smaller one on the sole; furthermore, the wound in the instep of the right foot was as large as that in the sole of the left. Thus it must certainly have been with our Saviour, supposing that both His Sacred Feet were fixed to the Cross with only one nail.

One feature which was specially remarkable in Gemma Galgani was the manner of the disappearance of the stigmata each week. In many cases, as for example in that of Domenica Lazzari, referred to above, the stigmata, when the flow of blood ceased, remained nevertheless very perceptible in the form of a raised cicatrice or a conspicuous white or red scar. In Gemma's case at ordinary times hardly any trace was to be seen of the marvellous phenomenon, which was of weekly occurrence.

> As soon [says Fr. Germanus] as the ecstasy of the Friday was over, the flow of blood from all the five wounds ceased immediately; the raw flesh healed; the lacerated tissues healed too, and the following day, or at latest on the Sunday, not a vestige remained of those deep cavities, neither at their centres, nor around their edges; the skin having grown quite uniformly with that of the uninjured part. In colour, however, there remained whitish marks.

It may be well to add that even in the same subject the phenomena of stigmatization are not always uniform. In Gemma Galgani this was especially the case with regard to the "fleshy nail-heads" in the palms of the hands, described in the above quotation. Father Germanus is at pains to insist upon this point.

He says:

> In order to be accurate, I wish to mention here, as I said before when treating of this particular (the nail-heads), that this last phenomenon was only observed a few times, and only in the palms of the hands, never on the feet; and that occasionally the stigmata bled without any laceration of the surface. The fleshy nail-heads, however, showed themselves, though seldom, and the deep wounds were the more usual state of Gemma Galgani's stigmata. I say, the more usual state.

In juxtaposition to this carefully weighed statement, made by one who was the continuous observer of Gemma's ecstasies, it is interesting to set down the account given by Dr. Gerald Molloy in 1873 of the stigmata of Louise Lateau. After describing how when a certain amount of blood had exuded from the wounds, the spectators wiped it away with linen cloths brought for the purpose, Dr. Molloy continues:

> The nature of the stigmata was then more distinctly seen. They are oval marks of a bright red hue, appearing on the back and palm of each hand about the centre. Speaking roughly, each stigma is about an inch in length and somewhat more than half an inch in breadth. There is no wound properly so-called, but the blood seemed to force its way through the unbroken skin. In a very short time, sufficient blood had flowed again to gratify the devotion of other pilgrims, who applied their handkerchiefs as had been done before, until all the blood had been wiped away a second time. This process was repeated several times during the course of our visit.

Much capital has been made controversially of the fact that in Louise Lateau's case there were no real flesh wounds but only *de petites plaies dorsales et palmaires qui reposent sur de légères indurations mobiles.* Dr. Dumas, for example, in the *Revue des deux Mondes* has made this admitted fact the basis of his theory that a local haemorrhage of this nature can be explained by suggestion and purely pathological conditions. But there are many well observed cases of stigmatization which exhibit wounds of a quite different character, much more radical and deep seated. Gemma Galgani supplies one instance in point, Domenica Lazzari, also mentioned above, furnishes another. To take an eighteenth century example, it seems certain that at times the hands of Saint Maria Francesca delle Cinque Piaghe were completely perforated in the places of the stigmata. At any rate one of her confessors, Don Paschal Nitti, deposed upon oath in the process of beatification:

> I have seen them, I have touched them, and to say the truth I, as the apostle St. Thomas did, have put in my finger into the wounds of her hands and I have seen that the hole extended right through, for in inserting my first finger into the wound it met the thumb which I held underneath on the other side of the hand (*mentre nel porre l'indice dentro la piaga s'incontrava col pollice che ienevo sottoposto dall'altra parte della mano*). And this experiment I have made in many Lents, and on many Fridays in March, because it was on such days that the said wounds were most fully developed.

It must, I think, be obvious enough that these are not mere cases of rubefaction and vesication. Whatever such investigators as Bourru, Burot, Charcot and Bourneville have succeeded in producing by suggestion in their hysterical patients falls very far short of what is recorded of Gemma Galgani, Domenica Lazzari and a dozen more whose manifestations cannot here be described.

But to return to St. Francis. If the orifices of his wounds, like those of Gemma Galgani, were round in front and narrow behind, and if they had closed, as in many other recorded cases, by leaving a raised scab or scar where blood had previously flowed, we should undoubtedly have something which on one side resembled the head of a nail, and on the other the point of the nail beaten down.

This supposition, it seems to me, will suffice to explain the language of Celano's *Vita Prima* and I do not know that we can safely ask for more. It will at the same time be understood that the historical evidence leaves us absolutely no ground for doubting the reality of St. Francis' wound-marks. I am only contending that they are probably identical in nature with the phenomena observed in many later stigmatics. The element of the marvellous in all the best-attested cases is sufficiently pronounced to need no emphasizing.

We can certainly assert with confidence that the wounds could not possibly have been self-inflicted either consciously or unconsciously, and the material conditions have nearly always been such that collusion or fraud are unthinkable. It is difficult to suppose that any impartial inquirer could look into the evidence available, let us say, in the case of Domenica Lazzari, without being deeply impressed by its strangeness. We have here a crowd of witnesses, men of position and intelligence, like Bertram Earl of Shrewsbury, the Archbishop of Sydney, T. W. Allies, Dr. Weedall, Conan Doyle, M. Cazales, and a number of other French, English, and German pilgrims. They pay their visits at different times, form their impressions quite independently, and yet all attest the same wonderful phenomena which it was well within their competence to observe. They see the dry scars on the Thursday, and on the Friday the *addolorata* in agony, the wounds streaming with blood, and always at the same hour; they note the poverty of the surroundings, they bear witness to her shrinking from all notoriety, they agree in their accounts of more than one marvellous detail which seems in direct contravention of the physical laws of the universe. They at least convince us that a problem is there of the deepest and most complex nature, whether we look to the supernatural for an explanation or seek to invoke some abnormal psychic force of which the world has hitherto been ignorant.

3

THE GENESIS OF STIGMATA

There is nothing perhaps which is more remarkable in this enquiry than the extreme diversity of the manifestations capable of being grouped under the general head of stigmatization. No two cases are precisely alike. Each needs to be examined by itself and to be judged upon its own merits. Hence in any attempt to provide a general view of the phenomena in question the first thing to be done is to give some idea of the wide range of those external appearances within the limits of which variation exists. To begin with, stigmatization is by no means confined to those openings in hands, feet and side which are commonly regarded as the five principal wound-marks of our Saviour's Passion. A large number of stigmatics also bear across the forehead and around the head a circlet of punctures, such as might have been caused by the wearing of a crown of thorns, and these punctures are often the channels of a profuse flow of blood. It is certainly a remarkable fact that the man who was condemned, as we have seen, at the Council of Oxford in 1222, is stated by the Barnwell chronicler, a contemporary, to have shown wounds, not only in his hands and feet, but on the head as well. This is the more remarkable because St. Francis of Assisi's various biographers mention nothing of the sort in his case, and it is therefore highly improbable that the Barnwell chronicler can have introduced this detail at a later date in imitation of anything he had heard of St. Francis. Apart from this very puzzling instance of the alleged impostor of 1222, the earliest example of a stigmatic crown of thorns appears to be that of Elizabeth of Herkenrode, the Cistercian nun, whose dramatic enacting of the scenes of the Passion has been described in a previous chapter. Abbot Philip of Clairvaux, who, after being for a time incredulous, came to witness the phenomena for himself, has left a minute account of her stigmata and of the blood which under his own eyes flowed from the wounds. The crown of thorns, however, he did not see—this manifestation was apparently of comparatively rare occurrence in Elizabeth's case—but he tells us in the following terms what he heard from the Benedictine Abbot of St. Trond, who was her confessor and neighbour.

> The aforesaid Abbot related to me and to my companions how on Good Friday in the year 1266 the virgin of whom we speak, in an interval

between two of the ecclesiastical hours, a time when ordinarily she had a respite from her sufferings, began to feel a pain in her head and was quite unable to keep it still upon her pillow in the same position, but continued turning it incessantly this way and that. Whereupon the Reverend Mother and sisters aforesaid, noticing this, lit a lamp and closely and attentively examined the maiden's head. Then they perceived and pointed out to those present the punctures as it were of thorns, reddened with drops of blood, encircling that virginal head like a crown and figuring the thorny crown of our Saviour.

This would under normal circumstances be rightly considered very unsatisfactory evidence, but when we remember that Abbot Philip, writing in the third quarter of the thirteenth century, had no precedent before him for any such phenomenon, and that it exactly agrees with the numerous descriptions given by medical eye-witnesses of the coronal stigmata perceptible in a score of modern ecstatics, it is unreasonable to doubt that the narrative reproduces the facts with all desirable accuracy. Here, for example, is the summary which Dr. Gerald Molloy furnishes of this feature in the case of Louise Lateau:

> As to the coronet around the head, it consists of a large number of bleeding points which are visible on Fridays only, and which present an appearance peculiar to themselves. They cannot be conveniently examined under the hair. But on the forehead where they are from twelve to fifteen in number, they form a band about an inch wide, midway between the roots of the hair and the eyebrows. There is no permanent discoloration of the surface, no appearance of a blister, no exposure of the under skin. But with the aid of a magnifying glass, it is possible to detect exceedingly minute punctures of the epidermis, through which the blood escapes.

Dr. Imbert-Gourbeyre, who had innumerable opportunities during nearly twenty years of studying the case of Marie-Julie Jahenny, describes the punctures round her head as being as large as hemp seeds, but in Domenica Lazzari and a good many other instances the punctures were still larger and the flow of blood much greater and more continuous. In a considerable proportion of the stigmatics whose history has been minutely recorded, the reproduction of the crown of thorns formed the first stage in the development of the whole series of stigmata; in some few other cases the crown of thorns remained visible externally when the stigmata in the hands disappeared, apparently because it would ordinarily be hidden by the wimple of a nun's headdress, and in large measure, of course, by the hair. This matter of concealment, as we shall have occasion to notice later on, seems, in a vast number of instances, to have had a decisive influence upon the appearance, disappearance, and development of the stigmata. Many of the holiest of such mystics, finding that the wounds upon their hands could not be hidden and that they attracted general respect and veneration, prayed earnestly to God to be freed from such a snare to their humility. They asked that they might still share the pain which their crucified Saviour felt in His hands and feet, without any external manifestation of their privileged condition. As a result we find that in a considerable number of cases the wound-marks disappeared within a short time of their first infliction and before the attention of anyone, except perhaps the confessor, the superior, or some trusted confidant, had been directed to the matter. Whether this withdrawal of the external manifestations ought to be described as miraculous, or whether it was the natural result of concentration upon the fixed idea that all such outward marks of God's favour were dangerous to the soul and ought to be repressed, is perhaps not the least perplexing of the many problems which beset the inquirer into these psycho-physical phenomena.

Whatever be the conclusion arrived at, it is noteworthy that in a large number of cases, some of them dating back to the earliest times, the stigmatic has declared—and there is absolutely no reason to doubt her sincerity—that the sense of interior pain in the part affected preceded by many months, or even by years, the visible appearance of scars or bleeding wounds. The life of Lukardis of Oberweimar, already referred to in previous pages, is peculiarly interesting in this connection. Somewhere about the year 1298 she seems to have been possessed with a most ardent longing to share the sufferings of Jesus Christ and to have made incessant prayer that the memory of His Passion might never fade from her heart. In the end, says her contemporary biographer, she was heard according to her desire:

> For she saw in the spirit that she ought to pass through a certain door in which she found Jesus Christ as it were recently fastened to the cross, scored with the weals of the scourges and most pitifully dripping with blood. As she looked intently upon Him the servant of God fell at His feet swooning and almost lifeless. Then our Lord said to her: "Rise up, My child, and help Me," by which she understood that she

ought not to be content with merely calling His sufferings to mind but that she was meant to help Him by voluntarily sharing in His Passion. At Christ's word, accordingly, recovering at last something of her strength, she answered tremblingly: "How can I help Thee, my Lord?" And thereupon raising her eyes she saw His right arm loosened from the cross and hanging feebly down, by which it seemed to her that the pain of the suffering Christ was greatly intensified. So the beloved handmaiden, drawing near in tender compassion, strove to tie up the arm again to the cross with a thread of silk, but she could not succeed. Accordingly she began to lift His arm with her hands and with deep groanings to hold it in its place. Then our Lord said to her: "Place thy hands against My hands, and thy feet against My feet, and thy breast against My breast, and in such wise I shall be so much helped by thee that My pain will be less." And when the servant of God had done this she felt interiorly the most bitter pain of the wounds both in her hands and in her feet and in her breast, although the wounds were not yet manifest to the outward eye. It was after this that she formed the habit of knocking her hands together with great force so that the noise was heard far and wide as from the collision of two planks.

I have recounted in previous pages how Lukardis was accustomed to bore, as it were, the palms of her hands by striking them violently with the opposite forefinger. Still, some two years seem to have elapsed after the above incident before any wound showed itself outwardly. The first was in the right hand and it is said to have appeared quite suddenly after a vision. Ten days later a similar wound showed itself in the left hand and after this, with intervals between, wounds also in the feet and side. The last of these charismata to be made manifest outwardly was the crown of thorns. The biographer's account of this is also interesting.

> When thus there appeared one after another upon the body of the servant of God the traces of the anguish of Christ's Passion which long before had been engraved upon her heart by constant remembrance, it happened on one occasion that a certain nun questioned that blessed one, saying to her: "Tell me, dear Sister Lukardis, since, in accordance with what thy confessors, Brother Henry and Brother Eberhard foretold, many marks of Christ." Passion have now successively appeared upon thy body, is not the time near at hand for the imprint of the thorny crown to show itself upon thy brow? "To whom that blessed one

answered thus and said: "You must know that I have long felt and still feel a very piercing and wondrous pain like a crown of thorns tightly bound to my head and running into it with its sharp spikes." Whereupon, being asked how far across her head she felt this pain, she answered: "I feel that pain as far as my hair extends and a little further, just as if all my hairs were so many sharp needles planted in my skull and penetrating right to the brain." Accordingly, the traces of this suffering often became visible, for there somehow appeared from time to time upon her brow the punctures as it were of sharp points. Moreover, the veins of her forehead and temples at times showed themselves so swollen that you would think that her whole head was tightly compressed with a band.

These accounts compiled by obscure mediaeval chroniclers seem to me nevertheless of great value, because on the one hand they were written down at a period when no tradition could yet have been formed as to the course of development commonly followed by the phenomena of stigmatization, and on the other because they never attained any notable publicity. Indeed, it may be said that these details have only been printed and given to the world within quite recent times. Nevertheless, they accurately agree in their more general features with the description furnished by numerous witnesses of the manifestations common among the more remarkable stigmatics of the seventeenth and eighteenth centuries, and still frequently to be met with in our own day.

Let me add, before we leave the subject of the crown of thorns, that in the case of at least some few stigmatics, this sign alone has been perceptible externally. This, for example, is recorded of Mary of the Holy Trinity, a Dominican nun in Spain, who died in 1660, and much the same may be said of the Blessed Osanna Andreasi (1505) who experienced the pain of the crown of thorns before any of the other sufferings of the Passion. Osanna, however, endured the pangs of the other stigmata as well, and they occasionally showed externally, so that Don Genesio, Archpriest of Rivarolo, was able to depose that he had sometimes seen in the palms of her hands, on Wednesdays and Fridays or during Holy Week, "a small black swelling which looked as if it were full of blood." However this may be, Osanna's stigmata became plainly visible in her dead body, and more than a century and a half later Father Janning, the Bollandist, visiting the Saint's incorrupt remains at Mantua, wrote that the wounds of the hands and feet could still be seen. Mother Francis Raphael (Drane) mentions in her *Life of St. Catherine of Siena* that in Catherine's dead body also the stigmata were traceable by a sort of transparency in the tissues, and she states that she possessed a photograph of one of the hands which showed this remarkable detail. It will be remembered that St. Catherine's special share in the sufferings of the Passion began in 1373 with the choice of the crown of thorns in preference to the golden crown which our Lord in a vision proffered her at the same time. Pressing it down upon her head, we are told that "for a long space after she felt a sensible pain by the pricking of those thorns." In the case of one of the latest stigmatics of whom we have record, Sister Maria della Passione, her confessor relates that her initiation began in Holy Week, 1903, when our Saviour took off His own crown of thorns and gave it to her. The other stigmata were bestowed later in the same year and as a rule these bled every Friday until her death in 1912. A very curious modern example, remarkable for the range and variety, though not for the intensity, of the manifestations, is that of Marie-Julie Jahenny, already spoken of, a Breton peasant girl in the village of La Fraudais (LoireInferieure). The case was closely watched for more than twenty years by Dr. Imbert-Gourbeyre at the request and with the full sanction of her diocesan, Monseigneur Fournier, the Bishop of Nantes, who himself seems to have had no doubt of the supernatural character of the phenomena observed. Dr. Imbert-Gourbeyre was a man who in historical matters entirely lacked the critical sense, but seeing that for thirty-six years he was a professor at the Medical School of Clermont-Ferrand, he cannot have been wholly incompetent as a witness to pathological facts, and his good faith was questioned by none. From his own personal observations he wrote in 1894 the following summary of Marie-Julie's successive experiences in the matter of the stigmata.

On the 21st March, 1873, she received the marks of the five wounds; the crown of thorns followed on Oct. 5th; on the 25th of November appeared an imprint on the left shoulder, and on the 6th of December the dorsal stigmata in hands and feet. On Jan. 12th, 1874, her wrists showed marks corresponding to those which the cords must have produced when our Saviour's arms were bound, and on the same day a sort of emblematic pattern developed in front of her heart. By Jan. 14th stripes had appeared on her ankles, legs and forearms in memory of the scourging, and a few days afterwards there were two weals on her side. On the 20th February a stigmatic ring was seen on the fourth finger of the right hand1 in token of her mystic espousals; later on there appeared various inscriptions on the breast, and finally on Dec, 7th, 1875, the words *O Crux ave* with a cross and a flower.

When speaking more in detail of this last incident, the same writer tells us that in 1875 Marie-Julie—

> announced a month beforehand, and several times over, that she was shortly to receive a new stigmatization, and that a cross and a flower with the words *O Crux ave* were to be impressed upon her breast. More than a week before the event occurred she named the precise day: it was to be the 7th of December. The day before this her breast was examined, when it was ascertained that the emblems spoken of had not yet made their appearance. On the morrow, before the ecstasy came on, she offered to submit to another examination, but this was considered unnecessary; she had the right to expect that we should take her word for it. Soon after she passed into a state of trance, and while this wonderful device was developing, her family and the witnesses who were present were able to testify to the incomparable fragrance which exuded from her body and made itself perceptible through her clothes. When the ecstasy was over, the cross, the flower and the inscription could be clearly seen upon her breast.

Dr. Imbert-Gourbeyre adds, writing in 1894, nearly twenty years after, "the flower and the inscription are visible still"

I have quoted this description on purpose, because there are elements in it which certainly do not inspire confidence. The keen interest which Marie-Julie seems to have taken in the impression she was making and the readiness to offer herself for medical examination, contrast strangely with the intense reluctance to direct attention to themselves or to allow any part of their bodies to be uncovered even for the inspection of a doctor or a bishop, which is conspicuous in almost every line written by such Saints as St. Veronica Giuliani, St. Teresa, or St. Catherine of Ricci. St. Veronica, for example, when her veil, contrary to the rigid traditions of the Capuchin Order to which she belonged, was removed, to enable the Bishop and other ecclesiastics to inspect the marks of her crown of thorns, could only console herself by recalling to mind how our Lord was stripped of His garments. Indeed, I might say in general that this intense unwillingness to court notoriety for any supernatural favour bestowed by God is the trait which has impressed me most deeply, and has seemed most uniform in the lives of those whom popular esteem, as well as the sentence of the Church, has proclaimed to be the truest followers of their Lord and heavenly Spouse. At the same time, to return to the case of Marie-Julie, she seems undoubtedly to have lived in obscurity for more than twenty years, and to have retained during that time the good opinion of ecclesiastical authority. Further, it Is difficult to believe that a physician of some standing in the medical world could have been imposed upon for all that long space of time by a peasant girl in a remote country village who had simply tattooed herself with a needle or had recourse to some other obvious trick. Or. Imbert-Gourbeyre had also had a good deal to do with Louise Lateau, and it must be remembered that in her case fraud is not imputed. Critics only object that the phenomena were insignificant in themselves and that they can be adequately explained by pathological causes. In any case we may admit that patterns and inscriptions, though evanescent in their nature, have been produced at the Salpêtrière upon the flesh of hysterical subjects by simple suggestion. This is the "dermographisme" of T. Bathélèmy and other French medical scientists, and though of comparatively rare occurrence, the fact is not to be denied.

The reference made above to St. Veronica Giuliani reminds me that we ought to touch at least briefly upon three manifestations occasionally present in stigmatic subjects which in her case were specially emphasized and particularly well attested. The first was the wound in the shoulder, corresponding to that which tradition ascribes to our Lord as the result of His carrying of the cross. The Saint herself in one of her Relations, that written by the command of her Bishop, Mgr. Eustachi, in 1700, gives an account of the first occasion on which she felt this pain, which was afterwards frequently renewed. At her death there was found upon the right shoulder *una lividura ben grande*, marking the seat of a former wound, and besides this the shoulder-blade was seen to be bent and depressed in an extraordinary degree, so much so that the two surgeons who inspected it declared in their formal depositions that it was inexplicable to them how she could have retained the natural use of her arm. It should, however, be mentioned that the Saint, in making the stations and in other pious exercises, used to drag about with her a heavy cross of wood, which may be in part responsible for the effects observed. Several other Saints (for example St. Catherine of Ricci) also had the wound on the shoulder, in some cases on the right, in others on the left, and, we may notice in passing, that there is a similar or even greater variation regarding the positions of the wound in the side. Some stigmatics have had it opposite or even above the heart, others almost under the arm, and either on the right side or on the left, while in form the aperture has sometimes been a straight cut, sometimes triangular and sometimes crescent-shaped.

A second notable feature in the stigmatization of St. Veronica Giuliani is the control which her Confessor seemed to be able to exercise over the outward manifestations. Veronica received the stigmata in hands, feet and side, as we learn from herself, in the course of a long ecstasy on April 5, 1697. She was subjected to rigorous examinations by Bishop Eustachi and by the Holy Office, the details of which caused her so much mental anguish that again and again she prayed to God that these external manifestations might cease. It seemed to her, however, that our Lord told her in a vision that the stigmata must remain visible for three years, and so in fact it happened, for on the 5th of April, 1700, the scars in hands and feet disappeared, though the open wound in the side still remained and sometimes bled profusely. After that date the opening of the stigmata was only intermittent, but, as we have already seen in the case of Gemma Galgani, even those wounds in hands and feet on occasion would manifest themselves and bleed and then close again without leaving any trace. With regard to the side, she herself states in her Relation:

> There were times when the Father Confessor said to me, "How long will the perforation in the side remain open?" I replied, "Our Lord seems to wish it should remain open for so many hours or days" according as I had been given to understand, and exactly at that time it would close again. But sometimes he (the Confessor) said to me, "I do not wish it to close before such a day or such an hour." And in fact it would happen so. . . . If I am not mistaken the Bishop on one occasion did the same thing. He came here with certain of God's servants and they wished to see this wound in the side open, to my great sorrow. Then the Bishop told me that he would come again the next day but wished the wound to be closed. And so precisely it came about.. These things have been a very great suffering for me. May it be all for the glory of God.

The third point suggested by the history of St. Veronica Giuliani is one which is far too perplexing and wide in its applications to be dealt with adequately here without a long digression. It is concerned with the appearances alleged to be found after death in the heart and viscera of many of the servants of God who have been honoured with the stigmata. Veronica seems to have had before her mind throughout the last years of her life a sort of clairvoyant mental picture of the physical state of her heart. She believed that the tissues of that organ had in some marvellous way hardened into the likeness of the holy objects which had filled her thoughts during life. There was the figure of a cross and a crown of thorns, a chalice, three nails, a little pillar, seven swords, and a number of letters, the initials of certain virtues. So real was this mental picture that by command of her Confessor she actually drew plans of it, using the help of two of the Sisters who were especially dear to her and in her confidence. Still more curious is the fact that she believed that her heart had been in this state for more than twenty years and that the arrangement of these emblems had often been altered in regard to their relative position, fresh ones also being added. The rough designs traced upon paper cut in the form of a heart are still preserved, and they represent the supposed arrangement of these emblems in 1715, 1718, 1719, 1720, and 1727, the year of her death. The most astounding part of the story is, however, the fact that some thirty hours after death her body was opened by two professors of medicine and surgery, in the presence of the Governor, Mgr. Torregiani, afterwards Cardinal, with a number of other ecclesiastics of note.

The medical witnesses and the rest drew up a formal instrument testifying to the fact that these emblems were actually found in her heart in positions corresponding to the last of the drawings made by the Saint. I can express no opinion as to this occurrence, but it is certain that similar wonders have been recounted of many other Saints and holy persons. St. Teresa tells us quite plainly in her autobiography[1] that she had a vision of a glorious angel who thrust a long golden spear with a fiery point right into her heart.

We have also some indication of the impression this incident produced upon the Saint in the fact that she made it the subject of a hymn still preserved to us. Now Teresa's heart was extracted after death and in that heart was found a wide horizontal fissure, as those may see to this day who visit the relic in its shrine at Alba de Tormes, or who procure one of the many photographs of it which are in circulation.' Another instance, very remarkable as resting upon the clear evidence of several eye-witnesses whose depositions are still preserved to us, is the wound in the heart of Caterina Savelli of Sezze.

This is a stigmatic (she died in 1691) who has escaped the researches of Dr. Imbert-Gourbeyre. When kneeling before the Blessed Sacrament exposed in the Jesuit church of Sezze in 1659, she saw in a trance five rays come from the Sacred Host which wounded her hands, feet and side. She prayed that the stigmata might not become known, and her prayer was so far heard that no marks appeared in the hands, though the side remained open, and blood or serum flowed from it at intervals. After death, however, the traces of wounds in the hands and feet became perfectly plain, and, what was most noteworthy, the heart being extracted, there was found in it a deep fissure of old date. The physician and the surgeon, who with many ecclesiastics signed the final attestation, declared that without supernatural intervention it would have been impossible for anyone to live with such a wound. And there appear to have been quite a number of similar cases, though not all equally well vouched for by contemporary evidence. Of Blessed Charles of Sezze, who, curiously enough, was a contemporary and fellow-townsman of Caterina Savelli, but who died twenty years before her, it is stated that the Pope ordered that a post-mortem examination should be made of his remains. Thereupon they found a wound in the heart completely piercing it, also the figure of a crucifix and the exact facsimile of a nail buried in the heart and four or five inches in length. A document formally attesting these facts is said to have been signed by several physicians and surgeons, but I have unfortunately not been able to meet with any copy of it. Charles of Sezze's claims to heroic virtue have, however, been fully discussed by the Congregation of Rites, and he was beatified in our own days by Pius IX.

Blessed Charles of Sezze's case possesses an additional interest from the fact that, apart from St. Francis of Assisi, no reliable example can be quoted of a male person who has had visible stigmata in hands, feet and side. Even in St. Francis we have no evidence of periodic bleeding, though this feature is found in almost all the best attested instances of female stigmatics from Elizabeth of Herkenrode and Lukardis in the thirteenth century, to Domenica Lazzari, Mme. Miollis, Louise Lateau, Marie-Julie, Gemma Galgani, and Maria della Passione in our own day. There seems to be fair evidence that a certain discalced Carmelite, Father Julian of the Cross († 1663), had stigmatic marks, like round nail-heads, in his feet, but it is not stated that they ever bled. Blessed Charles of Sezze, though he, like some other male ascetics, may have shared internally the pains of Christ's wounds, had no visible marks during his lifetime. When we consider the extreme austerity of life and the intense sympathy with the Passion of Christ conspicuous in such Saints as St. John of the Cross, St. Peter of Alcantara, St. Bernardine of Siena, St. Philip Neri, St. Paul of the Cross, St. Leonard of Port Maurice, St. Alphonsus Liguori, not to speak of all the Carthusian and Trappist contemplatives, this pronounced inequality between the sexes cannot but be regarded as a very extraordinary fact. Perhaps there is only one thing more remarkable in the strange phenomena of stigmatization, and that is that in all these numerous examples of open wounds, some of them bleeding continuously, not a single instance seems yet to have been pointed out in which the wound has suppurated.

4

Stigmata and Sanctity

As previously explained, it is not the purpose of the present chapters to propound any theory regarding the origin or supernatural character of the manifestations we are considering. My principal aim is to give an idea of the physical phenomena for which good evidence can be produced, and to leave the interpretation of the facts to the judicious reader himself. None the less, while excluding, so far as may be, all data of doubtful authenticity, it would be quite possible to convey a misleading impression regarding the mystical quality of those who are the subjects of these abnormal experiences. It is often as important to ascertain the whole truth as to take precautions that the records upon which our investigation is based contain the truth and nothing but the truth. This, I fancy, is a point in which hagiographers, aiming at edification, are sometimes a little negligent, but it ought not to be overlooked in the present inquiry. Stigmatization is a very wonderful thing, and it is generally found associated with holiness of an exalted kind, but it does not seem in itself to constitute a guarantee of sanctity. In this respect it resembles telepathic clairvoyance. Very often we find it recorded in Saints' lives that the subject of the biography possessed a knowledge of things happening at a distance, or that he penetrated the secret thoughts of his interlocutors. Indeed, such facts are frequently adduced in the process of beatification as proof of heroic virtue under the heading *charismata or gratia gratis* data. None the less we meet with a good deal of evidence that such knowledge of distant events is occasionally possessed under abnormal conditions by persons in whose lives religion plays a very small part, and who are equally removed from the suspicion of diabolical influences. It cannot be too often repeated that the Church has set an example of extreme caution in the interpretation of all such apparently supernatural favours. In all the great work of Benedict XIV on the Beatification and Canonization of the Saints hardly more than a few sentences are devoted to the question of stigmatization, though he admits, of course, that in some cases, as, for example, that of St. Francis of Assisi, it bears a supernatural character.

That some instances of alleged stigmatization are simply fraudulent is not to be disputed. The two notorious religious imposters of the sixteenth century, Magdalena de la Cruz and Maria de la Visitacion, both professed to bear the marks of the Passion in hands, feet, and side. When sentenced by the Inquisition each wrote out a detailed confession of hypocrisy and fraud, though in view of the many similar confessions made by reputed witches of riding through the air on broomsticks, etc., this acknowledgment of guilt cannot in itself be regarded as quite conclusive. In relatively modern times there seem to have been quite a number of similar pretenders, some of whom, it is stated, have been convicted by the law courts of patent imposture. I have not found it possible to obtain detailed information regarding any of these cases, though there appears no reason to question the justice of the sentences passed by the magistrates upon Rose Tamisier in France and upon Teresa Stadeln in Switzerland, both pretended stigmatics, in the course of the last century. A somewhat more doubtful example of the same kind is mentioned by Debreyne. It was the case of a girl of eighteen subject to frequent hysterical attacks, who in 1840 was a patient in a religious institution in Normandy.

According to the detailed account written by the chaplain, this girl, when in a state of trance, received, or pretended to receive, lumps of sugar and other dainties from some mysterious source.

The sugar undoubtedly was there, but where it came from nobody could find out. They repeatedly searched her and everything belonging to her, but discovered nothing. The sugar never became visible until it was quite close to her hands (*On ne le voyait que lorsqu' il était trés prés des mains*), and she declared that it came from heaven and was given her by our Blessed Lady, or by the Infant Jesus, or by St. John the Baptist. Thinking she might have some confederate in the institution in which she was detained, they removed her to another house, but the phenomena did not cease.

On the contrary, under the new conditions the sugar appeared more frequently than before, and she is said to have received it as often as twenty times in an hour. The girl also professed to be marked with the stigmata, not in the hands, but in the breast and in the feet. A trickle of blood came from the wounds every Friday.

In order to make sure [says the account from which I quote] that she had not made the wounds herself and had done nothing to re-open them, the foot was tightly bandaged, the bandage being sewn up in such a way that she could not have removed it without betraying the fact. Further, an unconsecrated host was placed under the bandage to prevent her stabbing the wound undetected by means of a pin or needle, but on the Friday evening it was found that blood had flowed from the wound, that the bandage had not been moved or interfered with, and that the host was quite intact just as it had been placed there.

This girl [the chaplain goes on] is not a Saint, she appears to be half-witted, but of that I have my doubts. There is reason to think her both spiteful and sly.

Obviously in this case everything points to imposture, and the precautions adopted to detect it were probably quite inadequate. But there are many instances of stigmatization where imposture out of the question but in which many of the details recorded are suggestive rather of disease than of that showing forth of the divine attributes which we associate with the idea of a miracle. I have already more than once referred to Domenica Lazzari, the "Addolorata" of Capriana in the Tyrol. No case is better attested.

The witnesses were men of high position, quite independent of each other, and their reports, which are in absolute accord regarding the main features of the case, cover a period of more than ten years. Still, the medical history of Domenica is a very curious one.

As a child she was a good girl who worked hard and loved to pray and read books of devotion, but she "exhibited no marks of extraordinary fervour, nor anything to distinguish her as different from what any good and pious girl ought to be." She heard Mass daily, attended all the services of the church and "communicated at least once a month." At the age of 13, shortly after her father's death, when she is stated to have wept almost continuously for four days and four nights and to have eaten next to nothing during the same time, she had a very serious illness, which Dr. Dei Cloche, from the account given to him at a later date, believed to be hysteria marked by violent convulsions. It should be remembered that this doctor writes as a devout Catholic and was apparently in entire sympathy with his patient, treating of her stigmata in minute detail. On June 3, 1833, at the age of eighteen, she had a very severe fright which led to her spending the night alone in a mill, a prey to abject terror. Nine days later she was seized with a sort of cataleptic attack in the fields, and from that time forward she seems hardly to have left her bed until her death in 1848. Dr. Dei Cloche was called to the case in April 1834, after another doctor had treated the patient for some months without any beneficial result. He gives a description of her extraordinary aversion for food and of the strange hyperaesthesia which manifested itself in all her senses. She could not endure anything but the most subdued light. The slightest pressure upon the abdomen caused her intense pain. When she consented reluctantly at his request to allow a small fragment of sugar to be placed upon her tongue, she at once had an attack which lasted for twenty minutes, in the course of which the fit of vomiting was so violent that she almost choked. Already for some weeks she had taken next to no nourishment at all, and from the 10th of April, 1834, until her death it seems that she neither ate nor drank. Dr. Dei Cloche induced her to smell some toast, but this also caused her extreme discomfort. She pressed a handkerchief to her nostrils, suffered contortion of all the muscles of her face, and for a short time fainted away. When a tumbler was struck with a key, she uttered a loud cry and stopped her ears, declaring that the noise stunned her (*mi ha intronata la testa*). A light object resting upon the stomach was enough to set her sobbing and to produce convulsions

in the whole body, while she also complained of agonizing pain.

Dr. Dei Cloche visited her once more in six months' time, and reports that at that date—

> she could endure neither light, nor scents, nor noise, without breaking out into groans, sobs and convulsive movements. She could not articulate a single word without extreme difficulty, and then only in a faint voice. She reluctantly allowed a few intimates near her bed, but if anyone out of mere curiosity drew close to her without precautions and against her wishes, her trembling grew more violent and her pain became more acute. She took no nourishment of any kind . . . but though her expression was dejected her limbs were not emaciated.

In January 1837 it was reported that wonderful supernatural phenomena (i.e., the stigmata) were manifesting themselves in Domenica, and Dr. Dei Cloche, who was now head of an important hospital in the city of Trent, was led to pay her another visit early in the May of that year. From a medical point of view he found her still in much the same condition, and extraordinary sensitive to any form of sense impression. Even the slight contact involved in feeling her pulse made her tremble all over and break out into groans. Night and day, not excepting the bitterest winter weather, when the thermometer stood at —13 degrees Reaumur (*i.e.*, 29 degrees of frost Fahrenheit), she lay with the window wide open, and in summer she only found relief from the heat in being continually fanned. On the Friday morning, when the anguish of the stigmata was beginning, Dei Cloche on approaching the house declared that more than a hundred paces away I could hear piercing cries which came from the window of her room looking out upon the road, and as I drew near I could distinguish the words, repeated again and again, "O God come to my assistance." At ten o'clock the unfortunate sufferer was still repeating the same invocation in vibrant tones. Now and again she returned laconic answers to questions addressed to her, but at once resumed her distressing ejaculation. ... At four o'clock in the afternoon, though the blood had then ceased to flow from the stigmata, she continued to utter her piteous cry with unabated energy. When asked why she never stopped this clamour, "It is," she answered, "because I never cease feeling intense pain all over my body and particularly in the places of the wounds, and I find relief in crying as I do."

Of the stigmata I have already spoken in a previous chapter. I will only add that Domenica's face was usually covered with a mask of blood which had trickled on Fridays from the circlet of punctures representing the crown of thorns. Lord Shrewsbury, in his published account of the Addolorata, tells us, on the authority of a German physician who in 1841 was studying the case, that "the face is never washed, she not being able to bear the use of water either hot or cold," though the blood gradually disappears of itself. We may also learn from the same authority that "there was a strong smell of coagulated blood in the room." At half-past three on the Friday afternoon "the blood was still oozing perceptibly from the wounds in the back of her hands," and Lord Shrewsbury adds:

> Her fingers were so firmly clasped that, to judge from appearances, she had not the power to loose them; but on the clergyman who accompanied us asking her to let us see the inside of the hands, she immediately opened them from underneath, without unclasping her fingers, as a shell opens upon its hinges, so that we distinctly saw the wounds, and the blood and serum, quite fresh and flowing down over the wrist.

The same writer was also permitted to see the feet, and noticed that "instead of taking its natural course, the blood flowed upwards over the toes, as it would do were she suspended on the cross." I cannot, however, help thinking that this appearance may be sufficiently accounted for without any miracle, by the fact, carefully noted by Dei Cloche, that in the acute stage of the stigmatization agony "the sole of the foot took a position nearly horizontal with her legs." At the hour when the feet were shown to Lord Shrewsbury and other visitors the rigidity of this attitude had probably somewhat relaxed. Still I am not sure how far this point ought to be pressed, for Mr. T. W. Allies, in his minute description of what he saw in 1847 (he was then still an Anglican), insists much that the course followed by the blood flowing from the forehead and from the hands was not that which it would naturally take in Domenica's recumbent posture. Dr. Dei Cloche's medical study of the case was printed ten years before the visit of Mr. Allies. When the last-named observer and his friends made their pilgrimage to Capriana, Domenica was within nine months of her death, and her physical vigour was apparently much less than it had been in 1837. At the earlier period she was shaken for hours together with convulsive movements which affected every part of her frame and which culminated in a prostration so complete that, as Dei Cloche says, "you might have taken her for death personified." Amid these convulsions, as the same medical observer notes,

> Domenica with her tightly clasped hands often showered blows upon her breast with intense violence, so that the noise was past belief. On one occasion amongst the rest she struck her chin with so much force that her gums were badly cut and her mouth was filled with blood.... The gnashing of her teeth was continuous, and so loud that it might be compared to the noise of a furious and hungry dog gnawing a bone, or to the grinding of an enormous file applied by vigorous arms to a great bar of iron.

Dei Cloche goes on to tell us that, as he learned on good authority, in the convulsive attacks of 1836, from June 24th to July 2nd, the noise of the blows which Domenica gave herself could be heard not only throughout the house but also in the road distant four perches from the building. Someone who had taken the trouble to count them declared that there were as many as 409 in a single hour. It is impossible not to be reminded of the exactly similar behaviour of Elizabeth of Herkenrode, of which details were given in an earlier chapter. But the question inevitably arises: Is this disease, or are these the strange ways in which the soul is led on to higher union with God? However extraordinary the phenomena which attended Domenica Lazzari's fourteen years of martyrdom there has never, so far as I can ascertain, been any question of introducing the cause of her beatification. She does not seem to have impressed either visitors or intimates with any sense of exceptional holiness. Her sister who looked after her, so Mr. Pollen wrote, "was perfectly simple, wanted no money, and treated Domenica more as an invalid than anything else." Mr. Wynne (afterwards Father Wynne, S.J.), the third member of Mr. Allies' party, wrote, two days after, to a correspondent as follows:

> We have been very much impressed, and what to me makes it more peculiar is that in former cases in which the stigmata have been granted, they appeared ... as the seal of consummate sanctity, or the reward of intense meditation on the Passion, whereas in the present instance there is nothing to lead one to suppose either the one or the other in any extraordinary degree. The impression conveyed to me ... was more one of great suffering and resignation than of any extraordinary tokens of grace. There is, I take it, no necessary connection between the extraordinary phenomena which her body bears and extreme sanctity, though one might expect it.
>
> Her life has always been extremely virtuous and pious ... but nothing that I saw led me to suppose the lofty religious abstraction, the spiritual fervour, or superhuman yearning of the soul for God, which one looks for in the female Saint.

But this in some sense only adds to the mystery. Sabatier, Georges Dumas, Dr. Merkt and others admit the physical reality of the stigmata, but explain them as the result of intense concentration of thought upon the wounds of our Saviour. But here apparently we have the phenomena without any such concentration. It seems, at any rate, certain from the concurrent testimony of many witnesses that in Domenica's case there was no proper ecstasy or trance, though I doubt if this can be said of any other stigmatic whose life is fully known to us.

Not less perplexing, though for different reasons, is the case of Palma Matarrelli, of Oria, near Brindisi, who was born in 1825 and died in 1888. Here the good faith of the subject of the phenomena is gravely in doubt, and it is open to the critic to suggest that the wonders recorded of her, if real, are due to diabolical agency. Perhaps I cannot supply a better account of Palma in short space than by translating the few sentences in which Dr. Imbert-Gourbeyre, in contrast to the 200 pages devoted to her in his earlier work, sums up the chief features of her case for the readers of Lai Stigmatisation. Palma was born in the little town of Oria, in which she also died. She was a girl of the peasant class who never learned to read or write. She married, had three daughters, who all died young, and then in 1853, at the age of twenty-eight, found herself a widow.

She seems [Dr. Gourbeyre continues] to have had extraordinary graces from early youth. It was on May 3rd, 1857, that she first received the stigmata. These somewhat later became apparent externally, but only to disappear again in 1865, with the exception of the wound in the side, which still remained at the time of my journey to Oria. Of the four stigmatics I have personally known, Palma's case is that in which I have witnessed the most extraordinary manifestations during the few days I spent in her vicinity in 1871. I have twice seen her on fire inside her clothes, ascertaining afterwards that there were real burns in her flesh similar to those caused by a boiling liquid. I have also seen the linen cloths laid upon her heart during this conflagration (*incendie*) marked with extraordinary patterns when they were removed. I have further seen the blood trickle from the circlet of punctures upon her forehead, and as it was caught in the handkerchief I held under it I watched it trace out patterns like those of the "conflagration." I have reproduced these patterns in my book *Les Stigmatiseés,* and to this I refer the reader. They also showed me at Oria beakers full of a liquid that had come from Palma's mouth, and in which solid bodies had formed which looked like hosts. I still keep a flask full of this species of balm, and to my great astonishment it has never putrified.

Dr. Imbert-Gourbeyre then adds a few words concerning the death of Palma, which took place in March 1888. He had been informed that she received the last Sacraments a few days before her death, that crowds of people flocked to Oria to do her honour, and that her body remained flexible and without sign of putrefaction until she was laid in the tomb. Dr. Gourbeyre is not, of course, the only witness who vouches for such marvels as those recorded above. A pilgrim who visited Oria in April 1872 wrote to the Abbé Curicque:

> Palma no longer has the stigmata regularly. During this last Lent they reappeared, but then the stigmatization, so far as any discharge of blood is concerned, came to an end. Still it recurs at times for the sake of her visitors (*elle revient pour et selon ses visiteurs*).

During our first two visits to her, her forehead was without any mark, then, after her thanksgiving, my companions and myself saw four trickles of blood, as broad as one's little finger, oozing from four punctures in the middle of the forehead, which wetted her face and hands. A white cloth was given her to wipe it off, and this wiping left upon the linen not simple bloodstains, but emblems clearly outlined, representing inflamed hearts, nails and swords. This is truly a marvel and I saw it with my own eyes.

Other witnesses testified to the marks of the wounds seen in her hands, and especially to the fact that cloths pressed against her breast were burnt away in many places so as to leave clearly defined patterns, representing hearts, flames, and other pious symbols. But not the least astonishing of the marvels recorded of Palma were her miraculous Communions, often twice or three times in the day, and at all sorts of hours. As it is asserted that she never took solid food, and but little liquid, she was nearly always fasting. In his *Stigmatisées* Dr. Imbert-Gourbeyre describes one such Communion which took place in his presence:

> At this moment I was conversing directly with Canon de Angelis on the subject of bilocation. I was sitting sideways to Palma talking to the Canon who was opposite me when I felt her hand gently tap me on the forearm. At the same instant the Canon fell upon his knees. I turned to look at Palma, and I saw her eyes shut, her hands joined, her mouth wide open, and on her tongue I perceived a host. I kneel down at once, I adore and I watch her. Palma puts out her tongue still further as if she was bent on making me see the host clearly, then she swallows it, shuts her mouth and remains profoundly recollected in her chair. It might at this moment have been about half-past four. The day was closing in, the oratory was badly lit by a small window very high up. The miraculous host appeared to me as white as wax and rather thick.

These circumstances apparently awakened no suspicion in the good doctor's mind, though the conditions were ideal for a sleight-of-hand deception. But this was not all. Palma having received this miraculous Communion, usage prescribed that for a short space she should be left alone in the oratory to make her thanksgiving. Soon she summons them back and they find blood trickling from her forehead. The stigmata have appeared once more in their absence. The next day Palma has a long conversation with Dr. Gourbeyre about her miraculous Communions. She explains that the Host is brought to her by our Lord, or by one of the Saints, who remains invisible but who has taken the consecrated particle from some tabernacle, sometimes from St. Peter's at Rome, or even from churches as far off as Milan. She also receives Communion in the ordinary way every morning at Mass, but our Lord bestows this special privilege on account of the needs of her soul. I must confess that the details of this and other conversations with Palma which Dr. Gourbeyre records with the utmost simplicity produce upon me a very unfavourable impression, but it is impossible to enlarge upon this theme. I will content myself with calling attention to certain comments on Palma, reprinted in 1892 in the fifth volume of the (*Euvres Completes* of Mgr. Barbier de Montault. In an article printed in 1877, before the death of Pius IX, Mgr. Barbier recalls a conversation with His Holiness, in the course of which the Pontiff said:

> Since you write in the Press say out loud, and say it many times over, that the Pope condemns all these visionaries with revelations, Palma, Cantiamille, and those others who mislead and deceive the faithful. It is all the work of the devil. I have documents to prove it.

In 1879 the Jesuit Pere Pouplard, in the French *Messager du S. Coeur de Jesus*, described how he had tried to learn what was thought in Rome of a certain "voyante " who lived in the South of Italy and who was supposed to be favoured with the most extraordinary manifestations. In answer, the very eminent and respected Roman theologian whom he consulted replied that he believed the whole thing to be only a snare of the devil. Quoting this passage in full, Mgr. Barbier de Montault dots the i's by declaring that the question undoubtedly referred to Palma d'Oria. Thereupon he professes to cite the very grave words spoken by Pius IX to himself in a special private audience which took place in 1875.

> I have had an investigation made concerning Palma [the Pope told him]. In consequence of the report which was then drawn up I have left the matter in the hands of the Holy Office, and the Holy Office has pronounced that the whole business is diabolic. The Holy Office is pledged to secrecy, but I am not pledged. Take good heed, then, of what I tell you. What Palma is doing is the work of the devil, and her pretended miraculous Communions with hosts taken from St.

Peter's are a pure piece of trickery. It is all imposture, and I have the proofs there in the drawer of my bureau. She has befooled a whole crowd of pious and credulous souls. One of your fellow-countrymen has written a book about her which has been delated to the Holy Office. Out of consideration for the author, who is a good Catholic and whose intentions are excellent, the Holy Office decided not to condemn him publicly, but has begged him to withdraw the book from circulation to prevent any new denunciation which might lead to its being formally censured.

There can be no doubt that the book referred to was the second volume of Dr. Imbert-Gourbeyre's *Les Stigmatisées*. In point of fact this book was not reprinted after 1873, and in the new work, *La Stigmatisation*, which replaced it in 1894, comparatively little is said of Palma d'Oria, in particular a complete silence is maintained with regard to her supposed miraculous Communions.

It must be confessed that there is a good deal of evidence, even on the surface, which confirms the unfavourable estimate of Palma formed by Pius IX. Her patronizing tone in speaking of Louise Lateau, her obvious fishing for information regarding Louise and other stigmatics, her prophecy that Napoleon III would return to France and suffer a violent death on French soil, her supposed miraculous Communions two or three times in the same day, the telepathic communications alleged to exist between her and that very unsatisfactory person Mélanie Mathieu, the little shepherdess of La Salette, her thinly veiled desire to make a display of the supernatural favours accorded to her, all these things are in conflict with the self-effacement characteristic of true sanctity. On the other hand, if her manifestations were diabolical in origin, one would have expected Satan to produce something less crude than the childish patterns of flames, hearts, etc., reproduced in *Les Stigmatisées*. Furthermore, there is evidence that Palma sometimes influenced souls for good. For example, a friend writes to me:

> There was a married woman, a cousin of mine, living a very frivolous and worldly life in Paris. She went to see Palma as a new excitement, not with a serious purpose. Palma knew all about her and had a message for her from our Lord. She was to return to Paris and seek a certain Father, whose name I forget, and make a general confession in preparation for death, for she was not to live long. While with Palma, my cousin saw the Sacred Host come miraculously and enter

Palma's mouth. Overwhelmed with astonishment and fear, she was at once converted. Returning to Paris she did as Palma had desired and lived a most holy life for a few weeks or months, and then died a very edifying death. She was about thirty years of age. All this happened about fifty years ago.

I repeat this statement as I received it, only adding that I am fully assured of the good faith of the writer, who has been known to me personally and by repute for more than thirty years.

5

A Stigmatization Imposture?

In an article on "Impostors" which I contributed to the *Catholic Encyclopaedia* I had occasion to make reference to the Spanish nun, Magdalena de la Cruz, who was sentenced by the Inquisition in 1546 for her alleged hypocritical pretence of sanctity supported by counterfeit stigmata and other phenomena. Magdalena's story is a very curious one. She was a girl of humble origin who was received into a Franciscan convent at Cordova in 1504 at the age of seventeen. Her ecstasies, penitential practices, miraculous communions and alleged abstention from food, attracted attention both within and without her own community. She was believed to have the stigmata and to be raised from the ground in prayer. She was elected prioress in 1533 when she was forty-six years old, and re-elected to the same office in 1536 and 1539. So universal was the veneration in which she was held that ladies of the highest rank, when about to be confined, sent to her the cradles or garments prepared for the expected infant that she might bless them. This homage was paid her even by the Empress Isabel in 1527 before the birth of Philip II. There were, however, those who regarded the nun with distrust, and St. Ignatius Loyola in particular lent her no countenance. Falling dangerously ill in 1543, it is alleged that Magdalena confessed to a long career of hypocrisy, and after a trial lasting nearly two years the Inquisition sentenced her to lifelong confinement in the convent of another Order where she was subject to many penalties including deprivation for a time of Holy Communion. It seems certain, however, that she accepted her lot with complete submission and in a spirit of the most edifying piety. She regained the respect of those who lived with her and is said to have died a very holy death.

Similar to this in many aspects, and causing probably an even greater sensation, was the case of the Dominican nun, Sor Maria de la Visitacion. Unlike Magdalena she belonged to a distinguished family, though she was a Portuguese, not a Spaniard.

At the age of twelve she entered the convent of the Annunciation in Lisbon and made her profession there in 1568 when she was seventeen. Through the reputation she acquired for virtue and intelligence, but possibly helped by family influence, she, though still a very young nun, was elected prioress in 1582, and from that time forward began to be famous. It is much to be regretted that the Life which the celebrated Dominican, Father Luis de Granada, is said to have written of her and which still exists in manuscript, seems never to have been published. Apart from a few casual notices, almost all that we hear of Sor Maria de la Visitacion belongs to the period subsequent to her downfall and loss of credit.

One would very much like to know the impression she made upon her fellow-religious during the fifteen years or more which she spent at the convent of the Annunciation before she became Superior. There can be no question that at the time preparations were being made for the mustering of the great Armada which was to conquer England, Sor Maria was a very influential personage.

The reputation which then attached to the name of the nun of Lisbon is convincingly attested in the reports which Lippomano, the Venetian Ambassador in Spain, dispatched to the Doge and Senate in 1587 and 1588. The Spaniards in 1587 were suffering from the attacks made by Drake upon the galleons returning from the Indies. The naval command, under the direction of the Marquis of Santa Cruz, was able to do very little to counter this menace, and on July 1587 Lippomano reports:

> The Marquis will go to the Azores, but little good is expected from his presence beyond securing the fleet from New Spain, though they say that he visited the holy nun of Lisbon, and that she bade him go with a good heart, taking with him the cross and promised him victory in all his actions.

In February of the next year Lippomano thinks it worth while to insert in his official dispatch the following item of gossip:

> Evil persons having spread a rumour that the stigmata of the holy nun are spurious, the General of her Order has made a new examination, with many tests, and sent the result to His Majesty.

> They find that beyond all doubt the stigmata are genuine and miraculous. Fra Luigi di Granada has written a book describing her divine operations.

After destruction had fallen upon the Armada, we have a letter from Lippomano to the Doge on December 14, 1588. It is written in a very different sense, and Mr. Brown summarizes the contents as follows:

> The Nun of Portugal who was universally held for a saint has been found out at last. The stigmata are proved to be artificial and the whole trick invented to gain credit in the world. She was induced to act thus by two friars of her Order of St. Dominic, with a view to being able some day to tell the King that unless he handed Portugal over to Don Antonio he would be damned for ever, and with the further object of raising a rebellion against the King. The friars are in the prisons of the Inquisition, the nun in a convent awaiting sentence.

There can be no doubt that Sor Maria's declared sympathy for the party which advocated the independence of Portugal from Spanish rule must have prejudiced her cause. If she had entertained such views before, she had dissimulated them, but in the depression and political agitation which settled down upon the peninsula after the great naval disaster she seems to have spoken more freely. No doubt this consideration was not forgotten by the Inquisitors; but in the sentence they pronounced no reference is made to political matters. The verdict was summarized by Lippomano thus:

> First she is condemned to perpetual prison in a convent not of her own Order outside the city.
>
> She may not receive the sacraments for five years, except on the three Easters [tre Pasque] or in articulo mortis, or in a papal jubilee.
>
> Every Wednesday and Friday in public in the nuns' chapter house, she shall receive the discipline for as long as it takes to chant the Miserere.
>
> She shall eat in the refectory in public on the ground, and no one may eat what she leaves. She shall lie on the ground at the door of the refectory, and all the nuns shall walk over her as they come in and go out.
>
> She shall fast perpetually; she may not be elected to any office, but shall take rank below the meanest nun in the convent.

She may not speak to any of the nuns or to anyone else without leave of the prioress.

The bread she uses, the drinking cups and all else shall be given to the Inquisition or its delegate.

She shall not wear a veil. On Wednesdays and Fridays she shall have nothing but bread and water.

Each time she leaves her cell to eat she shall recite her sin aloud.

In forwarding this summary, Lippomano not only makes reference to the fact that the nun had been previously held for a saint, but tells the Doge that she "had received several letters in King Philips own hand, one of them commending his action to her prayers, and declaring that he desired to come to Portugal to visit her and kiss her hand."

The exposure and condemnation of *Sor Maria de la Visitacion* not unnaturally had their repercussions. We may, in the first place, attribute to this cause the death of Father Luis de Granada himself. He had been Provincial of the Dominicans in Portugal and also a notable professor of theology. As a spiritual writer he was famous beyond any man of that generation. His books were printed in numberless editions and reproduced in many languages.

Even in Elizabethan England they were highly popular, and not only Catholics, but Protestants also, had busied themselves with the task of translating or adapting them. Sor Maria professed to be under his direction. He undoubtedly knew her well, used to hear her confession and required her to show him her stigmata. It seems to be beyond question that he made himself guarantee of her good faith by writing not only to Pope Gregory XIII, but to King Philip II, to Blessed John de Ribera, who was Archbishop of Valencia, and to many others. Himself recognized on all hands as a master of the spiritual life, he was satisfied that his penitent in Lisbon was one of the holiest of God's servants. There is no suggestion that, when the sentence passed by the Inquisition was made public, Luis de Granada fell under any suspicion of connivance in a fraud. He was himself a Spaniard, and in any case kept aloof from politics. There may, however, have been other members of the Order, as stated in Lippomano's dispatch quoted above, who were less discreet and who were ardent in the cause of Portuguese independence.

What is certain is that Fray Luis in 1588 was a very old man— he was born in 1504—and that the shock of this condemnation of the stigmatica for whose sincerity he had pledged his word must have been a very serious one. All that we know is that the sentence of the Inquisition was delivered on December 8th and that Fray Luis died before the close of the same month. Pére Mortier suggests that the old man's sight had been failing him in his last years. Hence it is probable that he might easily have been imposed upon when Sor Maria exhibited her seemingly wounded hands to him from the other side of the convent grille. This seems to be a reasonable explanation, but one would like to know more about the early relations between the venerable priest and his ecstatic penitent.

We are rather better informed concerning the case of Father Sisto Fabri, the General of the Dominicans, who, as Lippomano reported to the Doge, "made a new examination with many tests," and convinced himself that "beyond all doubt the stigmata are genuine and miraculous." Father Fabri's deposition from the high office which he held was unquestionably connected with the scandal of Sor Maria's alleged imposture. He was an Italian by birth, and there is nothing to suggest that he had ever known much of the prioress of the Annunciation convent at Lisbon. But when rumours of trickery had begun to circulate again, even after Luis de Granada had written so strongly in the nun's favour, the Dominican General, who happened to be in Spain at the time, thought it desirable to verify the matter for himself. He accordingly went to Portugal armed with full powers, and on November 18, 1587, he saw the stigmata of Maria de la Visitacion, of which he has left a description in Italian. There were punctures all round the nun's forehead, dark scabs as of protruding nailheads in the hands and feet, and in Maria's side he tells us that he saw a wound a little less than an inch in length and rather more than half an inch wide (*longo poco mem di un dito per longo, et larga poco piu di mezzo dito per traverso*). What he calls a *dito* was possibly rather more than an English inch, but the point is of no consequence. He had come provided with a piece of soap, but the attempt made to wash away the marks on the hands was unsuccessful. At the same time, it seems that as the nun protested that the slightest touch upon the affected parts caused her intense anguish, he felt obliged for pity's sake to desist from any too violent application of the detergent. This could not have been a very satisfactory test of the genuineness of the phenomenon, but the favourable verdict of this new investigation, as we have seen, was made generally known. In spite of unfriendly rumours and the hostility of a minority of her own community, the reputation of the prioress during those months which witnessed the concentration of the vast armada in the mouth of the Tagus still stood very high. The Cardinal Albert of Austria, Philip II's viceroy in Portugal, took no step, we are told, without consulting her, and she was formally asked to bless the great enterprise they had in hand.

Very possibly the fact that the five wounds were figured in the arms of Portugal may have led to the belief that the stigmata of this reputed saint were in some sense an omen of the victory of those arms. We know in particular that pieces of linen marked with her blood were eagerly sought for and were believed to work many astonishing cures. On these memorials, venerated as relics, five spots of blood were seen arranged so as to suggest the extremities of a cross, the largest spot being in the centre. Paramo, a contemporary and himself a high official of the Inquisition, describes Maria de la Visitacion as "famous throughout all the provinces of Spain and Italy and indeed even as far as the most distant confines of the eastern ocean." He also informs us of a clause which is not mentioned in Lippomano's summary of the sentence of the Inquisition, This was an explicit ordinance that all portraits of the pretended stigmatica or fragments of the linen she had used were to be given up and destroyed. But Paramo goes on to say that in spite of this he came to know, when he was Inquisitor in Sicily that Mary, the wife of Diego de Guzman, Count of Alba, and Viceroy of that province, still treasured some pieces of linen of this nature, as well as a portrait of the nun and a long written account of her life. This would seem to show that the verdict of the Inquisition had not entirely succeeded in persuading the admirers of the former Dominican prioress that she was no more than an impostor.

And here let me confess that I also am not convinced that the truth of the matter was brought to light in the course of the Inquisition inquiry. I do not for a moment suggest that Sor Maria was a saint, or even a woman of exceptional holiness, but I think it possible that she was honestly deluded and that some at least of the phenomena attributed to her were genuine. There are many cases in which it would seem to me difficult to question the reality of the strange manifestations, notably the ecstatic condition and stigmata, which observers declare themselves to have witnessed as they developed under their own eyes. Fraud and deception may in some measure intervene, and it is nearly always difficult to decide at what definite point the trickery begins. None the less, I do venture very positively to affirm that there are visionaries who have genuine ecstasies and genuine stigmata, but who for all that are by no means saints. In that case it does not seem to me that Maria de la Visitacion can quite definitely be set down as an impostor upon such slender evidence as is at present available in the printed accounts preserved of her.

What weighs, of course most heavily in the scale is her own confession of deliberate trickery, and her explanation of how she did it. But one may well ask whether the avowals of an accused on trial before the Inquisition are in any way more convincing than the confessions of witches obtained in the prosecutions which such staunch Protestants as Matthew Hopkins and the other English witch finders conducted in the seventeenth century. There cannot be a shadow of doubt that the unfortunate people brought to trial on the charge of witchcraft made these confessions, which are still preserved to us in court records, and that they included in them the most incredible details about their animal familiars, pacts with the devil, riding through the air and ritual observances of indescribable filthiness. The most astonishing feature in the case is the fact that it must have been perfectly well known to the accused witches that the avowal of such evil practices saved them from nothing. They were even more liable to be hanged if they confessed than if they denied everything, and in the English prosecutions torture, as a rule, does not seem to have been employed or threatened.

In the case, however, of a trial before the Inquisition, confession, even apart from any question of torture, brought a very definite gain to the accused, supposing always that there had been no previous condemnation and relapse. If Maria de la Visitacion— and the same seems to have been true of Magdalena de la Cruz— had stoutly maintained that her stigmata, levitations, miraculous communions and other phenomena were of supernatural origin, the court, once satisfied that she was unsound in any point of faith, would almost certainly have decided that if these marvels had occurred they must have been diabolical in their origin and that Maria was a sorceress who had made a pact with the devil. Now this was a much more serious offence than any imposture or trickery, however profane in character. Hypocrisy and even blasphemous pretences involved no denial of the Faith. The culprit might have to face the very severest ecclesiastical penalties, but there would be no relaxation to the secular arm, and no burning in an *auto da fé*.

Sor Maria, I assume, would have been quite shrewd enough to know how these things were regarded by Inquisitorial eyes. According to the received accounts suspicion of her fraudulent phenomena had first been kindled by one of her nuns who, looking through a chink in the door of the prioress's cell, had detected the reverend mother in the act of painting the semblance of a wound in one of her hands. Father Luis de Granada and the General of the Dominicans, who professed to have investigated the reality of these wounds, had, owing to her pretence of suffering intense pain, been deterred from applying any effective test. When, however, Sor Maria was brought before the Inquisition, the officials, we are told, tolerated no nonsense of this sort, but, scrubbing vigorously, removed the paint and found the flesh beneath perfectly sound and normal. Being thus detected in manifest fraud, she withdrew her previous denials, owned herself guilty and wrote out an explanation of the various forms of trickery by which she had succeeded in imposing upon her credulous admirers. This saved her from the stake, but not from a rude penance which lasted to the end of her days. It is noteworthy that she, like Magdalena de la Cruz, is said to have accepted her lot with complete resignation and to have died an exceptionally holy death.

In writing his account of the generalate of Father Sisto Fabri, Pére Mortier has naturally found occasion to discuss this scandal of the Lisbon nun which was so closely connected with the Generals deposition from office. I must own that his treatment of the subject does not convince me. Pére Mortier is apparently satisfied that the report of the washing away of the marks of Sor Maria's stigmata when she appeared before the officials of the Inquisition proves beyond dispute that these pretended wounds were a mere imposture. But in the Life of Blessed Gemma Galgani we may learn that Gemma told her first confessor, Mgr. Volpi, that if he sent a doctor to examine her he would see nothing. The confessor persisted and the doctor came one Friday when Gemma was in ecstasy and the stigmata were already bleeding. "The doctor took a towel, dipped it in water, and wiped Gemma's hands forehead. The blood immediately disappeared and the skin showed no signs of cicatrix, scratch or puncture, as if there had never been any laceration." Of course, a grave suspicion of fraud rested for a while on Gemma's stigmata, but there can be no question of the reality of her wound-marks as examined on other occasions, and her beatification, though it is explicitly affirmed that this pronounces no verdict upon the supernatural character of the phenomena attributed to her, must at any rate exonerate her from anything like conscious deception. We know practically nothing about the conditions under which these wound-marks appear, or are suddenly healed. So far as I may venture to express any opinion on the subject, all these questions are extremely difficult and must be left unresolved to the specialists in neuropathology of a future generation.

There are also several other matters which must raise doubts in the minds of those who are at all familiar with the records of stigmatization phenomena. It is difficult to understand how Sor Maria, if conscious of fraud, could have presented herself before the Inquisitors with stigmata painted on her hands. It would always have been easy for her to declare that, as happens so frequently in these cases, the stigmata had not developed. Even with those who normally have this experience every Friday, there is an intermission in paschal time and also on other occasions. Moreover, I find it hard to accept the statement that the prioress produced the effect of rising in the air by some mechanical apparatus which she worked by gently turning a handle, or that candles could have been so arranged in her cell as to surround her face with a mysterious halo of light. On the other hand, this was the sort of story she would be likely to tell when faced with the dire necessity of giving some natural explanation of happenings which she herself understood no better than those who were questioning her.

The points which seem to be the most clearly established are that thirty-two nuns and four servants testified before the Inquisitors in her favour, while only ten nuns and four other servants declared the manifestations fraudulent; further, that not only Luis de Granada, but also the Provincial Albert Agayo and the General Sisto Fabri, were favourably impressed; and perhaps most weighty of all that when Sor Maria was found to have declared herself in favour of the independence of Portugal, it became a matter of urgency with the Government of Philip II to use every means in their power to discredit her and to destroy the influence she was still able to exercise upon public opinion. It must not be forgotten that the Inquisition in the Spanish peninsula was in an exceptional degree a State institution.

As has been stated above, I am very far from maintaining that Sor Maria was a saint. She may indeed have been the cunning impostor that we have been commonly taught to believe. But it seems, on the other hand, at least equally possible that she belonged to that class of neurotic or hysterical visionaries who, being free from conscious deception, remain sincerely pious in spite of their delusions, and who in so many cases develop phenomena which are almost inevitably hailed by simple-minded enthusiasts as miraculous manifestations of the divine favour.

Let me conclude this chapter by giving an account of a very recent case of stigmatization which I have personally had the opportunity of investigating.

The girl, let us call her Lizzie Smith, lived in a manufacturing town in the north of England and belonged to the artisan class. She was then, I should judge, about thirty-seven years of age.

She was born a Protestant, but when she was in her teens she came across some nuns and eventually was instructed by them and received into the Catholic Church. About the same time she had a fit or a paralytic stroke which affected her whole left side. The leg gradually recovered, but the arm obstinately remained rigid; the hand was clenched and the nails even began to grow into the palm. She remained in this condition for some time until a pilgrimage to Holywell was suggested to her. She went and was there rather dramatically cured. As the latest *miraculée*, she thus attracted a good deal of attention; her photograph appeared in local newspapers, and she became an object of veneration to many of the more humble pilgrims, several of whom made friends with her and invited her to stay with them in their homes. After this she began to be visited by the spirits of the dead. Some came to ask her prayers that they might obtain their release from purgatory; others—and in particular a little girl who had died just after her first Communion and whose photograph she had seen in the house of one of her new friends—came from heaven to watch over and direct her. From the guardian spirit last referred to she received warning that she would soon be favoured by an apparition of our Lady and afterwards of our Saviour Himself. When our Saviour came, she was instructed to have some pieces of clean linen ready, and also a number of little pictures and objects of piety; for our Lord, she was told, would bless them. After some postponement, the vision of our Saviour duly occurred. He showed Himself as He was in His Passion, His wounds dripping with blood.

This blood (she was of course alone when the vision appeared) He allowed to drip on to the strips of linen, and He blessed the pictures by touching them with His fingers, leaving on each four drops of blood, roughly indicating the extremities of a cross. I have in my possession a number of these pictures. There is no doubt that the marks they bear are those of congealed human blood. Sometime later she professed to have received the stigmata, which were renewed from time to time on such days as Good Friday and festivals of the Passion. The wounds were not deep, neither did anyone ever see them forming. It is practically certain that they were self-inflicted; but there were wounds and they bled.

When I saw Lizzie Smith in August 1920, arriving at her house without any notification of my intended visit, she showed me in the palms of her hands slight but quite perceptible traces of a stigmatization which she averred had occurred on the previous Friday. One curious development may be mentioned here, though it has no direct connection with our present subject. In the November of 1919, the soul of a priest from purgatory, so she stated, came to her to ask for prayers. He laid his right hand upon her right arm, and the hand burnt through the blouse which she was wearing and left the impress of the thumb and fingers upon her forearm. There can be no question as to the burning of the sleeve of the blouse, or as to the marks upon her arm. Several persons, some of them quite sceptical as to the supernatural character of these manifestations (her parish priest was one of the latter number), saw the impression when it was quite fresh. They assured me that the imprint, as of four fingers and a thumb, was unmistakable. I myself saw the marks nine months after the event, though at that time they were blurred and fading. Finally, on the afternoon of March 17, 1920, another manifestation occurred. She declared that the metal figure of a large crucifix, which hung beside her prie-dieu, suddenly began to sweat blood.

The whole figure was dripping with blood. She covered the crucifix with a piece of clean linen and next day took it to her director, a priest in another town many miles away. There in his presbytery I saw it five months later, the linen still adhering to the figure and only detached from it with difficulty owing to the coagulation of the blood. Subsequent developments, upon the nature of which I need not enter, have (I believe) satisfied even those who formerly looked upon these various occurrences as supernatural, that the incidents of the story I have just narrated were all due either to imposture or self-delusion. Still, Lizzie brought into the Catholic Church nearly all the members of her family, and every evening a crowd of humble people assembled in the room she occupied and there recited the rosary with great devotion.

The story, it seems to me, is interesting as an illustration of the extravagances of which the hysterical temperament is capable. The predominance of the blood idea is in this case especially noticeable. At Lizzie's instigation, or certainly with her sanction, a convent of hard-working nuns, among whom she passed for a hidden saint, busied themselves in cutting the blood-stained linen cloth, which our Lord was said to have blessed, into fragments and sewing them up in little covers of American cloth to be worn around the neck or given to the sick as relics. The clergy lent no encouragement to this sort of propaganda, but a little band of followers seem to have been very zealous in the cause. It will be noticed that the incident of the crucifix sweating blood occurred some months before anything was made public concerning the happenings at Templemore. Moreover, curiously enough, on that very morning (St. Patrick's Day, March 17, 1920), on which the figure of Lizzie's crucifix was bathed in blood, a photograph had appeared in the Daily Herald representing the miraculous flow of blood from a picture in a French village church. Of this last very puzzling phenomenon I do not here propose to speak. No adequate investigation of the occurrence has yet taken place, although the Society for Psychical Research has for some time contemplated the idea of a systematic enquiry. It may be sufficient for my present readers to state that the curé in whose church these manifestations continued to take place was not only suspended by his Bishop, but persisted in saying Mass in defiance of this suspension.

The photograph, however, with a brief account of the phenomenon, appeared in the *Daily Herald*, and it is certainly a strange coincidence that on that very evening Lizzie Smith invited the attention of her parish clergy and others to the fact that a wonderful prodigy had occurred in her room and that the figure of her big crucifix was dripping with blood.

6

The Case of Padre Pio

A short article which appeared in the *Daily Mail* of June 19th, 1920, gave a curiously perverse account of the concourse of people who made their way to Foggia, in Apulia, attracted by the renown of Father Pio da Pietrelcina, the saintly Capuchin friar whose stigmata provoked a good deal of discussion in Italy and elsewhere. *The Daily Mail* correspondent let us know that:

> Extraordinary scenes are being witnessed in Foggia from day to day. The peasants refuse to confess to any but the young friar or to receive Communion from another's hand, and in consequence the rest of the monastery is idle, while long queues besiege the young Franciscan and gaze in wonder at the markings on his hands, sandaled feet, and head (sic).

And it added that—

> The Vatican is not enamoured of such "revivals," especially when they lead to a complaint from the head of the monastery that the ordinary life of the place is being interrupted; and so Monsignor Cheretti (sic) was sent over hill and dale for three days and nights in a motor-car to seek to calm the devout of Foggia, speaking in the name of Pope Benedict.

There seems, in this case, to be no doubt that Father Pio is a man of remarkable sanctity. He has sometimes spent as much as eighteen hours at a stretch in the confessional. The people throng to him to seek his spiritual direction, just as in years gone by they used to journey from all parts of France to consult M. Vianney in the little village church of Ars. There are many stories, which seem to be well substantiated, of the miracles worked by his intercession, as also of frequent ecstasies, and in one or two instances, of bilocation. Further, there is no question that from September 1918 he bore upon his body the five wound-marks of our Saviour. The fact is particularly interesting because the cases of complete stigmatization in male subjects are exceedingly rare. It may indeed be said that no perfectly satisfactory example has been known, except that of the seraphic Father, St. Francis, himself. But the Roman authorities, guided by the experience of many centuries, are wisely distrustful of abnormal favours of the psychophysical order in which hysteria and other pathological causes, or the action of evil spirits, or even fraudulent simulation, may at any time play a part. The Church never canonizes any of her children in their lifetime, and even after death she does not accept such manifestations, however well-grounded may be the belief in their supernatural origin, as the sole or principal foundation for her favourable judgment.

The truth is that history supplies many sad examples of ecstatics and stigmatics, long held in high repute of sanctity, who have afterwards fallen away. The two sixteenth-century Spanish nuns Magdalena de la Cruz and Maria de la Visitacion, whose pretended revelations and unusual gifts stirred the whole peninsula to its depths, may, no doubt, have been impostors from the outset, but also, quite as probably, were at first truly privileged servants of God, until the homage which was paid them sapped their virtue and filled them with conceit. In the chronicles of the Franciscan Order there is the extraordinary case of Friar Justin of Hungary (c. 1445), who had many ecstasies, and who on one occasion, in the presence of St. John Capistran and the whole community, as they sat in the refectory, was raised up in the air above their heads in a kneeling posture and floated to a picture of Our Lady, which hung high upon the wall. Nevertheless, shortly afterwards, yielding to spiritual pride, he left the Order and died miserably. In this connection it seems worth while to call attention to the only other alleged case of complete masculine stigmatization known to us in modem times. It is that of a youth who was then a Jesuit novice in the Sicilian Province. Strong measures were taken at the time by the General of the Jesuits and other superiors to protect the novice from the consequences of such publicity as had been given to the matter, but the individual in question, having long ago left the Order and being now completely lost sight of, there can be no harm in printing the following letter from the Rector of the English Jesuit College in Malta:

St. Ignatius' College, Malta.
Ap. 26, 1886.

Dear Father Provincial,

P.C.

The young scholastic novice whose eyes were cured in December last is now all the talk of this island. He appears to have the stigmata. I went to see him yesterday and conversed with him for about two hours. I saw the five wounds. On Good Friday Dr. Schembri tells me that he and eleven other medical men saw these wounds wide open and bleeding. The Father Provincial [of the Sicilian Province] told me that whenever he receives Holy Communion, blood flows copiously from his breast; he showed me three handkerchiefs quite saturated with blood; these handkerchiefs had been taken from his heart at the end of Mass. The bleeding began on the 1st of February last, and has continued on all Communion days since, except on Easter Sunday. The young man is in great pain, he is obliged to walk on his heels on account of the wound in the feet. He says that he has been through and taken part in all the sufferings of Christ's Passion. The marks of the scourges, Father Provincial tells us, were seen on his back.

He is often seen in a trance, and the body perfectly stiff, the face smiling. I asked him a great number of questions about the events of the Passion. His answers coincided exactly in every detail with the Gospel narrative, he speaks as one who had been a spectator of all the events he is recounting, without the least hesitation. He is only a child and apparently quite incapable of deceit. An officer asked the Provincial to put his beads on the novice's arm during the time he was in a trance; this being done, the young man took the beads in his hand which no one had hitherto been able to open. When he came to himself, he said our Lady had commissioned him to send word to the officer, mentioning his name, that he (the novice) was not a saint and that therefore such honour should not be showed to him. I was very much struck with the conversation I had with the novice. It is undoubtedly a very extraordinary case which is a source of great anxiety to his Superiors. I have asked our community to be very careful in talking with externs on this subject. Our enemies are saying that it is a piece of Jesuit cunning to deceive the public. Wishing your Reverence all paschal joys, Yours sincerely in Xt.,

Henry Martin, S.J.

The writer of this letter seems to have been entirely satisfied of the genuineness of the phenomena he referred to, and a friend of the present writer's, who also saw the novice, told him that, although quite prepared to believe the case was fraudulent, he had not been able to detect any suspicious circumstance in what he saw or heard. According to the account of all, the novice, whose name, to prevent any danger of unpleasant consequences, we refrain from printing, was, at any rate at first, a very simple lad, giving no great promise of success as a student. Both before his entrance into the Society of Jesus and at the beginning of his noviceship he had suffered from what a contemporary account describes as "violent convulsions." A few months later his eyes had gradually begun to fail him, until almost complete blindness had set in, and then he had been instantaneously cured. Not very long afterwards he left the Order, is known to have been drafted under the conscription law into the Italian army, but since then nothing seems to be known of him.

If we mention this case, it is not, as the reader will readily believe, because we have the slightest inclination to include the stigmata of Father Pio in the same category, but simply to illustrate how it happens that ecclesiastical authority is, and for two or three centuries past has always been, extremely cautious in bestowing any sort of formal sanction or recognition upon what are usually considered the outward manifestations of sanctity. In the processes of beatification the student will find the Promotor Fidei, popularly known as the "Devil's Advocate," again and again insisting that, while such marvels as levitation, stigmatization, bilocation, the knowledge of future or distant events, and above all, ecstasies and revelations, may all be legitimately submitted in evidence in confirmation of what has been otherwise proved, the fact of the heroic virtue of the servant of God must be established by testimony of quite another kind, to wit, by the depositions of those who have been the daily witnesses of his life and actions.

A pronouncement of the Sacred Congregation of the Holy Office made public in the *Acta Apostolicae Sedis* in 1923 must, for all interested in the phenomena of mysticism, claim attention as a decision of considerable significance. True, its wording was negative in form. It merely stated that this supreme ecclesiastical tribunal, "after due investigation," declared that the happenings (*facta*) associated with the name of the devout Capuchin, Padre Pio da Pietralcina of San Giovanni Rotondo, near Foggia, have not been proved to be supernatural in origin (*non constare de eorundem factorum supernaturalitate*), and the Faithful were accordingly exhorted to maintain such an attitude as is in accordance with this "declaration." An utterance of this kind, it will be seen, reflects no sort of censure upon Padre Pio, and requires no one to modify any conviction he may have formed of that mystic's personal holiness.

On the other hand, it does amount to something more than a precaution taken to safeguard the good Father from the indiscreet attentions of his ardent clients. If the Roman authorities had only meant to protect him from importunities, they could have accomplished their purpose by simpler means. They thought it worthwhile to hold a formal investigation, and the conclusion of that inquiry was that the evidence so far available does not prove that the stigmata, the works of healing and the alleged bilocations can be safely considered miraculous.

Now, of the bilocations and the cures I do not propose to say anything here. From the nature of the case the character of such occurrences can be judged only when we are in the presence of very full and exact evidence. But the stigmata are a somewhat different matter. As I have said, there can be no doubt that Padre Pio bears, and has borne for some years (since September 1918), in hands, feet and side, marks corresponding to the wounds of our Lord's sacred Passion. Not only have I conversed with several visitors to San Giovanni Rotondo, who have seen these marks, at any rate those in the hands, at different times and under different conditions, but I have also before me a copy of the medical reports made by two distinguished Roman doctors, who travelled to Foggia at the invitation of the Capuchin Superiors expressly to investigate the phenomena. One of these, by Professor A. Bignami, an agnostic pathologist of the Roman University, is dated July 26, 1919. Although some difficulty was caused by the fact that Padre Pio at that date had been using iodine as an astringent to cheek the bleeding, and that the marks in consequence might have been judged by a careless observer to be merely the stain of the iodine, Professor Bignami attests the existence of superficial scars upon the hands and feet and the form of a cross upon the left breast. He finds that these points are marked by extreme sensitiveness (hyperaesthesia), and does not consider them to have been artificially produced. The lesions are described by him as due to a necrosis of the epidermis of neurotic origin, and their symmetrical arrangement he considers to be probably attributable to unconscious suggestion. In his view there is nothing in the case which cannot be fully accounted for by natural causes.

Though Professor Bignami learnt from the Father himself that there had been a slight discharge of blood from the wounds at an earlier time, nothing of the sort was perceptible at the date of his visit in July 1919. Dr. George Festa, a distinguished Catholic physician of Rome, who travelled to Foggia four or five months later, was in this respect more fortunate. Drops of blood were trickling from the cross-shaped scar on the breast (to call it a wound might suggest a false idea of a rift in the flesh with open lips) and there were also a few drops oozing from the scab on one of the hands.

In other respects the descriptions given by the two doctors of the appearances observed are concordant enough. There were no deep fissures penetrating the extremities, no copious and periodical haemorrhages. As compared with the wounds of Domenica Lazzari, St. Veronica Giuliani and several other famous stigmatisées, the phenomena in Padre Pio's case are not in any way remarkable; but the stigmata are there. Moreover, this particular manifestation in subjects of the male sex is extremely rare. In writing on this subject I have stated that I knew of no quite satisfactory example since the days of St. Francis of Assisi. Fuller investigation has only confirmed this view, and, if on no other ground than its exceptional character, the case of the Capuchin ascetic of Foggia is always likely to claim from students an unwonted share of attention. But to say that a phenomenon is rare, or even exceedingly rare, is by no means the same thing as to show that it is miraculous. The Congregation of the Holy Office must certainly have had before them the reports of Drs. Bignami and Festa, and probably an immense amount of other evidence, proving the reality of those lesions which, when Padre Pio celebrates Mass, everyone near him can discern in his hands, and the presence of which in his feet is attested by his laboured and painful gait.

None the less, the sacred tribunal has decided that these marks are not necessarily supernatural in their origin, a pronouncement which must give pause to many over-enthusiastic believers in the marvellous who nourish their piety upon the disquisitions of the late Dr.Imbert-Gourbeyre or Padre Germano, C.P. But if the formation of these wounds is not a miraculous effect, to what natural cause can they be traced? You surely will not suggest, some of my readers may exclaim, that such phenomena are of hysterical origin. In the case of Padre Pio, not only Dr. George Festa, but even Professor Bignami, attests that, apart from the hyperaesthesia in the region of the lesions themselves, there are no hysterical symptoms. Padre Pio is always exceptionally calm and composed. There is no bad family history. He himself, with a candid simplicity which evidently made a profound impression upon the rationalist Professor, declared that he had never suffered from any nervous malady. He has never been subject to fainting fits or convulsions or tremors. He sleeps well and is not troubled with dreams. Similarly, the author of the *Life of Gemma Galgani* is at pains to show through many pages that none of the symptoms usually associated with hysteria were present in her case. I am not in a position to challenge these statements, and indeed there is no strict need to challenge them. What is realized by comparatively few persons outside the medical profession is the fact that a new and, as it seems, a much more exact conception of the neurosis still commonly called hysteria has come to prevail within the last thirty years, and that these views have been immensely developed and corroborated by the experiences of the Four Years' War. The associations of the word hysteria, as it is commonly understood by the public at large, are so misleading and so disparaging to the patient that many neurologists have urged that a new name should be found for it. "Suggestion Neurosis" being inconveniently cumbersome, the term "Pithiatism" (i.e., a state curable by persuasion), which is used by Babinski, and is introduced by him into the title of one of his books, seems likely in time to win acceptance. No doubt it cannot be maintained that even now all the great authorities are agreed as to the essential nature of hysteria. Pierre Janet is inclined to lay special stress upon "the retraction of the field of consciousness " and its accompanying amnesias. Freud, besides his insistence on conversion and symbolism, emphasizes the repression, "the driving back " into the sub-consciousness, of ideas that are painful. In Babinski's view the outstanding feature of hysteria is that it is a disorder which can be cured by simple "persuasion,' i.e., by counter-suggestion; while Dr. Bernheim, of Nancy, whose early contributions to the discussion were printed in 1884, declares that the word "hysterical" ought to be strictly confined to the fits (crises) of this nature, seeing that these same fits have no necessary connection with that unbalanced and emotional type of character with which the name is associated in the popular mind. On the other hand, practically all neurologists are now unanimous in affirming the great truth that "hysteria is before everything else a mental disease consisting chiefly in an exaggeration of suggestibility." Science is indebted to Liebault and Charcot for the demonstration of this principle, though Charcot's shibboleths of diagnosis (his "stigmata") are now given up, precisely because his hysterical patients were more suggestible than he himself realized. Further, there is at present an almost equally general agreement in the view that this suggestibility, manifesting itself on occasion through such disorders as aphasia, nervous anaesthesias, palsies, inhibitions of hearing and vision, etc., frequently occur in subjects who are in no way unbalanced and have never had a fit of hysterics in their lives. Though we need not necessarily identify ourselves with the precise standpoint of Bernheim, we can only pay tribute to his wide practical experience during some forty years in dealing with every form of psychoneurosis. We cannot, therefore, fail to be impressed when we find him in 1917 writing as follows:

> The immense majority of hysterical women, as the term is popularly understood, have no fits. They may, of course, occasionally have them, as others do, but there is no greater proportion of such fits among subjects who are silly and unbalanced than there is amongst ordinary folk. On the other hand the women who do suffer from hysterics (*crises de nerfs*) are not as a rule of this type. Many are thoughtful people with well-ordered minds; many are warm-hearted, full of feeling and inspired by the highest moral ideals, neither untruthful nor addicted to simulation (*simulatrices*), nor erotic. Beyond question, they are impressionable and are affected by emotional stimuli which are specifically hysteriogenetic. But outside of their fits I have never found it possible to identify them with any special type of character. In all ordinary relations they may have the same temperament, the same virtues, the same vices as other people.

Similarly, an English neurologist, Dr. A. F. Hurst, in his Croonian Lectures, tells us:

> It is so common to regard certain mental qualities as hysterical, and to apply the term hysterical to a certain type of individual, that it requires considerable courage to reject altogether the doctrine of a specific psychical disorder to which the name hysteria can be given.... For several years I accepted the definition of hysteria as an abnormal mental condition in which the individual is unduly prone to develop symptoms as a result of suggestion. But the experience of the war has taught us that, given a sufficiently powerful suggestion, there are probably no individuals who would not develop hysterical symptoms.... Many cases of gross hysterical symptoms occurred in soldiers who had no family or personal history of neuroses, and who

were perfectly fit until the moment that one of the exceptionally powerful exciting causes, such as occur comparatively rarely apart from war, suggested some hysterical symptom. After its disappearance as a result of psychotherapy the man was once more perfectly fit, and his subsequent history showed that he remained no more liable than any of his companions to develop new symptoms.... Many cases of hysteria will be missed if it is only looked for in so-called hysterical persons.

We must give up the idea, then, that hysterical disorders are only to be met with in subjects who are conspicuously neurotic, unbalanced, untruthful, selfish and weak-minded, and it consequently follows that there is no necessary disparagement in the association of even exalted sanctity with pithiatism, that is to say, with the emergence of certain neuroses commonly classed as hysterical. The holiness of Padre Pio or of Gemma Galgani or of such famous mystics of an earlier age as Maria Agreda and Anne Catherine Emmerich may be real enough, and yet this fact is not inconsistent with a liability to the occurrence of suggestion neuroses, manifested at times by startling phenomena which very naturally have often been misinterpreted by their contemporaries. Long before medical science in these matters had reached its present development the Church manifested a sound instinct in the regulation of her processes of beatification and canonization. No amount of evidence as to alleged marvels, the charismata or gratiae gratis datae as they were sometimes called, could be accepted in lieu of testimony to the virtuous conduct of those who were to be solemnly proposed for the veneration of the Faithful. Such phenomena as the stigmata, bilocation, a knowledge of distant and future events, ecstasies, aerial raptures, and so on, were accepted and welcomed as part of the proofs submitted, but they could not stand alone. They were only regarded as confirmatory of the testimony of those who from personal knowledge bore witness to the heroic standard of virtue practised by the Servant of God during his lifetime in all relations.

Further, there is the more need of caution because, while, as in the case of Padre Pio, we often find strange physical and psychic phenomena apparently free from any association with hysterical extravagance, there are also other cases where similar phenomena are exhibited in the lives of pious ascetics whose medical history seems to be a chronicle of almost every hysterical symptom known to neurologists. In this connection it may be interesting to give some account of a rare and very curious biography which I have lately had an opportunity of perusing. It is not by any means the only case of the sort I have met with, but there are features in this story which specially recommend it as a convenient illustration.

Anna Maria Castreca was born at Fabriano in the Marches of Ancona on November 13, 1670. She became a Religious, embracing the somewhat austere rule of the Capuchin nuns, in their convent in that city, on May 13, 1697, being then 26½ years old. Eventually, after long ruling the Community as Abbess, la Madre Costante Maria, as she was called in religion, died there in her 66th year on January 22, 1736. Her Life, forming a substantial quarto volume of more than 400 pages, was written shortly afterwards by Canon Angelagostino Buti from the materials collected by her confessor and others, and was printed at Fabriano in 1745. Credulous and enthusiastic though the author undoubtedly was, he leaves, nevertheless, an impression of simple candour, and he was in a position to obtain full information about one who had never travelled more than a few miles away from the town in which both she and her biographer were born and died. At the age of three, Anna Maria was taught to read by an uncle of whom she was so frightened that the sound of his step made her turn pale and cold and throw herself into her mother's arms. Her father and mother died when she was eight: hence she was sent to school at a Benedictine Convent where two of her aunts were nuns. Here her terrors were augmented, for one of these aunts inspired her with such awe that if this elderly relative met her in the corridor or looked at her when she was taking her supper in the refectory, the child dropped everything she had in her hands, whether it was a full basin of soup or a pile of books. But what (in accord with the theories of Janet at any rate) must be counted a much more unmistakable symptom of hysterical neurosis is the strange amnesia which came upon Anna Maria when she was eight years old. She was, it appears, particularly clever at reading aloud, so much so that the nuns employed her sometimes in reading to the community. One day, shortly after having experienced some kind of vision, she suddenly and completely lost the memory of everything she had learnt. Whether this amounted to a dissociation of personality it is hard to say, but the child had to begin to learn her a, b, c over again, and though she had been skilful at her needle, she found herself incapable of the simplest piece of sewing. A year later, with equal suddenness, the remembrance came back to her of all that she had previously forgotten.' Hardly less significant were the perversities she exhibited in the matter of diet, both in her childhood and throughout her early life. Even before the loss of memory just referred to we hear of strange disorders which puzzled the doctors, in the course of which she often passed two or three days at a time without taking any sort of food. Later on, when she was about eighteen, she was unable for a year together to eat either meat or eggs. Her diet consisted of nothing but curds (ricotte) and figs. She drank no wine, but only water with sometimes a little vinegar in it. If she forced herself in obedience to her doctor to depart from this regimen, all that she took was at once returned. Moreover, as the experience of similar cases at the present day would lead us to anticipate, there were many other vomitings, and occasionally hematemesis, which last were complicated by the eructation of balls of hair, bits of string and scraps of paper. The excretory processes were also interfered with. We read of periods of six or eight days together when absolutely nothing passed.

It was hardly to be expected that in a book which is ostensibly a spiritual biography written nearly two centuries ago we should find any accurate details about such matters as anaesthesias, or hemiplegias and paraplegias. But there is every reason to suppose that in the maladies which utterly baffled the skill of her numerous doctors these hysterical symptoms were often present. We read of a long illness, when she was about twenty, in which she was for a time "devoid of all external feeling", we also learn that for months she was unable to stand upon her feet, but was afterwards able to go about on crutches, we are told how at this period she suffered from strange phobias and would never allow herself to be left alone for a moment unless the door was securely locked. Most of these attacks, in which she was often believed to be at death's door and more than once received the Last Sacraments, were cured suddenly and, as she thought, miraculously. Anna Maria herself, and her pious advisers, were content to believe that all her disorders, physical and mental, were the direct work of the devil. "It would have touched a heart of stone," says her biographer, "to see how she was often violently hurled from the chair on which she was sitting, sometimes dragged along the ground, sometimes so dazed and bewildered that she was led to run about the house, barefoot and only half-clothed, in order to throw herself out of a window or do herself some other desperate mischief." At the same time there seems to be no evidence that Anna Maria had at this period manifested any unwonted signs of piety, except perhaps a tendency to have visions. It was one of these which brought to a head a latent desire she had for some time entertained of consecrating herself to God as a nun. She was, we are told, fond of pretty and quaint coiffures (or possibly hats), for which purpose "she often spent some hours before the mirror." One day, when she was thus engaged, she suddenly saw in the glass, not her own countenance merely, but the face of our Saviour crowned with thorns and dripping with blood. Moreover, she thought He spoke to her and bade her hesitate no longer, but consecrate herself to Him in the habit of St. Francis. Owing to her infirmities and other complications, some years passed before she could carry her purpose into effect, but when she eventually became a novice, things from a medical point of view grew worse rather than better. On the very first morning her head was found all swollen and bruised—this, it is averred, being the work of the devil, who had beaten her. In choir the most extraordinary things happened. She would suddenly be thrown down flat on her face.

As she stood singing the Office her breviary would fly out of her hands to the other end of the room. In the presence of all the nuns she would fall down in a fit, marked with the most horrible spasms and contortions, her neck twisted awry and "her leg bending the wrong way, so that sometimes the point of her foot touched the upper part of the abdomen.", Whether this was the *grande hystérie* of Charcot with its four well-marked stages, the details given do not enable us to decide, but such phrases as "hearing her choke with indescribable misery " would seem to point to the *globus*, if it were not that her tongue was found "forced back into her throat." But the full story of the excitements which disturbed the peace of the cloister on the coming of Suor Costante Maria would be endless. There were swellings and contusions, alternations of heat and cold, blisterings as if her limbs had been dipped in scalding water. She wanted to say Office properly, but for more than a month together her lips could only frame profanities and curses. When she tried to go to confession or to approach the altar for Communion, the way seemed to be strewn with red-hot ashes, the fire of which could only be quenched by a plentiful besprinkling with holy water. All the same, she felt this fire so intensely that long draughts of cool water were afterwards needed to revive her. At other times the way to Communion was barred by a ruffian with a drawn sword, visible of course to her alone.

But among all the incidents which filled the first seven years of her life as a nun, two are especially interesting in the light of modem investigations of the hysteria neurosis. Very naturally, in the case of such a novice, she was not admitted to make .her profession at the end of one year, and shortly afterwards a new infirmity manifested itself which lasted for some months. During this time "she ceased to be her natural self (*restava fuori di se*), and whatever was said or done she paid no heed to anything, but prattled away with a most charming grace of manner, seeming in look, in language and in all she did, to be just a little child of five years old." When we recall the amnesia which the novice had experienced twenty years earlier, during which she had to learn the alphabet again, this looks very like a case of dissociation and a return to the secondary personality which had manifested itself at that time.

The other set of incidents to which I refer point either to somnambulism or to a "fugue" prematurely arrested. It seems certain that Suor Gostante Maria was several times found wandering about the house during the night in a dazed state, though this was commonly attributed to diabolical malice, and was connected with weird happenings and acts of physical violence which cannot here be discussed. But on one occasion the Mistress of Novices met her in the middle of the night with the keys of the enclosure in her hand. She asked her where she was going, and Suor Gostante replied that Father Bosdari, the Extraordinary, was waiting for her in the parlour to take her home. Again, on another night, the novice, once more taking the keys, went of her own accord to the bedside of one of the nuns and told her the same story. The nun thus awakened was terribly shocked and spoke so strongly that Suor Costante was completely roused and retired in confusion. At yet another time it is stated that she had actually hunted out her secular clothes and was in the act of opening the door with the keys which she had again taken, when some sudden shock, or the presence of some of the nuns, seems to have brought her to herself. On the other hand, we are told that when her uncle and her brother, hearing of the disturbances her presence in the convent had aroused, came in the daytime to fetch her away, she absolutely refused to go with them.

In spite of all these agitations which destroyed the peace of the cloister and affected even the bishop and the whole diocese, Suor Costante eventually won the confidence of her fellow nuns, and she seems not only to have given proof of a strange knowledge of distant and future events, but to have been credited with many psycho-physical phenomena. Though the majority of the nuns inclined at first to the belief that she was possessed by the devil, she was after some years elected abbess, contrary to her own wish, and again subsequently re-elected, dying eventually in the odour of sanctity in that office. The evidence for the fact that she was (seemingly about 1715) marked with the stigmata, retaining more particularly a permanent wound in her side, cannot easily be rejected. We also read of her being mysteriously supported in the air, and that an unaccountable perfume exhaled from her person, particularly on certain feasts. I cannot here discuss the authenticity of these marvels, but I am satisfied that, just as not infrequently happens in certain stages of hypnosis (perhaps through some form of hyperaesthesia not yet sufficiently investigated), Suor Costante Maria did possess strange supernormal knowledge of a kind hard to explain, more particularly in regard to matters affecting her confessor, Don Filippo Gionantonj. It is also difficult to resist the conviction that she was not only eminently suggestible, but that the confessor occupied towards her a relation closely analogous to that of the hypnotiser to the hypnotised subject. For example, during one of her maladies she lost the sense of sight—an obviously hysterical blindness. The confessor commanded her to stand up and read the hour of None, and she at once did so without difficulty. Similarly, when she came to receive Holy Communion she sometimes was unable to open her mouth, or having opened it, to close it again. Here again the confessor eventually found that he could help her. Also, in some instances, the superior of the convent was able to exercise a similar influence.

There is much more which seems to call for comment in this curious case, but at the close of an already too long chapter, I can only leave the facts to speak for themselves. They certainly seem to justify, if such justification were needed, the caution shown by ecclesiastical authority in affirming the supernatural character of any phenomena with which "pithiatism" may be associated.

7

Hysteria and Dual Personality

The Strange Case of Dr. Jekyll and Mr. Hyde has familiarized English readers with the idea of what is now most commonly called "dissociation," a condition which suggests the possible co-existence of two or more personalities in one human subject. Though R. L. Stevenson's story is said to have originated in a dream, the essential feature of the fiction, viz., that the same man may show himself in two entirely different characters, neither of which is necessarily conscious of the existence of the other, is a fact which no psychologist at the present time will venture to dispute. We may readily admit that in real life two personalities so diametrically opposed in their attitude to good and evil as the Jekyll and Hyde of the story are rarely, if ever, exhibited by the same individual. But we do, all the same, find astonishing contrasts.

For example, the case of "Georges Marasco" has been rather fully discussed by me in *The Month* for December 1924 and January 1925. Here was a young woman, an unmarried mother, who later developed an extraordinary mystical tendency, seemingly without any violent crisis of conversion. She had been by turns a *dompteuse de lions* in a menagerie, a contortionist (*femme serpent*) a lightning-sketch artist, a *diseuse*, and a secret service agent during the War. Then we find her practising asceticism, lying bed-ridden, paralysed and apparently at death's door, until she was suddenly and miraculously restored to health at the shrine of Our Lady of Hals. She gathered round her a small clientele of admirers, and kept them busy taking down her endless revelations which were to be communicated to the Pope. She starved herself and developed stigmata in hands, feet and side, as well as the bleeding punctures of the crown of thorns—it is not quite easy in the light of existing photographs to believe the wounds artifact— and she officiated as a sort of high priestess at religious rites of her own devising. The climax was reached when Bertha Mrazek (alias Georges Marasco) was arrested by the police on a charge of obtaining money under false pretences, and her whole history after long investigation came out in court. The money does not seem to have been squandered or misappropriated, and the medical experts appointed by the Brussels tribunal to inquire into her mental condition reported that she was suffering from a *dedoublement de personnalité*, in other words, from a dissociation or disintegration of consciousness. They recommended her seclusion in some sanatorium on the ground that "she exercises an unhealthy influence over people of weak mind because they are contagiously affected by her own mental state.

This is undoubtedly a less usual type of psychosis, but one specially interesting to Catholics on account of its mystical features. On the other hand, examples of an entirely secular character are numerous, and during the last fifty years or more they have been very carefully recorded. To the case of Mollie Fancher I have made reference in another chapter; but the evidence for Mollie's five distinct personalities is lacking in precision and is much inferior to that presented for the extraordinary phenomena observed in Dr. Morton Prince's Sally Beauchamp, in the Léonie of Pierre Janet, in Azam's patient Félida X, in Louis Vive at Rochefort, or in Lurancy Vennum, the Illinois girl. All these remarkable examples of dissociation may be conveniently studied in F. W. H. Myers's *Human Personality*. But there has been no dearth of similar abnormalities since Myers, who died in 1901, left his great undertaking still unfinished. For instance, the Doris Fisher case, recounted at immense length by Dr. W. Franklin Prince and Professor Hyslop in three volumes of the American S.P.R. Proceedings (1915-17) is especially interesting. For fuller illustration one classical example, which is quoted by Professor Pierre Janet as the earliest known story of the kind, may be reproduced here because it is conveniently devoid of complications, and resembles the abnormal experience which forms the main subject of the present article. It was narrated in Dr. MacNish's *Philosophy of Sleep* (1830), but I give it as repeated by Pierre Janet:

> A well-informed, well-bred young lady of a good constitution was suddenly seized, without previous warning, with a profound sleep, which lasted several hours longer than usual. On awaking, she had forgotten all she knew; her memory was like a tabula rasa and had preserved no notion either of words or things; it was necessary to teach her everything anew. Thus she was obliged to learn again reading, writing, ciphering. Little by little she became familiarized with the persons and things surrounding her, which were for her as if she saw them for the first time. Her progress was rapid. After a rather long time she was, without any known cause, seized with a sleep similar to that which had preceded her new life.

On awaking, she found herself in the same state in which she was before her first sleep. She had no remembrance of anything that had passed during the interval. In a word, in the old state she was ignorant of the new state. It was thus that she called her two lives, which were continued separately and alternatively through remembrance. During more than four years this young lady presented these phenomena almost periodically. In one state or in the other, she did not remember her double character, any more than two distinct persons remember their respective natures. For instance, in the periods of her old state, she possessed all the knowledge she acquired in her childhood and youth; in her new state she knew only what she had learned since. ... In her old state she had a very fine handwriting, the one she had always had, while in her new state her handwriting was bad, awkward, childish as it were, because she had neither the time nor the means to perfect it.

Let us remember further that Theresa Neumann of Konnersreuth, according to the testimony of her most ardent devotees, exhibits from time to time a similar change of personality. In the condition which her compatriots describe as *Zustand des Eingenommenseins* (state of absorption) she acts and speaks as a child of five would do. She is unable to grasp the meaning of the word Pope, and instead of announcing that she sees six people she says one and one and one, etc., six times.

But it may be interesting to describe from a quite recent account how these dissociations of personality come about quite unexpectedly. Theresa, we learn, was on one occasion sitting on a sofa talking with Pfarrer Naber (her confessor) and two other priests about indifferent matters. Suddenly she had a vision of the later history of St. Mary Magdalen.

Theresa saw how Magdalen, together with two other women and two men, were placed on a ship without sails or rudder and set adrift on the sea, destined to inevitable death. A storm arose, and Theresa became filled with terror as she saw how the vessel was tossed about. Then, the vision ending for the moment, Resl [her pet name] who had been sitting in the middle of the sofa, leans backward. Father Naber suggested that she lie down. Perhaps because she was still vividly aware of what she had seen, she imagined that Father Naber had ordered her to be thrown into the water. She protested, to the amusement of those present: "No, no, not in the water! I don't want to lie in the water!" She was quieted by the words of the pastor and the others, and by the realization at length that all was well. Then, in answer to our questioning, she told what had taken place, and since she expresses herself and thinks and feels as a child when she is in the state of prepossession [presumably *Zustand des Eingenommenseins*], it was not astonishing that she broke off suddenly and turned with a mischievous smile to Father Hartl, the curate, to speak about his approaching nameday celebration. ... In the midst of this jovial, trivial interlude she became rapt into ecstasy again.

Later on she saw "the cave " (no doubt the *sainte baume*, where, according to the legend, St. Mary Magdalen spent long years of penance and died). She peeped "through a hole into the room out of stone" and saw Magdalen, a very old woman, hover in ecstasy above the ground; then her body sank to earth and her soul soared with the Redeemer to heaven. After this Theresa, speaking as a little child, began a conversation with our Saviour. "She begged Him to give her the 'little room' that was Mary Magdalen's, who does not need it any more. It would suit her [Theresa] exactly. There was water to wash oneself. To be sure, one would have to get a stove, a table and a bed, etc." And the witness assures us that he would not tire "listening for hours to this childlike prattle." The entrance to the cave seemed not to have been very broad. " She said Mother could not get in;' and when asked why, she hesitated lest she offend the reverence due to her parent. Then she answered, She is too plump.'" Neither could another priest present get in, "he was too tall," but "a very thin one," indicating Kaplan Fahsel, "he might squeeze through."

In the case of Theresa Neumann observers are unanimous in affirming that another form of dissociation must also be recognized. They call it the Zustand der erhobenen Rube (state of exalted repose). In this condition a voice speaking through her lips replied to a question put to her by no less a personage than her confessor: "Thou [du] canst not speak to Resl now, she is asleep." This utterance and the use of the second person singular astonished the good priest considerably, for the normal Theresa was always very respectful in her form of address. But in "exalted repose" the words spoken are very few; they are authoritative in tone and seem to emanate from a personality distinct from Theresa herself.' Thus the voice says "this afternoon at four o'clock her suffering will begin," or "she will have a vision this evening at eight." When she returns to her normal state Theresa remembers nothing of what her lips have spoken in exalted repose. Some of her most ardent champions, e.g., Pfarrer Naber, Kaplan Fahsel and the late Dr. Gerlich, have actually drawn the inference that the words spoken in this state are the words of Jesus Christ Himself; but they surely cannot know how common it is in these cases of dissociation for one personality to treat any other personality appearing in the same subject as something entirely remote and external, in fact, as a different being. Dr. R. Osgood Mason, commenting on two such cases, remarks:

In neither of the cases described had the primary self any knowledge of the second personality except from the report of others or letters from the second self.... The second personality, on the other hand, in each case, knew of the primary self, but only as another person—never as forming a part of, or in any way belonging to, their own personalities.

I have been led to embark upon this little disquisition by a biography I have lately come across which purports to recount the history of a Spanish nun, the Venerable Mother Beatrice Mary of Jesus, Abbess of a convent of Poor Clares of the strict observance, in the city of Granada. The book must have cost a considerable sum to produce, for it is a small folio printed in double columns, running to over 500 pages and adorned with a portrait. This narrative recounts the spiritual experiences of a religious who, however holy and supernaturally gifted she may have been, exhibited throughout all her early life the most pronounced symptoms of hysteria. Beatrice, born in 1632, was the daughter of Don Lorenco de Enciso y Navarette, a man of good position and a very devout Catholic. Up to the age of thirty-five she lived at home with her parents as a Franciscan tertiary, but in 1667 she was accepted as a postulant by a convent of Poor Clares and eventually became Abbess. The title-page of the biography describes her as "Venerable," but I cannot find any evidence that the cause was proceeded with and that she was at any time beatified. She died in 1702, and as the facts which Father Thomas de Montalvo has put on record profess to be derived from the depositions of the witnesses who gave evidence in the informative process begun with a view to her canonization, it is clear that this testimony must have been taken within a few years of her death. Dates are entered throughout the biography with a display of exactitude which points to the use of some contemporary journal kept by her confessors or her fellow religious. Of her mystical phenomena a word may be said later, but the one incident in the Life which specially caught my attention in glancing through its pages is a dissociation of consciousness closely similar to that recorded of Costante Maria Castreca.

On March I, 1665, before she entered the convent, after experiencing certain ecstasies of rather unusual duration, she, at the age of thirty-three, fell, we are told, into an extraordinary condition in which she exhibited all the external characteristics of a little child of three or four years old. Her language, her manner of speech, her conduct, movements, and the expression of her features, were those which would be expected of a little girl still in the nursery. She knew the inmates of the household by their faces, but could not give them names. This state had only lasted four days when the "Provisor," or Vicar-General, a man well known to her family and appointed by the Archbishop to investigate this curious case, came to see her." Finding her talking like a child, he commanded her in virtue of holy obedience to resume the natural use of her reason with all the powers God had given her, because he had to speak to her of matters which concerned the direction of her soul. Hardly had he given the order when her whole countenance changed, and it at once became manifest from the gravity of her expression that she had returned to her normal state." The Provisor spoke to her seriously and directed her to go to Confession and Communion. This she promised to do and was, in fact, enabled to do next morning. But no sooner had the Provisor left the house than Beatrice had a fit (*parasismo*) and when she recovered from it the child personality returned. This puerile condition, with slight interruptions, lasted for ten days. She was not ill and went about the house amusing her parents and her sisters very much by her mistakes and her childish replies to their questions.

She was sometimes gloomy, sometimes boisterously cheerful, but in either case without any apparent cause. When, at the end of ten days, this young woman of thirty-three came to herself again after the occurrence of another fit, a notable melancholy and taciturnity seems to have settled down upon her. From an early age she had been subject to ecstasies or trances, which sometimes lasted a whole day. She also suffered at frequent intervals from paralytic seizures; sometimes the right side was affected, sometimes the left, any small shock being sufficient to transfer the hemiplegia from one side to the other. We hear more than once of uncontrollable and persistent vomiting which the doctors were powerless to relieve. She was, no doubt, always abstemious and mortified in her diet, but there were also occasions when to please her mother or her confessor she wished to eat but was physically incapable of swallowing anything. So pronounced were her hyperaesthesias, nearly always associated with some quaint but dominant idea of moral wrongfulness, that we find recorded in her Life such an incident as the following.

During the time when she was living at home, her brother fell ill. This was in Lent, but the doctors considered it necessary for his health that he should eat meat. A joint was accordingly cooked, but unfortunately the smell of the roast flesh reached the nostrils of his sister Beatrice, and she was thereupon seized with so terrible a convulsion and loathing that they thought she would have died on the spot.

No pathologist, I fancy, would hesitate to pronounce that we are here in presence of an almost typical case of conversion-hysteria and it was complicated, as nearly always happens with mystics of this class, by all sorts of diabolical infestations of the "grappin" order which beset the unfortunate victim at frequent intervals. Nevertheless, though she seemed to be continually at death's door, Beatrice's life was prolonged to what was in those days accounted the good old age of seventy years. Let it also be remembered that the story is certainly not a mere romance. This folio, written less than seventeen years after her death, was based upon the sworn evidence of witnesses, and was published at the expense of the city of Granada where all her life had been passed. She was evidently regarded as a sort of spiritual asset, reflecting glory upon her birthplace. There was nothing to prompt any panegyrist to invent such an incident as that of the secondary personality which reduced Beatrice for ten days to the mental condition of a little child. On the other hand, the similar experience of Costante Maria Castreca at Fabriano, in Central Italy, could not have been known to the biographer of Beatrice in the south of Spain. Both these holy women, though they led the most austere lives and eventually came to rule over the convents which they had entered, presented almost every symptom of pronounced hysteria.

Was it a consequence of the hysteria or, in despite of this psychophysical condition, that they also exhibited remarkable phenomena of the mystical order? For those of Mother Costante Maria I must refer to my previous chapter, but a few words may here be said concerning the "charismata" which the Spanish biographer claims for Mother Beatrice. It will be sufficient to touch on her stigmata, her abstention from food and her levitations. With regard to the first of these, Beatrice, though she greatly desired to have the pain of Our Lord's wounds, is said to have prayed that no external marks might be perceptible for fear that they would attract notice to herself. In accord with this, on certain feasts of each year, she had intense suffering in her hands, feet and side, without any external indication which betrayed her condition. But there were exceptions. While still living at home, on Friday, May 30, 1664, after her crucifixion agony of three hours, she was wounded by St. Francis with a dart which pierced her heart. As she was still unconscious, her mother and sisters, who suspected from a gesture of hers that something had happened to her side, undressed her and found a crescent-shaped wound on her left breast. The confessor came and saw it, and the Provisor, the representative of the Archbishop, was also summoned, but by the time he got there there was no longer a trace of any such wound. After this a short ecstasy followed; the mother was led to examine her daughter's breast again, and found the wound as it was before. Once more the Provisor was called to bear testimony and he and a number of other ecclesiastics of high standing definitely bore witness to what their eyes had clearly seen. This inspection, we are told, was renewed on two subsequent occasions with the same satisfactory result. Moreover, there were other later instances when marks were perceptible in her feet and hands.

Further, we learn that among Beatrice's many fasts, one which she observed from November 3rd to December 25th of the year 1664, before she entered convent walls, was rigorously tested.

During these fifty-one days she ate nothing at all, but on four or five occasions when she was consumed by one of those interior conflagrations which were occasionally characteristic of her ecstatic state, she took a draught of water. To submit the matter to the control of reliable witnesses, she was lodged for a month in the house of Don Inigo de Azevedo, a judicial functionary, "Alcalde del Crimen de la Real Chancilleria de Granada," and her good faith was thereby triumphantly vindicated.

Of her levitations I will only say that her fellow-Religious describe her as kneeling for long periods raised a few inches above the ground, but in such a way that her habit and cloak prevented the onlooker from noticing that she was not really in contact with the earth. The truth, however, was betrayed by the fact that the slightest breath of air caused her to sway in this direction or that, just as if she were a feather or the leaf of a tree. If one of the nuns got up from her place and left the chapel a little swiftly, she was moved like a straw by the draught thus created. There were a number of other analogous physical phenomena recorded of Mother Beatrice, and with these also an inexplicable knowledge of distant events and of the future. How far these claims were justified no investigator at this distance of time can now hope to decide.

But to come back to the question of double or multiple personality, it is curious that, in the case both of mystics and of hysterical patients in general, this liability to dissociation of consciousness seems often to be combined with abnormal gifts of prevision and clairvoyance, or with some other strange type of phenomenon. If I mention Mollie Fancher in particular, that is because her case is to be dealt with in these pages; but quite a number of hystericals, such as Lurancy Vennum, Anna Winsor, or Doris Fisher, offer problems very difficult to explain on the basis of natural causation. And why, again, should so many of them be afflicted with an inability to eat, to speak, or to use normal sight? Paralysis also and catalepsy are often very pronounced. Theresa Neumann was paralysed for six years, in addition to blindness and loss of hearing. Costante Maria and Beatrice suffered frequently, even if intermittently, from the same disabilities. Mollie Fancher, during more than twenty years, was unable to leave her bed, having no use of one arm, and having her leg doubled beneath her. Of Anna Winsor we are told that among her constantly recurring spasms "all the muscles of the body and limbs were rigid except those of the right arm." There is, it seems to me, much still to be learnt about morbid psychology before we can safely talk of the supernatural in cases where a dissociation of consciousness is either indicated or apprehended.

8

Some Conclusions About Stigmata

The role of Devil's Advocate is a thankless one and does not make for popularity, Indeed, I may confess that, when writing somewhat in the character of a doubting Thomas, I have felt at times, in spite of good intentions, that I was even playing a mean and an unworthy part.

Why, I have asked myself, should a sceptical line of argument be put forward which may possibly trouble the simple faith of many good people much nearer and dearer to God than I can ever hope to be? And yet in these days of widespread education, universal questioning and free discussion, a premature and ill grounded credulity cannot in the long run be of advantage to the Church. The Christian has to be able to justify his beliefs, and adequate equipment for an encounter with rationalists or agnostics requires some previous study both of the position which it is intended to take up and of the form of attack to which that position may be exposed. Catholic apologetic must always be based at least in part on the reality of miracles. Any attempt to explain away the greater miracles of our Lord, or to the possibility that true miracles may be wrought even in our own day, would be incompatible with an honest acceptance of the Church's teaching. But, on the other hand, when new and remarkable manifestations are reported in connection with people of conspicuously holy life, there is often a tendency to acclaim them without further ado as if they must necessarily be of supernatural origin. It is quite possible, of course, that as faith weakens and science discovers marvels previously undreamed of, God in His good providence may have willed to come to the rescue of our unbelief and may multiply evidence to prove that His arm is not shortened. But in accepting such phenomena as a reinforcement of the *motiva credendi* prudence enjoins that we must make sure of our ground. We have to meet adversaries who of late years have paid a vast amount of attention to the study of psycho-pathology, and even a very slender acquaintance with the literature of hysteria and other nervous disorders suffices to show how extensive is the vista of possibilities which has been opened up, and also how great are the perplexities with which the whole subject is beset.

In the periodical *Etudes Carmélitaines* for 1932 much space was devoted to the case of Theresa Neumann. Among other contributions an article of Dr. R. van der Elst concerned itself specially with the stigmata, giving less prominence to the attendant manifestations (inedia, xenoglossia, hierognosis, etc.) "It will be much to the point," this writer said, "to consider the stigmata by themselves, because the stigmata are evidently the principal fact round which all the others turn. The stigmatization is the central phenomenon, which the others may complicate, but which is itself capable of explaining all the rest." Without necessarily agreeing with this dictum, it affords a convenient basis for orderly treatment, and it is plain that we must take things one at a time.

On the other hand, I venture to urge that to obtain a just view we cannot possibly discuss Theresa Neumann's stigmata as if hers were the only case known in history. There have been literally hundreds of other cases, regarding some fifty of which we are fully informed, although the rest are inadequately recorded. It is the neglect of kindred examples which strikes me as the weak point of nearly all that has been written about the stigmatica of Konnersreuth. Reference is occasionally made to a few well-known mystics who have exhibited similar phenomena— to Anne Catherine Emmerich, for example, to Louise Lateau or to Gemma Galgani; but what is to be said about the stigmatizations of the same external character occurring in other persons in whom we find them associated with much that is strange and disconcerting? None of the writers who treat of Theresa Neumann in accord with the views of the Konnersreuth Kreis take any notice of such people as Marie-Julie Jahenny, Palma d'Oria, la Madre Costante, Juliana Weiskircher, Georges Marasco, etc. It is the occurrence in these cases of a pronounced type of to "conversion hysteria" which constitutes to my mind the real difficulty of the problem.

If I propose then to set down here certain doubts which suggest themselves concerning the supernatural character of stigmata in general, this is not because I entertain any misgivings as to the facts recorded of Theresa Neumann's phenomena or as to the holy life which she leads, but simply because in the literature accessible to me I find no indication that these difficulties have been taken into account. The difficulties are not conclusive arguments, and they may quite possibly have an adequate answer; but on the surface they seem to me to point to the conclusion that stigmatization may be the result of what I will venture to call a "crucifixion complex " working itself out in subjects whose abnormal suggestibility may be inferred from the unmistakable symptoms of hysteria which they had previously exhibited.

I

And first of all we have the striking fact that not a single case of stigmatization was heard of before the beginning of the thirteenth century. No sooner, however, was the extraordinary phenomenon which marked the last days of the seraphic St. Francis published throughout the world, than other unquestionable cases of stigmata began to occur among quite simple people and have continued to occur without intermission ever since. What I infer is that the example of St. Francis created what I have called the "crucifixion complex." Once it had been brought home to contemplatives that it was possible to be physically conformed to the sufferings of Christ by bearing His wound-marks in hands, feet and side, then the idea of this form of union with their Divine Master took shape in the minds of many. It became in fact a pious obsession; much so that in a few exceptionally sensitive individuals the idea conceived in the mind was realised in the flesh.

II

If the suggestion just made were well-founded, we should expect to find that the exteriorisation of the "crucifixion complex" would vary much in degree according to the suggestibility of the particular subject. But this is in fact what actually happens. It is noteworthy that in a good many cases the development never goes any further than a certain deep reddening of the skin or the formation of something resembling a blood-blister in the site of each of the wounds. It is equally noteworthy that the form and position of these wounds or markings vary greatly. In some instances the wound in the side is on the right, in others on the left. Sometimes we have a round puncture, sometimes a straight cut, sometimes a crescent-shaped wound. When Gemma Galgani showed in her body the marks of the scourging, marks which bled profusely, we are told that these wounds closely corresponded in size and in position with the wounds depicted in a big crucifix before which she was accustomed to pray. When Anne Catherine Emmerich was first marked with a cross on her breast, it is stated that this was a Y-shaped cross, reproducing the form of a crucifix at Coesfeld to which she had great devotion in her childhood. All these things seem to point to an auto-suggested effect rather than to the operation of an external cause whatever its nature.

III

Again, although the war of 1914-18 showed us that hysteria is not, as was once supposed, an exclusively feminine disorder, still it remains true that at normal times, and especially under the conditions in which girls were formerly brought up, women were and are much more subject to hysterical fits than men. Now, while in the course of the last seven centuries there have been an immense number of female mystics about whose complete stigmatization no doubt is possible, there are only two quite clear cases of men being externally marked with all the five wounds. Moreover, even here we have no evidence of periodic bleeding on successive Fridays, such as is common in female stigmatics. The natural inference would seem to be that what predisposes to the reception of the stigmata is not unusual virtue, but some form of nervous susceptibility, more often met with in women than in men.

The physically vigorous saints, such as St. Vincent of Paul, St Francis Xavier, the great mystic St. John of the Cross, St. Alphonsus Liguori, St, Paul of the Cross, St. Francis of Sales, St. Philip Neri, St. John Baptist Vianney, and countless others were not favoured with the stigmata, in spite of the devotion to our Lord's Passion and the intense desire of suffering conspicuous in all of them. But not a few devout women who have never been beatified and whose history points to a certain extravagance of sensibility, have been thus honoured and have periodically enacted the scenes of the Passion, with bleeding from all the five wounds.

IV

So far as records are preserved concerning the early history of stigmatized persons I venture to say that there is hardly a single case in which there is not evidence of the previous existence of a complication of nervous disorders before the stigmata developed. That does not mean that the person thus bearing the marks of Christ s Passion was otherwise than good and even saintly from the very beginning. It is simply a question of the pathological conditions. I have called attention elsewhere to the health record in their early years of Gemma Galgani and of the Syrian Carmelite, Sister Mary of Jesus Crucified. Let me illustrate my point now by a reference to a very much earlier case, that of the nun Lukardis at Oberweimar, who is said to have been stigmatized for twenty-eight years, dying on 22nd March, 1309, less than a hundred years after St. Francis of Assisi. Her biographer was a contemporary who knew her personally, and the modern Bollandists who have edited the Life pronounce the narrative to be fully worthy of credit. We are told that, having entered a Cistercian convent when only a child, Lukardis, still in her 'teens, was made infirmarian for half a year, and then fell ill. She lost all power of grasping things with her hands. She could not even hold a stick to support herself with. "She had all the pains of the stone, of quartan and tertian fevers, and she frequently fainted away. The doctors could make nothing of her case. "At times she seemed, as it were, to be beaten in each hand, so that her fingers, knocking against each other, resounded like castanets" Most unmistakable of all, we are told that "when she was lying in bed there were occasions when her feet became rooted underneath her and her head sank down, while her stomach and chest were thrust upwards, so that she made a sort of arch of herself with a sharp curvature." This is surely a remarkable description of the opisthonic spasm well known in hospitals for nervous disorders. She was paralysed and bed-ridden for eleven years; but while she had the use of her limbs, it is stated that "the servant of God, sometimes in the day-time, sometimes at night, started running with such headlong speed that the most vigorous of men could not have kept it up without getting exhausted. At one time she ran round and round, at another straight on . . . when she had not space to run she came into violent collision with the wall.

There were also occasions when lying down she spun round for a long time like a joint roasting before the fire." Perhaps the most extraordinary feature of all, one which I hold it impossible for the biographer to have invented, is the allegation that for a considerable space of time she used to stand upon her head, or more precisely upon her head and shoulder, with her feet in the air, but nevertheless with her dress clinging to her legs as if it had been tightly sewn to them. It certainly would be hard to maintain that Lukardis was a quite normal person either before she received the stigmata or afterwards.

Another case of a stigmatica with pronounced hysterical symptoms is that of la Madre Costante (Anna Maria Castreca). She died (A.D, 1736) in the odour of sanctity as Abbess of an austere community of Capuchin nuns, but in her early life, both as a girl in the world and as a young religious, she exhibited every characteristic of this form of malady. She had paralysis, an anorexia and vomiting, as well as amnesias and fugues. When a novice of over twenty years of age, a dissociated personality suddenly emerged, and for several months together Anna Mana prattled away like a child of five and had to begin to learn the alphabet over again. Further, we are told how, in the presence of all the nuns, she would fall down in a fit marked with the most Horrible spasms and contortions, "her neck twisted awry and her leg bending the wrong way, so that sometimes the point of her foot touched the abdomen."

V

No doubt such attacks as those just described occur independently of the stigmatization and for the most part are antecedent to it, but they belong to the atmosphere, and one asks whether God can have chosen such a setting for a miracle to manifest His glory. In the case of Lukardis it is impossible to determine exactly the order of events, but this at least we know, that the good nun whilst still bedridden, when the Friday ecstasy came on, used, in a state of rigid catalepsy, to stretch out her arms as if she were being crucified, and to put one foot over the other. After eleven years she suddenly recovered from her paralysis and could then stand and walk. In future the cataleptic seizure on Fridays came upon her when she was erect, and we are told that each time for something like three hours she stood upon one foot, but otherwise unsupported, with her arms stretched out horizontally from the shoulders and with the second foot pressed tightly upon the instep of the first. During Lent she stood thus every day, but the stigmata only bled on Fridays.

In the case of other stigmaticas we read of scenes hardly less strange. Elizabeth of Herkenrode (1275), in enacting the scenes of the Passion, her stigmata bleeding the while, used to pull herself by the hair and beat her head against the ground over and over again. Also, when lying on her back at these seasons in a state of unconsciousness—whether we call it ecstasy or trance—she used to rain blows upon her breast with extraordinary force and violence. Nearly six hundred years later Dr. Dei Cloche, a devout Catholic, who printed a medical report upon the case of Domenica Lazzari, tells us how u with tightly clasped hands she often showered blows upon her breast with intense violence, so that the noise was past belief.... The gnashing of her teeth was continuous and so loud that it might be compared to the noise of a furious and hungry dog gnawing a bone, or to the grinding of an enormous file applied by vigorous arms to a bar of iron." None the less, Domenica, like Theresa Neumann, maintained an absolute fast from food and drink. It began in 1834 and lasted to her death in 1848.

When on one occasion the doctor persuaded her to allow a small fragment of sugar to be placed upon her tongue, she at once had a fit which continued for twenty minutes, in the course of which the spasm of vomiting was so violent that she almost choked. Even the smell of a piece of toast brought about a contortion of all the muscles of her face and for a short time she fainted away. Was not this simply hysteria, or are we to regard it as a supernatural manifestation of God's almighty power? The bleeding of the wounds in Domenica's case was almost continuous on Fridays.

No one has ever suggested that she was otherwise than a good and devout woman. She was bedridden, she sought no publicity, she accepted no presents, and I for one find it impossible to believe that the devil can have been allowed for all those long years to deceive priests and people by a counterfeit holiness.

VI

Yet another difficulty offers itself in connection with the "revelations " of such stigmaticas as A. C. Emmerich and Theresa Neumann. In both cases we have not only visions of our Lord's Passion, but also of the sufferings of the saints—for example, of the martyrdom of St. Catherine of Alexandria. Now in this instance both the visionaries simply reproduce the traditional legend. They recount the public debate between Catherine and the fifty philosophers, most of whom are converted and then perish as martyrs in the flames, the bursting of the wheel by which she was to have been put to death, finally her decapitation and the flowing of blood and milk from her neck. Similarly Theresa Neumann sees Lazarus, Mary Magdalen, Martha and others put into a boat without sails or rudder, but nevertheless traversing the Mediterranean in safety and landing in the south of France, where Mary Magdalen hides herself in a cave and lives for another thirty years before death comes to release her. Both these legends are, on the best of grounds, rejected by modem hagiographers as pure romance, but Theresa Neumann sees them in her visions, exactly, no doubt, as Pfarrer Naber pictures them to himself in accord with the story current in popular lives of the saints. Have we any ground for supposing that

Theresa's descriptions of the Passion, which conflict in many points with other revelations—e.g. with those of St. Bridget of Sweden—are more veridical than those of earlier mystics? And if she may be deceived here, can we put trust in her pronouncements regarding relics and other matters as if she were speaking in the name of our Lord Himself?

VII

Lastly, I venture to lay some stress upon the resemblance between Theresa Neumann's different phases of consciousness and those cases of multiple personality which recent study of abnormal psychology has made familiar. We find that when Theresa ("Resl") is in "the state of exalted repose" (*Zustand der erhobenen Ruhe*) a voice speaking through her lips may reply to a questioner: "Thou (*du*) canst not speak to Resl now, she is asleep," or "This afternoon at four o'clock she will enter on the Passion." What intelligence is it which thus makes answer and utters prophecies about the future which are regularly verified? Kaplan Fahsel and Dr. Gerlich do not hesitate to maintain that it is Christ our Lord who speaks. But surely anyone who has studied, for example, the Doris Fisher case of multiple personality, so competently observed and expounded by Dr. Walter Franklin Prince, must pause before accepting this conclusion. When Doris was to all appearance at the very point of death "a voice suddenly issued from her lips, though no other feature moved: 'You must get her out of this; she is in danger"; and then 'shake her harder; hurry, hurry!'" Psychologists are satisfied that this voice was only that of another personality of the real Doris, a personality which afterwards came to be known as "Sleeping Margaret." I can see no reason to suppose that the spoken words uttered by Theresa in the state of exalted repose come from any other source than a dissociated personality of Theresa herself. One might be more inclined to doubt if it were not perfectly plain that a second dissociated personality comes into play in the so-called "state of absorption" (*Zustand des Eingenommenseins*), when, as we know, Theresa speaks like a little child of five might speak, when she cannot understand what the word Pope means, and instead of announcing that she sees six people, says one and one and one, etc., six times.

These are some of the doubts which suggest themselves in connexion with the alleged supernatural character of the stigmatization phenomena. Let me repeat that I quite recognise that an answer may be fortheoming, but it seems to me a pity that little has been said on these matters in such big books as those of Gerlich and de Hovre; not to speak of the many minor publications and articles in which the case of Theresa Neumann has been discussed. There are some other points upon which I should have liked to dwell if space had admitted. The intense desire of Lukardis to have the marks of our Saviour's Passion imprinted on her own members, a desire which led her even to seek to bore holes in her hands and feet by gesture and act, is a very striking fact; for this preceded by a long time the actual development of the stigmata. There is much that is beautiful in the vision which attended the gratification of her longings. Hysterical though she was, no one can read the account without realising that she was a deeply religious woman.

And it is noteworthy that she was greatly revered by her fellow religious and that both in life and after her death she was believed to work many miracles. Finally, let me observe that, so far as regards Theresa Neumann, doubts similar to those here expressed have been strongly urged in other quarters. An article by Father E. Raitz von Frentz, S.J., in the *Revue d'AscStique et di Mystique* for April 1933, is especially worthy of notice.

CHAPTER III
TOKENS OF ESPOUSAL

Closely akin in some respects to the phenomenon of stigmatization, but in other features very different, the spontaneous appearance of a miraculous ring upon the finger of certain virgins of holy life is not infrequently mentioned in hagiographical records. In nearly all such cases the outward manifestation is preceded by an ecstasy in which the soul thus favoured believes herself to have gone through some form of mystic espousal with Christ our Saviour. This last experience is one which is met with repeatedly in the lives of holy women, but we do not by any means always hear that the ceremony left behind it any permanent or physical token of its occurrence. Even when some abiding memorial of this union remains, it is very often purely subjective; just as happens in the case of many stigmatized persons, who feel the pain of the wounds, even though no outward sign appears of the cause of these sufferings. The best known example of an invisible espousal ring is that of St. Catherine of Siena. In the year 1367, so her biographers tell us, the Saint had a vision in which she saw our Saviour with His Blessed Mother, St. John the Evangelist, St. Paul, and St. Dominic. Our Lord addressed her and made known His intention of "espousing her soul to Him in faith." Thereupon our Lady took Catherine's right hand and held it out to her Son, and He placed on the ring-finger a ring of gold which was set with four pearls and a diamond. Then the vision disappeared, but the ring, though invisible to all other eyes but her own, remained upon her finger. Raymond of Capua, her confessor and biographer, tells us how "She many times admitted to me, though with bashfulness, that she always saw that ring on her finger, and that there never was a time when she did not perceive it." Furthermore, a curious statement is made in a manuscript which belonged to the Carthusians of Pontignano, where St, Catherine's ring-finger was kept as a relic, to the effect that sundry devout persons, in venerating the relic, saw the ring upon it, though generally speaking the ring was invisible to all.

Perhaps the best way of setting about the investigation before us will be to start with an account of two cases of mystic espousals of comparatively recent date. For both of these I am indebted to the work of Dr. Imbert-Gourbeyre, and although, as I have previously explained, the writer referred to is utterly wanting in the critical faculty, still his good faith is beyond question. When he is merely reporting the words of others or describing what he has seen with his own eyes, his statements may be received with every confidence. The first whom he mentions of the two modern recipients of this favour is Gelestine Fenouil, born at Manosque (Basses Alpes) in 1849. She received the stigmata, it appears, at the age of seventeen, and three years later was marked with the crown of thorns. In 1874 took place her mystical espousals with Jesus Christ, and on this occasion she is believed to have received a ring from Him. Eye-witnesses described it to Dr. Imbert Gourbeyre as follows:

> It is a vivid red line encircling the finger, with tiny crosses occurring at intervals. The bezel represents a heart pierced with three swords. This ring shows much more conspicuously on Sundays, when it shines with extraordinary brilliance. It is not formed of little clots of blood adhering to the skin, but it is just a red mark, probably accompanied with a thickening of the epidermis.

One might feel some doubt as to the accuracy of this account, were it not that confirmation is forthcoming from a paper contributed to a medical journal, the *Annales de Dermatologies* The writer, a local physician named Dauvergne, had seen Célestine on some few occasions after she had received the stigmata, but as there was much talk and prejudice in the neighbourhood, the mother had raised an objection against further visits. None the less, Dr. Dauvergne, in the medical study referred to, remarks:

> Witnesses whose trustworthiness I cannot question assure me that recently, since I last saw the patient, a sort of ring with a bezel develops on her ring finger every Sunday. The ring then disappears,

only to manifest itself again at the same fixed day and hour, without changing the day or interfering with the appearance of the ordinary wounds on Fridays.... What pathogenical influence can we invoke to explain this new phenomenon? Is it a girl's fantasy to which her thoughts persistently cling? And yet she is a simple child whose mind is fixed upon the Host and the ciborium. Why, in that case, does not the picture of one of these develop upon her breast? Or must we believe that Jesus Christ has chosen to mark out His chosen spouse in this way? Imagination and science become lost in inextricable confusion when we study manifestations of this sort.

In the case of Célestine Fenouil, Dr. Imbert-Gourbeyre was unable to verify the facts for himself, but in that of Marie-Julie Jahenny, of whose stigmata we have already spoken, every facility was afforded him for personal inspection. Marie-Julie, then about twenty-three years old, exhibited in successive stages the various phenomena of stigmatization, beginning in March 1873. These were crowned in the February of the following year by the appearance of a mystical ring, i.e., a hoop of vivid red encircling the ring finger of her right hand. After four years' interval this appearance was further enhanced by the addition of three black points in the place where the bezel of the ring would naturally be looked for; but at a somewhat later date the circlet was transformed into a pattern of dots and dashes, a facsimile of which is also given by Dr. Imbert-Gourbeyre (*La Stigmatisation*, II, p. 86). The first appearance of the ring was formally made known to Marie-Julie some time beforehand, and when in ecstasy she spoke of these fortheoming mystic espousals and declared that witnesses ought to be present when they occurred. The actual day was named (February 20, 1874), and Dr. Gourbeyre explains that he had in his possession a letter from her confessor, the Abbe David, written in January and definitely announcing this date. On Friday, February 20th, everything occurred as had been foretold, and two days afterwards, says Dr. Gourbeyre, I received the following letter:

> God be praised. Yesterday we had the most consoling day imaginable. Everything previously foretold has been realized.... In accordance with the directions of Monseigneur (the Bishop) I had made arrangements beforehand. There were fourteen men there to act as witnesses, seven from Blain, one from Cambon, two from Gavre, three from Nantes sent from the Cathedral, and one from La Fraudais [the hamlet in

which Marie-Julie resided]. At half-past eight we had satisfied ourselves that the wounds were quite dry, that the ring-finger of the right hand was in a healthy state, pale as death without any trace of a ring. At nine o'clock all the wounds [the stigmata] began to bleed. At about a quarter past we perceived that the finger was becoming swollen and reddening under the skin. About a quarter to ten blood was running from the upper and lower surface of the finger, and by degrees we saw the ring take shape. It is now clearly marked for all her life to come. . . . Monseigneur is full of enthusiasm.

Dr. Imbert-Gourbeyre, writing in 1894, remarks: "Marie- Julie's ring remains to the present day. I saw it again in October 1891, still a ring made in the fleshy tissues (tourj ours fait darts les chairs), like a hoop of red coral which had sunk into the skin."

With this definite evidence before us of the reality of such happenings in modern times, it becomes difficult to reject as mere fable a score of similar incidents which are described in hagiographical records of earlier date. Among the more noteworthy of these is the series of mystic espousals recounted in the Life of St. Veronica Giuliani. We have her own narrative of these events, most reluctantly written down by her on various occasions in deference to the commands of her confessors and other ecclesiastical superiors. She herself describes the espousals as begun on Easter Day, 11th April, 1694, and several times renewed, and she is also our authority for a change in the form and fashion of the rings which she received in these visions from the hand of our Saviour. What interests us most here, however, is not the Saint's impressions of what she herself saw, but rather what was seen by others after the ecstasy had passed and she had returned to her normal state. Ordinarily it would seem that nothing was perceptible, but there are at the same time two quite definite pieces of testimony given under oath by her fellow religious in the process of canonization. Sister Mary Spanaciani deposed that on one occasion she, when a novice, had seen the ring quite distinctly.

It encircled her ring-finger exactly as ordinary rings do. On the outside there appeared to be a raised stone, as large as a pea, and of a red colour, which inspired me with fear and veneration, as is usual when we see anything supernatural or miraculous. Several times I was on the point of asking her what it was, but I never ventured to do so; and meantime, the countenance of the servant of God was glowing and radiant, as though she were in a sort of rapture, and this proved to be the case, for though I asked her various questions, she never answered to the point. It was, however, remarkable that a few hours after, though I looked at her hand carefully, there was no ring or jewel there; and now that it had disappeared, she was herself again and able to give connected replies to my enquiries.

Still more valuable is the testimony of the holy nun, Florida Ceoli, a confidant of the Saint, and herself a candidate for beatification. According to her account also, the ring was not ordinarily visible, but became perceptible at times. Suor Florida had been ordered by Father Tassinari and Father Crivelli to keep a look out for any such manifestations.

> I know, as I have also heard from our confessors, that this servant of God was espoused by Our Lord and I have been frequently desired by our authorities to ascertain if there was any outward sign of the Ring of Espousals. Five or six times in Padre Tassinari's time she came to my cell to let me examine the finger of her right hand which would wear the ring and at other times I made the examination in her cell. Every time I felt her finger just where a ring would be and I felt quite distinctly a small circle which was under the outer skin and I could also see that there was a mark round her finger like a vein in size and colour but quite hard.
>
> When Padre Crivelli was here, he sent for me one day to the confessional when Suor Veronica was there and told me to feel her finger very carefully and tell him what I found. This I did, telling him that I could feel the circle quite plainly. I remember once, I was talking to her and I suddenly noticed the circle on her finger and said without thinking, "Oh Gesu, what have you done to your finger?" I then remembered what had already happened and taking her hand, I said, "Have you had this fresh grace from Our Lord and you have not told me? " She drew her hand away and hid it, blushing and saying, "Just think, if it is true."
>
> I noticed another time that just where the precious stone would be in a ring, there was a small lump like a gem, white and yellow in colour, about the size of a small bean. This lasted some days.

Our Lord renewed these Espousals and gave her sometimes the ring she called the Ring of Love, at other times what she called the Ring of the Cross. By this latter she was warned of her sufferings.

All this I saw myself and notified to the various directors.

Of the good faith of this extremely scrupulous and truthful Sister there can be no possible doubt, and as her testimony is in close agreement with much other evidence of the same kind, we are fairly justified in believing in the objective validity of the fact thus attested concordantly by sight and touch.

But probably the most interesting of all the cases of mystic espousals accompanied by physical and external phenomena is that of St Catherine de' Ricci. AH the evidence is accessible in the printed *Positio super Viriutibus*, of which a copy may be found in the British Museum Library. The Promoter of the Faith, at the time when the cause was brought before the Congregation of Rites, was the famous Prosper Lambertini, even better known afterwards as Pope Benedict XIV. The question of St. Catherine's ring attracted his particular attention, and he made several criticisms which were replied to in detail by the Postulator of the Cause. St. Catherine, it should be noted, was born in 1522 and died in 1589. Unfortunately it was only in 1614 that the first juridical examination of witnesses took place in connection with the cause of beatification.

As the ring had originally become manifest in April 1542, it was practically impossible that any of the nuns who had formed part of the community when this wonder first occurred could be living to give evidence in 1614, seventy-two years afterwards. But the phenomenon showed itself at least intermittently throughout Catherine's life, and apart from written and second-hand testimony, some few witnesses were able to give evidence of what they themselves had seen. A few brief notes upon this, apparently somewhat conflicting, evidence may not be unacceptable.

Sister Dorothea Vecchi, aged eighty-three, deposed that she had herself seen the ring, and she described it as having a hoop of gold, but in the place of the bezel a protuberance in the flesh of the finger.

Sister Mary Magdalen Ricasoli, aged sixty-eight, had seen the ring twice, once when a child—but of this occasion she remembered little or nothing—the second time after the Saint's death. Then when the body was lying before the altar she clearly saw, and continued to see until the body was buried, a livid mark (*un livido*) round the index finger of the left hand.

Donna Isabella de' Bonsignori, aged fifty, saw the hand of the Saint one day at the gate of the convent, not long before her death. There was a ring on the index finger of the left hand—at least it had the form of a ring, but it appeared to her entirely of flesh raised up like a ridge. The Saint, noticing that her eyes were fixed on the ring, at once hid her hand again under her scapular, where she usually kept it.

Sister Angela Arrighetti, aged fifty-eight, once saw an extraordinary radiance coming from one finger of the Saint's hand when she chanced to raise it in prayer in the Oratory. The splendour so dazzled her that she could not see what sort of a ring it was.

Donna Dianora, wife of Paul de Salis, aged sixty, saw it two years before Catherine's death. She saw it when the Saint chanced to rest her left hand on the grille. It was a ring of gold, very dazzling, and she could not help asking herself what ring this could be, but she thought that perhaps prioresses and superiors wore such a ring.

Sister Elizabeth Dardinelli, aged sixty-seven, had seen a red circle round the ring finger.

Sister Serafina Baroncini, aged seventy-seven, saw the ring when a girl before she entered the Order. It was under her eyes for half an hour when she had been sent into the Scriptorium, and Catherine took her by the hand. It was a gold ring with a brilliant white stone, "so that I could see myself reflected in it" (*che io mi specchiavo dentro*).

Sister Frances Serafina Strozzi, aged forty-three, saw the ring as a child. It was a fold of the flesh of the finger in the shape of a ring.

This practically exhausts the list of witnesses *de visu*. From an evidential point of view, however, the two most valuable testimonies produced in the canonization process were written documents. The one was a copy of a letter written by Father Thomas Neri, a Dominican, in 1549. The other an excerpt from certain notes upon the life of Catherine, which had been compiled by Sister Mary Magdalen Strozzi, her privileged companion and nurse in illness. Father Neri had evidently been much impressed by the account he had obtained of the wonderful manifestations of which Catherine was the subject, and his letter was penned in quite early days, forty years before Catherine's death and seven years after the mystic nuptials first took place. He repeats in some detail the story of Catherine's vision, going into such particulars as these:

Then Jesus took from His left hand and from the finger next to the little finger a ring as described above (viz., a gold ring adorned with a magnificent diamond and enamelled in red), and while the Queen of Heaven continued to hold Catherine's hand Jesus Christ placed this most beautiful ring upon the finger which is called the index, next to the long finger of her left hand, saying, "I give thee this in token that thou shalt always remain my spouse and in token that thou shalt never be led astray by the tempter in anything," and He added, "Now thou art my bride indeed." Then Jesus kissed her on the mouth, and Our Lady in the same spot and moment did likewise, and Catherine, excusing herself to Jesus that she had no words to thank Him as her heart desired, only said, "My Lord I thank Thee that Thou hast deigned to take this wretched creature for Thy Bride."

The details, however, which particularly interest us in our present inquiry are those set out in the following passage. It should be remembered that the espousals took place during an ecstasy on Easter Sunday:

Within a fortnight of Easter, the true ring, that is to say the ring of gold with its diamond, was seen by three very holy sisters at different times, each of them being over forty-five years of age.

One was Sister Potentiana of Florence, the second Sister Mary Magdalen of Prato [this was Mary Magdalen Strozzi, who left the manuscript account of her beloved Mother Catherine], the third Sister Aurelia of Florence, so the Superiors of our Province have ascertained.

A command was laid upon this holy virgin (Catherine) by her superior to ask a favour of Jesus Christ; and by Him the favour was granted that all the sisters saw the ring, or at least a counterfeit presentment of it, in this sense, that for three days continuously, i.e., the Monday, Tuesday and Wednesday of Easter week, all the sisters beheld on the finger beside the long finger of the left hand, and in the place where she said the ring was, a red lozenge (*quadretto*) to represent the stone or diamond, and similarly they saw a red circlet around the finger in place of the ring, which lozenge and circlet Catherine averred she had never seen in the same way as the sisters, because she always beheld the ring of gold and enamel with its diamond. Also the ring was seen in this way as a reddening of the flesh throughout the whole of Ascension Day 1542, and also on the day of *Corpus Christi*, when it was accompanied by a most wonderful perfume which was perceived by all.

Father Neri also goes on to remark that this reddening of the finger could not have been due to any paint or dye, for on Corpus Christi day, as he relates, Catherine was brought into the church that the Governor of the city might see this wonderful red circlet. But all traces of it disappeared in his presence, though immediately afterwards it showed itself again to the nuns.

Regarding Father Neri's statement that three of the elder nuns were privileged to see the real ring of gold and red enamel, it is curious that no confirmation of this seems to be found in Sister Mary Magdalen Strozzi's own notes, though she is one of the three Sisters mentioned. What she does make perfectly clear is that for three days after Easter there was a red circle round Catherine's finger, which she describes as a ring "between skin and skin," corresponding closely to what Dr. Imbert-Gourbeyre tells of Marie Julie that her finger looked as if a red coral ring had been buried in the flesh. Again, Sister Mary Magdalen's notes give a curiously touching impression of her solicitude lest Catherine had become the dupe of some wile of the devil. She went to the confessor about it, and together they made experiments with cinnabar and other pigments, but they found they could produce nothing in the least like the reddening on Catherine's finger. Then Sister Mary Magdalen went to Catherine herself, and seems frankly to have told her doubts and scruples. These abnormal manifestations, she urged, were contrary to the spirit and traditions of the convent and were very dangerous to humility and to that desire for self-effacement which was so important in the religious life. Catherine agreed, and was delighted to let her do anything she pleased in order to get rid of the mark. She only blamed herself and begged their pardon for being the cause of so much trouble and disquiet of mind among the rest of the community. So Sister Mary Magdalen put the finger into her mouth to find if the red mark had any taste, and also left it to steep in water, and then tried to wash out the mark with soap—all, of course, without any effect.

On the other hand, Catherine declared quite simply that she saw on her finger a gold ring set with a pointed diamond, and could see nothing else. "I have to take it on faith," she said to her friend, "when you tell me that you simply perceive a red mark." The fact that St. Catherine continually saw the ring and its stone with her bodily eyes and could not see the circle of red is also definitely mentioned in the letter of Father Neri in 1549.

The facts are very puzzling. There is apparently overwhelming evidence that at certain times the marks of a red circle and lozenge showed themselves on Catherine's finger in a way that could be perceived by all. It also appears to be certain that she always with her bodily eyes saw on that finger a gold ring set with a diamond, but I cannot feel satisfied that the testimony recorded is sufficient to establish the fact that the golden ring was really seen by any others beside herself. There are so many well-attested instances of a supernatural radiance shining from the faces, hands and garments of mystics when rapt in ecstasy that we may readily agree that this is likely to have happened in the case of Catherine's finger. If so, casual witnesses may very well have persuaded themselves that in the midst of this radiance they discerned the gold ring and the diamond of which they had previously heard mention. It can only be said that the evidence is not sufficient to allow us to come to a definite conclusion.

The various other recorded examples of mystical espousal rings seem to be of much the same character. In the case of the Venerable Giovanna Maria della Croce (Bemardine Floriani), Abbess of the Poor Clares of Roveredo, who had received from our Saviour in 1644 an espousal ring with five diamonds, there was nothing which appeared outwardly to attract the attention of the observers. But one of her most devoted subjects, Sister Ursula, who often found a pretext for kissing the hand of this venerated superior, experienced in doing so an intense spiritual emotion.

Moreover, when her lips came in contact with the ring finger she noticed a roughness suggestive of the points of a hoop of gems.

She made some comment on this strange fact to the Mother herself, but Giovanna at once imposed silence upon her, and would never afterwards allow her to kiss her hand. It seems, however, that the news spread to other members of the community. A certain Sister Frances, with the connivance of the confessor, tried to put a ring on that particular finger, but found that it was impossible to push it beyond the second joint. The attempt was renewed after Giovanna's death, but the base of the finger was so swollen that, even when a large ring was used, it was impossible to press it home.

In the case of Marina de Escobar, who also is said, during the course of an ecstasy, to have received a ring of espousals from our Lord, the ring was so plain to her bodily eyes that she covered her hand with a cloth to hide it from herself. This vivid and sensible realization of its presence, however, lasted but a few days, and after that it was only seen by her occasionally and at intervals.

No other person beside herself is known to have beheld it.

Finally, a brief reference may be made to the ring of Columba Schonath in 1763. Here we are told that a material ring showed itself, which was of a red colour. The Dominican Provincial is said to have seen it radiant with light on the middle finger of her left hand. It is added that he washed it with water and tried to cut it with a knife, but could not make out of what material it was. However, all these details, it must be confessed, do not seem to rest on very satisfactory evidence.

CHAPTER IV
TELEKINESIS

It is not the purpose of this book to propound any theory as to the origin or nature of the phenomena discussed, or even to defend their supernatural character. My service is simply that of a *bureau de constatation*, to sift good evidence from bad, to separate the grain from the chaff. My contention, however, is that in the mystical state things really happen which are not reconcilable with nature's laws as commonly understood, and further that there is better published evidence of such occurrences in our hagiographical records than any which has yet been produced by Spiritualists.

From this point of view it is desirable to insist upon the point that the Church has never pronounced that the suspension, for example, of a man's body in the air is a miraculous fact which can be admitted as a proof of his sanctity. As the *Promotor Fidei* urges in one of the beatification processes to which we shall have occasion to refer, "these alleged charismata and supernatural favours are common to good and bad alike, and they cannot be accepted as validating an otherwise defective proof of virtuous life and conduct."

Telekinesis is a convenient term introduced of late years in the discussion of psychic phenomena, and is defined by the *Oxford English Dictionary* as "movement of or in a body, alleged to occur at a distance from, and without material connexion with, the motive cause or agent." The word has been used in a rather wider and vaguer sense by some writers, e.g., by F. W. Myers in his *Human Personality*, but the particular type of phenomenon which I propose to illustrate here comes strictly under this definition. It is the alleged transference of the Host through the air by some unexplained agency from the altar or the hands of the officiating priest to the lips of the expectant communicant.

It hardly needs saying that the evidence for such occurrences requires to be carefully scrutinized; for while on the one hand it would undoubtedly be rash to reject a *priori* the possibility of marvels of this description, it is certain on the other that fraud and hysterical delusion have often availed themselves of similar manifestations to establish a very ill-deserved reputation for holiness.

The notorious Magdalena de la Cruz (1487-1560), a nun who for many years was venerated as a saint throughout the Spanish peninsula—so much so that she was invited to bless the christening robes prepared for the infant prince, afterwards Philip II—was not only believed to have the stigmata, to live without food except the Blessed Sacrament, and to be raised in the air during some of her ecstasies, but it was also asserted that she received Holy Communion miraculously. More than once, we are told, when the number of particles in the ciborium had been carefully counted, one was found to be missing when the priest next inspected them and meanwhile Magdalena had exhibited a host on her tongue which had come to her no one knew how. A closely analogous deception or illusion was charged against, and apparently confessed by, the other hardly less famous Spanish pseudo-mystic, Maria de la Visitacion, during the reign of Philip II. In both these cases the Inquisition eventually intervened, and inflicted a severe penance on the culprits. Nearer our own time is the sensation caused by the "miraculous" communions of Palma Matarrelli d'Oria. It seems certain that Pius IX, after reading the reports submitted to him by the Congregation of the Holy Office, was convinced that all the Eucharistic phenomena were fraudulent. "What Palma is doing," he told Mgr. Barbier de Montault, "is the work of the devil, and her pretended miraculous Communions with hosts taken from St. Peter's are a pure piece of trickery. It is all imposture and I have the proofs there in the drawer of my bureau. She has befooled a whole crowd of pious and credulous souls." Certainly the account given by Dr. Imbert-Gourbeyre in his book, *Les Stigmatisees*, of Palma's Communion in the middle of a conversation which she was holding with him and Canon de Angelis, is of itself calculated to arouse vehement suspicion of fraudulent practices.

> I was sitting sideways to Palma talking to the Canon who was opposite me when I felt her hand gently tap me on the forearm. At the same

instant the Canon fell upon his knees. I turned to look at Palma, and I saw her eyes shut, her hands joined, her mouth wide open, and on her tongue I perceived a host. I kneel down at once, I adore, and I watch her. Palma puts out her tongue still further as if she was bent on making me see the host clearly, then she swallows it, shuts her mouth, and remains profoundly recollected in her chair.

There seem to have been a good many cases in which public attention has been directed to alleged manifestations of this sort and in which the Holy See, combining in former times both civil and religious authority, has inflicted severe punishment upon those within the States of the Church who were found after inquiry to have imposed upon the credulity of the faithful by pretended miracles. In the *Annali Universali di Medicina* for 1847 there is mention of a certain Vittoria Biondi who in the time of Pope Benedict XIV pretended to have received the stigmata, to have continued for a long period without taking food and to have been communicated supernaturally. A raid, it appears, was made by the authorities and in her room they found a number of small hosts carefully secreted which she used artfully to place upon her tongue, alleging that she had received Communion from an angel.

The culprit, after full confession of her impostures, was admitted to mercy and leniently dealt with, but a formal statement of the offences with which she was charged and of the sentence passed upon her was made public under the heading "Notificazione di affettata Santita." We cannot do better than begin our examination of the better known cases by citing the testimony of the saintly Curé of Ars, a man whose veracity and good faith will hardly appear doubtful to even the most determined sceptic. In one of his public catechisms the good Curé, as his biographer notes, delivered himself as follows on the subject of the real presence:

> Two Protestant ministers came here the other day who disbelieved our Lord's real presence in the Blessed Sacrament. I said to them, "Do you believe that a piece of bread could detach itself and, of its own accord, place itself upon the tongue of a person who was approaching to receive it?" "No." "Then this is not bread." A man had doubts about the real presence. He said to himself, What do we know about it? It is not certain. What is the Consecration? What takes place upon the Altar at that time? But he desired to believe, and he prayed to the Blessed

Virgin to obtain the gift of faith for him. Now listen well to what I am going to tell you. I do not say that it happened *somewhere or other*, but I say that it happened to me. When that man presented himself to receive Holy Communion, the Sacred Host detached Itself from my fingers while I was yet a good distance from him, and went and placed Itself upon the tongue of that man.

Two centuries earlier we find that another famous French priest, hardly less universally venerated for his holiness, had had a similar experience. In the year 1637-1638 Monsieur Olier, the founder of Saint Sulpice, spent some months at Nantes. He had been seriously ill, and by the invitation of the Rev. Mother took up his quarters in a gardener's cottage belonging to the Convent of the Visitation in that city. Among other members of the community at that time was a holy nun, Frangoise-Madeleine de la Roussié re, a memoir of whom was printed some years later. In this occurs the following passage:

> Our Lord used to manifest in an unmistakable way the pleasure He felt in visiting this holy soul. We learned this from many priests who gave her Communion, amongst others from the late Abbé Olier, who, being in the town and lodging in our little gardener's cottage, often said Mass in our church and distributed Holy Communion to the community. One day he asked our Rev. Mother, Mère de Bressand, what was the name of one of the sisters who had a patch of red on her face (it was a mark she had had from birth); and after hearing the name he remarked that she must be a very holy soul since the sacred Host had detached itself from his fingers and had travelled of itself to the mouth of that dear sister. Another ecclesiastic, the Rector of the parish of Nort, who is still living, said that the nun with the mark on her face was certainly a saint, and that he believed her to be such because he had seen the Sacred Host fly into her mouth when he was giving her Communion.

It is probable that M. Olier had already had some experience of similar happenings through his close spiritual friendship with the Dominican ecstatica, Mother Agnes of Jesus, who, like many canonized Saints, is believed to have repeatedly received Communion miraculously from the hands of angels or the Blessed in Heaven. Seeing that for most of these Communions we have no other evidence than the percipient's subjective persuasion that she had been so favoured, the trustworthiness of which may be questioned, I do not propose to discuss them here except when independent confirmation is forthcoming from other sources. But for one, at least, of Mother Agnes' miraculous Communions we have the statement of M. Martinon, Archpriest of Langeac, that, having refused to allow Mother Agnes to communicate at his Mass, he learnt from her afterwards that she had been communicated by an angel, whereupon going to examine the ciborium in which he distinctly remembered that he had left four hosts, he now found that there were only three. But without dwelling further upon French examples, let me go back nearly another three centuries to the famous case of St. Catherine of Siena. Our principal witness is the Dominican, Blessed Raymund of Capua, St. Catherine's confessor, and afterwards General of the Order. His writings leave a strong impression of a naturally sober and scrupulously truthful mind, though, of course, like all other men of his age, he readily believed in the interference of the devil and other supernatural agencies in human affairs. Before, however, we come to the detailed account he has left of his own experience in connection with St. Catherine's Communions, we may note briefly the evidence of Father Bartholomew Dominic given in the process of canonization. His account at once recalls the impressions received so many hundred years later by M. Olier, the Curé d'Ars, and others to whom we shall have occasion to refer further on. I quote from Mother Francis Raphael's *Life of St. Catherine*:

> Fr, Bartholomew Dominic tells us in his deposition that he frequently gave her Holy Communion, and that often at the moment of doing so he felt the Sacred Host agitated, as it were, in his fingers, and escape from them of Itself. "This at first troubled me," he says, cc for I feared lest the Sacred Host should fall to the ground; but It seemed to fly into her mouth. Several persons have told me that the like happened to them when giving her Holy Communion."

Not less striking is the following:

> I often saw her communicate [says Francesco Malevolti, another witness in the process] and always in ecstasy; and I beheld how when the priest was about to give her the Body of our Lord, before he had drawn more than a palm's length near her, the Sacred Host would depart out of his hands and like an arrow shoot into the mouth of the holy virgin. A wise man named Anastasius of Monte Altino also took

notice of this wonderful circumstance and introduced it into certain rhythmical verses which he composed on things appertaining to her which he had heard and personally seen.

Blessed Raymund's own account of St. Catherine's Communions is too long to be translated entire, and even Mother Francis Raphael does not reproduce the whole of it. Still it is unfortunate that the actual terms in which he narrates the story cannot be given, for almost every sentence unconsciously bears witness to his desire to tell the exact truth and avoid exaggeration. He explains first of all how on one occasion he had travelled back with St. Catherine from Avignon and had reached Siena on St. Mark's day utterly worn out with fatigue. It was not too late in the morning to say Mass, and so, in order to gratify her intense desire of receiving Communion, he put on his vestments and proceeded to celebrate the Holy Sacrifice, consecrating a small Host for her which lay on the corporal in front of him. When he turned round to give the general absolution before Communion he saw her face radiant and transformed with light. He was almost overpowered at the spectacle, and on once more facing towards the altar in order to take up the sacred particle he apostrophized It mentally, saying "Come, O Lord, to Thy spouse." "The thought" he goes on, "had hardly framed itself in my mind when, before I touched It, the Sacred Host, as I clearly perceived, moved forward of Itself, the distance of three inches or more, coming close to the paten which I was holding in my hand." Whether It then leaped on to the paten, Raymund tells us he is unable to say. He was too startled by what he had already observed to notice or remember exactly.

But after quoting the words "God and the Father of our Lord Jesus Christ knoweth and is my witness that I lie not," he repeats very solemnly, "I know and am certain that I saw the Sacred Host move of Itself without the intervention of anyone and come towards me." On another occasion, which belongs, it appears, to the early period of Blessed Raymund's acquaintance with St. Catherine, he had been waiting to begin Mass until the Saint, who was ill, could come to the church. Finally receiving a message that she was unable to communicate, he concluded that she had not left her house, and he thereupon offered the Holy Sacrifice believing, erroneously, that she was not present. She was, however, in point of fact, at the extreme end of the church in a place in which he could not, or did not, see her.

After the consecration and the *Pater noster* [says Raymund], I proceeded according to the rubrics to divide the Host. At the first fraction, the Sacred Host, instead of separating into two portions, divided into three, two large and one small, which seemed to me about the length of a bean but not so wide. This particle which I attentively observed, appeared to fall on the corporal by the side of the chalice above which I had broken the Host; I clearly saw it descend towards the altar, but I could not afterwards distinguish it on the corporal. Presuming that it was the whiteness of the corporal which prevented my discerning this particle, I broke off another, and after saying the *Agnus Dei*, consumed the Sacred Host. As soon as my right hand was at liberty, I felt on the corporal for the particle on the spot where it had fallen; but I found nothing.

Raymund then gives an account of his profound distress of mind and the fruitless search he instituted, in the course of which he examined minutely not only the corporal but every part of the altar and the floor. As he was giving up the quest in despair, he was interrupted by a visitor, a Carthusian Prior, desirous of having an immediate interview with St. Catherine. Believing her to be in her own house, Raymund conducted the Prior thither, and then for the first time discovered, to his great surprise, that she had gone out to church and had not yet returned. Retracing their steps with all haste, they found the Saint kneeling with some of her companions at the far end of the building remote from the altar.

St. Catherine was in an ecstasy, but, as the need seemed urgent, Raymund persuaded her companions to try to rouse her.

> They obeyed [he goes on], and when we were seated with the Prior I told her my anxiety in a low voice and in few words. She smiled gently and replied just as if she had known all the particulars. "Did you not search for it diligently?" On my answering that I had done so: "Why then are you so troubled?" she said, and again she smiled. I already felt more tranquil, and said, "Mother, I verily believe that it was you who took that consecrated particle." "Nay, Father," she replied, "do not accuse me of that; it was not I but Another; all I can tell you is, you will never find it again." Then I pressed her to explain what had happened. "Father," she said, "trouble yourself no more about that particle; I will tell you the truth as to my spiritual father; it was brought me by our Divine Lord Himself. My companions urged me not to communicate this morning in order to avoid certain murmurs. I was unwilling to

be troublesome to anyone, but I had recourse to our Lord; and He deigned to appear and gave me with His own sacred hands the particle which you consecrated."

I do not feel that we are called upon to pronounce any opinion for or against the correctness of St. Catherine's impression of the agency by which Holy Communion was brought her. The point which concerns us immediately in connection with our present inquiry is the fact that the sacred particle which disappeared from the altar was conveyed to and consumed by her. There are so many instances on record of the same kind of marvel that it would be difficult, it seems to me, to explain them as the concurrent hallucinations of two minds which happen to be in some kind of telepathic *rapport*. Let us take one, for example, which was recorded forty-one years after Catherine's death, and the scene of which lay far away from Siena, in Upper Suabia. Blessed Elizabeth von Reute (*die gute Beta*) was a mystic who died in 1420, and whose Life was written by her confessor, one Konrad Kügelin, almost immediately afterwards. He lets us know that Elizabeth lived with three companions, and that he, when he had said Mass, used to communicate these and afterwards take the fourth Host to Elizabeth in her sick room. On one occasion when he had given the three Communion he set out for the suffering ecstatica's cell carrying the remaining particle on the paten. The server went before, with a candle and a bell, but as he (Konrad) followed he suddenly missed the Host from the paten in his hand. Retracing his steps he made a great search but without result, though he was convinced that he had consecrated four Hosts. Finally, he made up his mind to go to the good Beta herself and tell her of the loss and of his sorrow and anxiety. When he entered her cell he found her radiant and smiling. "You laugh," he said to her, "whilst I am in deep distress." On this she at once replied: "Do not be troubled any more; our Lord has already revealed to me that you fear you have lost the sacred Host. You have not lost It. I must tell you that Jesus Christ, my beloved Spouse, came to me in human form, preceded by an angel magnificently clad, and that He gave me the Blessed Sacrament with His own Hand."

As the influences which surrounded Elizabeth of Reute were not Dominican, it does not seem to me likely that at this early date the incident can have been suggested by the story just related of St. Catherine of Siena. No doubt, as previously remarked, we cannot safely attach any importance to the account given by the nun of the channel through which the favour was received. The gift itself was objective and material, the vision was subjective and spiritual, and no one lays more stress upon the need of caution in interpreting such apparitions than the great authority on canonization, Pope Benedict XIV. But when we have the conviction of a preternatural reception of the Eucharist confirmed by the simultaneous and unaccountable disappearance of a consecrated Host, it does not seem irrational to believe that in some mysterious way the object of such intense longing and desire may have been physically transported through the intervening space. Certainly if telekinesis exists at all upon this earth—and levitation itself is sometimes reckoned as a particular development of it—it is difficult to imagine any conditions under which the power of spirit over matter is more likely to be displayed than in relation to those consecrated species which already in some way belong simultaneously to the two realms of soul and of sense.

Although there is a great family resemblance between most of these stories, I shall be excused, I hope, if I quote a few more illustrations. The evidence is not of the highest order—the element of cross-examination, for example, is almost always wanting—still it is first hand and good of its kind. Perhaps one of the most interesting, though not one of the most satisfactory, examples of these telekinetic communions is that presented by the case of Suor Domeniea dal Paradiso, a Florentine nun, who died in 1553. Almost all that we know about her is derived either directly or indirectly from the manuscripts of Father Francesco Onesti di Castiglione, who was her confessor for something like half a century. He had known her, he declared, almost from her cradle, and the account I am about to quote was written after he had been in intimate relations with her for thirty-four years. He declared that he had prayed for a long time that if the wonderful things he had recorded concerning the same Sister came from God and the spirit of truth, a sign might be given him in this form, *viz.*, that an angel should take her Communion from the Eucharist which he himself had consecrated. He prayed thus for many months without any answer to his prayer, and losing heart he began to think he had been guilty of presumption or curiosity.

But one Holy Saturday, when he was singing the Mass,

> I was about [he writes] to receive the Sacred Host, and I had It there upon the paten, when, after repeating the *Domine non sum dignus*, I remembered to utter the petition I usually made to obtain the sign I desired. Suddenly I noticed that a fragment of the Host the size of a large bean was lying on the paten a good two inches away from the

Host itself. At this I began to wonder how It could have separated Itself so far, and I resolved to take care not to let It fall off the paten, when lo! in an instant, I saw the same fragment upon my left hand, the hand with which I was holding the paten. It lay upon the back of my thumb at the highest point between the juncture with the hand and the knuckle.

At this I was much more astonished and so dumbfounded that I thought no more of the sign I had asked for. But whilst I stood gaping, the fragment as if It had been snatched away by an invisible hand disappeared and was nowhere to be seen either there, or on the paten, or on the altar. Not to cause further delay I consumed the sacred species, but I looked again to see if by some negligence of mine the fragment had fallen on to the corporal, for It could not have fallen anywhere else, but I saw no signs of it. Much troubled I finished the Mass, and after taking off my vestments and making my thanksgiving, I let my mind drift back again to the subject, being inclined to blame myself for negligence, but quite sure that I had not been either sleepy or distracted. Then suddenly I remembered the sign I had asked for, and in better spirits I determined to pay a visit to Sister Domenica and to find out if my prayer had been granted. I went, and she at last, joyfully smiling at my perplexity, made known to me that she had received the fragment of the Eucharist from her angel guardian as my messenger (*nomine meo*) on that same day and at the very hour at which I was celebrating.

It must be admitted that this is not a very convincing story, but taking the writer's narrative as a whole he leaves the impression, for reasons it would take too long to develop here, of a perfectly honest witness. On the other hand, Sister Domenica, though the communications she believed herself to have with celestial beings are of the most extravagant order, and though her delusions, I should be inclined to say, are in some cases patent, was nevertheless devoted to good works, beloved by her community and most austere in her life. She died at the age of eighty, the foundress of a great convent which maintained its fervour for many generations, and she was venerated by all as a saint. Her body, which had not been in any way embalmed, still remained incorrupt nearly sixty years after her death. It is impossible to believe that with such a record Suor Domenica could have been a vulgar hypocrite or impostor. And yet among Father Onesti's other stories concerning her, we find such a plain and unequivocal statement as this:

> When she knelt at my Mass, ravenous with spiritual hunger, I often saw the Eucharist in her mouth taken from the Sacrifice which I had consecrated. This was conveyed to her by the ministry of an angel. And this I knew not only from what I saw, but also from the number of the Hosts, for one was missing from the number which I had counted.

Onesti also declares that her fellow-nuns who had seen the same thing came to tell him of the fact, also that on one occasion she put out her tongue, at the command, as she believed, of the Archangel Gabriel, to show Canon Benivieni the Host she had miraculously received. Another example of much the same kind is that of the Venerable Gertrude Salandri, of whom her anonymous but most capable biographer writes as follows:

> Being forbidden to communicate on a certain day, she was gazing from afar at the Eueharistic table and deploring her misfortune. As she was unable to partake in act she sought comfort in the banquet of desire, when suddenly a particle escaped from the ciborium, passed of Itself through the Communion window, and flew straight to Sister Gertrude to gratify her longing. What her consolation was I have no words to describe. I only know that the nun who was privileged to be the witness of this extraordinary prodigy remained so overwhelmed with astonishment and so carried away by a flood of devotion that she ran at once to give an account of it to their Confessor and afterwards bore testimony to the fact upon oath in the process of beatification. Neither was this nun full of fancies nor one of commonplace virtue, but she was the great Servant of God, Sister Angela Maria di Gesu, called in the world Anna Maria Sarnini, of whose solid and eminent virtue we have spoken elsewhere more at large.

Even more wonderful are the Eucharistic marvels recorded in the Life of St. Maria Francesca delle Cinque Piaghe, who is still nearer our own times. Her biographer writes:

> For her the moments before Communion passed with intolerable slowness, so much so that she once went so far as to beg her confessor, Don Antonio Cervellini, to say a Mass for the dead or a votive Mass, in order to shorten things, and when he objected that the rite of that day did not allow it, "Your Mass," she told him, "goes on for ever; it is too long, for pity's sake say it quicker."

Such language, the good priest declared, would have troubled me had I not known the virginal innocence of her soul and her extraordinary austerity of life, and if I had not also realised that she was carried away by her love and thirsted only for Jesus Christ. Accordingly I made my preparation at once and to gratify her I hastened my Mass as much as I could. When, however, I came to the point of giving her Communion, hardly had I turned round and pronounced the words *Ecce Agnus Dei* when I perceived that the Host was no longer between my fingers. I was terribly upset and I stood there anxiously examining the paten and the ground, but she signed to me that she already had the Host upon her tongue, and I on seeing this was able to set my mind at rest. The server of the Mass, Signor Francesco Boreili, was also a witness of the incident and was as startled by it as the priest himself.

But the story told by another of the confessors of the same Saint is stranger than any we have yet met, and it gains authority from the fact that the said confessor, the holy Barnabite, F. S. M. Bianchi, has himself also been beatified. Since he made this deposition in the process of canonization of Saint Maria Francesca, and speaks not from report but of his own personal experience, his testimony, extraordinary as it is, cannot lightly be set aside. I quote the abbreviated account given in the *Analecta Juris Pontijicii.*

The longing for Communion in her case was so extraordinary that at times during my Mass God vouchsafed to console her by the ministry of angels, even so far as to allow her to participate in the precious Blood which was in the chalice. In fact the Archangel Raphael, after the consecration, or at any rate before my Communion, took her the chalice from the altar and allowed her to drink of it as she knelt at home. Sometimes she drank very little, only a few drops, but it was enough to lead me to question her and satisfy myself of the fact. On one occasion when she drank almost the half I noticed the clear and unmistakable absence of a part of the contents of the chalice, and I was extremely surprised. When I questioned her as to what had happened, she replied: "If it had not been that the Archangel reminded me that the Holy Sacrifice must be properly consummated I should have drunk the whole." At other times things happened differently.

For example, she received by the intermediary of angels the fragment of the Host which I had put into the chalice. On some rare occasions

I noticed this, not feeling the fragment on my tongue or against my palate. Then I asked the Servant of God about it, and she satisfied me that our Lord had willed that It should be brought to her.

I am unable to understand how Blessed Francesco Bianchi came to suppose that the chalice itself could have been removed from the altar while his Mass was proceeding, but no doubt it is difficult to imagine a liquid transported through the air as the Host might be transported. Curiously enough, the only parallel I am able to produce of this astounding conveyance of the species of wine to a communicant at a distance is to be found in the life of a nun in Southern Italy, who was born in 1866 and died only in 1912. Her biographer, who was also her director, writes of her as follows:

> On more than one occasion she received Communion under the two species of bread and wine. The fact of her having communicated was made known in various ways, first because at such times her look became angelic, indeed seraphic, to such a degree that she no longer seemed a creature of earth. From this transformation in her appearance it was evident to her intimates that she had been regaled with the most holy Eucharist. But that she had also been permitted to partake of the Precious Blood of Jesus was detected by the Superior General of the Order, and by some of the nuns, who, when kneeling beside her, remarked that an extraordinary fragrance of wine was perceptible all around.
>
> An astonishing fact was also noticed by one of her confessors who is now dead, and afterwards by her director [the writer of the biography] as well. Whilst he was saying Mass in the church of the convent, when the moment came for receiving the contents of the chalice he observed to his intense surprise that a considerable portion of the Precious Blood had already been consumed by some invisible agency. His suspicions, which turned in her direction, became a reality after Mass on his learning from some of the nuns that in conversing with Suor Maria della Passione they had perceived a fragrance of wine. This was further confirmed by the privileged Sister herself, who came to him and said smilingly: "Have you seen what Jesus has done? Oh! how good He is to me!" Thus in the fullness of her grateful heart she bore witness to the wonderful thing that had happened to her.

Another confirmation is furnished by a nun of the same community, Sister Maria della S. Sindone, who was the confidant of many of the secrets of the Servant of God. She has stated in writing: "One day Sister Maria della Passione was wreathed in smiles and I asked her what new thing had happened to her... she was silent, but afterwards, moved by the word of obedience, she bowed her head and said:... 'the Confessor this morning had a fright when he received the Chalice at Mass, because he perceived that the wine was diminished in quantity and he looked to see if It had been spilt upon the altar, but it was useless, because I drank It and I left very little in the Chalice, but I do not know... how it all happened'"

I have no means of gauging the trustworthiness of the writer of these things, but the book at least has appeared in a second edition with full episcopal sanction, and it seems that the beatification of Suor Maria is already being talked of as likely to come to pass at no very remote date. This, of course, is mere gossip, but with regard to another Italian mystic, Anna Maria Taigi, who was beatified in 1920, we have what seems good evidence that the Sacred Host on more than one occasion flew to her lips. The same is also true of a French ecstatic and foundress of our days, Mdre Marie de Jesus (Madame du Bourg), who died in 1862. In her case the fact of both levitation and telekinetic Communion appears to rest on the testimony of many of her religious sisters who were eye-witnesses. It may be worth while now to devote rather more space to the discussion of a particular eucharistic miracle which is somewhat different in character from those to which I have just been alluding, but which is widely known, first because it is recounted in one of the lessons of the Roman Breviary, and secondly, because its memory is perpetuated in the device which adorns the habit of the "Mantellate" or nuns of the Third Order of Servites. The prodigy is connected with the last moments of Saint Juliana Falconieri, the foundress of the Mantellate, who died on June 19, 1341. I cannot do better than quote the Breviary lesson just referred to.

The self-inflicted hardships of her life brought upon her a disease of the stomach, whereby, when she was seventy years of age, she was brought to the point of death. She bore the daily sufferings of her illness with a smiling face and a brave heart. The only thing of which she was heard to complain was that her stomach being so weak that she could not keep down any food, she was withheld by reverence for the Sacrament from drawing near to the Lord's Table. Finding herself in these straits she begged the priest to bring the Bread of God, and as she dared not take It into her mouth, to put It as near as possible to her heart. The priest did as she wished, and, to the amazement of all present, the Divine Bread at once disappeared from sight, and at the same instant a smile of joyous peace crossed the face of Juliana, and she gave up the ghost. All were confounded until the virgin body was being laid out after death in the accustomed manner. Then there was found upon the left side of the bosom, a mark like the stamp of a seal reproducing the form of the Sacred Host, the mould of which was one of those that bear a figure of Christ crucified.

This is the story which is told in the Breviary in accord with the various published Lives of the saintly foundress and the miracle is regarded by the Bollandists and others as peculiarly well authenticated because a document is in existence, said to have been drawn up in Latin eighteen days later, giving an account of what had happened. I reproduce with a few slight modifications the translation of it which is furnished by Father Soulier, O.S.M.

"He hath made a memorial of His wonderful works" [Ps. ex. 4].

Let it be placed on record how eighteen days ago our Sister Juliana died and flew to heaven with her spouse Jesus; and it was in this manner.

Being more than seventy years old, her stomach had become so weakened from her voluntary sharp penances, from fasts, from chains, from an iron girdle, disciplines, nightly vigils and spare diet, that she was no longer able to take or retain food. When she knew that because of this she must be deprived of the Viaticum of the most sacred Body of Christ, no one could believe how much she grieved and wept, so much so that they were afraid she would die from the vehemence of her sorrow.

She, therefore, most humbly begged Father James de Campo Regio that at least he would bring the most Holy Sacrament in a pyx and set it before her, and this was done. But when the priest appeared carrying the Body of our Lord, she straightaway prostrated herself upon the ground in the form of a cross and adored her Master.

Then her face became like the face of an angel. She desired, since she was not allowed to unite herself to Jesus, at least to kiss Him, but this the priest refused. She then begged piteously that over the burning furnace of her breast they would spread a veil upon which they might put the Host. This was granted her. But —O wonderful prodigy!—scarcely had the Host touched this loving heart than it was lost to sight and never more was found. Then Juliana when the Host had disappeared, with a tender and joyous face, as if she were rapt in ecstasy, died in the Kiss of her Lord, to the amazement and admiration of those who were present—to wit, of Sister Johanna, Sister Mary, Sister Elizabeth, Father James and others of the house.

One would deeply regret to disturb the reader's faith in so pretty a story. But we must not shut our eyes to two rather serious difficulties. In the first place, it is surely a very curious fact that in this quasi-official memorandum nothing whatever is said concerning "the mark like the stamp of a seal reproducing the form of the Sacred Host " which was found "on the left side of her bosom." They can hardly have forgotten the circumstance in eighteen days, and this was after all the only conclusive evidence that so stupendous a miracle had taken place. The month was June, the place Florence, it is hardly likely that the windows would have been kept closed in the room where the Saint was breathing her last. Consequently a slight puff of air or some convulsive movement of the invalid might easily have accounted for the disappearance of a Host so insecurely resting upon her breast.

How could the witnesses of such a marvel as the miraculous imprint upon her bosom have neglected to make the slightest reference to this detail, so much more startling in itself than the mere inability to find the sacred particle?

The first to mention the device stamped upon the virginal flesh of the Saint, so far as we can now ascertain, is Father Nicholas Mati, a Servite Religious, who somewhere about the year 1384 left behind him a manuscript volume, written in Italian and still, we are told, in existence, which he entitled *Giornale e Ricordi* (Journal and Memoirs). In this he included a very brief notice of St. Juliana and of Blessed Joanna Soderini; and one of the few definite things which he finds to say about the latter is embodied in this sentence.

"She was the happy disciple who, sooner than Sister Elizabeth and the others discovered upon the breast of St. Juliana that astounding marvel of the figure of Christ nailed to the cross impressed upon her flesh within a circle like a Host." Nevertheless, this testimony was probably not written down until some forty years after St. Juliana's death, neither is there any reason to believe that Father Nicholas was personally acquainted either with Juliana or with her devoted disciple Joanna Soderini. His information was presumably derived from his fellow Servites or some of the Mantellate nuns, and we know how easily a story of this kind may grow up and how quickly it spreads and is improved upon.

But what has so far been said is by no means the most serious difficulty which meets us in investigating the truth of this miracle. Much more upsetting is the fact that the story of the miraculous penetration of a Host through the breast was not new, but just at that period was widely diffused throughout western Christendom. The pious Franciscan tale to which I refer seems to have had its origin before St. Juliana was born. What we know for certain is that it recurs twice in the collection of stories known as the *Speculum Laicorum* (Mirror of Layfolk), which was almost certainly compiled by an English friar between 1279 and 1292. It is recounted there in a very summary fashion, but in other books of the same class plenty of detail is supplied, though, as might be expected, the circumstances vary in almost every example which we meet. Following the indications given in Mr. J. A. Herbert's *Catalogue of Romances*, Vol. Ill, I have copied one version of the story from MS. Sloane, a manuscript of the early fourteenth century. This account may be translated rather freely as follows:

> Brother Peter de Swynesfeld, of holy memory, who was formerly "Minister" [i.e., Provincial] of the Friars Minor in England, was accustomed to tell—and indeed he himself left the story in writing—how when he was returning from the General Chapter [at Assisi] in passing through the pleasant town of Rimini upon the Adriatic, in company with Brother Adam de Maddol, it happened that the lord of the said township fell ill. He was a nobleman (comes) and very pious, a true Catholic in faith, most earnest in hearing Mass and in looking upon the Body of our Lord (*precipuus in missis audiendis et in dominici corporis aspectu*) and amongst other things it was his daily custom to pray to God that at the hour of death he might be found worthy to be fortified by the Body and Blood of Christ as a precious viaticum. Before long the end drew near, for he suffered from continual vomiting and his stomach could retain no form of either liquid or solid food. Being thus bereft of the use of medicine and of all hope of recovery, he begged that the Viaticum of Salvation might be brought to his room by priests and religious, for he pleaded that his

eyes at least might be refreshed by the sight of the Body of our Lord, since he dared not partake of It as food.

Before this divine Presence he prostrated himself on the ground and poured out his lament that it was not permitted him to receive the Viaticum, for which every day of his life he had made petition with such intense desire. At last after many sighs and tears, he asked that his left side might be washed by the priest and covered with a linen cloth, humbly begging that since he was not worthy to receive the Body of Christ with his lips, the priest, if that could be allowed, might take It and lay It upon his heart. So it was done; and when the priest had reverently placed the most holy Eucharist upon the chest of the sick man just under the left breast, behold his chest opened of itself and the adorable Body of Christ, escaping from the priest's fingers, passed through the aperture; while in the same moment this truly Catholic nobleman fell asleep in the Lord. This took place about the year of our Saviour 1268.

As already stated, there can be no room for doubt that this story, though variously told, was in circulation long before the death of St. Juliana. In several of the texts of the *Speculum Laicorum* the prodigy is said to have happened near Marseilles. A narrative preserved in MS. Royal 7.C., which is somewhat fuller than that just translated, tells us that the nobleman was called Albert of Venice, and that his title was Count of Panne. In this version the narrator mentions that after the nobleman's breast had closed again "a certain red scar was left behind to prove the truth of the miracle" (*remamnte tamen cicatrice quadam rubea ad tanti miraculi Jidem faciendarri*). The friars also in this case are said to have been on their way to, not returning from, the General Chapter at Assisi, and the year assigned for the miracle is 1267.

Whether there is any historical foundation for this incident, or whether it is—like so many other tales included in these mediaeval collections of "exempla," such as *Convertimini* or the *Speculum Laicorum*—just a pious story, is very hard to decide. There can be no question that in spite of the protests of many learned theologians (Lyndwode, the great English canonist, among the number) the practice of bringing the Blessed Sacrament to be gazed upon by a dying man who was unable to receive Viaticum was a very common one in the Middle Ages. We have one famous example in the case of another Juliana, Juliana of Mount Comillon (1258), who was mainly responsible for the institution of the Feast of Corpus Christi, but no miracle is recorded on that occasion. Similarly of our own King Henry VII, St. John Fisher in one of his sermons tells us how:

> Two days next before his departing, he was of that feebleness that he might not receive the Sacrament again, nevertheless he desired to see the monstrant wherein It was contained. The good father, his confessor, in goodly manner, as was convenient, brought It unto him. He with such a reverence, with so many knockings and beatings of his breast, with so quick and lively a countenance, with so desirous a heart, made his humble obeisance thereunto; with so great humbleness and devotion kissed, not the self place where the Blessed Body of our Lord was contained, but the lowest part of the foot of the monstrant, that all that stood about him scarcely might contain them from prayers and weeping.

It is undoubtedly with a reference to such practices that the twenty-fifth of the Thirty-nine Articles of Religion laid down that "the Sacraments were not ordained of Christ to be gazed upon, or to be carried about, but that we should daily use them." Of course there is no absolute impossibility that both in the case of the Host laid upon the breast of the Italian nobleman and in that brought to St. Juliana Falconieri, the same miracle of absorption through the intervening barrier of flesh may have been wrought by the Divine power; but those who are best acquainted with the mediaeval practice of unconsciously adapting older legends to fresh cases and famous names, will be least disposed to regard the evidence offered for the marvel which we have here been discussing as adequate or convincing. The very fact that St. Juliana was so deeply venerated would be sufficient to render it likely that any accident or confusion occurring amid the deep emotional excitement of such a death-bed scene might be transfigured into a supernatural prodigy of profound significance.

CHAPTER V
THE LUMINOUS PHENOMENA OF MYSTICISM

The case of the "luminous woman" of Pirano in 1934 attracted a certain amount of attention in the English newspapers. Presented at first as a purely pathological abnormality, this manifestation now seems to be attributed, at least in part, to psychological conditions of religious origin. In a communication from Milan which appeared in *The Times* for May 5th of that year, we learn that a cinematograph apparatus has been brought into play, by means of which it has been possible to obtain an exact record of the nature and duration of the luminous appearances. With the aid of the film thus provided, Dr. Protti has submitted a provisional report of the case to a medical society connected with the University of Padua. This investigator, we are told, has convinced himself that the woman "has a fixed idea of a religious character," and he also holds that "these fixed ideas can in particular subjects produce profound changes in the vegetative life system." In illustration of this he appeals to the chill resulting from intense fear, to the bleaching of the hair which is sometimes caused by an unforeseen shock, to the emotions which increase the heart beats, to the effect of protracted suffering upon the gastric secretions with those of the thyroid gland, etc. All these things go to show what influence can be exercised by the stimuli which act on the brain in determining changes, sometimes of a lasting nature, in the visceral functions. That some disturbing conditions of this sort are present in the case, seems to the investigator we are quoting, to be a matter beyond dispute. In the words of *The Times* correspondent's report:

> These disturbances of the vegetative life in the woman are evident. It is enough to recall that the frequency of her breathing and her heart beats are redoubled when the luminous phenomenon is manifested, after which a heavy perspiration is noted. This increased frequency is probably determined by sudden additions to the blood stream of glandular substances tending to excite these functions. The woman fasted very strictly during Lent, and Dr. Protti attaches much importance to this circumstance. The radiant power of her blood is three times the normal, as Dr. Protti was able to verify.
>
> The doctor is, therefore, inclined to believe that, during fasting, conditions are established in the woman favourable to the production of an excess of sulphides, the presence of which is revealed usually by a dark mark left on the skin of those who wear a silver necklace. Sulphides have the property of becoming luminous when they are excited by ultra-violet radiations. As the radiant power of the blood is of an ultra-violet nature and as the woman possesses a very high radiant power, which rises still higher with the increase of the combustions produced by the acceleration of the heart beats, if seems possible to Dr. Protti that the ultra-violet radiation of the blood may excite the sulphides produced in the organism of the woman and thus bring about the periodical luminosity. Dr. Protti holds, therefore, that if it were possible to show that energies of equal intensity to the ultra-violet ones existed in the blood of the woman, it would be possible to believe that a plausible explanation of the luminous phenomenon had been found.

It is rather interesting to compare these remarks with certain comments which occur in the great treatise on Beatification and Canonization of Prosper Lambertini (Pope Benedict XIV).

That high authority is quite prepared to attribute to natural causes many of the luminous emanations said to have been witnessed now and again in the case of God's chosen servants. Appealing to the statements made by Gassendi, Conrad Gesner and T. Bartolini, the Pope says: "It seems to be a fact that there are natural flames which at times visibly encircle the human head, and also that from a man's whole person fire may on occasion radiate naturally, not, however, like a flame which streams upwards, but rather in the form of sparks which are given off all round; further, that some people become resplendent with a blaze of light, though this is not inherent in themselves, but attaches rather to their clothes, or to the staff or to the spear which they are carrying." It must be confessed that no very satisfactory evidence is adduced for this. The portents described in the early books of Livy are not exactly convincing as historical sources. Such a modern authority as Dr. E. N. Harvey shows no disposition to admit the existence of any radiant phenomena of this sort. The utmost he seems to recognize in the human subject is "the occasional presence of luminous bacteria in wounds," and the fact that "the skin may sometimes be a source of light, especially after sweating." This, he says, "is due to luminous bacteria upon the accumulations of substances passed out in the sweat which serves as a nutrient medium." But the phosphorescence which results from such causes is very faint and barely perceptible.

In any case, Prosper Lambertini is somewhat chary about admitting isolated cases of such effulgence to be incontestably miraculous, though, in view of the recognized holiness of such servants of God as St. Philip Neri, St. Charles Borromeo, St. Ignatius of Loyola, St. Francis of Sales and many more, he does not dispute that the brilliant light which was seen on occasion to surround them when preaching, or when offering the holy sacrifice, was of supernatural origin. It is unquestionably true, as he tells us, that there are hundreds of such examples to be found in our hagiographical records, and although a great number of these rest upon quite insufficient testimony, there are others which cannot lightly be set aside. As I have met no other instances in which the evidence is equally good, I trust I may be pardoned for referring to these two striking cases, both belonging to the seventeenth century.

The *processus ordinarius* for the beatification of Blessed Bernardino Realini, who died at Lecce in 1616, was begun in Naples in 1621. Amongst the witnesses examined on that occasion was a certain Signor Tobias da Ponte, a gentleman of rank, whose good standing was made clear by other evidence. He deposed that in the year 1608, or thereabouts, he had come to consult Father Bernardino, but finding his door closed, had waited for some time outside his room. The door, however, was not completely shut, and Signor Tobias noticed an extraordinary radiance which streamed through the slight aperture, and through certain chinks in the boards, all of which set him wondering what could have led the Father to have a fire lighted at midday in the month of April. In his curiosity he pushed the door a little further open and then perceived the holy man kneeling rapt in ecstasy and raised in the air a couple of feet or more above the floor. The witness was too awe-stricken to advance further, or even to remain peeping in as a spectator, but he sat down again upon a bench outside and contented himself for a while with watching the light as it issued through the crannies. He described himself as so dazed by what he had seen that when he had more or less recovered from his emotion he decided that the only thing to be done was to return home again. After giving this testimony, Don Tobias was closely cross-examined, but his evidence, given, of course, upon oath, was in no way shaken. He described how he had argued with himself that the radiance must be his own imagination, or that it was caused by some curious reflection of the sunlight outside, but he said that he had only become more convinced that neither of these things was possible. Although no other witness had shared this experience, there was some confirmation provided by the deposition of a certain Father Beatillo, who was able to testify that he had heard the story from Don Tobias several years before.

Even so, one may hesitate to regard the evidence as entirely satisfactory, but it must not be overlooked that quite a number of people bore witness to the extraordinary radiance with which Father Bernardino's countenance was at times transformed. They had not beheld him raised in the air, but some declared that they had seen sparks coming from all over his body like sparks from a fire (*scintillava da tutto il corpo come scintille di fuoco*), and others asserted that the dazzling glow from his countenance on one or two occasions was such that they could not rightly distinguish his features, but had to turn their eyes away. Similarly, a Father in Naples described how, one day, when he had gone to call Father Bernardino in the early morning he found him on his knees and with his face so radiant that it lit up the darkness of the room.

There were other witnesses, no doubt, who had lived with him in his later years, and who stated very frankly that they had never themselves seen the radiance spoken of, though they quoted the testimony of several Fathers, no longer living, who had been more privileged. But it must be remembered that Bernardino was eighty-six when he died, and that no official examination of witnesses took place until five years later. Consequently, few could have been in a position to give evidence concerning the period of his more vigorous activity; but they remembered what those who had been his contemporaries declared that they had themselves seen.

The case of Father Francis Suarez, the great theologian, depends upon the testimony of only a single witness, but it is in many remarkable. A laybrother, Jerome da Silva, who was acting as porter in the Jesuit college at Coimbra, came about two o'clock in the afternoon to let Father Suarez know that a distinguished visitor sought to speak with him. A stick placed across the door served to indicate that the Father did not wish to be disturbed, but as the Brother had received instructions that whenever this visitor called he was to inform Father Suarez at once, he pushed on, disregarding the signal, and found the outer room in darkness, the shutters being closed against the afternoon heat. Then the Brother's account goes on:

> I called the Father, but he made no answer. As the curtain which shut off his working room was drawn, I saw through the space left between the curtain and the jambs of the door a very great brightness. I pushed aside the curtain and entered the inner apartment. Then I perceived that a blinding light was coming from the crucifix, so intense that it was like the reflection of the sun from glass windows, and I felt that I could not have remained looking at it without being completely dazzled. This light streamed from the crucifix upon the face and breast of Father Suarez, and in the brightness I saw him in a kneeling position in front of the crucifix, his head uncovered, his hands joined and his body in the air lifted five palms above the floor on a level with the table on which the crucifix stood.

The Brother then withdrew in great agitation and waited near the door to recover himself. After a quarter of an hour Father Suarez came out, and finding the Brother porter outside asked him why he had not let him know. The Brother explained that he had called him and had come into the inner room, but that there had been no reply. Then Father Suarez, showing much emotion, tried to extort a promise from Brother da Silva that he would say nothing of what he had seen. The Brother, in turn, asked him to allow him to consult Father de Morales, who acted as confessor to both of them, and it was then arranged, at the suggestion of the confessor in question, that the Brother should draw up a signed and sealed statement in writing, but with an endorsement on the cover of the document that it was on no account to be opened until after Father Suarez's death. As both the laybrother da Silva and Father de Morales were themselves held in deep veneration for their well-known holiness of life, it seems to me that this is a piece of evidence which cannot lightly be rejected.

It may be noted, too, that the luminous phenomena connected with holy people take a very great variety of forms. Amongst many others, that wonderful model of patient suffering, St. Lidwina of Schiedam, was famous in this way. Thomas à Kempis who, though not her earliest biographer, has left a seemingly reliable account of the mystical experiences of his compatriot and contemporary, speaks of her as follows:

> Apart from her mental illumination, over which great men of letters and religious, versed in spiritual studies... wondered exceedingly, very often by day and night when she was visited by the angel, or returned from the contemplation of the things above, she was discovered by her companions to be surrounded by so great a divine brightness that, seeing the splendour and struck with exceeding fear, they dared not approach nigh to her. And although she always lay in darkness and material light was unbearable to her eyes, nevertheless, the divine light was very agreeable to her, whereby her cell was often so wondrously flooded by night that to the beholders the cell itself appeared full of material lamps or fires. Nor is it strange if she overflowed even in the body with divine brightness, who, according to the expression of Blessed Paul, beholding the glory of the Lord with open face, was daily transformed into the same image from brightness to brightness as by the spirit of the Lord (2 Cor. iii, 18). And not only was she wont to be surrounded by divine brightness, but with a wondrous sweetness also both herself and her cell were found to be redolent, so that those who entered thought that divers aromatic simples had been brought in and scattered there.

It is undoubtedly necessary in most of these cases to scrutinize the evidence narrowly even when it is presented on oath in a process of beatification. We cannot shut our eyes to the fact that after the lapse of years many people, without conscious insincerity, do very easily persuade themselves that they have heard, seen or said things which have no better foundation than their own imagination, or their wish to believe. Still, there are not a few cases in which the evidence seems strong, even though the persons so favoured are not Saints widely famous throughout the Church.

There can, therefore, be no adequate reason for refusing credence to the report of similar phenomena when they are recorded of those whose eminent holiness and marvellous gifts of grace are universally recognized. The radiance which at times is said to have surrounded St. Philip Neri, St. Catherine de Ricci, St. Francis of Paula, St. Alphonsus Liguori and many more, seems antecedently likely, assuming the fact that such a favour has been bestowed upon other holy people who are less eminent. No doubt it is easy to exaggerate the impression left in such cases. A man who speaks with power and intense conviction is apt to be flushed. His countenance is transformed, his eyes flame, his vehemence seems almost to surround him with a halo. In the very sober Life of St. Philip Neri, by the Abbes Ponnelle and Bordet, a biography which possibly pushes the critical spirit somewhat further than is necessary, we find, if I mistake not, no definite mention of the radiance which is said often to have lit up the face of the Apostle of Rome. There is a discussion, of course, of the extraordinary palpitations from which the Saint suffered, of the displacement of his ribs and of the sense of consuming heat which continually attended him, but we hear nothing of the radiant aureole with which, according to his early biographer and friend, Father Bacci, his features were not infrequently glorified. Moreover, in alluding to the acquaintance of St. Philip with St. Ignatius, the authors say:

> Philip was not in the habit of dating his recollections, but he gladly spoke of the impression made upon him by "Father Ignatius of holy memory." "His face," he said, "was all resplendent." Thus did interior perfection show itself to him in the faces of men. He observed the same phenomenon in St. Charles Borromeo, and in the Carthusians of Santa Maria degli Angeli, when they came away from their prayer.
>
> There is no need to suppose that he saw a material aureole, and Philip's words may be understood either of a countenance full of fervour, or of impassioned gestures, such as St. Ignatius made use of in his first sermons in Rome. Did not St. Ignatius himself say in the Constitutions which he drew up in 1539 (*sic*) that "the flame of the spirit and the eyes make more impression upon the masses than elegant discourses and nicely-chosen words?" Wandering about the streets of Rome in search of the things of God, Philip cannot have failed to attend, during 1538, the sermons at Santa Maria di Monserrato, when the Spaniard, by his vehemence and his "authority," was carrying off their feet even those of his hearers who did not understand his tongue.

This may be so, but I find it rather difficult to believe that St. Philip and those who used similar expressions, not only of St. Ignatius, but of

St. Charles and many others, were only speaking metaphorically. There are so many stories of holy priests who lit up a dark cell or a whole chapel by the light which streamed from them or upon them, that I am strongly inclined to adhere to the more literal interpretation. For example, we read of the fourteenth-century Carthusian, John Tornerius, then at the Grande Chartreuse near Grenoble, that when his non-arrival in time to celebrate his first Mass, led the sacristan to go to his cell to fetch him, he found the little room radiant with light which seemed to be diffused all round the good Father as if the midday sun was shining there. Similarly, in the process of beatification of the holy Franciscan Observant, Blessed Thomas da Cori, witnesses stated that the whole church on a dark morning was lit up by the radiance which glowed in the Father's countenance *(che sembrava un sole il quale tutta quella chiesa luminosa e risplendente rendesse)*. Further, we learn from what is seemingly the earliest account preserved to us of Blessed Giles of Assisi, that in the night time on one occasion "so great a light shone round him that the light of the moon was wholly eclipsed thereby." So, again, that the house of Blessed Aleidis of Scarbeke seemed to be on fire when she, with a radiant countenance, was praying within; or, once more, that the cell of St. Lewis Bertrand, as Captain de Betancourt bore witness, "appeared as if the whole room was illuminated with the most powerful lamps." And such alleged examples are numerous.

Let me add that the frequent occurrence of luminous phenomena in mediumistic seances—many of these being well attested in circumstances where the strictness of the control seems to preclude the possibility of fraud—strongly inclines me to believe that similar manifestations are not likely to be lacking in the records of mysticism. As the wonders contrived by Pharaoh's magicians followed closely the type of the miracles wrought by Moses and Aaron, so no careful student of psychical research can fail to notice a very close resemblance between the marvels recorded in the lives of the Saints, and the phenomena of what is loosely termed spiritualism. What the connexion is, I am not here concerned to inquire, nor do I believe that we yet possess data enough to be able to deal adequately with the problem.

CHAPTER VI
HUMAN SALAMANDERS

1

At the time of the excitement caused in Paris by the phenomena of the *Convulsionnaires* of Saint-Medard a certain Marie Sonet became famous under the nickname of Marie "la Salamandre." It was stated of her that she used to remain suspended for more than half an hour above a fiery brazier, enveloped only in a sheet, and that, although in that position the flames played directly upon her, neither she nor the sheet which covered her, sustained any damage. In a booklet contributed to the series "Questions Disputees." M. Olivier Leroy published in 1931 an interesting essay upon the question of human incombustibility, borrowing his title from the nickname above mentioned. The fact that in the lives of many of the Saints, their immunity from injury when exposed to burning heat is assumed to be explainable only as a miraculous interference with the laws of nature, has led M. Leroy to make a study of some of the more striking of such cases and to bring them into relation with other examples of impassibility in subjects who were not ascetics. I propose in the present chapter to follow in that writer's footsteps, adding some fresh material which has possibly escaped his researches.

Almost the earliest martyr, regarding the manner of whose death we possess quite authentic information is St. Polycarp of Smyrna, who suffered in a.d. 155 or 156. He was condemned to be burnt at the stake, and the pile of logs when lighted blazed fiercely. It is stated, however, that the flames, forming into an arch, gently encircled the body of the martyr, inflicting no injury; so that his persecutors, to dispatch him, sent a spearman to pierce him through the breast with a lance. The gush of blood is said to have extinguished the conflagration, but when he was dead and the pile was rekindled, his body, except for the bones, was reduced to ashes. This would seem to show that it was no mere accidental current of air which had previously saved the martyr from destruction. More directly relevant, however, to our present purpose is the case, recounted in the sixth century by St. Gregory of Tours, of a Catholic who, in the course of a dispute with an Arian opponent, threw a gold ring into the fire, and as a test of the truth or falsehood of the doctrine repudiated, challenged his adversary to pick it out again. The Arian declined the contest, but the champion of orthodoxy, invoking the Trinity, plunged his arm into the flame and recovered the ring, now red-hot. He held it for some time in the palm of his hand, but, so Gregory assures us, sustained no injury. In another similar challenge recorded by the same writer, a ring was fished out of a cauldron of boiling water, and again the faith of the Catholic who did this protected him from harm. It may be admitted that no great reliance can be placed on the historical accuracy of these stories; but the next to be noticed is both better known and better attested.

This also was in some sense a challenge. In the early days of the Patarine and Investiture controversy strong feeling was aroused in many localities against simoniaeally intruded prelates. In 1062, after the death of Bishop Gerard of Florence, an unworthy candidate by a huge bribe secured the appointment for himself, but thereby provoked a series of riots among the citizens, some favouring his cause and others opposing it. As the only means of restoring peace, it was decided that an appeal should be made to the judgment of heaven. St. John Gualbert, Abbot of Vallombrosa, directed one of his monks, Peter Aldobrandini, afterwards Cardinal and now venerated as St. Peter Igneus, to submit himself to a fiery ordeal in order that right and truth might prevail. Two great piles of wood were formed, ten feet in length, with only the narrowest path between them. These were kindled until they burnt fiercely, and even the path itself was strewn with red-hot embers. Then Peter, having offered Mass and divested himself of his chasuble, but retaining the other sacred vestments, walked slowly along the passageway between the two blazing piles. Not a hair of his head was injured, nor was his alb even scorched. He would have returned the same way, but the people were satisfied that God's will had been made manifest. The simoniacal bishop was deposed and afterwards gave proof of sincere repentance.

There seems to be good contemporary evidence for this incident, and Mgr. Mann, for example, in his *Lives of the Popes*, accepts it as historical.

But now let us turn to a well authenticated case of somewhat later date which M. Leroy has extracted from the life of the Augustinian hermit, Blessed Giovanni Buono—whether Buono was his family name or only a sobriquet (John the Good) does not seem to be quite clear. We happen, by good fortune, to possess a copy of the evidence given by the witnesses in the cause of his beatification in 1251, two years after his death. First amongst these we have the testimony of one Father Salveti, who tells us how a Brother, named Jachim, was violently tempted to give up his vocation and to leave the Order. It happened, however, one cold day in winter, when a number of the brethren were gathered round a great fire, that John Buono began to hold forth upon the supreme importance of being faithful to one's religious profession. They ought, he said, to fear nothing, neither cold, nor heat, nor hardships, nor tribulations, being assured that God would always come to their aid when help was really needed.

> And saying this [the witness went on] John suddenly rose up and stepping into the lire he began to shuffle the embers about with his feet just as if they were water, and there he remained standing for as long a time as it would take to say the Miserere half way through. Then, quitting the fire, he went back to his cell and sent for Brother Matthew, as well as for this deponent and two other brothers of the same Order whose names he has forgotten. He told them that they must be the friends of God and love Him dearly; but since this deponent was convinced that Brother John Buono had suffered hurt from the said embers, he purposely came close to the same John that he might the better examine and observe whether any damage had been done to his feet or his legs or his tunic, but, though he scrutinized them narrowly, he saw no trace of burning or of any injury.

It is interesting to note from the same record that the deponent, Father Salveti, was subjected to a rather minute cross-examination.

He was asked where the incident had occurred, and precisely when, how many of the brethren were present and their names, and also what he knew about the Brother Jachim who was said to have been confirmed in his vocation by witnessing this prodigy. One regrets to learn that about eighteen years had elasped since the scene occurred which Father Salveti described; but there was another witness, Brother Matthew, who also had been present on the occasion, and his account is in substantial accord with the first. He declares that there was a deep bed of embers on the hearth—it will be remembered, of course, that no fires but wood fires were then known—and that John Buono stood barefoot in these embers for a considerable space of time, shuffling about in them like a man who was washing his feet in a brook. Another striking series of manifestations, similarly assumed to be proof of the special sanctity of the holy man for whom fire had no terrors, is cited by M. Leroy from the canonization process of St. Francis of Paula. These have a certain special interest because this immunity from burning seems to have been habitual with the Saint, and because he also seems to have possessed the power of communicating the same immunity to others. A large number of incidents are on record proving his own insensibility to the effects of fire, and although unfortunately the evidence in most cases was not put on record until some thirty to fifty years after the event, still it was evidence given on oath and concerned with matters which are likely to have made a deep impression upon those who had been eye-witnesses. We learn, for example, from a certain Bemardinus de Raymundo that he had been sent by his master to a smithy to get one of his animals shod. A large piece of red-hot iron remained over after the operation, and thereupon Francis, who chanced to come in, asked the man if he had enough iron left to serve for another similar job he wanted done. The smith pointed to the bar which had been heated, whereupon Francis calmly took it up in his hands. They shouted to him, "Father, don't do that. You'll be burnt," but the Saint replied, "By your leave, I am just holding it to warm myself." So again, when a lime-kiln had fallen in, we hear of his sending the people away to dinner while he, single-handed, entered the kiln to repair the damage. More directly perhaps to the point is the story of how two distinguished ecclesiastics who were charged by the Bishop to report on Francis of Paula and his way of life, began, in order to test him, by making light of the austerities practised by himself and his followers. "It is quite easy for you to do these things," they said, "because you are a peasant and used to hardship. But if you were of gentle blood you would not be able to live in this way." Whereupon the account goes on:

The said Brother Francis replied "It is quite true that I am a peasant, and if I were not, I should not be able to do things like this." And as he so spoke, he bent down to the fire, which was a big one and burning fiercely. Filling his hands with the brands and live coals, he held them there while he turned to the Canon and remarked: "You see, I could not do this if I were not a peasant." ... Then the Canon threw himself down before the said Brother Francis and wanted to kiss his feet and his hands, but the Brother would not allow it.

The incidents of this kind recorded in the life of Francis of Paula are very numerous. We hear of his putting his arm into a kettle of boiling oil, and on another occasion into boiling lye. We are told that when red-hot charcoal was brought him in two wooden trays to make a fire he carried off the burning charcoal in his hands but rejected the trays. There is also a story of certain charcoal burners who had covered their stack so unskilfully with soil that the flames burst out through several crannies. Francis put his bare foot over each cranny in turn to keep the fire in until fresh earth could be brought to close the orifice. He took up in his hands a large fragment of lime from a burning kiln, and when at another time something went wrong with the kiln, he entered it ten or twelve hours after it was opened, though it was usually found necessary to wait five days before it had cooled sufficiently.

In 1516 when the Count of Grotteria wrote to Leo X to urge the canonization of Francis of Paula—he had died in 1507—the Count, among other pleas, averred that it was known to himself and to his wife that Francis, like the three youths of Babylon, had passed unscathed through more than one fiery furnace. In particular he attested that the holy man "carried coals in his hands to warm some of those who had no faith in him, and that the unscorched condition of these same hands [*immaculatio manuum*] had brought them to unhesitating belief."

This fetching of coals to warm people without mention of a chafing dish suggests to me that he really meant them to take the red-hot charcoal and hold it; for it is common to find that those who are themselves immune have the power to extend this immunity to others. Those so requested to warm themselves seem to have declined the invitation, but a case was mentioned by Maestro Confortus de Affriento, an eye-witness, in which the test was apparently successful. He declared in his evidence that when a house of the Minims was being constructed at Paternio, and a lime-kiln had been made there and had already been fired, news was brought to the Saint that it was falling in. Upon this Francis ordered a diminutive Brother [*monachulus*—possibly the door was so low that a grown man could not have crept in] to take a stick which he gave him and to set it up inside. He told the boy to have no fear, and in fact no harm resulted but the kiln was saved. Although hagiographers record many isolated examples of this insensibility of the saints to the effects of fire, some of these cases are certainly inadequately attested, while in most other instances the privilege seems only to have been accorded for some special emergency. M. Leroy does well to refer to the well-known story of St. Catherine of Siena. Mother Francis Raphael recounts the incident thus:

> Another day, being engaged in the kitchen according to her custom, she sat down by the fire and began to turn the spit; as she did so she was rapt in ecstasy.... When supper was ended Lisa returned to Catherine, intending to watch by her until she should recover consciousness. On re-entering the kitchen, however, she was terrified to find that Catherine had fallen forwards, and was lying with her body on the burning coals. The fire was large and fierce, for an unusual quantity of wood was always kept burning in the house for the sake of preparing the dyes. "Alas" cried Lisa, "Catherine is all burnt," and so saying she ran and drew her out of the smoking embers, but found to her wonder that she had received no injury either in her person, or even her clothes, on which the "smell of fire had not passed." "And yet," says her old English biographer, "it was a great fire and she a long time in it." But the fire of God's love that burnt within her heart was of such force and virtue that it would not suffer that outward fire to prevail over her.

These instances may suffice as illustrations of the kind of episode which meets us not infrequently in the Lives of the Saints, and which is habitually treated by hagiographers as miraculous. M. Leroy in his booklet gives references to other examples in the *Acta Sanctorum*, and he might have added many more. There is, for instance, a curious story in the historically respectable biography of St. Austreberta who died in a.d. 705. Again we hear that in a number of cases live charcoal was carried in the hands from one place to another, *e.g.,* this is mentioned in the Life of Domenica dal Paradiso, and in that of Margaret Parisot, while Blessed Angelina di Marsciano is said to have brought the whole burning contents of a stove hidden under her mantle into the presence of the King of Naples in order to convince him that she was not frightened by his threats to burn her for a witch. Of the holy people who seemed to be consumed with some interior fire and who radiated such intense physical heat that their propinquity was often the source of considerable discomfort to their neighbours, I have written in a later chapter.

Taking a general view of these alleged examples of human incombustibility, they may, I think, be conveniently divided into four classes. There are in the first place the cases of which I have so far been speaking which are usually considered to be a miraculous testimony to exceptional holiness of life. Secondly, there are those for which no more is claimed than that the individual so endowed appears by some freak of nature to be unaffected by the action of intense heat. Thirdly, we have many stories of spiritualistic marvels which recount how certain mediums when entranced are able with impunity to handle fire and to protect others from its action. Lastly, there are the "fire-walks," associated it would seem nearly always with some pagan religious rite, but recurring in almost every part of the world among barbarous peoples, and traceable even in remote antiquity. I am not here considering the fire Ordeals of the Middle Ages which would belong properly to the first category. Such tests were conducted by ecclesiastics, and they formally made appeal to the Divine justice, trusting that God would not allow the innocent to perish. Incidentally it may be noted that the case of Queen Emma, the mother of St. Edward the Confessor, which M. Leroy has cited at length, is rather an unfortunate selection. There is no mention in contemporary history of this walking of the Queen over nine red-hot plough-shares, and it is now universally rejected as a fable.

The question remains whether there is any evidence for the belief that some exceptional individuals are impervious to the effects of heat, and even for a while to flame, assuming that the trial is not indefinitely prolonged.

Let me quote in the first place a well-known passage from *Evelyn's Diary* which M. Leroy also has transcribed. Obviously the performer in this case made no pretence of any religious mission. He was simply a common juggler, but it is difficult to see how such feats could be executed in a private drawing-room if they were entirely faked. Where there is a stage and the opportunity of using apparatus, illusions might be produced much more easily. Be this as it may, Evelyn records:

> Oct. 8, 1672. I tooke leave of my Lady Sunderland, who was going to Paris to my Lord, now ambassador there. She made me stay dinner at Leicester House, and afterwards sent for Richardson the famous fire-

eater. He devoured brimston on glowing coales before us, chewing and swallowing them; he mealted a beareglasse and eate it quite up; then taking a live coale on his tongue, he put it on a raw oyster, the coal was blown on with bellows till it flamed and sparkled in his mouth, and so remained until the oyster gaped and was quite boiled; then he melted pitch and wax with sulphur, which he drank downe as it flamed; I saw it flaming in his mouth a good while; he also took up a thick piece of iron, such as laundresses use to put in their smoothing-boxes, when it was fiery hot, held it between his teeth, then in his hand, and threw it about like a stone, but this I observed he cared not to hold very long; then he stood on a small pot, and bending his body, took a glowing yron with his mouth from between his feete, without touching the pot or ground with his hands; with divers other prodigious feates.

Richardson, it appears, was well known in France as well as in England, and an article was devoted to him in the *Journal des Savants* for 1677. The account given of this juggler's performance is in exact accord with Evelyn's description, but it magnifies rather than attenuates the wonder, saying for example that "he holds a red-hot iron in his hands for a long time without any mark being left by it afterwards." Side by side with this we may range an extraordinary report furnished by a correspondent of the *New York Herald* concerning a negro in Talbot County, Maryland. The writer names several prominent inhabitants of Easton, as well as the editor of a local newspaper, and states that in their company he was present at an exhibition of the negro's powers which took place, not in the performer's own home, but "at Dr. Stack's Office."

> A brisk fire of anthracite coal was burning in a common coal stove and an iron shovel was placed in the stove and heated to a white heat. When all was ready, the negro pulled off his boots and placed the hot shovel on the soles of his feet, and kept it there until the shovel became black. His feet were then examined by the physicians—three were present—but no burns could be found and all declared that no evidence of a heated substance having come in contact with them was visible.
>
> The shovel was again heated red-hot, taken from the stove and handed to him. He ran out his tongue as far as he could, and laid the shovel upon it, licking the iron until it became cooled. The physicians examined the

tongue but found nothing to indicate that he had suffered in the least from the heated iron. A large handful of common squirrel shot was next placed in an iron receptacle and heated until melted. The negro then took the dish, poured the heated lead into the palm of his hand, and then put it into his mouth, allowing it to run all round his teeth and gums. He repeated the operation several times, each time keeping the melted lead in his mouth until solidified. After each operation the physicians examined him carefully, but could find nothing upon his flesh to indicate that he had been in the least affected.... Then he deliberately put his hand into the stove, in which was a very hot fire, took therefrom a handful of hot coals and passed them around the room to the gentlemen present, keeping them in his hand some time. Not the slightest evidence of a burn was visible upon his hands after he threw the coals back into the stove.

The writer goes on to say that all the people present had come with the express purpose of detecting trickery, if such there were, but that they were satisfied of the genuineness of the exhibition.

We are also told that two judges of the judicial circuit, who are named, had previously visited the negro in his own blacksmith's shop, and that they had subsequently declared that, to use their precise words, "he performed most astounding feats, such as handling red-hot iron with his bare hands, forging it into shape without the use of tongs, putting it upon his tongue, etc." Finally, after mentioning the names of other distinguished eye-witnesses, the correspondent terminates his account with this statement:

> After he [the negro] had concluded his performance in Dr. Stack's office, I sought an opportunity to converse with him. I found him very ignorant, not able to read or write, and in all respects an unadulterated negro. His name is Nathan Coker, and he is about fifty-eight years of age. He was born in the town of Hillsborough, Caroline County, Md., and was the slave of Henry L. Sellers of that place, by whom he was sold to Bishop Emery. In relation to his ability to handle fire, he said: "Boss, when I was about thirteen years old, Massa Emery hired me out to a lawyer, whose name was Purnell. He treated me badly, and did not give me enough to eat. I shied around the kitchen one day, and when the cook left, shot in, dipped my hand into the dinner pot, and pulled out a red-hot dumpling. The boiling water did not burn, and I could eat the hot pudding without winking; so after dat I often

got my dinner dat way. I has often got the hot fat off the boiling water and drank it. I drink my coffee when it is boiling and it does not give me half so much pain as it does to drink a glass of cold water. I always like it just as hot as I can get it."

When further questioned the negro added:

"I often take my iron out of the forge with my hand when red-hot, but it don't burn. Since I was a little boy I have never been afraid to handle fire."

It is unfortunate that I am only able to quote this account at second- or quite possibly at third-hand. It appears in The Spiritual Magazine for January 1872 (pp. 15-18), and no sort of reference is given to the precise number of the *New York Herald* in which presumably it first saw the light. Very probably it had been copied in an American spiritualistic journal and through that channel had found its way to England. None the less I have little doubt of its genuineness. Maryland is not so far distant from New York that the *New York Herald* could fail to circulate there, and the mention of the names of a score of residents, together with those of the circuit judges and a sheriff, would be sure to provoke emphatic protests if the account had been a fake. On the other hand the Spiritualists could have had no motive for inventing such a story.

It does not say a word about spiritualistic influences or mediumship. The negro's gift is represented as a purely natural faculty which was, of course, free from trance or anything of the sort.

But there will be occasion to say more of the insensibility of certain entranced mediums to the action of fire when we come to deal with the two other classes of immune persons who have already been mentioned above.

2

In the light of such cases as those already cited of the fire-eater Richardson and the negro of Maryland—to which many other examples might be added—it seems difficult to declare positively that a miracle is necessarily involved when human flesh in contact with flame sustains no injury. But our hesitation must unquestionably be augmented when account is taken of the feats of spiritualistic mediums and of the records of fire-walk ceremonies among primitive peoples. I propose in the pages which follow to call attention to some well-authenticated examples of both these classes of abnormal phenomena.

So far as regards the former category one naturally turns to the record of Daniel Dunglas Home, who is specially remembered for this kind of exploit. But it should be premised that he was neither the first nor by any means the only medium to offer similar manifestations. That such incidents did take place at Home's séances is established by a mass of evidence which it is impossible to reject. On more than twenty occasions his immunity from injury when in contact with red-hot coals was attested by witnesses of the highest standing, and, what is even more striking, he was able to impart the same immunity to those who had faith and were willing to take burning objects from his hands. From the many records available one may choose almost at random an incident recorded by the late Earl of Dunraven (then Lord Adare) in a contemporary account of a séance held on November 30, 1868, at Mrs. Hemmings house at Norwood. After some preliminary visits to the fireplace and poking the fire. Home, entranced—

> went back to the fire, and with his hands stirred the embers into a flame; then kneeling down, he placed his face right among the burning coals, moving it about as though bathing it in water.

> Then, getting up, he held his finger for some time in the flame of the candle. Presently he took the same lump of coal he had previously handled and came over to us, blowing upon it to make it brighter. He then walked slowly round the table, and said, "I want to see which of you will be the best subject. Ah! Adare will be the easiest because he has been most with Dan [i.e., himself]." Mr. Jencken held out his hand, saying, "Put it in mine." Home, said, "No, touch it and see". He touched it with the tip of his finger and burnt himself. Home then held it within four or five inches of Mr. Sari's and Mr. Hart's hands, and they could not endure the heat. He came to me and said, "Now, if you are not afraid, hold out your hand." I did so and having made two rapid passes over my hand, he placed the coal in it. I must have held it for half a minute, long enough to have burned my hand fearfully; the coal felt scarcely warm. Home then took it away, laughed and seemed much pleased. As he was going back to the fire-place, he suddenly turned round and said, "Why, just fancy, some of them think that only one side of the ember was hot." He told me to make a hollow of both my

hands; I did so, and he placed the coal in them, and then put both of his on the top of the coal, so that it was completely covered by our four hands, and we held it there some time. Upon this occasion hardly any heat at all could be perceived.

It should be pointed out that the Lord Adare who, at the age of twenty-seven, wrote this account for the benefit of his father (a convert to Catholicism) was by no means an intellectual nonentity. Moreover, before the description just quoted was printed in 1870, it was submitted to all those who had taken part in the séance, viz., Mrs. Hemmings, Mr. H. Jencken, Mr. Hart and Mr. Sari, and "the answers in every case were in the affirmative as to the correctness of the contents." No less weight must be accorded to the testimony of Lord Lindsay, afterwards 26th Earl of Crawford and Balcarres. Now Lord Lindsay in 1869 stated for the information of the Committee of the Dialectical Society, who were holding an investigation as to the reality of the alleged spiritualistic phenomena:

> I have frequently seen Home, when in a trance, go to the fire and take out large red-hot coals, and carry them about in his hands, put them inside his shirt, etc. Eight times I have myself held a red-hot coal in my hands without injury, when it scorched my face on raising my hand. Once, I wished to see if they really would burn, and I said so, and touched a coal with the middle finger of my right hand, and I got a blister as large as a sixpence; I instantly asked him to give me the coal, and I held the part that burnt me, in the middle of my hand, for three or four minutes, without the least inconvenience, A few weeks ago, I was at a séance with eight others. Of these, seven held a red-hot coal without pain, and the two others could not bear the approach of it; of the seven, four were ladies.

It is hard to believe that Lord Lindsay was hallucinated, or lying, and hardly less difficult to suppose that on each of these eight occasions Home was successful in slipping in, as Podmore suggests, a thin clinker or a pad of ashes between the burning coal and the hand. Also, if he put an innocuous substitute inside his own shirt, what became of the real red-hot coal in the meantime? Red-hot coals have a way of betraying their presence to more senses than that of sight if they are left lying on carpets or thrown into water. But what I would more especially insist upon is the audacity of all this playing about with fire. There seems to have been very little of the dare-devil, either physically or morally, in the normal Home when not entranced. Think of the social ruin to which he exposed himself if anything had gone wrong. Mr. Jencken stated: "Only within these last few days, a metal bell, heated to redness in the fire, was placed on a lady's head without causing injury," and, in the case of another lady on a different occasion, a red-hot coal "was dropped," she said, "on to my white muslin dress, where it remained for some seconds, as it was so hot we all feared to touch it. My dress though made of the finest muslin was not ignited, and we even failed to detect the slightest trace or mark of any kind after examination." Nothing was dearer to Home than the vogue he enjoyed in aristocratic circles, but if a lady had had to carry a scar for the rest of her life, or had had her dress set on fire as the result of one of these experiments, he must have known that such an incident would not easily have been forgiven or forgotten.

Perhaps the most famous of all D. D. Home's fire experiments was the occasion when, in the presence of several witnesses, he drew out of a blazing fire with his hands "a huge lump of live burning coal " so large that he had to hold it in both hands, and then deliberately placed it on the head of his friend, the aged Samuel Carter Hall, F.S.A., for many years editor of *The Art Journal*. Someone said, "Is it not hot?" and Mr. Hall answered, "Warm, but not hot." Whereupon Home proceeded "to draw up Mr. Hall's white hair over the red coal, the coal, still red, showing beneath the hair." Mrs. Hall, his wife, afterwards had the coal (which some of those present attempted to touch, but then shrank back after burning their fingers) placed in her own hand. She also found it warm but not unbearable. But let me take a final illustration of Home's extraordinary gift from another source.

In Stainton Moses' notes—the notes were written immediately afterwards—of a stance which took place at Miss Douglas' house, 81, South Audley Street, on April 30, 1873, we are told how after various phenomena with the accordion and with materialized hands which were both felt and seen—

> Mr. Home went to the fire-place, removed the guard, and sat down on the hearthrug. There he seemed to hold a conversation by signs with a spirit. He repeatedly bowed, and finally set to work to mesmerise his head again. He ruffled his bushy hair until it stood out like a mop, and then deliberately lay down and put his head in the bright wood fire. The hair was in the blaze, and must under ordinary circumstances

have been singed off. His head was in the grate and his neck on a level with the top bar. This was repeated several times. He also put his hand into the fire, smoothed away the wood and coal, and picked out a live coal, which he held in his hand for a few seconds, but replaced soon, saying the power was not sufficient. He tried to give a hot coal to Mr, Crookes, but was unable to do it. He then came to all of to satisfy us that there was no smell of fire on his hair. There was absolutely none. "The smell of fire had not passed on him."

Before Myers printed this account in the *Proceedings of the S.P.R.*, he consulted Sir William (then Mr.) Crookes as to its accuracy. The latter replied on March 9, 1893, in the following terms:

> I have a distinct recollection of the séance here described and can corroborate Mr. Stainton Moses account. I was not well placed for seeing the first part of the "fire test" here recorded.
>
> I knew, from experience, that when I Iome was in trance much movement or conversation on the part of others present was likely to interfere with the progress of the phenomena. My back was to the fire and I did not at first turn round to see what he was doing. Being told what was taking place, I looked and saw Home in the act of raising his head from the fire. Probably this was the last occasion of the "several times " it was repeated, as I have no recollection of seeing it more than once. On my expressing great disappointment at having missed this test, Mr. Home told me to leave my seat and come with him to the fire. He asked me if I should be afraid to take a live coal (ember) from his hand. I said No, I would take it if he would give it me. He then put his hand among the hot coals (embers) and deliberately picked out the brightest bit and held it in his hand for a few seconds. He appeared to deliberate for a time and then returned it to the grate, saying the power was too weak, and he was afraid I might be hurt. During this time I was kneeling on the hearthrug, and unable to explain how it was he was not severely burnt. The fire was of wood, Miss Douglas never burning coal in her reception rooms. At the commencement of the evening a log of wood had been put on, and this had been smouldering throughout the evening. My recollection of the fire is that it was not a particularly bright one.

What Mr. Crookes adds, seeing that he was one of the most famous chemists and physicists of his day, is particularly interesting.

I do not [he goes on] believe in the possibility of the ordinary skin of the hand being so prepared as to enable hot coals to be handled with impunity. School-boys books and mediaeval tales describe how this can be done with alum or certain other ingredients. It is possible that the skin may be so hardened and thickened by such preparations that superficial charring might take place without the pain becoming great, but the surface of the skin would certainly suffer severely. After Home had recovered from the trance I examined his hand with care to see if there were any sign of burning or of previous preparation. I could detect no trace of injury to the skin, which was soft and delicate like a woman's. Neither were there signs of any preparations having been previously applied. I have often seen conjurers and others handle red-hot coals and iron, but there' were always palpable signs of burning. A negro was once brought to my laboratory, who professed to be able to handle red-hot iron with impunity. I was asked to test his pretensions, and I did so carefully. There was no doubt he could touch and hold for a brief time red-hot iron without feeling much pain, and supposing his feet were as resisting as his hands, he could have triumphantly passed the "red-hot plough-share" ordeal. But the house was pervaded for hours after with the odour of roast negro.

I will only add here that other mediums since Home's day have exhibited the same powers in this matter of fire immunity, though they do not seem to have experimented quite so boldly. Some years ago I heard Mrs. Philip Champion de Crespigny recount in private conversation an experience of her own in which a log of wood in full combustion was not only taken out of the fire by a medium and carried round the room, but was left upon Mrs. de Crespigny's own hand for some seconds without her sustaining any injury or inconvenience. The name of this medium was Mrs. Annie Hunter, and we may note that there have been several others for whom the same power of handling fire has been claimed at various times.

I have myself heard from a friend in conversation a description of a Fire Walk at which he had personally assisted in Ceylon within the last half-dozen years, but whereas this last was quite normal and in accord with the accounts published by Mr, Andrew Lang and many others, M. Leroy's correspondent records several unusual features which I do not remember having met elsewhere. I will only notice that in the Ceylon case my friend insisted much upon the intense heat which was given out by the prepared bed of ashes.

Several officers and other Europeans of distinction were present at the spectacle and chairs had been prepared for them at a few yards distance from the little lake of fire, but they found themselves intolerably scorched in that position, and all the chairs had to be moved back before the ceremony could proceed.

The Fire Walk of which we read in M. Leroy's pages took place at Mysore, a native State in southern India about 250 miles from Madras. The account is contained in a letter sent him by Mgr. Despatures, the Catholic bishop of Mysore, who was himself an eye-witness. He had received beforehand a formal invitation from the Maharajah requesting the pleasure of his company, as if to a concert or a luncheon party, and with the view of fostering the excellent relations which existed between the sovereign and his Catholic subjects, the bishop accepted. The ceremony was fixed for six p.m., but Mgr. Despatures, suspicious of possible imposture, was there in good time and went to examine the preparations beforehand. He found that a shallow trench had been dug about a foot deep, some thirteen feet in length and a little more than six feet in width. This had been filled to a depth of about nine inches with red-wood charcoal. There was no question, he tells us, about the genuineness of the fire; the heat which exhaled from it was stifling. Close by was standing a Mohammedan from the north of India who was the hero of the occasion; but the bishop points out that the man had had nothing to do with the preparation of the fire-pit. The Maharajah, who was also suspicious of trickery, had seen to this himself. Incidentally, one gathers, not without surprise, that no religious significance attached to the rite in the minds at least of the more educated natives; it seems to have been for them, as for the European guests, simply a curious spectacle, like the performance of a conjurer. At the hour appointed the Maharajah with his family and suite arrived in state, and took up a position about twenty-five yards from the trench, a fact in itself significant of the heat evolved. After which the letter proceeds:

> The Mohammedan, according to Indian usage, came and prostrated himself before the sovereign and then went straight to the furnace. I thought that the man was going to enter the fire himself, but I was mistaken. He remained about a yard from the brink, and called upon one of the palace servants to step into the brazier. Having beckoned to him to come forward, he made an appeal into which he seemed to put all his powers of persuasion, but the man never stirred. In the

meanwhile, however, the Mohammedan had drawn closer to him, and then unexpectedly taking him by the shoulders he pushed him into the little lake of glowing ashes. For the first moment or two the Indian struggled to get out of the fire; then suddenly the look of terror on his face gave place to an astonished smile, and he proceeded to cross the trench lengthwise, without haste and as if he were taking a constitutional, beaming contentedly upon those who were standing round on either side of him. His feet and legs were perfectly bare. When he got out, his fellow servants crowded round him to ask what it felt like. His explanations must have been satisfactory, for one, two, five, and then ten of the palace household plunged into the trench. After this it was the turn of the bandsmen of the Maharajah's band, several of whom were Christians. They marched into the fire three by three. At this juncture several cartloads of dried palm-leaves were brought down and thrown upon the embers. They blazed up at once, breaking into tongues of flame higher than a man's head. The Mohammedan induced others of the palace servants to pass through the flames and they did it without taking harm. The bandsmen went through a second time, carrying their instruments in their hands and with their sheets of music on top. I noticed that the flames which rose to lick their faces bellied out round the different parts of the instruments and only flickered round the sheets of music without setting them on fire. There must, I think, have been two hundred people who passed over the embers, and a hundred who went right through the middle of the flames. Beside me were standing two Englishmen, the head of the Maharajah's police force (a Catholic), and a civil engineer. They went to ask the royal permission to try the experiment themselves. The Maharajah told them that they might do it on their own responsibility. Then they turned to the Mohammedan and he motioned to them to go forward. They crossed without any sign of burning. When they came back into my neighbourhood, I asked them what they thought of it. "Well," they said, "we felt we were in a furnace, but the fire did not burn us." When the Maharajah stood up to mark the close of the proceedings, the Mohammedan, who was still standing close to the trench, fell writhing upon the ground, as if in an agony of pain. He asked for water; they brought it and he drank greedily. A Brahmin who stood near me remarked: "He has taken upon himself the burning of the fire."

All this took place, in 1921 or 1922, in the park of the Maharajah's summer palace, but Mgr. Despatures goes on to mention that a fortnight later another performance took place in the town of Mysore itself. Many people again passed through the fire without injury; but at the close, in spite of the Mohammedan's warning that no others must make the attempt, three individuals pushed their way in. They were badly burnt and had to be taken to the Government hospital. The Mohammedan was held responsible and was in consequence prosecuted in the courts, but he pleaded that the sufferers had been warned and had disobeyed.

Speaking of the scene, at which he had been present, the bishop remarks that some people maintained that they must all have been hallucinated, but he himself emphatically rejects such a solution.

> I was [he writes] in full possession of my faculties. I went round the trench before the proceedings began; I went back to it again after all was over; I spoke with those who passed through the fire, and I even said a Hail Mary or two with the view of arresting any exhibition of diabolic power. ... It was beyond doubt a real burning fire which consumed the charcoal and sent up in flames the cartloads of palm leaves that were thrown upon it, but it was a fire which had lost its power of injuring those who crossed it and all that they took with them.... How can we account for it all? I do not think that any material cause can explain it. No expedient, at any rate, had been employed to produce such an effect. I am forced to believe in the influence of some spiritual agency which is not God.
>
> (SIGNED) M. DESPATURES, BISHOP OF MYSORE.

Very commendably, but with the full assent and even the assistance of the bishop, M. Leroy has sought to obtain confirmation of this story from others who were present. Four gentlemen, two of whom at least were Englishmen, have obligingly answered his questions. He tells us that in the broader features of the account all are agreed, but in the details which would not be likely to be noted carefully or remain very clearly in the mind of a casual observer there are the usual discrepancies. While Mr. H. Lingaraj Urs says that the trench was four feet wide, fifteen long and five feet deep, Mr. Macintosh writes that it was thirty yards long!, he must presumably have meant feet, and he estimates the number of those who passed through it at five hundred. Mr. H. Lingaraj Urs and Mr. J. C. Rollo (this last gentleman is the principal of Mysore College) passed through the trench with their boots on, but the fire left no trace, and they had no sensation of burning.

I must confess that the easy confidence with which rationalists like Sir James Frazer dismiss the fire-walking phenomena does not impress me very favourably in regard to their readiness to admit unpalatable evidence or their capacity for weighing it. "Strange as it may seem," says Sir James, in discussing this matter, "burns are comparatively rare. Inured from infancy to walking barefoot, the peasants can step with impunity over the glowing charcoal, provided they plant their feet squarely and do not stumble, for usage has so hardened their soles that the skin is converted into a sort of leathery or horny substance which is almost callous to heat." But a man who is pushed without warning into a bed of red-hot ashes does not plant his feet squarely, neither is there any reason to suppose that the dozen or more Europeans who are known upon good evidence to have taken part on different occasions in these fire walks, had feet which were callous to heat. Still less can we believe that Home, or Lord Lindsay, or Mrs. de Crespigny had hardened the palms of their hands into a sort of leathery or horny substance which rendered them impervious to the action of fire. Dr. B. Glanvill Corney, who was for many years the chief medical officer of the Fiji Group, and has written sundry official reports on the conditions of life in these islands, took a great interest in the form of fire walk (over flag-stones heated red-hot) which formerly prevailed in that part of the world. He writes on the subject as follows:

> I have seen the Fijian fire walk done five times and I have examined the feet of several of the performers immediately afterwards, without meeting with any trace of injury, or any trace of a protective application.
>
> On one occasion a boy of fourteen or fifteen years, who was doing it for the first time, was unable to complete the journey round the hot stones in the pit, either from the heat, or from imperfect knowledge or skill in evading the risk. He hopped briskly out of the line of men on to the brim of the pit and I examined his feet then and there. There was no injury whatever to be seen, though the stones were hot enough to have charred a pocket-handkerchief into a frizzled black ash in a few seconds, and some were still red-hot on their undersides, towards the middle of the pit. I cannot help thinking that some physical phenomenon takes place which has not been understood or explained.

It is unsatisfactory to have no solution to propound, but I am afraid that we have to leave this, like many another problem, to be cleared up by those who, with fuller and more accurate evidence before them, will be in a better position to form a judgment than we are to-day. I am not denying that the phenomena of incombustibility may have a diabolic origin, but the mere fact that we cannot explain them does not necessarily justify such an inference. M. Olivier Leroy seems to me to speak wisely when he protests against the assumption that the Mohammedan wonder-worker patronized by the Maharajah of Mysore can only be looked upon as a myrmidon of Satan.

CHAPTER VII
BODILY ELONGATION

If I have often inclined to a rationalistic explanation of phenomena commonly held to be supernatural, I may confess that my judgment in this matter has been influenced by the fact that many analogous phenomena, attested by good evidence, are to be met with in the annals of psychical research. The levitations of D. D. Home bear a close resemblance to the aerial flights of St Joseph of Copertino. The fragrance perceived during the séances of Stainton Moses has a hundred parallels in the sweet odours which were intermittently associated with the ecstasies of such saints as St. Catherine de Ricci or St. Veronica Giuliani. The many recorded cases in which the Blessed Sacrament has flown from the altar or from the hands of the priest to the lips of an enraptured communicant may be regarded as a form of the phenomenon familiar to psychic researchers as "telekinesis." The bilocations which are related in the story of St. Alphonsus Liguori or of St. Francis Xavier, would seem to be of quite ordinary occurrence if we may judge by the similar cases investigated by Gurney and Myers in their *Phantasms of the Living*. The luminous radiance spoken of in the lives of so many holy people from St. Catherine of Siena to the Curé d'Ars, is also of frequent occurrence in the manifestations of Home, Eglinton and other mediums. Even the remarkable "spirit drawings" executed by such people as Mr. F. L. Thompson and Miss Heron Maxwell, who have never had any sort of artistic teaching or practice, have their counterpart in two similar drawings still preserved which were made by the Blessed Crescentia Hoss at the beginning of the eighteenth century.

In one of Crescentia's ecstasies she had a vision of the scourging of Our Lord, and at her Superior's request she described to her the kind of implements employed. There were, according to her account, bundles of thorny boughs and also whips formed of a number of cords which had small metal sickles attached to their extremities. As a further test, her Superior commanded her to draw them while she stood looking on. The poor Sister (she was a weaver's daughter, a destitute girl who had only been received into the convent with reluctance as an act of charity) had never learnt to draw, but under obedience she set to work with a pencil and a sheet of paper, and produced two sketches which from the point of view of draughtsmanship are astounding for the delicacy and firmness of every line. Her biographer, who reproduces the two drawings in facsimile, declares that "many thousand people, including great artists, have expressed their astonishment that an untrained hand could have executed such work."

But among the phenomena of mysticism, the most impressive and, in some sense, the most convincing, are those which are least usual. One cannot help suspecting that the witnesses who gave evidence in processes of beatification may sometimes have been expecting the manifestations they report because they were well aware that such things often occurred in the lives of saints. Any indication which seemed to point to stigmatization, or elevation above the ground in prayer, or celestial radiance, or emanations of perfume, or blood portents after death, etc., was likely to be interpreted without discussion as something unquestionably miraculous. It is, therefore, a matter specially worthy of notice when we find some phenomenon recorded of a holy person which is not likely to have suggested itself to religious observers as a mark of sanctity, but which does at the same time hold a recognized place among the manifestations which psychical researchers have recorded in recent times. The point with which I propose particularly to deal in the present chapter is the elongation of the human body. One would, I think, be safe in saying that this is a prodigy which no devout client would be likely to invent in order to demonstrate the sanctity of the particular object of his veneration.

Even among mediums the phenomenon is not very common. It is true that since it was repeatedly witnessed in the person of D. D. Home appeal has been made to a passage in the *Mysteries* of the Neo-Platonist Iamblichus, but I am not satisfied that the pagan philosopher had in mind anything which could be strictly described as elongation. He tells us that, in the trances of the mystics whom he is describing, "the body also is seen lifted up, or increased in size, or borne along in mid air," but it is not clear that the word, which some scholars want to translate to "elongated," means anything more than distended. In any case, the point is of no particular consequence.

Let me begin, therefore, by giving some account of the elongations which are recorded of the famous medium D. D. Home. The evidence in his case is much more satisfactory than that produced in support of any similar claim made for other mediums. It may be noted, for example, that when "Dr." Monck, afterwards convicted of fraud in a court of law, professed to have been elongated, the whole performance took place in darkness. The alleged increase in height was only demonstrated by someone feeling the medium's head raised above its previous position while someone else professed to guarantee that his lower limbs remained undisturbed in the chair on which he was sitting. On the other hand, the intellectual standing of the witnesses who observed the elongations of Home, and the conditions they describe, make a much better impression. If I am to keep this chapter within reasonable limits it is only possible to quote a small part of the available evidence, but I may begin by an extract from the letter written by Mr. H. D. Jencken, a barrister of good reputation, to The *Spiritual Magazine* for January 1868. Internal evidence makes it clear that the incidents described had occurred only a week or so before the letter was written. Mr. Jencken declares that he had by that time been present on at least five occasions when Home was elongated and shortened. On the evening with which we are here concerned:

> Lord—— was seated next Mr. Home who had passed into a trance state, in which after uttering a most beautiful and solemn prayer, he alluded to the protecting spirits whose mission is to act as guardian angels to men. "The one who is to protect you," he said, addressing Lord——, "is as tall as this." And upon so saying, Mr. Home grew taller and taller; as I stood next him (my height is 6 feet) I hardly reached up to his shoulder, and in the glass opposite he appeared a full head taller than myself. The extension appeared to take place from the waist, and the clothing separated eight to ten inches. Walking to and fro, Mr. Home specially called our attention to the fact of his feet being firmly planted on the ground. He then grew shorter and shorter, until he only reached my shoulder, his waistcoat overlapping to the hip.

The name left blank by Mr. Jencken was unquestionably that of Lord Adare, for we have his own independent account of the same scene, which I propose to quote a little later. But Mr. Jencken also describes a similar incident which was then of even more recent date. Speaking in trance, Home, who in such circumstances always referred to himself in the third person by his Christian name, remarked:

> "Daniel has been elongated six times, he will be elongated thirty times during his life"; and encouraging every mode of testing the truth of this marvellous phenomenon, he made me hold his feet, whilst the Hon. Mr.—— placed his hands on his head and shoulders. The elongation was repeated three times, twice whilst he was standing. The extension measured on the wall by the Hon. Mr.—— showed eight inches; the extension at the waist, as measured by Mr.——, was six inches, and the third time the elongation occurred, Mr. Home was seated next to Mrs.———who, placing her hand on his head—and her feet on his feet—had the utmost difficulty in keeping her position, as Mr. Home's body grew higher and higher; the extreme extension reached being six inches.

There can be little doubt that the person here referred to as "the Hon. Mr.——," was the future 26th Earl of Crawford, then best known as the Master of Lindsay. But let me now turn to Lord Adare's account of the seance first mentioned. It is given in a letter to his father, the third Earl of Dunraven, written a few days after the occurrences described. The letter occupies several printed pages, and it must suffice to quote the passage which refers to the elongation.

> Home [wrote Lord Adare] stood up and said: "He (the guardian spirit) is very strong and tall," and standing there beside me, Home grew, I should say, at least six inches. Mr. Jencken, who is a taller man than Home, stood beside him, so there could be no mistake about it. Home's natural height is, I believe, 5 feet 10 inches. I should say he grew to 6 feet 4 inches, or 6 feet 6 inches. I placed my hands on his feet, and felt that they were fairly level on the ground. He had slippers on, and he said: "Daniel will show you how it is," and he unbuttoned his coat. He was elongated from the waist upwards; there was a space of, I suppose, four inches between his waistcoat and the waist-band of his trousers. He appeared also to grow in breadth and in size all over, but there was no way of testing that. He diminished down to his natural size, and said: "Daniel will grow tall again." He did so, and said: " Daniel's feet are on the ground." He walked about and stamped his feet, but returned shortly afterwards to his natural size.

BODILY ELONGATION

Neither in this nor in Mr. Jencken's account is anything said about the light, but they were certainly not sitting in complete darkness, for not only are Home's movements and gestures escribed in detail, but Mr. Jencken took long notes on the spot, recording the speech delivered by Home immediately before t e elongation began. Moreover, in Adare's description of some five or six other elongations occurring in similar conditions, there is definite mention in one case of the gas being lighted, in another of a fire that was brightly burning, and in a third of such measurements as would have been quite ridiculous if there had not been sufficient illumination to be able to see distinctly. For example, Adare remarks concerning Home's elongation on April 3, 1869, in the presence of six observers:

> While his arms appeared to be increasing in length, his chest became greatly expanded, and he said to me "You see how it is, the extension is from the chest." He then placed himself against the wall, and extended his arms to their full natural length; I made a pencil mark at the tips of his fingers. His left arm was then elongated. I held the pencil against the wall, suffering it to be pushed along by his fingers until he told me to make another mark. His right arm was then elongated, and I marked the movement in the same manner. The total elongation, as ascertained by this means, amounted to 9 1/2 inches.

It may suffice to add to these extracts the statement made by the Master of Lindsay, afterwards Earl of Crawford, in his evidence given before the Committee of the Dialectical Society on July 6, 1869.

> On another occasion I saw Mr. Home in a trance elongated eleven inches. I measured him standing up against the wall, and marked the place; not being satisfied with that, I put him in the middle of the room and placed a candle in front of him, so as to throw a shadow on the wall, which I also marked. When he was awake I measured him again in his natural size both directly and by the shadow, and the results were equal. I can swear that he was not off the ground or standing on tiptoe, as I had a full view of his feet and, moreover, a gentleman present had one of his feet placed over Home's insteps, one hand on his shoulder, and the other on his side where the false ribs come near the hip-bone.

Miss Douglas, another witness to Home's phenomena, who corroborated these statements, having been asked by one of the

Committee how she could be sure that Home was not standing on tiptoe, replied: "He stood in the middle of the room where all could see." At a later stage of the same sitting, the Master of Lindsay, answering further questions as to the manner of the elongation, explained:

> The top of the hip-bone and the short ribs separate. In Home they are unusually close together. There was no separation of the vertebrae of the spine; nor were the elongations at all like those resulting from expanding the chest with air; the shoulders did not move. Home looked as if he were pulled up by the neck; the muscles seemed in a state of tension. He stood firmly upright in the middle of the room, and before the elongation commenced I placed my foot on his instep. I will swear he never moved his heels from the ground. When Home was elongated against the wall, Lord Adare placed his foot on Home's instep, and I marked the place on the wall. I once saw him elongated horizontally along the ground. Lord Adare was present. Home seemed to grow at both ends, and pushed myself and Adare away.

There is a good deal more similar evidence, and it is noteworthy that on some occasions Home's body not only expanded but contracted. Mr. Jencken in particular declares, "I have witnessed Mr. Home shrinking down to about five feet," and Lord Adare also speaks of his being "shortened to less than his natural height." What I would specially insist upon is that we cannot treat such witnesses as Lord Adare and the Master of Lindsay as if they were mere nincompoops, even though they were both young men. Adare, in 1869, was twenty-eight years of age. He had acted as war correspondent for the *Daily Telegraph* in Abyssinia in 1867, he was to represent the same journal in Paris during the siege, and at a later date he served on two occasions as Under-Secretary of State for the Colonies. The Master of Lindsay was younger, but before he became Earl of Crawford, he was elected F.R.S. in 1879, at the age of thirty-one. He was then already President of the Royal Astronomical Society, and later on he became a trustee of the British Museum and an Honorary Associate of the Prussian Academy of Sciences. These are not distinctions which fall to the lot of cranks or silly enthusiasts, even though they be men of wealth, as Crawford was.

But I must turn now to the evidence for similar elongations in the case of mystics. The clearest example which I have met with is to be found in the printed *Summarium* of the depositions submitted to the Congregation of Rites in view of the hoped-for beatification of Sister

BODILY ELONGATION

Veronica Laparelli, a nun who died in 1620, at the age of eighty-three. Her ecstasies were very remarkable, lasting sometimes for as much as three days, and her fellow Religious asserted positively that on certain occasions she had been seen raised above the ground in prayer. While she was still living, a nun, Suor Marguerite Cortonesi, who, at a later date, was elected abbess, drew up a record of these unusual happenings, which is cited in the process referred to. One extract from this document runs as follows:

> On one occasion, among others, when she [Veronica] being in the trance state was reciting her Office alternately with some invisible being, she was observed gradually to stretch out until the length of her throat seemed to be out of all proportion [*pareva facesse una gola lungafuori di misura*] in such a way that she was altogether much taller than usual. We, noticing this strange occurrence, looked to see if she was raised from the ground, but this, so far as our eyes could tell, was not the case. So, to make sure, we took a yard-measure 'canna' and measured her height, and afterwards when she had come to herself we measured her again, and she was at least a "span " [ten inches or more] shorter. This we have seen with our own eyes, all of us nuns who were in the chapel.

Again, in the same process, we have the deposition of a lady, Donna Hortenzia Ghini, who, in 1629, stated on oath:

> Sister Lisabetta Pancrazi, formerly a nun in the same convent, told me that on one occasion, seeing that the said Sister Veronica when in ecstasy seemed taller than in her normal state, she took a yard-measure [cannd]and measured her height, and that after the said Sister Veronica came to herself she measured her again with the said yard-measure, and she found that she was half an arm's length [*un mezzo braccio*] shorter; and this I know because I heard the said Sister Lisabetta say it, as I mentioned above.

The *Promotor Fidei*, or "Devil's Advocate," whose business it is in such cases to raise difficulties, professed to be somewhat shocked by this manifestation:

> Furthermore [he comments] we may note a certain unlikelihood and incongruity in the fact as stated in the Summarium that on one

occasion the body of the servant of God, when in ecstasy, stretched out and grew beyond natural measure, while other witnesses extend the same phenomenon to occasions when she was praying without any ecstasy.

He goes on to remark that this elongation was not only intrinsically improbable, but that it could serve no purpose of edification or utility. It could not benefit the servant of God herself, and would excite repulsion and alarm rather than devotion in the beholder. These are very sensible observations, but they also go some way to prove the unlikelihood that the story was merely invented by the nuns without any foundation in fact.

It may be admitted that one would be glad to have more precise and detailed evidence, but the consideration that the cause of the candidate for beatification was not likely to be advanced by the narration of unrecognized phenomena which were more suggestive of the acrobat than of the saint, may have checked any keen interest in the subject. One would be almost inclined to treat these recollections of Veronica's Religious Sisters as without significance, were it not for the fact that traces of a similar elongation phenomenon are found elsewhere. For example, in the Life of Mother Maria Costante Castreca we hear of a fellow-novice of hers who came to tell the confessor, Don Filippo Gionantonj, a strange thing which she had seen. She reported that while Maria Costante was praying before a statue of the Infant Jesus she had watched her grow a considerable height from the ground, becoming a tall woman, while her whole body was a-tremble. This had happened somewhere about the year 1700. Canon Bud, her biographer, was a contemporary, and as he had in his keeping the copious notes which her confessor Gionantoni had taken for many years, we may regard the incident as fairly well attested. One cannot feel quite the same confidence in the details which are given of the mystical phenomena of the Venerable Domenica dal Paradiso, who lived two centuries earlier. The imposing volume which was published at Florence in 1719 from the pen of B. M. Borghigiani contains many extravagances the sources of which are not easy to trace. Still, there may be some foundation for a statement made by him in the following terms:

> Amongst the other remarkable features which have been recorded concerning that intoxication of divine love from which Domenica suffered, one was this, that the Spouse of Christ was made to appear

a taller woman than she really was. Castiglione, her director, noticed the same thing happen in many other ecstasies, though she returned to her normal stature afterwards, as soon as she was herself again.

Something of the same nature seems to have been observed in Domenica's contemporary, the Dominican nun, Blessed Stefana Quinzani. One of the most remarkable hagiographical documents ever printed is the account of one of Stefana's Friday ecstasies, drawn up with all legal formalities and signed and sealed by twenty-one ecclesiastics and gentlemen of distinction who had witnessed the whole series of scenes of the Passion enacted in her person. Only one detail, however, is directly relevant to our present subject, an incident connected with the fastening to the cross. After enduring the scourging at the pillar and the crowning with thorns, the ecstatica seems to have thrown herself on the ground:

> The right arm [we are told] is extended as if the hand were being really and immovably nailed, and at once the muscles [nervi] are seen stretched and tense, the veins swell and the hand grows black, and just as if it were indeed being fastened with a material nail, she utters a terrible shriek [*grido*] followed by a piteous moaning. Then the left is extended in a similar manner to the right, but stretched considerably beyond its natural length [*assai sopra la lungagine sua naturale*].

This elongation of one limb might seem to be a different matter from the growth of six inches or more in stature such as Home's intimates have described for us above, but the primitive text of the contemporary Life of Blessed Stefana, which has been printed for the first time only in recent years, tells something more. From her confessor, who is the author of this memoir, and who informs us that he had been familiar for five years with the weekly ecstasy in which she enacted the scenes of the Passion, we learn that when the right hand was, in imagination, pierced, her whole frame seemed to contract in that direction, and that when the left arm appeared to be dragged by violence to the opposite side "her bosom was clearly seen to open." I find it hard to decide whether this only means that the garment which she wore was stretched and possibly torn by the strain, or whether the writer wished to suggest that there was some sort of physical rupture in the sternum and the adjacent tissues. I give in a footnote the Italian text which at any rate states plainly that the bosom was distended. The arms, it is stated, became so rigid that, as we learn both from her biographer and from the twenty-one witnesses mentioned above, no man, though he used all his strength, could in the smallest degree bend or move them. We are also told that although, while these sufferings lasted, her features showed an extraordinary emaciation, Stefana became plump and round-faced (*grassa e piena*) as soon as ever the ordeal was at an end.

A similar and even more curious example of the alleged elongation of one limb meets us in the printed text of the *Vita e Dottrina di Santa Caterina da Genova*. In the terrible period of physical torment which preceded the death of the Saint, her spiritual daughter and handmaid, Argentina, told how she suffered intense pain in one arm "in such wise that the arm grew more than half a palm longer than it was by nature." It is true that this is one of the passages of the *Vita e Dottrina* which are not found in the earlier manuscript texts and that Baron F. von Hûgel contests their reliability on that ground. I may confess, however, that I am not convinced, as I have explained elsewhere, by the line of argument he has adopted.

Finally, without making any claim to produce another case of elongation, I venture, nevertheless, to direct attention to certain phenomena recorded of the French stigmatis'e Marie-Julic Jahenny. Although Dr. Imbert-Gourbeyre, who describes them, was in historical matters quite uncritical, still he was at the time a professor in a school of medicine of good standing, and he had retained this post for many years. He informs us that in the autumn of 1880, Marie-Julie habitually passed into a state of ecstasy or trance three times a week. In these ecstasies she foretold what particular form of suffering awaited her in her next spell of unconsciousness. On Friday, September 24, 1880, she gave warning that on the following Monday in expiation of the sins of mankind committed during the previous month, her body would be compressed and her limbs shortened, while her tongue would be swollen beyond measure. Dr. Imbert determined to be present, and five other persons of credit, one of them a priest, also assisted at the scene. He describes how, when the trance came on, Marie Julie's head seemed to sink into her body, while the shoulders notably protruded above it. Her whole frame shrank together into a sort of ball. After that there was an extraordinary movement of each shoulder in succession so that it seemed to stand at right angles to the collarbone. The tongue swelled to an incredible size, forcing itself out of the mouth between the clenched teeth. This was followed by a prodigious dilation of the whole of the right side of the body from the arm-pit to the hip. Dr. Imbert could feel through the nightdress that the left side of the trunk had shrunk to practically nothing. All these physical transformations succeeded each other with a certain deliberation, but in so short a space of time that Dr. Imbert, speaking as a pathologist, was positive in affirming that medical science could offer no explanation of them. It does not seem unreasonable to suppose that this variation in the bulk and form of organic structures may be of substantially the same nature as the phenomenon of elongation.

To draw any firm conclusion from such isolated happenings as those which I have here tried to bring together, is not easy. On the one hand, only a very robust scepticism will maintain that the alleged phenomenon has no better foundation than the hallucination of the observer. On the other, it would certainly require a great deal more evidence than we as yet possess to establish a presumption that such elongations as have been here described must be attributed to a preternatural cause, to the action, in fact, of either God or the devil. The one feature which is common to all the alleged examples is that these phenomena are only met with in the state of trance. Is it possible that in this condition certain vital processes, such as metabolism, etc., are capable of modifications of which science as yet knows little or nothing? In some susceptible subjects cataleptic conditions can undoubtedly be induced under hypnotism. Does anyone pretend to know precisely how this happens?

I have not yet met with a single case of stigmatization in a subject who was previously free from neurotic symptoms. There is a presumption in every instance that the recipient of the stigmata was highly suggestible, and now there has come to hand, quite recently, a booklet describing the case of the Lutheran girl Elizabeth. The subject is an Austrian peasant girl, apparently with no vicious propensities, but by nature religiously minded. She was highly neurotic, and had been an inmate of some half-dozen different *Kliniks*, where under hypnotic treatment she recovered sufficiently to be fit to go to work again, but soon after relapsed and had once more to go to hospital. She was for some time under the care of Dr. Lechler, who has published this detailed account, and he finally decided to take her into his own house as a domestic servant, so that he could still study the case and give her the treatment she needed. The most important fact is that on Good Friday 1932 she went to a cinema where some sort of representation of the Passion of our Lord was realistically depicted.

On returning home the doctor saw that she had been very intensely affected, and she complained of pain in her hands and feet. The idea then came to him of hypnotising the girl, as he frequently used hypnotism with her in his treatment, and of giving a direct suggestion that she like our Lord had her hands and feet pierced with nails. The suggestion had to be renewed more than once but it was entirely successful, and in this booklet Dr. Lechner reproduces photographs both of the palms of the hands and the soles of the feet with the wounds. Subsequently, by further suggestion, he induced a condition in which tears of blood streamed freely from the eyes and in which bleeding punctures appeared on the forehead corresponding to the crown of thorns. There also supervened an inflamed condition of the shoulder caused by her imaginary carrying of the cross. Of a wound in the side, if I mistake not, nothing is said.

The photographs have every appearance of being a trustworthy record of the results obtained. I see no presumption of any imposture, unless the fact that the book is written apparently in the hope of arresting the stream of conversions to Catholicism caused by the wide discussion of the phenomena at Konnersreuth, should be regarded as matter of suspicion. On the other hand, Dom Magei, a Benedictine professor at Salzburg, quotes the book with entire confidence, and I know of other Catholics interested in the subject who regard this publication as of the greatest importance in its bearing on the case of Theresa Neumann.

I need not say that I am quite incompetent to discuss the pathological aspects of the case in its early stages. I don't read German with sufficient facility to wade through pages and pages of technical description. The theory of a luxation of the lumbar vertebrae and injury to the spinal cord (*Wirbelverruckung or Ruckenmarksverletzung*) has for at least six years past been very severely criticized by Dr. Ewald and others. Unfortunately, in this out-of-the-way village no radiograph was ever taken. No one in the early stages of Theresa's illness could foresee the importance the case was afterwards to assume. My only contribution to the subject lies in a somewhat discursive study of the numerous other cases, some fifty or sixty altogether, where we have a detailed description of stigmata and of the circumstances in which they occurred. The impression left upon me has been that the subjects who were so favoured or afflicted were all suffering from pronounced and often extravagant hysterical neuroses. Many of them were intensely devout (of course it is only in the case of people whose thoughts were concentrated on religious motives that one would expect to find this type of manifestation) but in others piety was combined with eccentricities and with apparent dissociations of personality which were very strange and not exactly edifying. I find it difficult to believe that God could have worked miracles to accredit such people as His chosen friends and representatives.

With regard to the fact of the bleeding wound-marks in hands, feet and side of which we read in the accounts of Theresa Neumann and a multitude of others, there cannot be a shadow of doubt.

These wounds could not be artefact (though there are not infrequent cases of such deliberate imposture). Theresa has often been under observation during the whole time the ecstasy and bleeding have developed. Medical opinion was slow to admit the reality of stigmata as a demonstrated fact. A great discussion took place in the 'seventies of the last century over Louise Lateau. Many eminent pathologists, amongst others Professor Virchow, declared that the whole thing was trickery (*Betrug*). In the case of Theresa Neumann we have not only the bleeding wounds, but we have other phenomena, the most noteworthy of which is the alleged abstention from all food and drink, except the Blessed Sacrament, which has now (1933) lasted for six years. Further, it is claimed that she pronounces upon the authenticity of relics (hierognosis) and may read the secret thoughts of those who visit her. I do not propose to discuss this aspect of the question. I only know that it has been stated that the same relic has been pronounced by her on one occasion to be authentic and on another occasion to be spurious. I have no means of getting at the truth. Still more remarkable is the assertion that in her visions she echoes aloud the shouts of the crowd and repeats fragments of their conversation.

A distinguished Catholic professor of Semitic languages, Fr. Wutz, declares that the words can be recognized as Aramaic words belonging to the popular speech of Palestine in the time of our Lord. It may be so, but it would require a very thorough investigation to determine the fact satisfactorily.

Perhaps the most inexplicable of all these phenomena is the fast, and I must own that it has impressed me considerably to find that a Lutheran psychiatrist, Dr. Lechler, who has been mentioned already, accepts the fact of the fast without any reserve. In his booklet *Das Ratsel von Konnersreuth im Lichte eines neuen Falles von Stigmatisation*, he writes: "The fact which in my judgment seems to admit of no doubt, that Theresa since 1927 has taken no nourishment, not even the least sip of water, without at the same time losing weight or showing signs of exhaustion, will be regarded by unbelievers as a very startling phenomenon. Can this also be the result of a mental condition? If Theresa's stigmata can be explained by autosuggestion, the conclusion readily offers itself that her abstention from food has a similar origin. She has long been aware that such fasts are recorded of many devout Catholics."

Dr. Lechler then refers to the case of Blessed Nicholas von Fliie who is said to have taken neither food nor drink for twenty years. But he lived in the fifteenth century, and there are other examples more recent and better attested, even if not quite so prolonged. That of Anne Catherine Emmerich, which he also quotes, is more convincing. Theresa, he contends, must have persuaded herself that she, who received the Blessed Sacrament daily, needed no bodily food, while she also saw clearly that such abstinence was a silent homily to the world, proving that with the abiding presence of the Body of Christ man had little need of material nourishment. It is stated by Kaplan Fahsel, Canon de Hovre and others that St. Therese of Lisieux on the anniversary of her death (30th September, 927) appeared to her namesake, clothed as a Carmelite, and told her definitely that she no longer needed any earthly food.

On the question of this *inedia* I am not at all sure that I shall have the support of anyone who reads this chapter. Writing in The Month more than twenty-eight years ago, I ventured to propound the opinion that this claim of supporting life by the Blessed Sacrament alone, a claim which has been made for many holy people, in history. It is, I hold, an historical fact that such complete absence from both food and drink has continued in a number of or a long period of years but that it is not necessarily to be considered of supernatural origin. There is evidence that with Anne Catherine Emmerich, Domenica Lazzari, and Louise Lateau, all stigmaticas in the last century, it lasted for over ten years, but there are numerous other examples of such *inedia*, less well attested, and others again more satisfactory but for shorter periods, though always for twelve months or more. In adhering to this view, I may say that I have derived much encouragement from two non-Catholic examples. The first is that of Mollie Fancher of Brooklyn, in which, though the fast was not quite absolute, her doctors, who had the fullest opportunity of observing the case, declared publicly, first in 1878 after twelve years and again in 1893 when the abstinence had continued for another long period of years, that she "had lived for years together without sustenance enough to feed a baby for a week." As the patient was completely paralysed and for a large part of that time had always someone sitting with her at night, they must have been able to learn whether there were any excreta. But I cannot go into details here. The other case is much more recent. In the booklet just mentioned, published in 1933, Dr. Lechler discusses the phenomena of his patient, Elizabeth, a pious Lutheran girl, afflicted with all sorts of hysterical neuroses.

Concerning the nutrition of his patient, he says: "During the period of Elizabeth's illness it surprised me that when for six weeks together it was necessary to feed her artificially, owing to her refusal of all nourishment, she did not in that time lose any weight but actually gained half a pound. Considering the limited amount of food which could be administered in that way, a more healthy subject would undoubtedly have shown signs of wasting. When I, later on, asked her in the hypnotic state what was the cause of this unexpected result, she told me that she was at that time terrified at the idea of death. Since she was afraid that if she grew thin she would be sure to die, she had kept on repeating to herself day and night "I must not lose weight."

In order to investigate further whether metabolism in Elizabeth's case had any close dependence on her mental impressions, I conveyed to her waking state the suggestion that in the next week she would put on seven pounds. This suggestion was repeated several times each day. By the end of the week there was in fact a gain of seven pounds, though there was no increase in the amount of nutrition, and though Elizabeth while the experiment lasted, went on with her hard work the whole day long. On the other hand, on three different occasions I failed in an attempt to suggest that in spite of her refraining from food for several days together she should not lose weight. The decrease occurred, as it usually would do, in spite of the suggestion."

Dr. Lechler, in this case, inferred that the suggestion failed because it was not strong enough. He noticed that though the same amount of nourishment was given, his subject was liable to surprising and rapid fluctuations in her bodily condition. When she was mentally well-balanced, she at once began to put on flesh, but when an inferiority complex or a feeling of inadequacy took possession of her, a loss of weight immediately became perceptible.

Another surprising feature in the case was the fact that Elizabeth, like Theresa Neumann, and, I may add, like Teresa Higginson, seemed to have little need of sleep. On the average she slept only from two to three hours each night, but she got through a heavy task of work in the daytime (she acted as his domestic servant and also worked in the garden) without any notable exhaustion.

CHAPTER VIII

INCENDIUM AMORIS

That emotional ardours of a more intense type are often attended by an actual rise of bodily temperature may be regarded as a fact of everyday experience. There is nothing therefore particularly astonishing in the statements which we so often encounter in the lives of the great mystics, to the effect that when some transport of love took possession of their souls their countenances became inflamed, that they could hardly endure the clothing which seemed to stifle them, and that in the coldest of winter weather they threw open doors and windows, panting for air and half unconsciously seeking the same kind of relief as our Lord has indicated in His parable of Dives and Lazarus. Let us begin by taking a few well-known examples. In Father Goldie's *Story of St. Stanislaus Kostka* we read:

> St. Francis de Sales in his book on the Love of God, says, "Stanislaus was so violently assailed by the love of Our Saviour as often to faint and to suffer spasms in consequence, and he was obliged to apply cloths dipped in cold water to his breast in order to temper the violence of the love he felt." One day he was found by his Superior walking alone at night time in the little garden which the Novitiate then possessed, when a very bitter cold wind was blowing, and on being asked by the Father Rector what he was doing there, he replied with all simplicity and straightforwardness, "I am burning, I am burning," as he felt his heart still on fire with the love of God, although his prayer was over. Stephen Augusti bore witness to the fact that the Socius to the Master

of Novices, Father Lelius Sanguigni, had often to bathe his chest to temper the scorching heat.

Similarly in the ease of St. Mary Magdalen de' Pazzi, who was born in 1566, two years before St. Stanislaus died, we are told how her transports of love transformed her outward appearance, "for her face" says her biographer and confessor, Father Cepari, "losing in a moment the paleness which had been produced by her penances and austere religious life, became glowing, beaming and full; her eyes shone and sparkled like stars, and she cried out, saying, 'O Love! O God of Love!' etc." But, more in particular, the same biographer, whose statements are in every way confirmed by the depositions of the witnesses who gave evidence in the process of beatification, declares that:

> Sometimes, overpowered by the excess and abundance of this love, she said, "I can no longer bear so much love, retain it in Thyself"; and through the great and consuming flame of this Divine Love which she felt, she could find no rest, but tore her clothes, went into the garden and tore up the plants, or whatever came to hand. In the midst of winter she could not bear woollen garments, through that fire of love which burned in her breast, but cut and loosened her habit.

Or again:

> Feeling so great a flame in her face, she fanned herself with her veil, then ran to the well and drank a quantity of fresh water, bathed her face and arms, poured it into her bosom, and so great was the flame which burned in her breast that even externally she seemed to consume.

Not less remarkable was the devotional ardour of St. Philip Neri, the contemporary of both the saints last named.

> Philip [says Father Bacci] felt such a heat in the region of the heart, that it sometimes extended over his whole body, and for all thinness and spare diet, in the coldest days of winter it was necessary, even in the midst of the night, to open the windows, to cool the bed, to fan him while in bed, and in various ways to moderate the great heat. Sometimes it quite burned his throat, and in all his medicines something cooling was generally mixed to relieve him. Cardinal Crescenzi, one of his spiritual children, said that sometimes when he touched his hand,

it burned as if the saint was suffering from a raging fever.... Even in winter he almost always had his clothes open from the girdle upwards, and sometimes when they told him to fasten them lest he should do himself some injury, he used to say he really could not because of the excessive heat he felt. One day, at Rome, when a great quantity of snow had fallen, he was walking in the streets with his cassock unbuttoned; and when some of his penitents who were with him were hardly able to endure the cold, he laughed at them and said it was a shame for young men to feel cold when old men did not

Elsewhere the biographer records how—

Sometimes in saying office, or after Mass, or in any other spiritual action, sparks, as it were of fire, were seen to dart from his eyes and from his face. This inward fire was such that it sometimes made him swoon, forcing him to throw himself on his bed, where he is said to have lain occasionally a whole day without any other sickness than that of divine love. On one occasion it so burned his throat that he was ill for several days.

There can be little doubt that the discovery which was made in the autopsy performed after St. Philip's death must be closely connected with the same intense fervour of divine love. During more than fifty years of his long life he had suffered from a strange and inexplicable palpitation of the heart, which was noticed, not only by himself, but by many of his companions and friends whom in the tenderness of his affection for their souls he often pressed to his bosom. The surgeons, when they opened his body, found a swelling under his left breast, which proved to be due to the fact that two of his ribs were broken and thrust outwards. In view of the positive testimony of the surgeons, there can be no dispute that the injury was there and had been there for many years. His biographers seem therefore fully justified in tracing it to that strange incident of the coming to him of the Holy Ghost in 1544 under the guise of a globe of fire. "Thereupon," we are told, "he was suddenly surprised by such an ardour of love that, unable to bear it, he threw himself down upon the ground, and, like one trying to cool himself, bared his breast, to temper in some measure the flame which he felt." Certain it is in any case that from that time forth his body was liable in moments of deep emotional feeling to tremble convulsively with intense palpitations, while he became conscious of the presence of a swelling on the left breast, the size of a man's fist. This he retained for all the rest of his life. It is curious that a displacement of the ribs, similar in cause and character, but apparently less in degree, is recorded in the case of St. Paul of the Gross, the founder of the Passionists, who lived two centuries later. An even more striking modern example is that of Gemma Galgani, who died at Lucca in 1903.

Nevertheless, such physical manifestations as these, however wonderful in themselves, can hardly be regarded as witnessing to any abnormal increase of the temperature of the body. So long as we have no evidence of a more objective kind than the mystic's longing for fresh air or cool water, or his statement that he is suffering from a sensation of suffocation and burning heat, there obviously is nothing which takes us beyond the range of the symptoms which may be observed in any hospital fever-ward. None the less, the claim is made in many hagiographical writings that phenomena do occasionally occur for which no parallel can be found in the pathological records known to medical science. I have heard it stated, for example, that in the case of Padre Pio da Pietrelcina, the young Capuchin priest of Foggia, who is marked with the stigmata, the clinical thermometer used by his doctor in visiting him professionally has on more than one occasion been unable to register the high temperature of the patient, and has consequently been broken by the unprecedented expansion of the mercury within. The same allegation has also been made to me, by persons who seemed to be well informed, in connection with another modern mystic. But in neither case have I authority which I could quote in print. In earlier ages, of course, there were no clinical thermometers, and the only proofs which can be offered in evidence are of a much ruder description. Still, some such tests are recorded in hagiographical literature, and the authenticity of these alleged examples affords interesting matter for discussion.

Probably the best-known case is that of St. Catherine of Genoa, which, thanks in large measure to the very learned and painstaking study of Baron Friedrich von Hügel, has been brought to the notice of many English readers for whom the ordinary Saint's Life offers little attraction. St. Catherine was a mystic of the seraphic type, and perhaps nothing more beautiful has ever been printed about the love of God than is to be found in the utterances and writings attributed to this noble Genoese matron. Assuming for the moment the authenticity of the whole content of the *Vita e Dottrina di Santa Caterina da Genova*, which was first published in 1551, we find that the book abounds in references to the extraordinary physical state into which Catherine was frequently thrown by the intensity of her consuming love. Quite at the beginning, and in reference to her "great fasts," which lasted from 1476 to 1499, it is stated that, for twenty-three lents, and as many advents, the Saint took no solid food at all, but occasionally drank a glassful of a beverage compounded of water, vinegar and pounded salt.

> When she drank this mixture it seemed as if it were thrown upon a red-hot flag-stone and that it was at once dried up in the great fire which was burning within her. An astounding and unheard of thing! For no digestion, however healthy, could bear a drink of this kind fasting, but she declared that the interior sweetness she experienced was so great that even this unpalatable beverage gave refreshment to her body.

I omit chance references which seem to point to some similar state of suffering which recurred at intervals during the intervening years. What is certain is that in her last sickness, which continued from January to September 1510, she was over and over again the victim of sensations of intense burning. For example:

> On one day she was stabbed with a still sharper arrow of the divine love.... The wound (*ferita*) was so poignant that she lost speech and sight, and abode in this manner some three hours....

> She made signs with her hands of feeling as if it were red-hot pincers attacking her heart and other interior parts.

> Later on there was a day when she suffered such an intensity of burning that it was impossible to keep her in bed. She seemed like a creature placed in a great flame of fire, so much so that human eyes could not endure the spectacle of such a martyrdom. This anguish lasted a whole day and night and it was impossible to touch her skin because of the acute pain which she felt from any such touch.

But this was by no means all. We are told a little later of another attack (*assalto*)—

> This was so violent that her whole frame seemed to be in a tremble, especially her right shoulder (which appeared as though severed from her body, and similarly one rib seemed to be forced out of its place

with so much pain, anguish and racking of muscles and bones, that it was a terrible thing to look upon, and it seemed impossible that a human body could endure it).

The words which I have enclosed in brackets are regarded by Baron von Hügel as not forming part of the primitive text of the *Vita*, in spite of the fact—so at least I infer from him—that they are found in the manuscripts as well as in the first printed edition of 1551. He asserts, in regard both of the alleged injury to the shoulder and the displaced rib, that these details "have precisely the same "colour,' and no doubt proceed from the same contributor, as the longer passage relative to her supposed stigmatization, absent from all the MSS., but given in the printed Vita on the authority of Argentina." It requires, I think, a very robust sceptic to reject nowadays the possibility of the phenomena of stigmatization, and some injury to the shoulder is of frequent occurrence in the case of stigmatized persons. To take but a single example, the post mortem examination of the body of St. Veronica Giuliani attested the existence of "a very considerable curvature of the right shoulder, which bent the very bone just as the weight of a heavy cross might have done." The surgeon, Gentili, who performed the autopsy, stated in his sworn deposition that "if this curvature had occurred by natural means it would have prevented her moving her arm, but I have myself frequently seen Sister Veronica during her last illness move her right arm without the least difficulty." But whatever we may think of the inference thus drawn, there can be no reasonable doubt of the fact that some extraordinary deflection of St. Veronica's right shoulder was observable, together with the marks of the five wounds, when her body was examined on July io, 1727, thirty-four hours after her death. Now the Vita e Dottrina, as we have it, was actually printed in 1551, so that such precedents as St. Philip Neri's displaced ribs, and St. Veronica Giuliani's flexed clavicle could not possibly have been known to the compilers. Consequently it seems, in my judgment, much saner to suppose that these additional details, if additions they were, are derived from Argentina's faithful memory of what her eyes actually saw in St. Catherine's last illness, than to attribute them to the fervid imaginations of irresponsible panegyrists.

But the most curious and interesting record of the internal conflagration by which the last remnants of Catherine's vitality were consumed has still to be noticed. On August 28th, when the tragedy of suffering began to near its end, she was again all on fire. She cried aloud that "all the water which the world contain could not give me the least refreshment." Later her tongue and lips became so parched with the burning heat within that she could not move them or speak. At such times, if anyone touched a hair of her head, or even the edge of the bed, or the bedclothes, she would scream as if she had been stabbed. Her confessor sometimes hesitated to bring her Communion in this state, for she could swallow nothing, neither food or drink, "but, with a joyous face, she would make him a sign that she was not afraid, and then, when she had received, she remained with her countenance glowing and rosy, like that of a Seraph."

An explanation of all this suffering was afterwards given by her devoted handmaid, Argentina, who declared that Catherine had predicted it before it came about, and had confided to her that before her death she was destined to endure the sufferings of our Lord's Passion, together with the anguish of the five wounds (the Stigmata), at least interiorly, on account of the great love she bore to her Saviour and her desire to resemble Him in all things.

None the less, it is added that Catherine never allowed a word to escape her in public which could throw light upon the cause of these torments and betray their entirely supernatural character. When Argentina also bears witness that her mistress, throwing out her arms in the form of a cross, presented the counterpart of her crucified Saviour, one of her arms being stretched more than five inches beyond its natural length, I must confess that this detail, instead of discrediting her statement, as Baron von Hugel declares it to do, seems to me to supply a notable confirmation of the general trustworthiness of our witness. Certain it is, in any case, that when the Blessed Stefana Quinzani in 1497 represented in ecstasy the incidents of the Passion of our Lord, her left arm in the crucifixion scene was "stretched considerably beyond its natural length" (*assai sopra la lungagine sua naturale*). If Argentina was romancing, it is extraordinary that she should have embellished her story with just those striking features for which parallels, attested by the best of evidence, can be found in the case of other mystics. No doubt it may be said that Argentina might easily have read or heard an account of Blessed Stefana Quinzani's ecstasies which took place in 1497. This is true, but it is much more likely that the story would have been known to an educated lady like her mistress, St. Catherine, and in that case it is quite conceivable that the impression made upon Catherine's mind may have contributed to produce the same physical phenomenon in her own mystical transports.

During the whole of the Saint's last illness, and especially in its closing phases, these long-protracted seizures, characterized by a sensation of intense burning (*fuoco*), are a constantly recurring feature. In particular, the printed Vita records two special occasions when material proof was given of the intensity of the heat developed. Let me copy the first in Baron von Hügel's translation:

> In proof that this holy woman bore the stigmata interiorly, a large silver cup was ordered to be brought in, which had a very high standing saucer; the cup was full of cold water for refreshing her hands, in the palms of which, because of the great fire that burned within her, she felt intolerable pain. And on putting her hands into it, the water became so boiling that the cup and the very saucer were greatly heated.

One is conscious of a certain temerity in differing from an authority who has devoted so much time and so much learning to the elucidation of his subject; moreover, I can make no claim to any expert knowledge of Italian. Nevertheless, I find it hard to accept the Baron's rendering of this passage, and still more his rejection of the whole incident as unhistorical. To begin with, the "large silver cup" (*gran tazza d'argento*) was surely a standing cup with a stem and a shallow bowl, more or less like an exaggerated champagne glass in form, though probably the stem was shorter in proportion. Cups and saucers were not known in Europe until long afterwards, and, in any case, there is no mention of a "saucer," but simply of the *piede della tazza*, the stem or pedestal of the cup. Anyone who leaves a silver spoon in a cup of hot tea is apt to discover with a start that silver is an excellent conductor of heat.

It seems to me natural to suppose that Argentina made a similar discovery. She had carried the cup in by its pedestal full of the coolest water she could procure. After St. Catherine had bathed her hands Argentina came to remove it and the stem burned her when she touched it. Such an incident is likely to have impressed itself upon her memory, and the use of the word *bollente* (boiling) is only a very natural exaggeration. She was surprised to find that the stem had become unpleasantly hot.

Between the 13th of September and the 15th, on which last day she died, Catherine lost immense quantities of blood. The temperature of this discharge, we are told in the *Vita*, was such that (1) it heated the vessels in which it was caught; (2) it scalded her flesh wherever it touched it, so that the places had to be cooled with rose-water; (3)

being on one occasion received in a silver cup, it heated the base of the cup and left a mark which could never be washed out. Baron von Hugel comments that only the first of these observations is to be found in the manuscripts, and that "purely secondary, physical matters are thus, with a short-sighted good faith and admiration, eagerly utilized to naturalize and obscure a soaringly spiritual personality." No doubt it is true that these physical matters are "purely secondary" but after all, for our present inquiry, the question is, Is the statement accurate? If these things did happen they were worth recording, and while I agree that the evidence taken by itself is not conclusive, we cannot ignore the precisely similar declarations which have been made by eye-witnesses in the case of other mystics.

Let us take, for example, the instance of the Venerable Serafina di Dio, a Carmelite nun of Capri, who died in 1699. Her Life, which was written by the two Oratorian Fathers, Sguillante and Pagani, was published at Rome in 1748. They seem to have based it almost entirely upon the evidence furnished in the process of beatification. In this biography we read:

> Her nuns say that they have often seen her—for example, when she was in prayer, or after Communion—with her face glowing like a flame and her eyes sparkling. It scorched them if they touched her, even in winter time and even when she was quite old, and they declared that they had repeatedly heard her say that she was consumed with a living fire and that her blood was boiling.
>
> Her throat, palate and lips became so parched that it was necessary to cool them with fresh water; but this expedient by no means sufficed to allay the burning she felt. . . .
>
> The doctors, who did not understand the cause of her sufferings, applied many kinds of cooling remedies and frequently bled her; while our Saviour Himself, in order to give her some relief, especially when these blood-boilings (*li bollori del sangue*) lasted for two or three days, as was often the case at times when she entertained an intense desire to die a martyr, so disposed matters that she lost great quantities of blood through the nostrils or by the mouth. It was a matter of intense astonishment to all observers to see a body so emaciated as hers lose such a vast quantity of blood without being incapacitated for everyday duties.

Those who are familiar with the story of St. Catherine of Genoa will remember that, in her case too, her recoveries were as marvellous as the mysterious indispositions which repeatedly brought her to death's door. But the most striking phenomenon recorded in the Life of the Venerable Serafina is the statement made regarding her holy remains after she breathed her last:

> For the space of twenty hours the body retained so great a heat, particularly in the region of the heart, that one could comfortably warm one's hand by holding it there, as many of the nuns discovered on making the experiment. Indeed, the warmth was perceptible for thirty-three hours after death, though somewhat less in degree, in spite of the fact that the month was March and the weather chilly. The corpse did not completely lose its heat until it had been opened and the heart extracted.

One's first instinct is to conclude that the nuns and their doctor must have been mistaken in supposing that life was extinct, but there are a good many similar cases, and it is difficult to believe that mystics, after long and exhausting illnesses, were peculiarly exposed to the danger of being buried alive.

Take, for example, the case of the Dominican nun, Suor Maria Villani, at Naples. She died on March 26, 1670, at the age of eighty-six, and her Life was published four years afterwards, in a volume of more than 600 pages, by Father Francis Marchese, O.P. In his very first sentence the biographer informs us that his heroine was a furnace of love, and this is the note upon which he harps throughout the whole book. It is plain, also, from the letters and other writings of the Sister herself, that the idea that she was continually consumed by an almost insupportable flame of love dominated all her thoughts. The Life states that the physical effects of this interior conflagration were such as to compel her to drink as much as thirty-six, and sometimes even forty-five, litre of water in a day. I do not exactly know the English equivalent of the Neapolitan measure of a Libra, but thirty-six libber probably falls not much short of twenty-eight pints or three gallons and a half. Moreover, we are told that the drinking of this was attended by a hissing sound like that of water falling on a sheet of red-hot iron. It is impossible not to suspect a certain amount of exaggeration in all this, but on the other hand, there are definite physical facts connected with the case which cannot readily be explained away. Suor Maria believed that she had been wounded in the side and heart by a fiery spear of love, and there is good evidence that the wound was really there. At any rate, her biographer prints three formal depositions signed by three of her confessors, who had been permitted, at different times, to see, touch and even probe the external wound. These Fathers were well-known Dominicans, and one, Leonardo di Lettere, had a great reputation for sanctity, so that the cause of his beatification was introduced after his death. The Life of Maria Villani appeared with the fullest ecclesiastical sanction, and both the General of the Dominicans and the Cardinal Archbishop of Naples gave it their *imprimatur*. But perhaps the most remarkable statement which the book contains is the account of the opening of the body nine hours after death. The corpse of this woman of eighty-six, which, when she breathed her last, had been dried up, emaciated and dark in hue, became fresh-coloured and supple like that of a living person.

When the surgeon opened the breast, a quantity of bright fluid blood issued both from the incision made and from the heart.

Some of this blood, the biographer assures us, had been preserved in two little flasks, and at the time of writing (1673) still remained liquid and incorrupt. But what most astonished the onlookers present at the autopsy was "the smoke (*fumo*) and heat which exhaled from the heart, that veritable furnace of divine love." The surgeon found the heat too trying to proceed. He was compelled to draw back for a while, but afterwards returning, "he put in his hand to extract the heart, but he found it so hot that, burning himself (*scottandosi*), he was compelled to take his hand out again several times before he succeeded in effecting his purpose." The biographer declares that a formal affidavit regarding these facts was made by the surgeons Domenico Trifone and Francesco Pinto. With regard to the heart itself, an open wound was found in it of the very same form and shape as the dead nun had drawn with her own hand on a page of her tractate, *De tribus divinis flammis*. "This wound (in the heart)," the biographer goes on, "I have seen and touched and examined. The lips of the wound are hard and seared, just as happens when the cautery is used, to remind us, no doubt, that it was made with a spear of fire."

There are other examples more or less similar to those of Serafina di Dio and Maria Villani, but I have no room to discuss them at any length. It must be sufficient to note that in the case of the Franciscan missionary, the Ven. Antonio Margil, an apostle who was often seen raised in the air in his ecstasies of love, it is stated that after death "his face which had been pale during lifetime became of a beautiful rosy hue, his eyes remained bright and his limbs flexible, while his flesh continued warm down to the moment when his body was consigned to the tomb.'" So, again, we are told of Blessed Andrew Ibernon, another holy Franciscan who was entirely penetrated with the seraphic spirit of the Poor Man of Assisi, "it was observed when they laid his body in the coffin (three days after death) that the flesh was still warm and soft, and all the sinews and muscles flexible, just as if he had only expired the moment before.'" These two Lives last mentioned were written in each case by the Postulator of the Clause, who had all the sworn depositions before him.

Among other instances of phenomenal heat manifestations might be cited the case of the Venerable Rosa Maria Serio (1725), Prioress of the Carmelite convent of Fasano, who for seven successive years had an extraordinary experience on Whit-Sunday. On the first occasion a ball of fire descended upon her visibly in the sight of all the nuns. When they undressed her they found her underlinen above the breast burned in the form of a heart. The same burning took place for six other years, but there was no visible ball of fire. Again, in the Life of the Venerable Francesca dal Serrone (1601), a Franciscan nun of San Severino who, like Maria Villani, had a wound in the side, we read that the blood, which on certain occasions came from her side or was vomited by the mouth, was so hot that it cracked an earthenware vessel used to receive it, and had to be caught in a metal bowl. Similarly of St. Teresa's companion, the Carmelite Anne of Jesus, as well as of two or three other candidates for beatification, we are told that in some of her illnesses, the nuns who nursed her could hardly touch her flesh on account of the burning heat. The evidence for these cases is inconclusive, but it is certainly not contemptible.

CHAPTER IX
THE ODOUR OF SANCTITY

It would be a matter of some interest to investigate how and when the phrase "the odour of sanctity" first took its rise. St. Paul, of course, tells us in his second Epistle to the Corinthians (ii. 15): "we are the good odour of Christ unto God," and this perhaps might point more naturally to a metaphorical interpretation. But there is at the same time so much evidence of an early date which suggests that certain facts in the physical order have played their part in the evolution of this idea that it would certainly be rash to exclude the more literal explanation. Probably the earliest testimony which can be produced is that contained in the famous letter of the Christians of Smyrna, describing the martyrdom of their holy Bishop, St. Polycarp, in a.d. 155. They say:

> When he had offered up the Amen and finished his prayer, the firemen lighted the fire. And a mighty flame flashing forth, we to whom it was given to see, saw a marvel, yea and we were preserved that we might relate to the rest what happened. The fire, making the appearance of a vault, like the sail of a vessel filled by the wind, made a wall round about the body of the martyr; and it was there in the midst, not like flesh burning but like gold and silver refined in a furnace. For we perceived such a fragrant smell, as if it were the wafted odour of frankincense or some other precious spice.

So at length the lawless men, seeing that his body could not be consumed by fire, ordered an executioner to go up to him and stab him with a dagger. And when he had done this there came forth a quantity of blood so that it extinguished the fire, and all the multitude marvelled that there should be so great a difference between the unbelievers and the elect.

No critic nowadays contests the authenticity of this letter. It was undoubtedly written by those who were eye-witnesses of what happened. The same is also true of the letter which was despatched some twenty years later (i.e., about a.d. 177) by the Christians of Vienne and Lyons to their brethren in Asia Minor.

Here the survivors, speaking of the more heroic among their number who boldly defied the persecutors, say:

> They went out rejoicing, glory and grace being blended in their faces, so that even their bonds seemed like beautiful ornaments, as those of a bride adorned with variegated golden fringes; and they were fragrant with the sweet odour of Christ, so that some even supposed that they had been anointed with earthly ointment.

It appears, then, that already in the second century the idea was familiar throughout the Christian world that high virtue was in some cases miraculously associated with fragrance of body. Another example, equally attested by historical evidence of the highest class, may be cited from the accounts preserved to us of the death of St. Simeon Stylites in 459. From more than one source we learn that his privileged disciple Anthony, unable to obtain any response from his master, climbed to the platform of the column and found the Saint's body "exhaling the perfume as it were of many spices." So again St. Gregory the Great in his *Dialogues* tells us of the poor afflicted Servulus, whom he personally knew:

> While he lay giving ear within himself to that divine harmony, his holy soul departed this mortal life: at which time all that were there present felt a most pleasant and fragrant smell, whereby they perceived how true it was that Servulus said. A monk of mine, who yet liveth, was then present, and with many tears useth to tell us that the sweetness of that smell never went away, but that they felt it continually until the time of his burial.

Or to take an example from our own country in the early centuries, we are told of St. Guthlac, the hermit, in his last hours on earth, that "when he turned himself again and recovered his breath, there came fragrance from his mouth like the odour of the sweetest flowers." Further, after the Saint had expired, his disciple "heard angelic songs throw the regions of the air, and all the island (of Crowland) was profusely filled with the exceeding sweetness of a wondrous odour." Also we learn that when his sister St. Pega "came on the next day, according to the command of the blessed man, they found all the place and the buildings filled with the sweetness of the herb ambrosia." These statements are derived from the Life of the Saint by his contemporary Felix, and the general trustworthiness of the biography in question is disputed by no one.

Now while, of course, we are bound to recognize that one or other of these descriptions may owe something to the fervent imagination of a single reporter, writing possibly under deep emotional stimulus, still the accord among these witnesses, so widely separated in place and time, is not a little remarkable, and, what is perhaps more striking, there is a consensus of testimony as to the occurrence of similar manifestations in recent centuries which cannot be ignored. In a short account like the present it is impossible to give an adequate idea of the number of examples which have been recorded. The vast majority of cases have to do with the fragrance proceeding after death from the mortal remains of some of God's specially devoted servants, and this does not immediately concern us here, but there are also many instances of Saints whose person, dress, and cell have diffused sweet odours during life in such a way as to attract the general attention of their intimates and visitors.

What lends a certain confirmation to the accounts referred to is the occurrence of facts of a similar nature among spiritualistic phenomena, notably in the case of the medium, Mr. Stainton Moses. This gentleman, who, it must be remembered, was not a professional medium, and who is spoken of with the sincerest respect by all who knew him intimately, gives the following account of his own personal experience. It is contained in a letter to *The Spiritualist* newspaper for January 1, 1875:

> In every circle with which I am acquainted, some means is used for inducing harmonious conditions. This is usually done by means of music or singing. In our circle it has always been done by means of perfumes. From the very first we have been enjoined to stillness, and attempts at conversation have been repressed. We do not use a musical

box, nor has music been asked for. But no stance passes without perfumes being showered upon us or perfumed waves of air being wafted round the circle. These waves of air usually blow over my head, so that by putting up my hand I can feel the cold air blowing over my head twelve or eighteen inches above it. It is not until the waves of scented air come round to me that I detect the presence of perfume, except on rare occasions.

These perfumes are of various kinds, rose, sandal-wood, and verbena, being favourites. Any sweet-scented flowers in the room are utilized and their perfume extracted. This is notably the case in the country. We have noticed in such cases that the presence of a particular flower in the room would determine the prominent spirit odour; and that particular blossoms would have all the perfume extracted from them for the time, though the odour would return on the following day. Sometimes, however, a perfectly distinct odour would be extracted from—or, more precisely, be put upon—a particular flower. In this case the flower invariably withered and died in a short time.

It is now some months since I first noticed the presence of a perfumed atmosphere round myself, especially during times when I was suffering pain. I have been liable to neuralgia, and at such times those around me have noticed the presence of perfume of various kinds, such as those we observe during our seances. One evening I was standing at an open window through which the air was blowing, and the perfume of rose was so marked that friends who were present endeavoured to trace it to some definite source. It was found to be localised in a spot no bigger than a shilling at the top of my head. The spot was perceptibly wet with the perfume, which oozed out more freely on pressure. Since that time we have become familiar with the fact, and have ceased to wonder when the perfume shows itself, if I am suffering pain.

The process is, I am informed, remedial, and I have knowledge of at least one medium now living who has frequently observed a similar phenomenon, though not referable to perfume localised in one spot.

But, indeed, the fact is both new and old. We have not observed it of late years, perhaps because we have not searched for it, but in mediaeval days the fact was perfectly familiar. It is only now that we

THE ODOUR OF SANCTITY

are beginning to understand the phenomena of mediumship, which showed themselves among the monks, nuns and recluses of the middle ages. They were in many cases powerful mediums, they gave themselves the best conditions—seclusion, prayer, fasting—and the odour of sanctity became a well-known occurrence among them. Only they named it badly. There was no particular sanctity about them or about us now—frequently the reverse. The perfume had nothing to do with sanctity. It was a phenomenon of mediumship which was rife then, and which exists now, perhaps more frequently than we know.

Of course, we have more evidence for all this than Mr. Stainton Moses unsupported statement. His friends, and especially Dr and Mrs. Charlton Speer, confirm his statements in all material points. Neither is there any reason for suspecting these perfectly respectable people of conspiring to deceive the public. At the same time it should be noted that the fragrance which perfumed the air at the seances referred to was in many respects different from the phenomena I have found recorded in the Lives of the Saints. In the former case we seem to have the presence of certain material scents, definitely recognized as the perfume of particular flowers, which were, so to speak, sprayed upon the persons present, and which smarted, as we learn from other witnesses, when a few drops accidentally got into their eyes. Sometimes, again, the scent would be poured upon the heads or the handkerchiefs of the sitters. But the most striking difference between these phenomena of the seance-room and the odour of sanctity " with which Mr. Stainton Moses compares them is the fact that the ascetics so honoured, instead of making a display of their mysterious gifts, did their utmost to hide them from the knowledge of men. The exact opposite seems always to have been the case even with unpaid mediums like Stainton Moses and D. D. Home. They exploited their powers for their own credit, if not for their pecuniary emolument, and there is little of modesty to be found in anything they have written on the subject.

In selecting a few examples of more recent date to illustrate the olfactory phenomena which meet us in hagiographical literature, we may begin with an instance recounted by St. Teresa. In her *Book of Foundations* she speaks at some length of a contemporary of hers, the famous Spanish ascetic Catalina de Cardona, a lady of very high family, who, to the distress of her noble relations, embraced a life of solitude and extraordinary austerity. Catalina paid a short visit to the Carmelite convent of Toledo, and St. Teresa reports of her;

All our nuns assured me that there was about her a fragrance as that of relics, so strong that it moved them to give thanks to our Lord; it clung even to her habit and her girdle which she left behind, for they took her habit from her and gave her another; and the nearer they came to her the more strongly did they perceive it, though her dress, owing to the heat which then prevailed, was of a kind to be offensive rather than otherwise. I know they would not say anything which was not in every way true.

It is plain that St. Teresa herself fully believed in the reality of the phenomenon. Similar manifestations were afterwards to be recorded of many members of her own Order, and so far as regards the fragrance of the body after death there is probably no example in history in which the evidence is so abundant and so overwhelming as that which attests the wondrous perfume which for many years was exhaled by the mortal remains of St. Teresa herself.

One might almost infer, from the curious phrase she uses describing the scent as an "odour of relics," that she habitually perceived some such fragrance in all the relics which she venerated. It is one of the difficulties in this sort of investigation to decide how much is subjective and how much objective in a phenomenon which some witnesses perceive and others do not. In the case of the espousals ring I have mentioned earlier, there was at least the possibility o the concurrent testimony of the two senses of sight and touch. But for these olfactory marvels we are necessarily dependent upon one sense alone.

One saintly Carmelite nun in particular was renowned, like her mother, St. Teresa, for the wonderful perfume which for more than three years after her death proceeded from the cell which she had occupied. This was Donna Vittoria Colonna, the daughter of Don Filippo, Grand Constable of Naples, but known in religion as Mother Clare Mary of the Passion. Three medical men made depositions regarding the inexplicable perfume which they had perceived, not once, but many times, in the cell in which Mother Clare Mary had died, and the same fact was borne witness to by all the community. Moreover, in this case the marvel manifested itself occasionally during life, as, for example, when the holy nun was discoursing with great fervour on the love of God.

More widely-known, however, is the case of St. Catherine de' Ricci. In the official investigations, in view of her canonization, we find some twenty or thirty of the nuns in her convent at Prato bearing witness upon oath to the strange celestial odour which was especially noticeable in the chamber of death, although some of them had also perceived a similar perfume clinging to her on certain occasions in her life-time. Some of the nuns described it as resembling the scent of vivuole mammole, apparently a species of violet, though these flowers were not then in season, but most of them considered that it could not be compared to the odour of any flowers or to any artificial perfumes. It was perceptible around her tomb for more than a year, though the body had been enclosed in a leaden coffin.

In those cases in which a mysterious fragrance manifested itself during life, the phenomenon seems generally to have been connected with some ecstatic condition of the subject. Thus we read of St. Veronica Giuliani that the scent seemed to come from her stigmata. Father F. M. Salvatori, in the Life of St. Veronica, which he compiled mainly from the depositions of witnesses in the process of canonization, says of her:

> It is worthy of remark that when the above-mentioned wounds were open, they emitted so delicious a fragrance throughout the whole of the convent that this alone was sufficient to inform the nuns whenever the stigmata had been renewed, and on several occasions the religious were convinced by ocular demonstration that they had not been deceived. When the bandages which had been applied to these mysterious wounds were put away, they communicated the same sweet perfume to everything near them. The fact is attested by her confidant, the Blessed Florida Ceoli.

Still more remarkable in some respects is the case of Sister Giovanna Maria della Croce of Roveredo, who died in 1673. Her biographer, Weber, who seems to have had access to all the official documents and depositions of witnesses, after describing the incident of her mystic espousal to Jesus Christ, continues as follows:

> From this time onwards her finger exhaled a delicious fragrance, which she was unable to hide, and which all the community soon became aware of. Consequently they sought every opportunity to touch it and kiss it. The perfume which it gave out was so powerful that it communicated itself to the touch and persisted for a considerable time. Thus it happened that Sister Mary Ursula, having touched that finger in the holy nun's first illness, her hand for several days afterwards

retained an exquisite fragrance. This scent was particularly perceptible when Giovanna Maria was ill, because she could not then take any precautions to disguise it. From her finger the perfume extended gradually to the whole hand and then to her body, and communicated itself to all the objects which she touched. It could not be compared to any earthly scent because it was essentially different, and transfused soul and body with an indescribable sweetness. It was more powerful when she came back from Communion. It exuded not only from her body but also from her clothes long after she had ceased to wear them, from her straw mattress and from the objects in her room. It spread through the whole house and betrayed her comings and her goings and her every movement. The religious who were in choir were aware of her approach from the perfume which was wafted before her before she came into view. This phenomenon, which lasted for many years, was the more remarkable because naturally she could not endure any form of scent. It was necessary to keep all such things as musk and amber out of the house altogether, because they acted upon her from a considerable distance even though they were hidden in the cellar, and produced a most distressing effect, so much so that she would even faint away on the spot. The only scent which did her no harm was that which breathed from her own person. Often new novices who joined the Order came to the convent wearing, according to the fashion of the times, scented necklaces of pearl or coral. She was so painfully affected by these objects that she could not come near the wearers, and it was found necessary to require them to lay them aside at the convent gate in order to save the Mother Abbess from the risk of a swoon or some other indisposition.

One of the Sisters, when giving evidence in the inquiry which preceded the process of beatification, speaks of an occasion when the Mother Abbess, overcome when at prayer by a fit of weeping, found herself without a handkerchief. The Sister proffered hers, which the Abbess accepted gratefully and returned after wiping her eyes and cheeks. The handkerchief thus restored exhaled an inexplicable and delicious fragrance. Another characteristic of these phenomena in the case of Giovanna Maria was, as her biographer points out, that this mysterious perfume waxed and waned according to the events of the ecclesiastical year. The odour was notably more pronounced upon the feasts of our Lady and reached its climax on the great festivals of our Lord, but diminished on ordinary days.

THE ODOUR OF SANCTITY

This case is a fair specimen of several others which have been recorded. Perhaps the most striking is that of St. Maria Francesca delle Cinque Piaghe, a Franciscan nun, who died at Naples in Here again we are told of the delicious fragrance which clung not only to her habit, but to everything she touched. As her biographer states, after a careful study of the process of beatification:

> There is hardly one of the numerous witnesses whose evidence is reported in the Summarium who does not speak in explicit terms of this perfume, and in order that there might be no doubt that the favour came to her from her Mother Mary and from her divine Spouse, it was regularly observed that this phenomenon manifested itself with special intensity on the great festivals of our Lady and on the Fridays in March on which she participated mysteriously in the sufferings of Christ's Passion.

Some of my readers will perhaps remember that St. Maria Francesca was one of the more remarkable among stigmatized saints. In the case of the Dominican nun, Agnes of Jesus, Prioress of Langeac, who died in 1634, we have another example of a wonderful perfume, attested by many witnesses, including distinguished lay-folk and medical men. These manifestations were particularly remarked after death in connection with her tomb, and they seem to have been confined to certain exceptionally favoured individuals who suddenly were conscious of a heavenly fragrance and were moved by it to ardent devotion, though to others at the same time the fragrance was not perceptible. None the less, we further learn that during her lifetime her cell was as it were embalmed with perfume which also at times exhaled from her person. There are a considerable number of such cases in which little detail is available except by an examination of the processes of beatification, and these are not readily come by, but a general resemblance seems to run through them all, and what has already been said will probably suffice to illustrate the kind of evidence which they offer. But one example which ought not to pass without special mention is that of the Blessed Maria degli Angeli, who died at Turin in 1717. She was a lady of noble family, who became a Carmelite at the age of fifteen. The convent was especially dear to the royal house of Piedmont, and one of the Princesses of that family, in the process of beatification, made a deposition under oath to the following effect:

As a proof of the holiness of this servant of God I would appeal to the incomparable fragrance which made itself manifest in the places where she lived or through which she passed. The sweetness of this perfume resembled nothing earthly. The more one breathed it the more delicious it became. It was specially perceptible on the feasts of our Lady, of St. Joseph, of St. Teresa, during solemn novenas and at the holy seasons of Christmas, Easter and Pentecost. The ladies of my suite were conscious of it as well as myself, and what astonished me more than all else was the fact that after the death of the servant of God I noticed and still continue to notice this perfume in the cell she occupied, although every object which it formerly contained has been taken out of it.

A number of witnesses, so we learn from the Life of Blessed Maria gave evidence to the same effect in the process of beatification. "When we wanted Reverend Mother," said one of her nuns, "and could not find her in her cell, we tried to track her by the fragrance she had left behind." She, on her part, made every effort to conceal this continued miracle and even went so far as to carry evil-smelling objects to her cell, but it was all of no use. This sort of olfactory phenomenon does not seem to be met with quite so frequently in the records of modem ascetics, but I may call attention to at least two instances of comparatively recent date. Sister Mary of Jesus Crucified, the Carmelite nun of Pau, who died at Bethlehem in 1878, was favoured in this way. Her biographer, Père Estrate, tells us:

> Since the death of the holy Sister, several Carmelites both at Bethlehem and Pau have been conscious of a delicious perfume in many places which she once frequented. This fact reminds us that the same sweet fragrance was often noticed to proceed from her when she was still living.

The room in which she died was also inexplicably perfumed, and the odour clung to the dress of all who visited it.

CHAPTER X
INCORRUPTION

1

It may be said that nearly all the phenomena which we have been considering in this volume are characterized by a certain element of mystery. Why should these extraordinary gifts be conceded to some holy people and withheld from others? Not a few mystics in whom such manifestations as those of levitation, stigmatization, perfumed emanations, etc., have been most conspicuous, have never been canonized. On the other hand, many of those who, both by common estimation and the judgment of the Church, are held up for veneration as among the most eminent of God's servants, have been entirely devoid of these special marks of the Divine favour. As I have more than once previously noted, it is not the aim of this volume to solve problems, but to state and classify facts. But it seems particularly necessary to reiterate this caution in approaching a question where the apparent inconsistency of God's dealings with His elect is more than usually puzzling and difficult of explanation.

The phenomena may conveniently be divided into six different categories. They are: (1) a preternatural fragrance perceived in the neighbourhood of the body of the deceased, a fragrance which sometimes persists for months or even for years. A well-attested case is that of St. Teresa of Avila. (2) The alleged complete absence of cadaveric rigor. (3) Immunity from natural decay, lasting in some cases for centuries, though in those here to be considered such agencies as saponification, embalming, desiccation, the use of sealed metal coffins, etc., have to be excluded. (4) The bleeding of venerated corpses after an interval of weeks, months or even years. An instance in point is the flow of liquid blood from the nostrils of St. Catherine of Bologna three months after she had for a fortnight been buried in the earth and had been again exhumed. (5) Much less frequent, but occasionally reported on what seems reliable evidence, is the persistence of warmth, sometimes of a notably high temperature, in the cadaver long after life appears be extinct. When a surgeon opened the body of Maria Villani nine hours after death to extract the heart, the heat was such that he could not at first retain his hand in the abdominal cavity. (6) There are a few cases in which the dead saint is alleged to have raised his arm in benediction, or lifted his foot to be kissed, or turned his head towards the Blessed Sacrament, or covered the pudenda when the body was being reclothed. Very explicit evidence of this last marvel may be found in the account given by the Oratorian Fathers who prepared the body of St. Philip Neri for the grave. In this and some similar instances, the possibility of catalepsy or trance seems to be excluded by the circumstances of the case.

Already in the fourth century we find some familiarity with the idea of incorruption. Paulinus, the secretary, if we may so describe him, of the great St. Ambrose of Milan, has left us a memoir of his master in the form of a letter addressed to St. Augustine.

As to the authenticity of this document there is, practically speaking, no dispute. Opinions may differ widely as to the historical trustworthiness of the writer. He records many marvellous incidents, and we may suspect him of exaggerated panegyric, but he at any rate reflects the tone of thought of devout Christians at the close of the fourth century. Now, Paulinus in speaking of the discovery by St. Ambrose (c. 396) of the body of the martyr St. Nazarius, writes as follows:

> At this time he (Ambrose) found the body of the holy martyr Nazarius which had been interred in a garden outside the city (Milan), and he took it up and transferred it to the Basilica of the Apostles beside the highway which leads to Rome. Now, in the tomb in which the body of that martyr lay—as to the date at which he suffered we have down to the present been able to learn nothing—we saw the martyr's blood as fresh as if it had been shed that same day. Further, his head, which the wretches had cut off, was so perfect and free from corruption (*ita integrum atque incorruptum*) with all its hair and the beard, that it

looked to us, at the time we moved it, as if it had been washed and laid out for inspection there in the tomb. And why should we wonder, since our Lord long ago promised in the gospel that not a hair of their head should perish. Also we were overwhelmed at the same time with so heavy a fragrance that it surpassed all perfumes in sweetness.

As to the fact of some translation of the body of St. Nazarius we have confirmatory evidence in the writings of St. Paulinus of Nola (a contemporary) and also in St. Gregory of Tours, but it is only from Paulinus the secretary that we learn so definitely that the head of the martyr showed no trace of corruption. Whether this is the earliest recorded example of the phenomenon in Christian history I am unable to say, but the number of instances in which the same marvellous immunity from the horrors of the tomb has been observed in subsequent ages is almost incredibly great.

It will be sufficient in passing to recall, as connected with our own country, the famous cases of St. Cuthbert, St. Willibrord, St. Elphege, St. Edward the Confessor, St. Hugh, Bishop of Lincoln, St. Edmund, Archbishop of Canterbury, St. Etheldreda, of Ely, and St. Werburg, of Chester. Neither can it be said that this form of manifestation has ceased in modern times. St, Madeleine Sophie Barat, the foundress of the Society of the Sacred Heart, died in 1865. Twenty-eight years afterwards her body was found almost perfectly entire, although the coffin was partly decayed and covered with mildew. A similar immunity from corruption was bestowed on St. John Baptist Vianney, the famous Cure d'Ars, who died in 1859 and was beatified in 1905. Hardly less celebrated is the voyante of Lourdes, Bernadette Soubirous, with whose visions of Our Lady in the grotto of Massabieille the whole wonderful story of the fountain and its cures began. Bernadette died in the humble obscurity of the Convent of St. Gildard at Nevers in 1879, being then 34 years of age. In 1909 her body was exhumed, and we are told by an. eye-witness:

> Not the least trace of corruption nor any bad odour could be perceived in the corpse of our beloved sister. Even the habit in which she was buried was intact. The face was somewhat brown, the eyes slightly sunken, and she seemed to be sleeping. The damp funeral garments were exchanged for new ones. The body was placed in a new zinc coffin lined with white silk. Within it was placed a record enclosed in a glass tube and giving an account of the opening of the coffin and

the condition of the body. After this the coffin was again deposited in the mortuary chapel in our garden.

These last three examples are interesting because no one will pretend that the repute for sanctity which attaches to these names owes anything to the condition in which their mortal remains were discovered long after death. No doubt there may have been cases in the past where a supposed miracle of incorruption has started a whole cult. Baron Friedrich von Hügel is inclined to attribute to this cause the outburst of popular enthusiasm which eventually brought about the canonization of St. Catherine of Genoa. He tells us, quoting from the original sources, how Catherine's body was left for about eighteen months in its first resting-place by one of the walls of the hospital church. But then "it was found that the spot was damp, owing to a conduit of water running under the wall. And the resting-place was broken up, and the coffin was opened: and the holy body was found entire from head to foot without any kind of lesion." After that we learn that there was a great concourse of people to see the remains, which were left exposed for eight days and then were transported to another site. Baron von Hügel's final conclusion is that it was the incorruption which gave the first, and, as it turned out, an abiding impulse to the popular devotion. Indeed, as we shall see later on, it is highly improbable that, but for this condition of the body, a cultus would ever have arisen sufficiently popular and permanent to lead on to the Beatification and Canonization, But as things now stood, the movement had been set going, and it continued on and on.

This may quite conceivably be a just interpretation of the course of events so far as concerns the canonization of St. Catherine of Genoa, but it certainly cannot be maintained, and the learned critic referred to would not dream of suggesting, that in all such cases of incorruption it is the accidental immunity from physical decay which has first attracted popular attention and paved the way for a formal decree of canonization. It would be absurd to suppose that the veneration which attaches to the names of St. Teresa, St. Francis Xavier, St. Philip Neri, or St. Catherine of Siena, owed anything to the fact that their remains had not been allowed to see corruption in the ordinary course of nature. No reasonable person can doubt that these servants of God would have been canonized even if the common law of dust to dust had prevailed in their case from the first. But besides such names as those just mentioned, which are known to all the world independently of creed, there are scores of others, great missionaries, great founders of religious institutes, great preachers, great ascetics, great practises of the spiritual and corporal works of mercy, whose fame has owed nothing at all to the accident that, many years after their work was done and their histories written, the bodies in which they had moved amongst men were found immune from decay and sometimes fragrant. Take, for example, such a case as that of St. Vincent de Paul, whose holiness was famous all over France long before his life had ended. He died in 1660, and it was only after numberless petitions for his canonization had been addressed to Rome that the cause was begun, and that there took place in 1712 an official inspection of the remains. More than fifty years had elapsed since the burial, but none the less when the tomb was opened, "everything," to use the words of an eye-witness, "was as when he had been laid there. The eyes and nose alone showed some decay. I counted eighteen teeth. The body was not disturbed, but those who approached saw at once that it was entire and that the soutane was not in the least damaged by time. No offensive odour was perceived, and the doctors testified that the body could not thus have been preserved for so long a period by any natural means." It must be admitted that the integrity was not complete, and that when the tomb was again opened twenty-five years later most of the tissues had been resolved into dust, but the decay then observed seems to have been due to certain floods which had occurred during the interval. Similarly at about the same date we have remarkable accounts preserved to us of the translations of the famous Dominican Nun the Venerable Mother Agnes of Jesus, Prioress of Langeac. She was the friend and spiritual mother of Monsieur Olier, the founder of Saint Sulpice.

Her death took place October 19, 1634, and the body was buried, without evisceration or any process of embalming, like those of other members of the community, in the chapter house. After some years the bishop, in view of the procedure for her beatification, wished the remains to be interred apart. The body was then found entire and without trace of corruption. Other translations and inspections followed down to 1778. The flesh of the face and other uncovered parts disintegrated in time, but more than once, and notably in 1698 and in 1778, the scientific experts, surgeons and doctors of medicine, pronounced that the preservation of the body was, humanly speaking, inexplicable. In several of the reports, which are very fully given by her biographers, Lucot and Lantages, the emanation of an extraordinary perfume from the body is much insisted on.

Or let us take for another example the case of a great Spanish bishop, St. Thomas of Villanova, Archbishop of Valencia, who died in 1555. Twenty-three years after his burial a certain Canon of the Cathedral wished to manifest his devotion to the holy prelate by enclosing the tomb, up to this quite open, with a railing of bronze, and hanging a costly silver lamp above it. To carry out this work it was found necessary to disturb the tomb, and we are told that as a consequence of this digging the whole church was filled with perfume. Further it is stated that the body itself was uncovered and was found absolutely whole and entire, exactly as it had been on the day of the burial, the features still wearing the same sweet expression. This was the more remarkable because, with the view apparently of frustrating the plans of certain ecclesiastics who were suspected of a design to carry the treasure off, the corpse of the Archbishop had been buried at some depth and in the actual soil.

Of course it must be recognized throughout in dealing with this subject that cases of a remarkable and seemingly unaccountable preservation of human remains are sufficiently common to make it rather difficult to decide in any individual instance that the absence of corruption is due to anything more than mere coincidence. We have bodies strangely desiccated like the natural mummies of Peru, of which a good many specimens may be seen in the anthropological museum of the Trocadero in Paris. We have others preserved from pure *actionmguano*, of which Frank Buckland gives an account in the fourth series of his *Curiosities of Natural History*. Then there are the dried and shrivelled corpses in the gruesome Capuchin emetenes of Palermo and Malta. "They are all dressed in the clothes they usually wore... the skin and muscles become as dry and hard as a piece of stockfish, and though many of them have been here upwards of two hundred and fifty years, yet none are reduced to skeletons." Somewhat different from these are the bodies so curiously preserved in one of the Dublin churches.

> As is well known, the preservative qualities of the vaults under St. Michan's Church are most remarkable, and decay in the bodies committed to them is strangely arrested. The latest writer on the subject in a short notice of the church speaks of being struck (among others) "by a pathetic baby corpse, from whose plump wrists still hang the faded white ribbons of its funeral." This coffin bears the date 1679; yet the very finger and toe nails of the child are still distinct. The antiseptic qualities are believed to be largely attributable to the extreme

dryness of the vaults and to the great freedom of their atmosphere from dust particles.

Further, there are other corpses in which the normal process of decay is arrested by saponification, and there seems to be also a certain number of sporadic examples—perhaps the case of the body of the great English canonist Bishop Lyndwode, which was found centuries after his death, wrapped in cere-cloth but quite entire, may serve as an illustration—for which it is difficult to assign any adequate explanation. The Orthodox Russian Church includes amongst its saints a considerable number of bishops and other ascetics whose remains have been found entire some time after their deaths; indeed, this incorrupt condition seems to be regarded, theoretically at least, as a necessary condition for canonization in that Communion. The incorruption of the holy man's remains is officially set down as one of the conditions which have to be verified before any reputed servant of God can be canonized. Readers of Dostoyevsky's romance, *The Brothers Karamazov*, may remember the tremendous sensation caused when it was discovered that the corpse of a holy ascetic, one of the characters therein, was betraying unmistakable signs of the onset of putrefaction. It seemed to be taken for granted that he must have been a hypocrite. At Kiev there is a famous "laura," known as that of the Pescery, which has a sort of necropolis attached to it containing 73 bodies of "saints," all mummified and lying in open coffins, robed in rich vestments. The condition of these remains seems to be very similar to that of the corpses in the Capuchin burial crypt at Palermo. Similarly, Hassert, in his account of Montenegro, speaks of the incorrupt corpse of the hermit St. Basil of Ostrog, and notes how he was expected to kiss the dried-up (*vertrocknete*) hand. So also Schwarz saw the body of St. Peter I, the Vladika at Cetienje, who died in 1830. He speaks of "dieser dilrre, steinharte Kadaver." But such details exist in abundance in works dealing with travel through the regions in which the Orthodox Church is dominant.

But it is not only the multitude of examples of bodies naturally preserved from decay which creates a difficulty against any premature appeal to the interference of supernatural agencies. There is also the fact that the occurrence of the phenomenon is extremely arbitrary, and, to judge by human standards, inconsistent. So far as the available evidence allows us to speak positively, there is every reason to believe that this special privilege of incorruption was not accorded to some of the greatest saints who have glorified the Church in the course of the last eight centuries. Neither in the case of St. Bernard, nor St. Francis of Assisi, nor St. Dominic, nor St. Ignatius Loyola, nor St. Vincent Ferrer, nor St John Baptist de la Salle, nor St. Alphonsus Liguori, nor St. Clare, "the Seraphic Mother," nor St. Bridget of Sweden, have we any satisfactory evidence that their mortal remains were exempted from the common lot of humanity. On the other hand, while the privilege has been conferred upon a large number of simple and ecstatic souls, whose sojourn in this world seems to have been a continued anticipation of the angelic intuitions of Paradise, the majority of these who have been canonized for their innocence of life, and, if may so speak, for their precocious sanctity, have not been the recipients of this special favour. St. Aloysius Gonzaga, whose festival is celebrated by the Universal Church as that of the Patron of Youth, was not found incorrupt. Neither, again, was the holy Passionist, St. Gabriel (Possenti) of Our Lady of Sorrows, who was canonized recently. The same is true of St. John Berchmans.

Now St. Gabriel was just twenty-four when he died, St. Aloysius twenty-three, and St. John Berchmans twenty-two. One would have thought that if anything could be regarded as likely to exempt any son of man from the curse laid upon us through our father Adam, it would be the virginal innocence of lives such as these, and yet it is certain that in a very few years all these bodies were reduced to dust. In the case of holy virgins of the other sex we have perhaps rather more examples of incorruption at a relatively early age. St. Rose of Viterbo, whose body remained intact for many centuries, is commonly said to have died at the age of eighteen, but this is quite uncertain. We know that she died in the middle of the thirteenth century, but we have no record of the exact year, and still less of the year of her birth. St. Rose of Lima, whose body was exhumed and found quite entire six months after death, was thirty-one when she passed to a better world. St. Clare of Montefalco, one of the most famous Italian examples of immunity from putrefaction, lived to the age of thirty-three.

The following account of the body of St. Clare of Montefalco is given in the *Cornhill Magazine* for October 1881. The writer is—of all people in the world—Mr. John Addington Symonds:

> A handsome young man appeared who conducted us with decent gravity into a little darkened chamber behind the altar. There he lighted wax tapers, opened sliding doors in what looked like a long coffin, and drew curtains. Before us in the dim light there lay a woman covered with a black nun's dress. Only her hands and the exquisitely

beautiful pale outline of her face (forehead, nose, mouth, and chin, modelled in purest outline, as though the injury of death had never touched her) were visible. Her closed eyes seemed to sleep. She had the perfect peace of Luini's St. Catherine borne by angels to her grave on Sinai. I have rarely seen anything which surprised and touched me more. ... S. Chiara's shrine was hung round with her relics; and among these the heart extracted from her body was suspended. Upon it, apparently wrought into the very substance of the mummified flesh, were impressed a figure of the crucified Christ, the scourge, and the five stigmata. The guardian's faith in this miraculous witness to her sainthood, the gentle piety of the men and women who knelt before it, checked all expressions of incredulity.

St. Mary Magdalen of Pazzi, mentioned by Pope Benedict XIV as a celebrated instance of the same phenomenon, was forty-one at the time of her death. Blessed Mariana of Jesus, known as the "Lily of Quito," was relatively quite young. She went to heaven at the age of twenty-four. A month later, when her body was transferred to a new tomb, it was found beautiful and supple like that of one who had just died. However, three years afterwards (in 1646), the coffin was again opened, and all the flesh had then crumbled to dust, though there came from the remains a fragrant perfume which filled the whole church. Of more recent date is the rather extraordinary case of Maria Christina, the daughter of Victor Emmanuel I, King of Piedmont, and bride of Ferdinand II, King of the Two Sicilies. She had been married nearly four years when she died in 1836, at the age of twenty-four, shortly after the birth of her only child. Seventeen years later, when the cause of her beatification had been introduced as the result of many alleged miracles, the body is said to have been found intact. It is, of course, possible that some embalming process had been resorted to after death, but this is not stated, and it is difficult to suppose that the immunity of the remains from corruption could have been accounted in any way wonderful if this had taken place. Another curious instance, belonging still more nearly to our own times, is that of Father Paul Mary Pakenham, C.P. In 1850, Captain the Hon. Charles Pakenham, of the Grenadier Guards, who, through his aunt, Lady Katherine Pakenham, the wife of the first Duke of Wellington, was the nephew by marriage of the hero of Waterloo, was received into the Catholic Church. He entered the Passionist Order and became a priest, but after less than two years of very fervent ministry, he died in the beginning of March 1857 at the age of thirty-six. Now in the

Memoir of Father Paul Mary, published in 1915, we find the following interesting account of the exhumation of his remains:

> In March 1894, thirty-seven years after the happy death of Father Paul Mary, the chapel built by him, which had long stood useless, was finally removed to give way to a new cemetery for the use of the religious community at Mount Argus. During the removal of the remains of the dead religious from the old burial place to the new, the members of the then community, doubtless moved by holy curiosity, had the coffin containing the body of Father Paul Mary Pakenham opened. Whether it was due to natural or supernatural causes we do not care to conjecture, but the body was then found perfectly intact and incorrupt, and the face wore a most lifelike expression as of one who lay in a peaceful slumber. The writer had the happiness of being present on that occasion and will never forget the sight, nor the emotion of some members of the original community who stood by the coffin then as they stood by it in their fresh sorrow for their saintly father's loss almost forty years before. The coffin was afterwards closed and reverently lowered into its new resting place where now, close beneath the great Celtic cross which overshadows the cemetery, all that is mortal of Father Paul Mary Pakenham awaits the resurrection of the just.

It must not, of course, be supposed that we are always left so completely without guidance regarding the natural or supernatural origin of these interferences with the ordinary processes of decay, as in the two cases just cited. No examples would be more suggestive of design on the part of Divine Providence than those in which the exemption from corruption is only partial, as for instance in the preservation of the tongue of St. Anthony of Padua, when all the rest of the body had crumbled to dust. Unfortunately, in many cases of this class the historical evidence is apt to be defective on one side or the other. That St. Anthony's tongue was in reality found red, soft and entire can hardly be doubted. The Bollandists give an engraving of it in its reliquary as it existed in their day, more than 400 years after his lifetime. But after all, the recorded facts of the history of St. Anthony furnish no clear and outstanding reason why the tongue of the Saint should have been preserved, in preference, let us say, to his heart or his right hand. In the similar case of St. John Nepomucen, who died a martyr to the secrecy of the confessional, the preservation of the tongue is entirely appropriate and significant, but the evidence that this organ was specially singled out to be alone immune from corruption might perhaps be stronger than it is. Still, Benedict XIV tells us in his De Canonizations Sanctorum that a formal examination was ma e o this delicate member in 1725, 382 years after Nepomucen's martyrdom. The scientific experts found that it was entire, retaining the normal shape, size and colour of the tongue of a living man, an further that it was still both soft and flexible. Certainly it would seem very hard to suggest any natural explanation of the Pemenon, and Benedict, who, as he informs us, was *Promotor Fidei* (vulgarly "Devil's Advocate") at the time this investigation took place, after doing his best to argue against it, fully concurred in the decision of the Congregation of Sacred Rites that this wonderful conservation of the tongue might be accepted as an authentic miracle of the second class. Another example is the tongue of B. Battista Varani (see AA.SS. May, Vol. XXXI) alone preserved incorrupt. The body had been found incorrupt thirty years after death. A very arbitrary confessor ordered the nuns to rebury it between two planks and to water the earth thrown into the grave and beat it down, perhaps to blot out all memory of the place of burial. In 1593, some thirty-six years later, the grave was again opened and the bones of the beata were found, still fragrant, along with the dust of the body, while the tongue alone remained incorrupt, still moist and of a ruddy colour. So the event is recorded in Pascucci's Life (3, 13) which was written in 1630, and which is quoted by the Bollandists. Unfortunately, the evidence is not always so satisfactory, nor the application so obvious. The heart of St. Bridget of Sweden may have been found fresh and entire when all the rest save her bones was reduced to dust, but, apart from testimonies to prove the permanence of the heart in the same state, we cannot altogether rule out the possibility of coincidence.

Similarly for the alleged preservation of the hand of St. Stephen of Hungary, or again, of the hand of our own King Oswald, or of the thumb of St. Edith of Wilton, the evidence must be held to be lacking in that historical precision which can alone bring entire conviction. With regard, however, to the general question of immunity from corruption, and in particular with regard to certain specially chosen examples, there are still several considerations which would prevent us from regarding the phenomenon as in all cases explicable by natural causes.

2

In the light of the facts appealed to in the preceding pages, and of other facts observed, for example, in those fallen in battle who have been hastily interred and afterwards exhumed, it must be admitted that the laws which govern the decomposition of the human body are very complicated and are still imperfectly understood. The editors of the most authoritative English treatise on Medical Jurisprudence do not hesitate to speak as follows:

> The action of the environment, the inherent potentialities of the microbes, and the state of their vitality at any moment involve such an enormous number of varying and variable factors that it becomes quite impossible to explain on a rational basis of ascertained fact... the extraordinary variations in the circumstances of putrefaction that have been observed.

In the same standard work we may read that "sometimes one body has been found more decomposed after six or eight months burial than another which has lain interred for a period of eighteen months or two years." While a distinguished American authority says: "I have seen bodies buried two months that have shown fewer of the changes produced by putrefaction than others dead but a week." None the less, by common experience, it remains undoubtedly true that, apart from the occurrence of quite exceptional external conditions, e.g., of extreme cold, decomposition does set in sooner or later, and that unmistakable signs of its approach are in general discernible long before a fortnight has elapsed after death. Further, we seem to be justified in drawing the conclusion that all knowledge in this matter is still largely empirical. The medical expert of the present day cannot claim to be very much better informed than his brother of the seventeenth century. In the one case as in the other, he can only say, when confronted with an individual example of incorruption: "Here is a case which in my experience is extremely unusual. I cannot explain why the process of decay has been prevented or arrested. I can only state that something has happened here which does not occur in more than one dead body out of a thousand. We have not sufficient data to solve the problem."

Now the point of special interest which seems to me to emerge from a study of the presence or absence of decomposition in the bodies of mystics of recognized holiness lies in the extraordinary proportion of cases in which we observe some notable departure from the laws which usually govern the disintegration of the human cadaver. Anyone at all conversant with hagiographical literature will be aware that wherever mystics have died in repute of exceptional sanctity—I am speaking more particularly of Catholic countries—the intense and often quite extravagant devotion of the people has exercised great pressure in inducing the responsible authorities to keep these holy bodies above ground much beyond the period commonly assigned for inhumation. Nevertheless, out of hundreds of such cases of exceptional delay, I cannot recall more than two or three instances in which a hasty interment has had to be resorted to in consequence of the signs of decomposition making themselves perceptible. No doubt untoward incidents of this kind are apt to be ignored or glossed over in the panegyric which so often does duty for a spiritual biography, but in innumerable cases the exact contrary is explicitly affirmed. The only satisfactory way of testing the matter would be to make some kind of a census of all the devout servants of God who have been canonized or beatified during the last few centuries, taking careful note of what evidence is available regarding the condition of their mortal remains when exhumed after death. Unfortunately, this would be a long and rather difficult piece of research, for the beatifications and canonizations of modern times are more numerous than would be readily believed. Failing an investigation of this magnitude, I have attempted something of the same kind on a smaller scale. It will probably be known to most of my readers that of the saints who are formally raised to the altars of the Church by a solemn process of inquiry and a Bull of canonization, only a few are inserted in the Roman Calendar and have feasts which are kept by the Universal Church. For example, St. Lewis Bertrand, the great Dominican missionary, is specially honoured in Spain and by his own Order, but his festival is not kept by the Church at large. The same is true of such heroes of zeal and charity as St.

Peter Claver, S.J., the Apostle of the Negroes, or of St. Leonard of Port Maurice, O.S.F., the great preacher, or of such paragons of fervour as St. Veronica Giuliani, and St. Catherine de' Ricci, with innumerable others. Confining ourselves to the saints who have lived within the last five centuries (i.e., since the year 1400), we find that forty-two of these are included in the Roman Calendar and are honoured in Mass and Office by all priests who follow the Roman rite. To these forty-two I have confined my little census, and this limitation has the conspicuous advantage that we may be quite sure that the mere fact of the body remaining incorrupt has in none of these cases led to the inclusion of the saint in the Calendar followed by the Church at large. Each one of these forty-two has been chosen as remarkable in some other way, either as the founder of a religious Order or as a typical missionary or as a pattern of charity or innocence, etc. Anyway, here is the list:

SAINTS IN THE ROMAN CALENDAR
WHO LIVED BETWEEN 1400 AND 1900.[1]

Jan. 29.   S. FRANCIS OF SALES (1622). Embalmed, body found
B   entire in 1632; only fragrant dust in 1656. Hamon, *Vie*, II, pp. 481-2. Heart preserved apart; "oil" distils from it. Bougaud, *Vie de S. Chantal*, II, p. 566.

March 8.   S. JOHN OF GOD (1550). In 1570 body, except for
A   the tip of the nose, entire, and also fragrant. *AA.SS.* March, Vol. I, pp. 831 and 853.

March 9.   S. FRANCES OF ROME (1440). Body exhumed 4½
A   months after death; fresh and very fragrant. *AA.SS.* March, Vol. II, pp. 101 and 209.

March 28.   S. JOHN CAPISTRAN (1456). Evidence of exhumation
B   not satisfactory. *AA.SS.* Oct., Vol. X, pp. 432-6 and 915; but said to have been reliably identified with a still incorrupt body in 1765. See Léon, *Lives O.S.F.*, III, p. 419.

April 2.   S. FRANCIS OF PAULA (1507). Supple and fragrant
A   a week after death; body still entire in 1562 when burnt by the Hugenots. Dabert, *Vie*, pp. 443 and 463.

April 5.   S. VINCENT FERRER (1419). Fragrant and supple
C   after death, but in 1456 only bones and dust. Fages, *Vie*, II, p. 274; *Notes*, p. 416.

April 24.   S. FIDELIS A SIGMARINGA (1661). No evidence of
C   incorruption at exhumation eighteen months after death. F. della Scala, *Der H. Fidelis*, p. 179.

April 28.   S. PAUL OF THE CROSS (1775). Only skeleton left
C   when first exhumed in 1852, but fragrant and flexible twenty-four hours after death. Devine, *Life*, pp. 377-8.

May 5.   S. PIUS V (1572). Viscera removed, but body re-
C   mained supple, high-coloured and like that of a living man for four days. At translation in 1588 nothing left but skeleton. *AA.SS.* May, Vol. I, pp. 695-7.

---

[1] I have in each case given a reference to an authority where fuller details may be found. The reference *AA.SS.* stands for the Bollandist *Acta Sanctorum*. For convenience sake I have cited the modern reprint. The date given after each name is the year of death.

May 10. A		S. ANTONINUS OF FLORENCE (1459). Unburied for eight days, it remained flexible and fragrant; found in 1589 still incorrupt. *AA.SS.* May, Vol. I, pp. 328 and 360. Cf. T. Buonsegni, *Descrizzione, etc.*, published at the time of the translation, p. 17.
May 15. C		S. JOHN BAP. DE LA SALLE (1719). No phenomena. Translation in 1734; only skeleton found. *Vie* (1876), II, p. 321.
May 17. A		S. PASCHAL BAYLON (1592). Covered with quicklime, but found entire and incorrupt nine months later. In 1611 surgeons declared preservation miraculous; fragrant. Staniforth, *Life*, pp. 183-9.
May 20. A		S. BERNARDINE OF SIENA (1444). Kept above ground twenty-six days after death; fragrant; copious discharge of blood from nostrils after twenty-four days. Incorrupt in 1472. Amadio, *Life*, pp. 287-9, 325. Still incorrupt in seventeenth century. *AA.SS.* May, Vol. V, p. 148.
May 26. A		S. PHILIP NERI (1595). Viscera removed but body apparently not embalmed. Found perfectly free from corruption eight months after death. Still sound and entire in 1599, 1602, and 1639. Bacci, *Life*, II, pp. 124-5, 130. Capecelatro, *Life*, II, pp. 465-6 and 487.
May 29. A		S. MARY MAG. DE PAZZI (1607). Body exhumed 1608 on account of damp. Found entire and supple. Fragrant oily liquid exudes from it, but face darkening. Officially certified incorrupt in 1639 and 1663; flesh still supple. *AA.SS.* May, Vol. VI, p. 318.
May 31. A		S. ANGELA MERICI (1540). Fragrant and flexible for thirty days; intact, incorrupt and sweet smelling in 1672. Still entire in 1867.[1] B. O'Reilly, *Life*, pp. 247 and 253.
June 4. B		S. FRANCIS CARACCIOLO (1608). Flexible and fragrant, blood flowed when incision made. Embalmed, partly preserved in 1628. Cencelli, *Compendio*, p. 203.
June 12. C		S. JOHN A S. FACUNDO (1479). No evidence of incorruption but extraordinary fragrance at translation in 1533. Valauri, *Vita*, p. 143.
June 21. C		S. ALOYSIUS GONZAGA (1591). Nothing left but skeleton in 1598; no phenomena. Cepari-Goldie, *Life*, p. 244.

[1] But see Postel I, p. 220, who says that some of the limbs are those of a skeleton.

July	5.	S. Anthony M. Zaccaria (1539). Body remained entire, though kept above ground until 1566; then buried in damp earth, only skeleton in 1664. Teppa, *Vita*, p. 177.
A		
July	18.	S. Camillus de Lellis (1614). Body soft and flexible until interment. At official recognition in 1625 still found fresh and supple like a living body. A copious exudation of fragrant liquid. Cecatelli, *Life*, I, p. 216.
A		
July	19.	S. Vincent of Paul (1660). When exhumed in 1712 body incorrupt and entire, though eyes and nose had suffered. In 1737 flesh reduced to fragrant dust. Maynard, *Vie*, IV, pp. 370-1.
A		
July	20.	S. Jerome Æmiliani (1537). Alleged fragrance in 1566, but no other phenomena. *AA.SS.* Feb., Vol. II, p. 218.
C		
July	31.	S. Ignatius Loyola (1556). Viscera removed and body roughly embalmed. Translation 1568; no phenomena. Bartoli-Michel, *Vie*, II, p. 210. *AA.SS.* July, Vol. VII, p. 610.
C		
Aug.	2.	S. Alphonsus Liguori (1787). Apparently no phenomena except " ruddy countenance " before burial. Exhumed *c*. 1817. Berthe-Castle, *Life*, II, pp. 615, 683.
C		
Aug.	7.	S. Cajetan (1547). Body seemingly thrown into a common pit with others. No phenomena known. *AA.SS.* Aug., Vol. II, p. 324; Maulde de la Clavière, *Vie*, p. 154.
C		
Aug.	21.	S. Jane Frances de Chantal (1641). Embalmed; body found entire in 1722. Heart preserved separately; strange phenomena. Bougaud, *Vie*, pp. 538, 566, 585.
B		
Aug.	27.	S. Joseph Calasanctius (1648). Viscera removed after death. Heart and tongue still remain fresh and supple as in life. Losada, *Vida*, p. 215.
B		
Aug.	30.	S. Rose of Lima (1617). Body found entire, fresh-coloured and fragrant, eighteen months after death. Still fragrant but wasted and desiccated in 1630. Feuillet, *Life*, pp. 156-7; *AA.SS.* Aug., Vol. V, pp. 987-9.
A		

Sept. 5. A		S. LAWRENCE JUSTINIAN (1455). His body remained above ground and exposed to the air for sixty-seven days. There had been no embalming process, but it continued entire, fragrant and ruddy. *AA.SS.* Jan., Vol. I, p. 563.
Sept. 18. C		S. JOSEPH OF COPERTINO (1663). Embalmed in deference to suggestion of the Pope. No phenomena. *AA.SS.* Sept., Vol. V, p. 1043; Laing, *Life*, p. 118.
Sept. 22. A		S. THOMAS OF VILLANOVA (1555). Quite incorrupt in 1582; resolved into dust, but very fragrant, at later translation. *AA.SS.* Sept., Vol. V, pp. 958 and 976.
Oct. 10. C		S. FRANCIS BORGIA (1572). No phenomena. Body not disturbed until 1617. Newly enshrined 1625. Suau, *Vie*, pp. 541-2.
Oct. 15. A		S. TERESA (1582). Minute description of its incorrupt state and marvellous fragrance by Ribera in 1588, confirmed by Gracian. Phenomena of heart. Ribera, *Life*, Bk. V, chs. i, ii, iii; Mir, *Vida*, II, pp. 815-7.
Oct. 19. A		S. PETER OF ALCANTARA (1562). Incorrupt and fragrant in 1566, still intensely fragrant in 1616, but flesh consumed. *AA.SS.* Oct., Vol. VIII, pp. 651, 699, 783.
Oct. 20. B		S. JOHN CANTIUS (1473). Said to have been found incorrupt in 1539, evidence not satisfactory. Fragrant dust in 1603. *AA.SS.* Oct., Vol. VIII, p. 1059.
Nov. 4. B		S. CHARLES BORROMEO (1584). Body (embalmed) to a large extent entire in 1606, despite damp and leaky coffin. Doctors consider preservation supernatural. Giussano, *Life*, II, p.. 555. Body in 1880 still in same condition. Sylvain, *Vie*, III, pp. 387-8, 395.
Nov. 10. A		S. ANDREW AVELLINO (1608). Body found incorrupt a year after death. Curious phenomenon of blood remaining liquid and uncongealed. Fernandez Moreno, *Vida*, pp. 112-4.
Nov. 13. A		S. DIDACUS (1463). The body, dug up four days after death, remained above ground for six months supple and fragrant. It was still entire in 1562. Rottigni, *Vita*, pp. 87-90.

Nov. 14. S. Josaphat (1623). Martyred and thrown into the
A   river on the Sunday, body fished up beautiful and
           fresh-coloured on the Friday. In 1637 remains still
           almost completely incorrupt. Official verification in
           1637, and again in 1674. Guépin, *Vie*, II, pp. 105,
           355 and 402.

Nov. 24. S. John of the Cross (1591). Body found incorrupt
A   and fragrant nine months after death; bled when
           fingers cut off. Lime added; still incorrupt in 1859.
           Muñoz y Garnica, *Vida*, pp. 229-300. D. Lewis, *Life*,
           p. 293.

Dec. 3. S. Francis Xavier (1552). Buried in the earth at
A   Sancian, lime heaped on top. In Feb. 1553 body
           disinterred and found quite fresh as if just dead.
           Brought to Malacca, reburied, then in Dec. transferred
           to Goa. Formal medical attestation (Nov. 18, 1556)
           that it had not been embalmed but remained fresh,
           supple, and with natural colour. Some parts of the
           body still supple in 1615, the greater portion desic-
           cated. Brou, *Vie*, II, pp. 370, 385, 404.

As I have indicated by the capital letters A, B and C, which stand against these entries, our data may be divided into three classes. In no less than twenty-two cases out of the whole total of forty-two there is good evidence that the body of the saint was found incorrupt after an interval of time which in normal individuals almost invariably sees the development either of an advanced stage of decomposition or of complete decay. Again, there are seven more cases marked B, in which we have indications of the occurrence of unusual phenomena of a somewhat similar character.

Finally, even in the C class, where little or nothing out of the common is recorded, the negative testimony we possess is not always conclusive. In the instance of St. John a S. Facundo, fifty-four years, in that of St. Paul of the Cross, seventy-seven years, and in that of St. Francis Borgia, forty-five years, seem to have elapsed before any examination was made of their remains. But a body may pass through many transformations in half a century, and it is at least conceivable that the flesh of these or other saints, after remaining entire and unblemished for a decade or two, may have quietly crumbled into dust before ever they were disinterred. We know at any rate that something of this sort must have happened in the case of St. Thomas of Villanova, St. Peter of Alcantara, and others, which remained intact for a certain period and were afterwards reduced to skeletons. In more modern times an interesting example is furnished by the translations of Blessed Julie Billiart, the foundress of the Soeurs de Notre Dame (de Namur). She had died on April 8, 1816. In the July of that year, Soeur Anastasie, Superioress at Namur, with two other Sisters, obtained access to the remains and saw that the body was quite perfect. In July, 1817, the body, by way of precaution in the political disturbances of the times, was secretly removed to an underground hiding-place, and was then again found incorrupt, save that the finger-tips were somewhat shrivelled. We are further told that "from the remains exuded a quantity of clear oil which stained the cloths in which they were wrapped." But by 1842, "owing to an inundation," the flesh had crumbled to dust and only the skeleton remained.

To return, however, to our list, it will be seen that in this selection of prominent saints, extending from 1419 to 1787, drawn from many different countries and interred under the most diversified conditions, more than half enjoyed for some years, and often for vastly longer periods, the privilege of incorruption. Of course, if these holy people had been canonized or added to the Roman Calendar because their bodies had been exempt from decay, there would be nothing very wonderful in the high proportion of examples exhibiting this phenomenon, but this, it is necessary to repeat, is emphatically not the case. Although the supernatural preservation of the body of a saint is, under very exceptional circumstances, sometimes admitted to rank as one of the miracles which have to be established by evidence before a decree of beatification can be pronounced, I do not think that this form of miracle has been had recourse to in the case of any one of the names included in our list.

On the other hand, even if it were admitted that all the phenomena that we witness in the preservation of the bodies of holy mystics are at tunes found to occur spontaneously and naturally without any presumption of the intervention of miracle—and I may confess that I for one should find it very hard to accept this view—still, the high proportion of such cases amongst those who have led lives of heroic virtue cannot possibly be explained as the result of mere coincidence. No doubt we all have heard or read many stories concerning the discovery of human remains in an incorrupt state when coffins in vaults have accidentally been broken open or new graves have been dug. But the proportion of such instances to the thousands of skeletons which under certain systems of burial are constantly being cleared away from cemeteries to make room for other occupants, is extraordinarily small. In the city of Mexico and in some parts of the south of Europe, where the soil is unsuited to interment, a corpse after death is simply thrust into a horizontal cell in a solid mass of masonry and the end of the cell sealed up. Apart from those who pay for special privileges, the cell after a term of years is emptied of its contents and receives another tenant. In this way hundreds of receptacles are examined and cleared every year. Nevertheless, even so, the discovery of a fairly perfect body in a mummified condition is a rare event, and those that are occasionally met with are generally hideous objects with distorted features owing to the unequal contraction of the tissues. In the Museum of the City of Mexico one or two favourable specimens of desiccated human corpses brought to light in this way used to be exhibited in glass cases—evidently such objects were deemed not too common—and Sir H. Rider Haggard was hoaxed into the belief, which he subsequently published to the world in his novel *Montezuma's Daughter*, that these gruesome relics were the bodies of walled-up nuns.

The classical word Larva, which means both a wraith and a mask, might seem, not inaptly, to describe a somewhat rare form of incorruption which, though historically well-attested, hardly seems to belong to the phenomena of mysticism. Still, an illustration which has very kindly been sent to me is too interesting and curious to be passed over in silence.

My informant was Major Ernest Anne, of Burghwallis Hall, Doncaster, but formerly of Northumberland. When he was a young man, he once visited a friend who was a medical student in Newcastle, and was taken by him to see the dissecting-room, where various gruesome fragments of humanity were very much in evidence. On his return home, he chanced to give an account of his sensations, visual and olfactory, before a mixed company and in the hearing of one Thomas Turner, an outdoor servant on the family estate at Hesleyside; and when someone present raised a question as to the time which elapsed before a body committed to the earth was rendered unrecognizable by decay, old Turner chipped in with an experience of his early youth. He told them that as a boy he had lived at Haydon Bridge, and that there he, with other lads, had got some schooling from an old fellow who combined the functions of parish clerk, sexton and schoolmaster.

To quote verbatim from Turner's story as reported by Major Anne:

INCORRUPTION

It was the sexton's custom when he had to dig a grave to take half a dozen of us, his bigger scholars, to help him. In short, we did the digging, while he sat down, smoked his pipe, and generally directed operations. On this occasion the site for the new grave had been fixed upon in a remote part of the old churchyard where there was no vestige of any previous burial. Our schoolmaster showed us where to begin digging and removed a few of the top sods himself, just to set us going, and then we boys fell to with a will. Well! we had got down to maybe three feet, or thereabouts, when presently one of our picks struck wood, and we found that we were on top of an old coffin. Either from curiosity, or to see if it were not better to begin digging another grave in a different place, our schoolmaster jumped up, and ordering us out of the hole which we had already dug, took on the work of excavation himself. He removed the soil carefully from what was apparently the lid of a very, very old coffin, and when he had got this clear he set about prising the lid off with his pickaxe. There was little need of this, though, for after a heave or two the whole lid broke up into pieces. These the schoolmaster carefully removed and we then saw that there was a sheet of fine linen covering the remains, which lay in what was left of the old coffin. This he pulled away, and I shall never forget what we all looked upon then, since, apart from what I am telling you, it was the first time I had ever seen a corpse. Inside the coffin at our feet lay the body of a young lass of about my own age—and, would you believe it, Sir, she looked as if she had just fallen asleep. Her eyes were closed, and both her face, which was very beautiful, even in death, and her hands, which were crossed over her breast, were as if they were moulded of pure wax. Her hair was silky and golden, and flashed in the morning sunlight. Our schoolmaster was dumbfounded and told us that in all his long years of work in the graveyard he had never come across such an experience before. After considering a bit he replaced the cloth over the dead girl and laid some sacking over that. He bade us go home to our dinners, and on no account to go near the grave until he returned with the Rector, whom he then set off to fetch. The Parson happened, however, on that day to be away from home and did not return until late in e afternoon. Meanwhile, we had started upon and finished another grave in a different part of the churchyard. We none of us went near that we had begun upon in the morning. I think we were too awed after what we had seen—at least I know that I was. When the Rector and his wife at last arrived, we then accompanied them in a body to the graveside. The sexton removed the sacking; but of the beautiful girl whom we had gazed upon only a few hours before, there now only remained a skeleton. The face, the hands, the hair, aye, the very linen itself, everything, everything, had disappeared, and left no more than a disordered heap of what one calls dust.

Major Anne's friends knew him to possess an exceptionally retentive memory, and there can be no reason to doubt the substantial accuracy of the story thus told. Though more dramatic in its setting than some other similar narratives, there are a good many parallels which have been recorded elsewhere. We may mention, for example, a case referred to by J. C. Scholes in his *History of Bolton* (p. 157), where a body, exhumed apparently entire, fell to dust almost immediately on exposure to the air.

Some famous examples, alleged to belong to classical times, may be found recorded by the antiquaries of the Renaissance. One of them was identified, no doubt erroneously, with the body of Cicero's daughter Tulliola. It is to be noted, however, that in the case of many of the saints mentioned in the list that is given above, the bodies, even after protracted exposure, are stated to have remained for several years, not mummified, but still soft and flexible. The manner of preservation was, therefore, in some way different from that of the example just described.

In the case of ordinary interments in graveyards, the discovery of bodies in a good state of preservation is even more uncommon. Naturally it happens as a general rule that the bodies are never examined or disturbed, but now and then occasions arise when exhumations take place on a considerable scale. A very instructive example of this occurred in Paris in the year 1840. During the revolution of the last days of July 1830, barricades had been thrown up all over the city. There had been a good deal of fighting and many killed, some of them, women, children and noncombatants. The weather was hot and the barricades in many cases rendered the conveyance of bodies to any distance an impossibility. It therefore became necessary to bury the corpses hastily in any available spot near at hand, and this was generally carried out by the private enterprise of individual citizens. Ten years later some sort of panic occurred over the insanitary conditions resulting from these interments. The municipality intervened, and it was decided to exhume and to re-bury elsewhere all the bodies which had been disposed of in this irregular way. After the operation had been successfully carried out, a report was duly published by the medical officers who had directed the proceedings. In all 574 bodies were disinterred. They had been committed to the earth in 15 distinct localities, all over the city, and under the most widely different conditions. Rather more than a hundred had been buried in coffins, a considerable number had been rolled up in *serpilieres* (rough coverings of canvas), but the great majority had been buried as they had fallen, without any wrapping or protection. On the other hand, in many of the pits or trenches, where the corpses had been laid in rows, considerable quantities of lime had been heaped on top of them. Further, the soil to which they were committed differed widely in character.

In some cases it was sandy, in others clayey, and in others again, as in the Marche des Innocents, it seems to have been supersaturated with the products of the decomposition of other corpses which had been buried there for centuries back. It is impossible to go into details, but a tolerably full account may be found in the article published in 1843 by M. H. Gaultier de Chaubry, one of the medical officers in charge of the exhumation. The important fact which stands out is that of these 574 corpses, disinterred ten years after burial, not one was found in a state which could in any sense be called incorrupt. In the great majority of cases nothing remained but bones completely detached from each other. In a certain group of seven, buried in the lowest stratum of all, under a number of others, the features might still be recognized, but this was obviously due to the fact of the formation of considerable quantities of adipocere, a process probably helped by the decomposition of the bodies lying about them. I gather, however, that even these were rather unpleasant objects, and that putrefaction, though retarded on account of the saponification of the tissues, was unmistakably going on. They could hardly have been mistaken for incorrupt bodies. A fuller description, however, of the appearances presented by human remains converted into adipocere under conditions specially favouring its development is furnished by M. Thouret in his Rapport on the exhumations carried out on a vast scale at Paris in 1785, when the cemetery of the Church of the Holy Innocents, now the Marche des Innocents, was at last cleared of the bodies there interred, the accumulation of many centuries. Owing to the dampness of the soil and its complete saturation with the products of decomposition, almost every corpse buried in certain positions had been converted into adipocere. The interior of the coffins and the linen cloths with which the dead had been covered were perfectly preserved.

The bodies themselves, having lost nothing of their bulk, and appearing to be wrapped in their shrouds, like so many Larvae, had, to all seeming, suffered no decay. On tearing apart the grave-clothes which enveloped them, the only change one noticed consisted in this, that they had been converted into a flabby mass or substance (*une masse ou matiere mollasse*) the whiteness of which stood out the more clearly in contrast to the blackness of the soil in which they lay.

M. Thouret goes on to tell us that "these remarkable mummies preserve all the lines of the face with its features and expression. The eyes are unimpaired, and also the plumpness of the cheeks, together with the hair, eyelashes and eyebrows." Some of the most perfect had been there for five years or more. How far the remains could have been mistaken for bodies miraculously protected from corruption, it is not easy to decide from his description, but it seems certain that although the *fossoyeurs* of this particular cemetery were quite familiar with this extraordinary transformation of the fleshy parts into what they called *gras de cadavre*, still it was on this occasion that the existence of such a condition was scientifically recognized for the first time. Further, the name adipocere (from adeps fat, and cera wax) was then invented to describe it, and its true nature as an impure ammoniacal soap was at least suspected. In Taylor's *Medical Jurisprudence* adipocere is described as having an offensive odour, but this does not seem to be invariably the case. Many years ago a medical friend gave me three or four pounds weight of the substance taken from the trunk of a human cadaver, then under dissection, and I kept it in my room for some days in an ordinary brown-paper parcel without its making itself unpleasantly perceptible. It may therefore be that in some of the cases which are described by our hagiographical writers as instances of immunity from decomposition we have really to do with the phenomenon of saponification where their imperfect scientific knowledge did not enable them to recognize. A curious illustration of such a possibility seems to have occurred at the exhumation of the body of the Blessed Marie de Sainte Euphrasie Pelletier, the foundress of the Good Shepherd Nuns.

She died in April 1868, and her body, which had been enclosed in a leaden coffin, was exhumed in June 1903, thirty-five years afterwards. Dr. Herbert, one of the scientific experts present on the occasion, deposes that "the features could be recognized by those who had seen the Venerable Mother before her demise. The mouth was slightly open, the eyes shut, the eyelashes intact, the skin like that of a mummy," He further adds that, without entirely unclothing the body, "we were able to ascertain that the chest, the abdomen, the thighs and the legs, were covered with a skin like that of a mummy, under which was a mass of *gras de cadavre*, resulting from the saponification of the tissues underneath." The second expert, Dr. Thibault, remarks:

> I may say that, in general, the skin, becomes mummy-like, hard to the touch, and resonant when struck by a metal instrument, covers a substance spread over all the body. This substance is vulgarly called *gras de cadavre*, it covers the bones. In taking a fragment of linen off the feet, I detached two toes, which proves that at least in that part of the body the bones are not adherent. I think that probably the same is true of the other members. As I am called upon to indicate the general cause of the state in which the remains were found, I declare that in coffins hermetically closed the decomposition may be arrested, and this seems to me to have been the case in the present instance. It is to be feared that the opening of the coffin may bring on a more complete putrefaction.

Evidently the author of this statement did not believe that there was anything in the case which called for a supernatural explanation. None the less, we can hardly doubt that if the phenomenon had been observed in the Middle Ages, or even in the seventeenth century, it would have been accounted miraculous, at any rate, by less well-instructed enthusiasts. I do not dispute that some, possibly several, of the eases recorded in our census may be susceptible of the same explanation. But the difficulty still remains; Why is it that such an enormous proportion of the bodies of those who die in the odour of sanctity should be preserved from decay? Very few of them were enclosed in lead coffins hermetically sealed. Some of them had quicklime thrown on them, but the quicklime did not in a single case prevent the bodies of those who fell in the Revolution of July 1830, from being converted into skeletons.

Some also were buried in damp places, where adipocere may more easily form. But saponification is, after all, of very unusual occurrence, apart from bodies drowned and long submerged, or those thrown among heaps of others. Dr. Orfila, who perhaps paid more attention experimentally to this subject than any scientist has done before or since his time, gives a minute description of thirty-one bodies exhumed by him and expressly selected on account of the varying conditions under which they were interred. In every one of these cases decomposition, in its various stages, had been actively at work. Lastly, as I hope to show later, there are quite a number of instances of saintly persons whose incorrupt remains, when exhumed, present features entirely different from those recorded in cases of saponification or in mummies naturally desiccated.

3

The very large proportion of cases in which the bodies of saintly persons are preserved from decay may, I submit, fairly be urged as an argument of some weight against the view which would attribute this phenomenon entirely to natural causes. If it be contended that the abstemiousness with regard to food and drink characteristic of all such ascetics may profoundly modify the conditions of normal metabolism and tend to eliminate certain classes of microbes which are most active in the process of putrefaction, we may reply that the very poor are of dire necessity abstemious, while no observations point in their case to any similar immunity. Moreover, it ought to follow that when famine reigns in the land the corpses of its victims should be proof against the agents of corruption, but no recorded experience seems to bear this out, rather the contrary. I am inclined, therefore, to think that the argument must stand until definite evidence can be brought which would provide an explanation of the anomaly.

Moreover, as previously suggested, there are certain specific cases which seem to offer problems of peculiar difficulty to those who reject all intervention of the supernatural in this matter. Let me take, for example, the preservation of the body of Blessed Maria Anna (Ladroni) of Jesus, a tertiary of the Order of Our Lady of Ransom, born in 1565 Madrid, in which city she also died, a.d. 1624. Some little time after her decease, Cardinal Treso, Bishop of Malaga and President of Castile, who had known her well during life, drew up a deposition in writing in view of the impending process of her beatification. After bearing testimony to her virtues, and speaking of the miraculous cures attributed to her intercession, the Cardinal states that he was himself present at the first exhumation of her remains; whereat

> I saw [he says], and was greatly astonished to see, a body some years dead, which had never been opened or had any of the viscera removed or been embalmed in any way, so completely preserved that neither

in the abdomen nor in the face was there any trace of decay, except a spot on the lip, though this was something by which she had been marked in much the same way during life.

In 1731, a hundred and seven years after the death of the Servant of God, a much more thorough and official inspection of the body took place at the instance of the ecclesiastical authorities interested in the cause of her beatification. The remains were sound soft, supple, flexible and elastic to the touch, and emitting a remarkable perfume; while "from the whole body there exuded a certain oily fluid, like some kind of fragrant balsam, which moistened both the internal organs and the surface of the skin, and with which the clothing was also saturated." As this investigation took place in Madrid, there was no difficulty in bringing together a number of medical experts. To quote again from the Life which was published on the occasion of the beatification, and was based upon the sworn depositions of witnesses and other official documents:

> Not less than eleven professors of medicine and surgery, all of them among the first and most famous in the city and court of Madrid, took part in the proceedings and made deposition as witnesses. They took out their instruments and some made long and deep incisions in the fleshy parts, others laid open the breast, others scrutinized the cavities thus exposed to view, others explored any orifice by which it might have been possible to introduce preservatives against putrefaction. In fact, their united efforts resulted in what was not merely a rigorous examination but an absolute dissection of this innocent body. If these proceedings were irregular, irreverent and unwarranted, they were yet so useful in establishing the reality of the miracle that we cannot find it in our heart to condemn them.

After completing their investigations the doctors declared that—

> The interior organs, the viscera and the fleshy tissues were all of them entire, sound, moist and resilient. The fluid which was observed to exude from the body impregnated all the interior and all the substance of the flesh. The deeper the incisions which were made, the sweeter was the fragrance which was emitted from them, so much so that one of the surgeons would not for several days afterwards wash the hand with which he had manipulated the viscera for fear of losing the

supernatural perfume which it had thus acquired. During the whole of this time the odour remained quite perceptible both to himself and to all who came near him.

Upon this evidence the wonderful preservation of the body of Maria Anna was accepted as a miracle by the Congregation of Rites, despite the fact that thirty-five years later, long before the decree of beatification was actually issued, a third inspection of the remains revealed the fact that by this time the body was no longer flexible or soft to the touch. The tissues had hardened and wasted, though they were by no means reduced to dust.

One thing seems to be abundantly clear from the account just quoted—viz., that if the body of Blessed Maria Anna was preserved from corruption, this was not due either to any process of natural saponification or to its having dried up into a mummy. On the one hand it is incredible that experienced surgeons, after cutting into the flesh and thoroughly examining the viscera, should describe the various tissues as intact and sound if they had really found them converted into a mass of adipocere. On the other hand, they insist with much emphasis not only upon the fact that the body, a hundred years after death, was elastic and perfectly flexible, but that other corpses which had been buried in the same vault had all been subject to the common law of decay. Over and above this, there remains the phenomenon, by this time very familiar to us, of the inexplicable fragrance given forth, and, last but not least, the puzzling circumstance of the exudation of an oily liquid. As to this last feature something will have to be said later on.

The next example I propose to take is of a somewhat different character, the case of the Jesuit martyr, St. Andrew Bobola.

Father Bobola, born of a noble Polish family, at the time of his death in 1657, was sixty-seven years of age. For many years he had been combating by his preaching the propaganda of the Russian schismatics among his Ruthenian countrymen until he came to be known as the Apostle of Pinsk. His success had drawn down upon himself the special hatred of his religious opponents. During the course of an inroad of the Cossacks in 1657, Father Bobola fell into their hands. When he refused to conform to the Russian schism he was most cruelly tortured, being scourged and outraged in ways that cannot here be described. He was partially flayed alive, one hand was almost completely hacked off, splinters of wood were driven in under his nails, his tongue was torn out by the roots, and his face so disfigured with heavy blows that it hardly retained the semblance of humanity. "He bled," said an eyewitness, "like an ox in the slaughter-house." It was only after hours of torment, when the butchers had glutted their rage and when no signs of life remained but a convulsive twitching of the muscles, that the victim was finally despatched by a sword blow to the throat. After throwing the body upon a dung-heap, the Cossacks departed, leaving the Catholics free to gather up the mutilated remains, which were eventually conveyed to Pinsk and hastily interred in the vault beneath the Jesuit church in that town. Forty-four years later the Rector of the Jesuit College of was led by a vision or dream, which he deemed supernatural, to make search for the body of the martyred aposde. It was found eventually, to all appearance in exactly the same state in which it had been committed to the tomb. Apart from the mutilations of the martyrdom it was entire and quite incorrupt; the joints were flexible, the flesh in the less injured parts was resilient to the touch, while the blood with which it was still covered in many places looked as if it was freshly congealed. Other more or less formal inspections of the body took place during the next twenty years, but it was not until 1730 that the final and official examination was carried out under sanction of the Apostolic See. Six ecclesiastics and five medical experts subjected the remains to a close and prolonged scrutiny, and their depositions are still preserved to us. They agreed in declaring that the body, except for the wounds inflicted by the murderers, was entire, that the flesh was soft and flexible, and that its preservation could not be attributed to any natural cause. Although we are not told that the body was cut into, still its mutilated condition and the open wound in the throat would surely have betrayed the presence of adipocere, and this strange condition could hardly have failed to elicit some comment if any great mass of that substance had replaced the muscles and internal organs. Upon this evidence the case was debated at length, both in 1739 and in 1830, by successive Promoters of the Faith and Postulators of the cause, and in 1835 this preservation of the body was formally accepted by the Congregation of Rites as one of the miracles required for the beatification. I ought not to omit to state that more than one of the witnesses deposed that the other bodies buried in the same vault with that of Blessed Andrew Bobola were none of them preserved from corruption.

Among the many cases which might be quoted of quite exceptional immunity from the law of dust to dust, it is difficult to make a selection, but I will choose for my third example a case from a convent in the

Netherlands, chiefly because the nun so privileged was an English woman and a member of an English community. The Teresian Carmelites, now long domiciled at Lanherne, in Cornwall, were for nearly two centuries before the French Revolution established at Antwerp. There, in the year 1714, died the saintly Mother Prioress Mary Xaveria, by birth Catherine Burton, who, several years before her death, announced, apparently through some supernormal knowledge she possessed, that in the subterranean burial-place of the Religious there was one incorrupt body. This statement was accidentally verified a year or two later, when it became necessary to enlarge the crypt devoted to this purpose. Eleven or twelve receptacles had to be opened, and the remains were found either quite reduced to skeletons or in process of rapid decay, but one other, which was that of a nun who had died in great repute of sanctity, offered a very different spectacle. The tomb was that of Mother Mary Margaret of the Angels (Margaret Wake), who had been buried in 1678, thirty-eight years before. Although, as we are told, the vault was exceedingly damp and confined, this body was entire, in spite of the fact that the habit in which it was vested was rotten and saturated with moisture. The Bishop of Antwerp was informed of the occurrence, and came himself to examine into the facts, accompanied by three medical men. He insisted on viewing the other remains and satisfied himself that all were decayed. Afterwards he had the incorrupt body removed to a place where it could be more conveniently examined, and there, as the almost contemporary account informs us,—

> He ordered the surgeon to make an incision in the pit of the stomach through which they discovered the diaphragm perfectly sound. The prelate put his hand into the wound that was made and perceived a balsamic smell proceeding from the body, which his fingers retained two or three days after, though he washed them several times.

After an interval of ten days the same eminent dignitary ordered a second and more formal investigation to be made by four physicians and surgeons, of which we are told:

> They examined it again narrowly, opened the diaphragm, by which they found the heart, liver, lungs, and all the internal parts perfectly entire, with all the muscles, etc. They again declared that no corruption had ever entered that body, and that it must e supernatural, giving this on attestation in writing, with their own hands that it was beyond the

course of nature, leaving it to the divines to determine whether it was to be termed miraculous.

The narrator, Father Thomas Hunter, S.J., who was the confessor of the community, and undoubtedly himself an eye-witness, informs us further:

> This holy body appears of a brownish complexion, but full of flesh, which like a living body yields to any impression made upon it, and rises again of itself when it is pressed, the joints flexible. You find a little moisture when you touch the flesh, but this is not so sensible as when the grave was first opened, and this very frequently breathes out an odoriferous balsamic smell, which is not only perceptible to those about the body, but has sometimes filled the whole room. I mentioned before that it had been observed that blood flowed out of the grave after the body had been deposited in it. This happened about six weeks after her death, and when her body was found incorrupt, they all took notice that both the sides and lid of the coffin seemed all to be tinged with blood.

Here again we have a case in which, assuming (what I think we have no reason to doubt) that the account of the doctors' examination of the viscera is reliable, there can be no suggestion that the remarkable integrity of the remains was due to saponification.

For a fourth illustration it will be sufficient to refer to a medical report written in 1868 by Dr. Pietro Dettori at the time of the third exhumation of the remains of Blessed Anna Maria Taigi, a married woman, whose beatification took place in 1920. The account is too long to quote entire, but I translate the more significant passages. Anna Maria had died in Rome in 1837, at the age of sixty-eight, and she had consequently been buried for thirty-one years. Dr. Dettori begins by remarking that the body was quite perfect and that from the appearance of the corpse one would have said that death had taken place only two or three days before.

> The features are slightly bronzed, but only by the action of the light and the air. She looks about seventy, the head is a little bent back, the face is rather full, and the hair, excellently preserved, is white. In the general expression of the face may clearly be read the patience, resignation, gentleness, kindness, and goodness with which the Servant of God was so singularly endowed during her life.

The Doctor then goes on to say that on a more detailed examination he found the skin of the face dry and hard, but not shrivelled in any way. The hands were blackened and the skin of them dry.

There was a certain amount of flexibility about the shoulder and arm joints, but this freedom of movement could in no way be compared to that of the arm of a living person. Altogether the witness, so far, though impressed, was not prepared to draw any decisive conclusions from what he had seen. On being invited, however, to make an inspection of the lower limbs and trunk, he found more solid reason for expressing astonishment.

> I examined first the feet and the legs and I found them intact as was the case with the rest of the body, but there were also other phenomena which had not been apparent in the arms or the face.
>
> On the inner side of each leg there was a pronounced exudation, of a lymphatic humour, somewhat viscous, clear-coloured and with a peculiar odour. This liquid had saturated the stockings where it had come in contact with them. The legs yielded to the pressure of the finger and the muscles still possessed a consistence which was really wonderful in view of the fact that death had taken place more than thirty years before. But what astonished me more than all was the inspection of the abdomen. The skin in front was of a deep red colour and much distended. The muscles beneath it retained an extraordinary elasticity, in virtue of which, after yielding to the pressure of the finger, they recovered their former position immediately the pressure was removed, without any depression being left, all of which proves that the tissues within are in no state of putrefaction but are in their normal condition. The skin of the posterior face of the abdomen retains its natural whiteness. It is flabby and somewhat shrivelled, but it is soft and discharges a viscous humour which has no offensive smell.

Even if these appearances were consistent with extensive saponification of the trunk and viscera—a point upon which I can offer no opinion—no explanation is forthcoming why this extremely rare condition should develop in just those cases where a reputation for extraordinary sanctity has been established on quite other grounds. Just as in the instances previously referred to of Bernadette Soubirous the Curé d'Ars, and Mother Barat, so it is certain that Anna Maria Taigi, a humble uneducated woman of the servant class, was almost universally honoured as a saint long before her body was exhumed for the first time in 1855. Preparations for the cause of her beatification had already been made before that date, and a *Life of the Servant of God* had been published in 1849 by Mgr. Luquet, Bishop of Hesebon, which had been widely circulated in thousands of copies, not only in French, but also in Italian. Even in her lifetime, poor, humble and untaught as she was, Anna Maria had been consulted and venerated by some of the highest ecclesiastical dignitaries of Rome.

One would be tempted to go on quoting still further illustrations of the same phenomenon, for there are literally scores of other cases to which I have not yet made any sort of allusion, but it is plain that this catalogue cannot be indefinitely extended. One would also like to recall the details of some ancient examples, for instance, of the wonderful preservation of St. Cuthbert's body, which, though he died in the year 687, so exactly coincides in every feature with the modern evidence which I have been reproducing. The Venerable Bede, who had conversed with many eye-witnesses, records how, eleven years after Cuthbert's death, "on opening the sepulchre they found the whole body as entire as if he were yet living and more like one in a sound sleep (for the joints of the limbs were flexible) than one who was dead," while other trustworthy chroniclers, four centuries later, minutely describe the continuance of the same conditions, despite all the accidents of travel and exposure to air to which the shrine had been subjected during the intervening years. They speak of the flexibility of the joints, the solidity of the sinews (nervi), and the fragrance which pervaded all; or, to quote in particular the words of Reginald of Durham, "all his limbs are solid, flexible and whole, and as become a perfect man, folding with sinews, movable with veins full of blood, sweet in the softness of flesh, such as give the appearance of one living in the flesh, rather than dead in the body." There is, no doubt, some exaggeration in the phrasing, but the words beyond question faithfully reproduce the general impression which the onlookers carried away.

There is, however, one feature which has met us in several of the cases dealt with in these pages on Incorruption and which requires a word of notice. Space unfortunately fails me to discuss it with the thoroughness its importance seems to require, but it cannot be passed over altogether in silence. The phenomenon I refer to is that of the exuding of an oily fluid, which is mentioned for example in connection with the body of Maria Anna of Jesus, of Anna Maria Taigi, and of many others already canonized. Among the Greeks, in the early Middle Ages, before the Schism of the Eastern Church, the saints of whose remains this wonder was recorded, were known as unguent spouters.

One early and relatively famous Western example is that of St. Walburga, an Englishwoman by birth, who joined her brother, St. Winibald, when he was preaching the Gospel in Germany.

She became Abbess of Heidenheim, where she died in 779. Although there is no record of her body having been preserved entire, still from her bones, translated to Eichstadt, an oily fluid has trickled for more than a thousand years, and the phenomenon continues to this day. An interesting modern example of the same kind is furnished by the relics of St. Gerard Majella, C.SS.R., who died in 1756. We read that a century after this date:

> The ecclesiastical authorities having ordered that all the relics of the servant of God should be officially examined, Gerard's tomb was opened for the first time on June 26th, 1856. It was then noticed that a mysterious oil oozed forth in such abundance from the brain and bones as to fill up more than one basin. . . .. On Oct. 11th the body of the Saint was again examined in the presence of two doctors. They found the bones more or less damp, but as this could be attributed to the humidity of the soil, it attracted but little attention. They were dried with all due care, and then placed in a chest lined with white silk. Four hours later the chest having been opened, it was discovered that a kind of white oil, shedding a sweet fragrance, was coming forth anew from the holy relics, and resting like drops of dew upon the silk lining. After a short examination the physicians drew up an official report of this occurrence, which in their opinion was beyond the laws of nature.

More commonly, however, this oily fluid does not distil from the skeleton or relics, but from bodies which have been preserved from decay. It was so, for example, in the case of St. Mary Magdalen de' Pazzi and in that of St. Camillus de Lellis. Thus the body of St. Camillus was exhumed in 1625, ten years after his death. Whereupon, as his biographer reports:

> It was found quite fresh and perfect, like a living body, and a surgeon who was there felt moved to make an incision into the side, from which there came forth a great quantity of liquid with a most fragrant smell. This did not cease to flow for six days, during which the remains were exposed to the veneration of the faithful.

A very well-attested English example of the same phenomenon is that connected with the translation of the body of St. Hugh of Lincoln. A contemporary account tells us that when the cover of the marble tomb was removed—

> The body of the holy prelate, although it had been deposited there for well nigh eighty years, was found incorrupt and almost unchanged. As soon as the Archbishop laid his hand on the glorious head of the Saint, it separated from the shoulders, leaving the neck fresh and red just as if death had been recent. ... In the tomb where the body had rested there was found a great quantity of pure oil.... On the following morning in the course of the ceremony it happened that the Bishop of Lincoln took up the head of St. Hugh and held it for a while reverently before him. As he did this an abundance of the same pure oil flowed from the jaw over the Bishop's hands, and this notwithstanding that the venerable head had been carefully washed a few hours before and had been found quite dry in the morning. The oil only ceased to flow when the Bishop had placed his precious burden upon the silver dish upon which this relic was to be borne in procession.

Of both St. William of York and St. John of Beverley a similar prodigy is recorded, and only a little time before the date of the translation of St. Hugh it was stated that oil had begun to exude from the tomb of the famous Robert Grosseteste, also Bishop of Lincoln, whom many people of that age called "Saint " Robert, and to whom many miracles were ascribed.

Perhaps the most curious instance of this kind of phenomena, if we could only trust the evidence, is that of the body of Mère Marie Marguerite des Anges (Van Valckenissen), of whom Huysmans has written at length in *La Cathedrale*. We are told that she prayed that she might literally be burnt away as a sacrifice before the Blessed Sacrament, and that after her death oil exuded from her body for many years, which was regularly burnt in the sanctuary lamp of the convent. "On this point," says Huysmans, "there is abundant authentic evidence. More or less minute inquiries were made and the reports of medical experts are so precise that we can follow from day to day the state of the corpse until it had turned to oil and could be preserved in phials, from which a spoonful was poured every morning into the lamp." The story, then, is apparently not a pure legend, but unfortunately I have not been able to obtain access to the rather scarce Life in which this curious circumstance is narrated. But, however we may explain the phenomenon or fail to explain it, the exudation of some sort of viscous oily fluid from many incorrupt bodies seems to be a fact beyond dispute, and also a fact which has never been registered by medical science.

CHAPTER XI
THE ABSENCE OF CADAVERIC RIGIDITY

I had at one time thought that the first case in which the absence of *rigor mortis* had been noted was that of St. Francis of Assisi, but I have since come upon an earlier example. In the Life of St. Raynerius of Pisa written by a contemporary, and seemingly trustworthy, it is recorded that "his limbs after death showed no sign of any stiffening. They remained, on the contrary, moist and bedewed with perspiration, and they were as flexible as those of any living man." (*AA.SS.* Jun., Vol. iv, p. 370). It would seem that something out of the common must have been observed to prompt such a statement. This was in 1160.

Rather more than half a century later, we have the death (1226) of St. Francis. His brethren who gathered round to venerate his holy remains gazed with awe at the stigmata, and Brother Elias, who succeeded him as head of the Order, notified the sad tidings to all the Provinces. "From the beginning of ages," he wrote, Äúthere has not been heard so great a wonder, save only in the Son of God, who is Christ our God. For a long while before his death, our Father and Brother appeared crucified, bearing in his body the five wounds which are verily the stigmata of Christ." He describes them minutely, and then goes on to recount how during his last days his body was bent, he was unable to raise his head, and his limbs "were rigid as are wont to be the limbs of a dead man.

But after his death, his countenance was most beautiful, gleaming with a wondrous brightness and making glad them that saw it; and the limbs which before were rigid had been made exceeding supple, allowing them to be turned hither and thither according to his position like the limbs of a tender boy." Thomas of Celano, officially deputed to write the first Life of the saint, similarly states within three years of his death: "His sinews were not contracted as those of the dead are wont to be, his skin was not hardened, his limbs were not stiffened, but turned this way and that as they were placed." The scientists of the last century scoffed at the stigmata as a fairy tale, but the reality of these wounds is now practically undisputed. If we can trust our witnesses for this, which was in their eyes the greater marvel, there seems good reason to believe them accurate in what they tell us concerning the flexibility of the limbs.

But of course the real strength of the case, as with stigmata, lies in the multitude of later examples. I am sure I am not exaggerating when I say that I could give references to fifty cases of those in repute of sanctity in whose dead bodies the same complete absence of *rigor mortis* was observed. Moreover, in reading hagiographical records I am constantly coming across fresh examples. They occur in every subsequent century and in our own times. The question whether the limbs of a corpse are stiff or flexible does not require the testimony of a medical expert. This is a matter which even a child can observe for himself. But in many cases there is the evidence of doctors, who in the seventeenth and eighteenth centuries often declared the marvel to be inexplicable, and therefore in their eyes miraculous. A remarkable case of early date is that of Bl. Peter of Luxembourg, a youth of royal blood, who died (in 1387) at the age of eighteen, already created a Cardinal. We happen to have in his case the evidence taken on oath within three years of his death for the process of beatification. Witness after witness declared that the limbs could be moved in any direction, that the body was cold, that he was kept above ground for four days in the heat of summer at Avignon, that the countenance remained beautiful like that of a youth sleeping, and that there was no sign of corruption or rigidity.

Among modern instances I may call attention, in the first place, to the case of Sister Maria della Passione, a nun of Southern Italy, who died in 1912 at the age of forty-six, and who has already been mentioned more than once in the course of this book. It was about 7.40 in the morning of Saturday, July the 27th, that she breathed her last, and somewhat later in the day her remains were conveyed in a shallow, open coffin to the convent chapel, where they were visited by crowds of devout persons anxious to show their veneration for the deceased. Her biographer tells us:

> As the body of Sister Maria della Passione had remained perfectly flexible, as though it had been that of a living person, the pious visitors, men as well as women, took her hands, raised them up and kissed them with affection and veneration. Invalids who were suffering from some bodily infirmity pressed the hands to their reast or their throat, or to the place where they felt pain, exclaiming: " How beautiful she is! She looks like an angel. She is truly a vessel of election."

There can be no need to insist upon the fact that it would be impossible to move the hands of a normal corpse in this way eight or nine hours after death. Hearing that it had been determined to leave the body above ground for three days, the doctor came to lodge an indignant protest, but on examining the condition of things for himself he withdrew all opposition.

Notwithstanding the fact [her biographer continues] that it was the hottest season of the year (i.e., July 27, 28 and 29), that the scene was in Southern Italy, in a tiny church, and with a great concourse of people, the body remained throughout perfectly flexible, and although it was pulled about by the constant handling of those who stood close to it, to the astonishment of all, it remained without a trace of corruption and without giving off the least unpleasant odour; on the contrary it was remarked that the face became more and more beautiful and the features more clear-cut (*profilato*).

This continued to the end, and, indeed, it seems that the holy nun herself had predicted it. It may fairly be counted a point in favour of the truthfulness of this record that in this case there is no mention of any preternatural fragrance. Of the two phenomena the odour of sanctity seems to be of more common occurrence than the absence of rigor, perhaps because the former forces itself upon the attention of all present, while the latter may easily pass unperceived. If the whole story were merely the fabrication of an unscrupulous panegyrist, there would be no reason why he should not also claim for his heroine the privilege of perfumed emanations, which, as we shall see, play so prominent a part in many similar descriptions of older date. But before turning to any of these we may notice one or two other examples of cadaveric flexibility which apparently were unaccompanied by any perceptible fragrance.

Mother Margaret Hallahan, Foundress of the English Dominican Congregation of St. Catherine of Siena, died at Stone a few minutes after midnight on the morning of Monday, May 11, 1868.

The body was conveyed to the chapter-room early in the morning. Her devoted friend, biographer and successor in office, Mother Francis Raphael (Drane), writes of this as follows:

> During Monday and Tuesday, the body remained in the chapter room; every member remained flexible, and the countenance lost all appearance of suffering or emaciation, and assumed a beauty which rather increased than diminished as the hours went by. The expression was that of extraordinary majesty and strength, but mingled with childlike sweetness and serenity.

The body was transferred to the church on the Tuesday evening, and was not removed until the time of interment after the Solemn Requiem on Thursday. The people of the vicinity pressed up to look upon the remains of the holy nun and to touch them with their pictures and rosaries. "The features," says Mother Drane, remained unchanged in their singular beauty and the hands were still perfectly flexible." It may fairly be assumed that if the wnter here speaks only of the hands, this was because the body had now been laid in the coffin, albeit still uncovered, and any further experiments with the other limbs would have seemed unbecoming and uncalled for. No one who knows anything of the character or the writings of Mother Drane will be disposed to think lightly of the testimony thus given to facts of which she had been the eye-witness.

Not less conscientious and exact is the biography of Mother Maria Gertrude Salandri of Valentano. She died in 1748 at the age of fifty-eight. The body, we are told, became quite supple; there was an extraordinary beauty in the face and colour in the cheeks, though her sufferings and exhaustion during the previous six weeks had been extreme. In particular, it is stated that thirty-six hours after death the Sub-prioress, without any effort, took the hand of the dead nun as she lay on a bier, before she was finally placed in her coffin, and raising it aloft, gave a last blessing with it to the assembled nuns who had venerated her as their mother. Again, we read of Sister Marie de Saint-Pierre, a Carmelite nun of Tours, who died in July 1848, that her limbs, though they had been stiff and immovable during her illness, became, after death, as supple and flexible as those of a child, and the same is also told of another nun who was prioress of the same convent, and who went to her reward in 1863. In the case of this manifestation, unlike that of the stigmata, there seems to be no inequality between the sexes. Of Brother Grispino da Viterbo, for example, a Capuchin lay-Brother, who died at Rome in 1750 of gangrenous necrosis, it is stated that owing to the nature of the disease it had been decided to bury him at once, within a few hours after death. But, as his biographer tells us:

> Hardly had the corpse been laid out, when, as all could see for themselves, an incredibly surprising change took place in every part of the body. The blotches, the wounds, the unhealthy pallor and the other signs of the gangrene all disappeared at once; the flesh of the limbs became healthy, supple and white like that of a child; the knees unbent to their full extent, the hands and feet, which were before contracted and knotted, straightened out and became pliable like those of a man in health. In fact, the body was completely transformed, and as all present perceived, it was not only changed in appearance, but also flexible and comely in a degree which excited general attention and astonishment.

It is also stated that when the body was exhumed, six days after death, the same flexibility and complete absence of corruption were still observable. Yet another case was that of the Italian Carmelite, Angiolo Paoli (1720). Witnesses in the process of beatification attested on oath that for the two days that the body was left exposed to view after death, there was no trace of cadaveric rigidity. The flesh remained soft, fresh-looking and everywhere elastic. Still more satisfactory is the evidence in the case of the holy priest, Andre Hubert Fournet, the Founder of the religious congregation of the Soeurs de St. Andre. He died in the diocese of Poitiers on May 13, 1834, and I happen to have access, in this instance, to the printed *Positio super Introductione Causa*. In the *Summarium* annexed, three of the nuns who gave evidence deposed to the fact that when the body lay exposed after death, they were employed in taking the rosaries and other pious objects given them by visitors in order to touch the body with them. They testified to its perfect flexibility, and declared that there was not the least sign of corruption observable during the four days which elapsed before interment. One of them in particular specifies: "When touching the body with these objects I bent the fingers, the wrist and also the elbow of the Servant of God, and in each case I found that the joint was perfectly supple."

And this perhaps may be a suitable place to say a few words upon the physiological aspect of the question of cadaveric rigidity. So far as I can discover from various standard handbooks of medical jurisprudence, English, French, German, Spanish and Italian, which I have been able to consult, not one of them seems to recognize the possibility that in any human corpse rigor mortis may never set in at all. Considerable variation has been observed in the time after death at which it makes its appearance, and also in the duration of this condition of rigidity. Speaking presumably with reference to the conditions which usually obtain in Great Britain, Professor Glaister states:

> On the average, stiffening will probably have begun in the neck and jaw and face about five or six hours after death, will be definitely present in the upper part of the body in ten hours, and will be present over all the body between twelve to eighteen hours, and it will, in all likelihood, have passed off in the bulk of cases by the end of thirty-six hours.

The same high authority goes on to say that rigor has been delayed as long as sixteen hours, and has been present as long as twenty-one days, though these of course represent very extreme cases. Further, he states that in all exhausting diseases of long or short duration, cadaveric rigidity shows itself early and passes off quickly, and in the same conditions putrefaction also commences early. It would appear at the same time that all estimates such as those just quoted are somewhat tentative and uncertain. A German authority states that the stiffening (*Leichenstarre*) usually lasts three times twenty-four hours; another of more recent date, without committing himself to a precise estimate of the duration of the *rigor*, declares that in the majority of cases it becomes complete within five or six hours of death, and only disappears to give place to putrefaction. A standard Italian authority, no doubt basing his estimate upon the conditions prevailing in a more southern climate, states that rigor generally begins from two to three hours after death, and only disappears between thirty-six and forty-eight hours after life is extinct. But, as already noticed, amid all these variations, one nowhere finds any suggestion that cadaveric rigidity is ever entirely absent. Indeed, the work which is generally considered the primary English authority on the subject definitely pronounces that "the physiological data previously stated… have shown that this period of rigor mortis is absolutely certain to arrive sooner or later."

THE ABSENCE OF CADAVERIC RIGIDITY

In view of this very positive declaration the numerous cases occurring in our hagiographical records in which no signs of cadaveric rigidity seem to have been discernible, offer, to put it at its lowest, an extremely curious problem. It may, of course, be objected that the instances already described, or the others which we still have to consider, are only examples in which rigor has set m extremely late or has disappeared exceptionally early. Still, a little consideration will suffice to show that this suggestion does not provide a satisfactory solution of the difficulty. Apart from some rather uncertain data derived from suicides, who asphyxiated themselves with carbon dioxide (carbonic acid gas), where we are told that the bodies sometimes remained for two or three days at the Paris *Morgue* without *rigor* setting in, the best English authorities, such as Glaister, and Taylor and Smith, assign sixteen hours, or at most twenty-four hours, as the extreme limit of delay. Now in nearly all the cases of flexibility considered here we have explicit testimony that the limbs, and more particularly the hands and arms, had not stiffened, though one, two or three days had passed since the moment of death. It must be remembered that the members of a religious community are quite familiar with the ordinary physical phenomena of death. They do not employ extern nurses or servants to perform the last offices for the mortal remains of deceased members of the Order. Consequently, there is no likelihood that a slight, or even a considerable, delay in the normal time of the appearance of rigor would be proclaimed as anything supernatural. It is perhaps more easily conceivable that nuns or other religious might not be aware that the rigidity of a corpse is only temporary, and that it passes off after a certain interval, but as a rule it only passes off to give place to putrefaction, and in practically all the cases with which we are dealing the absence of any signs of approaching corruption is insisted upon just as strongly as the flexibility of the limbs. Moreover, in the vast majority of cases our evidence shows that the hands and arms of the deceased were perfectly supple just at that time, *i.e.*, between the 18th and 36th hour after death, when the normal dead body is *always* held fast by *rigor*. A particularly clear example of this may be found in the case of St. Leonard of Port Maurice. He died at Rome shortly before midnight on November 26, 1751, at the age of seventy-four. In order to avoid the tumult and disorder which often occurred when those who died in repute of sanctity were exposed in the church the populace were never admitted to visit the remains, but the body was laid in the tomb during the early hours of November 28th. Shortly before it was lowered into its place of sepulture, and consequently about twenty-four hours or more after death, a juridical examination took place at which were present the Father Provincial, a notary, a number of religious and Mgr. Giovardi. A formal instrument was drawn up and sealed which stated that the body was then flexible in every part as if still living. This document was produced with others in the process of beatification.

The cases we have so far considered involve nothing but the simple absence of *rigor*, but, as already insinuated, this phenomenon is frequently associated with other manifestations. Perhaps no more remarkable example can be cited than the occurrences which attended the death of St. Lewis Bertrand, the great Dominican missionary, which took place at Valencia on October 9, 1581. With regard to the absence of *rigor* we have apparently two distinct attestations, one concerning the time when the sacred remains were removed to the sacristy after the indiscreet devotion of the relic hunters in the church had exceeded all bounds, the other describing the condition of the body immediately before it was finally consigned to the tomb. The first of these occasions must have been not less than two, or more than six or seven, hours after the Saint breathed his last. Regarding this, Father Wilberforce says; at this time the limbs were perfectly flexible, the flesh feeling as if alive although without warmth." The examination of the remains before their final interment took place about thirty-six hours after death. Of the second inspection we are told that "the body was found unchanged, the flesh white as alabaster, the face shining with a peculiar and attractive beauty, while the limbs were perfectly flexible."

As already stated, the absence of *rigor* in the case of St. Lewis Bertrand was rendered specially remarkable from the number of other phenomena, apparently well attested, with which it was associated. For example, "at the moment in which his soul departed, a brilliant light flashed from his mouth, illuminating the whole cell with its splendour," this lasted "for about the length of time that is needed to recite a Hail Mary." Further, "a perfume of astounding sweetness . . . came from his dead body," and "heavenly music was heard by many in the church where the body was awaiting burial." This fact seems to have been made the subject of careful investigation, but it is also admitted that the harmony was not perceptible to all, and this seems also to have been the case with the effulgence which many witnesses observed with astonishment in the hands and other uncovered portions of the body as it lay exposed in the church.

In the case of the Jesuit, St. Peter Claver, "the Apostle of the Negroes," who died at Cartagena, in South America, about 2 a.m. on September 8, 1654, we have a similar combination of marvels.

THE ABSENCE OF CADAVERIC RIGIDITY

The flexibility of the body was conclusively demonstrated by the fact that while it lay exposed in the church, ten or twelve hours after death, the position of the hands and arms was altered for the greater convenience of those who came to venerate the remains.

Instead of the hands clasping a chalice as had at first been arranged, the chalice was removed, the arms were crossed and the hands allowed to hang down on either side in a position which allowed the people to kiss them. But they were not content with this.

Those who were afflicted with various infirmities, with sore eyes, with aching heads, with ulcers in the arms or breast, lifted up the hand of the dead man, and moved it to touch the part affected. It may fairly be counted as further proof of the abnormal character, to say the least, of this flexibility, that witnesses deposed to the marvellous fragrance observable in the hands and feet and to the copious perspiration which bedewed the whole surface of the body.

This same phenomenon is recorded of a number of other persons who died similarly in the odour of sanctity, for example, in the case of Blessed Gaspar de Bono, of St. Benedict Joseph Labre, and of St. Paschal Bay Ion. Blessed Gaspar de Bono, whose death occurred at Valencia in Spain on July 14, 1604, remained three days unburied, venerated in the extreme heat of summer by an unending stream of devotees, who filled the church and all its approaches. During all this time the body remained fragrant, supple and bedewed with a mysterious moisture. On the second day, some thirty-six hours after death, we have record of two miraculous cures worked by placing the hand of the corpse upon the injured limbs of suppliants present beside the bier.

Still better attested (by a number of witnesses whose depositions are very fully given in the process of beatification), is the case of St. Benedict Joseph Labre. He breathed his last in Rome on the evening of April 16, 1783. When we read of the perspiration which bedewed the brow as often as it was wiped away, of the perfect suppleness of the limbs, of the warmth which in four days never entirely gave place to the chill of death, of the hand automatically clutching a bench and supporting the weight of the body, it is difficult to believe that the Saint was really dead; and yet the surgeon, Valenti, opened a vein, and medical opinion seemed to be entirely satisfied that life was extinct. The case is not a little perplexing, but it seems certain that no trace could be perceived of the action of either heart or lungs. A trickle of blood came when the vein was opened.

A similar difficulty might be raised in the instance of St. Paschal aylon. Here also there was an extraordinary moisture bedewing the brow and an absolute flexibility of the limbs maintained during the three days the body was exposed. The eyes remained bright and unclouded, and it was easy to draw back the eyelids. The crowd of visitors was never weary of trying the experiment in order to look into the depths of those wonderful orbs.

But the number of cases in which no trace of *rigor* could be discovered is far too great to enumerate and discuss one by one, and this fact, as it seems to me, forms the best answer to the suggestion that these holy men and women were not really dead. That a mistake could have been made in one or two isolated instances is conceivable, but the idea of a whole series of blunders, or the supposition that holy people were peculiarly liable to pass into a comatose state without any perceptible sign of life (cataleptic rigidity *ex hypothesi* being also excluded) must surely be rejected. The same religious men and women who gave evidence of the passing away of these chosen souls and of the condition of their mortal remains while awaiting sepulture, are also those who were most likely to be familiar with the phenomena of trance or ecstasy. To take a striking example, I may quote the case of the nun, Veronica Laparelli, who died at Cortona in 1620. She often fell into ecstasies, which were sometimes continued for as much as sixty hours, or even longer. About five hours after death the body was opened and the viscera removed. One of the surgeons who performed this operation gave evidence upon oath in the process of beatification. He declared that there was no cadaveric rigidity at all, that the flesh remained supple without any trace of unpleasant odour and that the eyes were as beautiful and bright as if she were not dead. The removal of the heart and viscera in this case completely disposes of the hypothesis that life was not extinct. None the less, when visitors were admitted some hours after this operation to offer their tribute of respect to the deceased, we learn that the eyes were still so bright that the nuns kept raising the eyelids to look at them. The whole face, as one of them stated, was smiling (*pareva che ridesse*). Moreover, to quote another nun witness:

> The body, and particularly the hands and the face, never stiffened, although the weather was bitterly cold; and this I know because we put upon the fingers rings which were handed to us by the crowd who came there out of devotion, and the rings could be slipped on to her fingers and taken off again without difficulty. This I know because I saw it.

Again we have very conclusive evidence of the absence of rigidity in the account given of the scenes which followed upon the death of S. Felix of Cantalice in May 1587. He expired on the Monday afternoon. The body, when washed and laid out some hours later, was quite supple. When exposed in the church on the Tuesday the devotion of the people tore away almost all the habit in which the Saint was clothed, and a new habit had to be provided. It was noticed that not the least difficulty was found in dressing the body again, indeed, as the infirmarian declared, there was far less difficulty in dressing him now, owing to the perfect flexibility of the limbs, than there had been when he was lying ill before the final release came.

Perhaps the most interesting class of case in which the absence of rigidity has been observed is that which is concerned with the exudation and incorruption of the blood. But the present chapter threatens to exceed its proper limits, and these blood phenomena may very well claim a chapter to themselves.

CHAPTER XII
BLOOD PRODIGIES

If in discussing the problem of incorruption I was inclined to regard the phenomena so often observed in the bodies of saints as inexplicable by mere coincidence, it may be confessed that the analogous wonders recorded concerning the behaviour of their blood after death weighed with me much in forming that opinion. Many of these stories are of ancient date. In the account given by Paulinus, the biographer of St. Ambrose, concerning the discovery of the body of St. Nazarius, he declares that the martyr's blood after the lapse of many years was seen to be "as fresh as if it had been shed the same day." Similarly, St. Ambrose himself states that when the bodies of SS. Gervase and Protase were dug up, " very much blood " was found. Abbot Einhard, the biographer of Charlemagne, whose credit as a veracious chronicler stands high, declares, being himself an eye-witness, that when a translation of the remains of SS. Marcellinus and Peter took place in his own monastery, they exuded blood for several days, though the martyrdom had taken place 500 years earlier. There are a good many similar statements in Carolingian documents, some of them obvious fabrications, others made by authorities normally regarded as trustworthy. Still, it does not seem worth while to gather up evidence so remote which must always suggest many doubts, if only from the uncertainties which beset the process of transmission.

One example, however, belonging to the close of the twelfth century, seems worthy of notice, partly because it is an English example and partly because it rests on testimony which is undoubtedly contemporary and for most matters quite reliable. The Saint in question is the hermit St. Godric of Finchale. He died on May 21, 1170, and his life was written by his devoted friend and neighbour, Reginald of Durham. Godric, who must have been over ninety and had been bedridden for nearly eight years, passed away at dawn, and a full description is given of how the body was sewn up in various wrappings leaving the feet exposed. The news of the death of the holy man soon got wind, and certain personages of distinction (*nobiliores quidam*), with other less important folk, crowded to the hermitage before the day was out to beg for relics.

Under such constraint, we are told, his religious brethren were induced to cut away the nails from the toes, and "cutting rather too deep, the blood gushed forth, just as from a living man, so that the crimson flood besprinkled the hands of him who used the knife, although the dead body had long before grown cold, for it was now getting towards dusk and he had died at early dawn." Indeed, as the chronicler explains, at nine o'clock the next morning, when they were on the point of committing the body to the grave, a drop of fresh blood still showed on the toes, and a devout client, long afflicted with a disease called "anatrope"—this seems to have been an inability to retain any food, probably hysterical in its origin—was instantaneously cured upon contact with the blood when he kissed the dead Saint's feet. Although the effusion of blood here spoken of, some thirteen or fourteen hours after death, could not safely be described as without a parallel in medical experience, it certainly seems to be very unusual. For example, we are told by a high authority that in general after death—

> incisions fail to cause bleeding. Exceptions may be met with, e.g. apparent bleeding may occur in extreme cyanosis, or when at a later period development of gases in the trunk expresses blood from the trunk into the extremities.

Similarly in Taylor and Smith's *Medical Jurisprudence* we read:

> Blood coagulates more slowly in the dead body than in a vessel into which it has been drawn during life or after death. The blood may remain fluid in the vessels in a dead body from four to eight, or even as long as twelve, hours after death. It rarely begins to coagulate until after the lapse of four hours; but if drawn from a blood-vessel and exposed to air, it coagulates in a few minutes after its removal.

There seems to be no object in attempting to follow any chronological order in the illustrations of post-mortem haemorrhage which I propose to give in this article. So we may conveniently deal here with the case of St. Catherine of Bologna, whose incorrupt body, though now very blackened and unsightly, has been preserved intact down to our own day. St. Catherine, the abbess of a community of Franciscan nuns, died on March 9, 1463, at the age of forty-nine. According to the custom of the Order she was buried in the ground, without any coffin, only a few hours afterwards. Almost immediately a remarkable fragrance was perceived in the place where she was interred, and when miraculous cures were wrought there, the nuns began to doubt whether they ought not to have treated the body of their saintly abbess with more reverence. After eighteen days the confessor of the community gave the Sisters permission to exhume the body. The face was crushed and dirtied by the soil, but after the remains had been reverently washed and cared for, it recovered all its beauty and rosy cheeks replaced the pallor of death. Other marvels also happened, and Illuminata Bembi, who succeeded Saint Catherine in her office of Abbess, has left in the account she wrote at the time such details as the following:

> On Good Friday, feeling a devotion to see the precious remains, and having obtained our confessor's permission, we opened the sepulchre [in which they had now been honourably enshrined and on lifting up the silk veil which covered the virginal body, we found it quite bathed in sweat; while we were wiping it with linen cloths it exhaled a most agreeable odour. One of the Sisters seeing a little bit of skin, which hung from one of the feet, pulled it off, and instantly red blood flowed out from the place, as if the body were alive.... On the night preceding Easter we again opened the sepulchre, and what was our joy and surprise at seeing one of the eyes a little open and appearing quite beautiful; a moment afterwards the other also opened a little. When morning came the saint appeared more beautiful than ever; her forehead seemed to shine, her face was red as a rose and a mild light filled her eyes, which were quite open.... Three months after death, she twice bled at the nose so copiously as to fill a cup with the blood.

It must be confessed that there are many things in the Life of St. Catherine of Bologna, written a century and a half after her death by Father Grasset, which must strike the reader as very extravagant. The story there told in another chapter of the vocation of Leonora Poggi is in particular quite incredible. But the account abbreviated above is an insertion, a piece of first-hand evidence by an eye-witness who, even if fanciful and credulous, can hardly be suspected of deliberate fabrication. The change of colour in the face, and the bleeding at the nose after death, might possibly be caused by the existence of "hypostases," or accumulations of uncongealed blood; but Taylor and Smith, in dealing with similar phenomena, speak of a few *days*, not of three weeks and three months. "Shifting of an hypostasis," they say, "may cause a reddening in the face of a body which has been dead three days." I have no doubt that many of the curious post-mortem haemorrhages and strange flushings of the countenance, recorded in hagiographical documents, are due to hypostases, for I have noticed that these phenomena almost invariably occur after the corpse, in being transferred from one place to another, has been exposed to violent joltings. But the bleeding of a body in its extremities a month after death, and the persistence of these hypostases for weeks or even years without any sign of putrefaction is undoubtedly a matter for fuller investigation. Nothing can be more certain than the fact that the body of St. Catherine, fully exposed to the air, was kept for a time in the same by no means roomy chamber in which the nuns sang their Office and spent a notable proportion of every day in prayer. For two years they acted as if she were still their Abbess and elected no successor. A little later the body was placed seated in a recess where through a grating it looks upon the High Altar, and though blackened and shrivelled, it remains in the same position to this day. Grasset declares that for more than seventy years the nails of her fingers and toes grew like those of a living person and used regularly to be cut, but he adds that in his own time (1620) this growth had long since ceased, as the extremities of the body had become hard and dry.

But our concern is with the phenomena connected with the flow of blood from dead bodies, and it is to be noted that, though this type of manifestation is far less common than that of the absence of rigor, the number of alleged instances is still very considerable. In the majority of cases this flow of blood has been occasioned by an attempt to cut away some portion of the flesh, small or great, to preserve as a relic. The Life of St. Francis di Geronimo, the Neapolitan Jesuit, who died in 1716, provides a good example, seeing that we have here the depositions made under oath during the process of beatification by the persons principally concerned. The lay-Brother John de Giore, who, when giving his evidence three or four years after the event, was forty-eight years of age, tells the following story. It had been his duty to clothe and lay out the body of the Saint for burial.

Father Francis breathed his last about ten o'clock in the morning. His holy body remained soft and flexible and his face appeared much more beautiful than if it had been that of a living man. No one could have been afraid of it, and so I, though I have a horror of corpses, stood close to him and moved and clothed the limbs with my own hands, feeling nothing but delight and consolation all the time. There were two other Brothers helping me, and while we were trying to make him keep his hands upright and a little apart in order to receive and hold a chalice between them before carrying the body into the church, the arms and hands, being perfectly limp, kept falling back when we had set them in their place. So I said to him: "Father Francis, dear, keep those hands of yours quiet just as I put them," and in fact the hands now remained as I arranged them, without falling down as they had done twice before. Then a pious thought occurred to me, and together with the other two Brothers, one called Peter Miglietti, who is now dead, and the other, Francis Sala, we determined to cut out the corns which he had on the soles of his feet in order to keep them as relics. This we began to do, but in cutting the first corn—it was under the right foot, if I mistake not—blood began to flow, bright crimson blood, in such quantities that we had to use a number of cloths to mop it up, besides collecting two ounces of it in a little basin; and it would not stop running, for all the efforts made to check it by bathing it with *acquavita sflemmata*. In fact, as I have said, it went on flowing from about half-past ten until seven in the evening, in such a way that devout people dipped a multitude of little cloths in it, and in particular the handkerchief of the Signora Principessa della Roccella Cantelini was so dipped, and I have heard since that she preserves it with great veneration in the casket in which she keeps her jewels.

Now, although there is nothing extraordinary in the fact that an incision made in the foot half an hour after death should be followed by bleeding, I think it will be admitted that the continuance of this bleeding for eight or nine hours would be regarded as a most unusual occurrence, even if the trickle from the wound was very slight, as may have been the case here. It is in any case noteworthy that many of the witnesses speak of the extraordinary fragrance which during the three days before burial proceeded from the body and from the handkerchiefs steeped in his blood, as also of the flexibility which allowed the Saint's hands and arms to be freely moved by those who could get near the bier.

A very similar case is that of Sister Maria di Gesu, who died at Angelopolis in Mexico on June 11, 1637, aged fifty-eight. She passed away, we are told, at three in the afternoon, and the body was clothed and laid out a little more than three hours later. No death-pallor settled upon the features, the limbs remained perfectly supple, a wonderful fragrance made itself perceptible and a copious perspiration exuded from the face, which moisture, though constantly wiped away with handkerchiefs, continued until the body was laid in the grave. Sometime after midnight, one of the nuns, bent upon obtaining a relic, ventured secretly to cut off one of the toes, whereupon the blood flowed in abundance, and though she endeavoured to absorb it with linen cloths and then to catch the stream in an open vessel, it continued to trickle, until the nuns applied an astringent powder and prayed for the flow to cease.

As previously stated, the blood prodigies connected with the wounding of the bodies of saints are very numerous and belong to all periods. A contemporary Latin Life of St. Silvester, Abbot of Monte Fano, who died in 1267, recounts how a woman who came, forty-eight hours after he had expired, to venerate his remains, and attempted secretly to cut a portion of flesh from his foot, was detected by the stream of blood which flowed from the wound as copiously as it could have done from a living man." Similarly, St. Luchesius, a Franciscan tertiary, who died in 1260, had the big toe cut from his dead body, and the operation was followed by a profuse flow of blood. The legend containing this statement was compiled before 1320, and Father Papebroch, the Bollandist, apparently considers it a trustworthy document. Much more remarkable, however, are the cases in which the interval of time between death and the effusion of blood is a matter of months or years. St. Peter Regalatus, a Franciscan, died in 1456. In 1492 that is to say, thirty-six years afterwards, his body was exhumed and transferred to a more honourable resting place. At the instance of the Spanish Queen, Isabella, the hand, or at least several of the fingers, was severed from the arm, and it is stated that from both surfaces fresh blood (*recentissimus sanguis*) flowed as from a living body, and that this discharge continued for some time. Although the original sources from which this account is derived are not known to us, Father Anthony Daça, O.F.M., is a chronicler who had access to all the records of his Order and is generally considered trustworthy. In fact, in an epilogue appended to another work of his, the *Vida de Juana de la Cruz* (*Vazquez*), he takes very high ground indeed regarding the necessity of observing the strictest accuracy in all historical statements. Another very remarkable and apparently well attested case is that of the Dominican, Geronimo Batista de Lanuza, Bishop of Albarrazin. He died on December 15, 1624, and as he was in great repute of sanctity, there was the usual contest to retain possession of his mortal remains as a precious treasure. It will probably be remembered that, some forty years before, the body of his great countrywoman, St. Teresa, had given rise to similar disputes. Thirty-six days after his demise the body of the holy Bishop was exhumed and found without a trace of corruption. The face had none of the pallor of death, all the joints were supple, the flesh elastic, and the veins stood out as if they were charged with blood. A strange compromise had been adopted by which the city of Albarrazin was to retain possession of the lower limbs, while the body was to find its final resting place at Saragossa. A skilful surgeon was summoned to amputate the legs at the knees. Although some effusion of blood was foreseen and ligatures made to prevent it, the precautions were quite ineffectual. It is stated that a great quantity of blood flowed, as fluid and as vividly crimson as if the operation had been performed on a living subject. The biography of Lanuza, published twenty-four years later in a folio volume by Fray Geronimo Fuser, O.P., who had been his confessor, professes to give the names of seventeen persons who were present at this amputation, together with that of the surgeon, and it seems certain that the writer had access to the formal depositions made by them and by other medical authorities in the process of beatification. One would have liked to see the actual terms in which the faculty gave their evidence, but unfortunately these documents are not reproduced in the Life, and the process of beatification is inaccessible to me. There seems, however, no reason to doubt the substantial accuracy of the statements made. When the body, thus deprived of its lower extremities, arrived at Saragossa four days afterwards, the face was found to be bleeding. It must, they conjectured, have received some injury in the joltings of the transit. But there was still no trace of corruption, and the blood which flowed was fluid and crimson, like that of a living man freshly shed.

Very similar, but in my judgment much less well attested, is the story of the severed arms of St. Nicholas of Tolentino. It is narrated that they were cut from the venerable and incorrupt remains of the Saint in 1345, forty years after his death, by a lay-Brother who intended to carry them off to Germany, but that this sacrilegious act was the occasion of a stupendous flow of blood, which led to the discovery of the outrage and the arrest of the thief. What is more remarkable still, the two arms thus recovered, having been enshrined at Tolentino in precious reliquaries, it is averred that they continued to emit blood at intervals during the space of three hundred years and more, these effusions being regarded, for the most part, as portending some calamity. The evidence for the original prodigy at the severing of the limbs is certainly not satisfactory, but there can be no reasonable doubt that from the two arms, venerated at Tolentino as those of St. Nicholas, a curious exudation of a red fluid, described as "blood," did take place from time to time during the sixteenth and seventeenth centuries. In 1699, this discharge seems to have continued pretty constantly for four months together, and the effusions of 1671 and 1676 were also noteworthy. Pope Benedict XIV, in his famous treatise on the Beatification and Canonization of saints, accepts the marvel as an authentic fact and apparently pronounces it to be miraculous. It is obvious, however, that the science of that age was unable to apply any conclusive test to decide whether the fluid was really living blood, or a sort of darkened serum devoid of blood corpuscles. The fact seems to be that even modern science knows very little of the histology of a cadaver in which normal putrefaction does not take place.

On the whole, it must be said that the instances of the effusion of blood after death chronicled in our hagiographical records are fairly numerous, and that they differ widely as to the time at which the phenomenon has been observed. In the case of St. John of the Gross, the contemporary and friend of St. Theresa, we are told that his incorrupt body was exhumed nine months after it had been consigned to the tomb. On this occasion before it was restored to its resting place—

> The prior, at the request of Zevallos, cut off one of the three fingers of the right hand which held the pen when the saint was writing, that he might give it to Dona Ana as a proof of the story he had to tell. The hand was full of blood, and the blood flowed as freely as from the hand of a living man.

A still longer interval is recorded in the case of the Franciscan Saint, Pacificus di San Severino. He died on September 24, 1721, and in his case, as in that of so many other ecstatic saints, there was the usual fragrance and complete absence of cadaveric rigor, down to the time when burial took place. More than four years later his body was disinterred; when it was found quite incorrupt, flexible in every joint, and emitting a sweet perfume. In moving the body, however, an accident occurred. The head came into violent contact with the stairway and detached itself from the trunk, whereupon a stream of crimson blood flowed from the neck and bespattered the shirt of one Francesco Tarquinio, who was helping in the removal. Father Melchiorri, who wrote a Life of Saint Pacifico more than a century later, declares that this shirt was still preserved as a relic in the chapel of a noble family which he names.

In other cases, the flow of blood followed shortly after death, but still was judged by medical men, who, despite their very primitive conceptions of disease, had plenty of experience in practical anatomy, to be unprecedented and even miraculous. For example, St. Francis Caracciolo, the Founder of an Order of Clerks Regular, died on June 4, 1608, at six p.m. Three full days later it was decided to embalm the body, as it had to be conveyed some distance to its last resting place. The first incision of the surgeon's knife, to his very great astonishment, was attended with a copious flow of blood (*Jiuido, vigoroso e vermiglio*), while an inexplicable fragrance filled the whole room. In the case of St. Gerard Majella, the Redemptorist lay-Brother, the interval was shorter. Three hours after his death on October 15, 1756, a vein was opened by his Superior, and "there gushed forth a copious flow of ruby blood." Moreover, two days later, before finally consigning the body to the tomb, the Superior of the house again opened a vein, and again there gushed forth red blood that spoke of life rather than of death." Even though in such circumstances one may be tempted to doubt whether life was really extinct, it should be said that the community and the doctors seem to have been quite satisfied upon the point. Cases of this description are fairly numerous, and without going into details, it may be sufficient to mention that a copious flow of bright crimson blood occurred when a vein was opened in the dead body of Bernard da Corleone (f 1667), a Franciscan lay-Brother, of the Capuchin Father Antonio da Modena (1648) and Angelo di Acri, another Capuchin, in 1739.

There is another and a rather different type of blood-prodigy connected partly with the preservation of human blood, fluid and incorrupt, and partly with its apparent ebullition. I had intended to discuss it in the present chapter, but it would hardly be possible to go into any detail without extending this beyond normal limits. So I will end with the remark that some of the cases where blood has been drawn either from the living or the dead subject and has remained uncongealed and without any sign either of fermentation or putrescence, certainly do seem to present a curious analogy with the absence of cadaveric rigor and the freedom from normal decay which the student encounters over and over again in perusing our hagiographical records. Meanwhile, it may not be out of place to quote certain observations of a specialist who seems to have devoted considerable attention to this field of research, Professor Halliburton. He says:

> The coagulation of the blood after it is shed is, in many points, similar to the stiffening of the muscles which occurs after death called *rigor mortis*. The blood plasma is, during life, a liquid; the muscle plasma, *i.e.* the contents of the sarcolemma, is also, during life, a liquid. Both contain various albuminous matters of a complex nature. In both, certain of these proteid or albuminous substances undergo a change after death; this change is a solidification; and the solid substance is called the clot; the liquid residue being called the serum.
>
> In the case of blood, the clot is composed of fibrine (with entangled corpuscles), and after coagulation has occurred it floats in blood serum. In the case of muscle plasma the clot is composed of myosin, and the liquid residue is termed the muscle serum.

After specifying certain conditions which prevent the coagulation of muscle plasma as well as that of blood plasma, Professor Halliburton proceeds:

> This similarity between the behaviour of muscle plasma and blood plasma suggested to me that the cause of the coagulation was the same in both cases, viz., a ferment action. . . . The question of the cause of the disappearance of rigor mortis at a certain time after its onset is a question which I am at present engaged in investigating, the commonly accepted theory that it is due to putrefactive changes appearing to me unsatisfactory.

This seems to promise that science may some day be in a position to explain by natural causes the curious phenomena which we have been considering. But scientists themselves would probably be very willing to admit that at present the whole subject of the coagulation of the blood and its resolution in the cadaver is very obscure and that all theorizing is hazardous.

CHAPTER XIII
THE CASE OF MOLLIE FANCHER

1

The present chapter aims at illustrating the difficulty of assigning precise limits to the range of those natural but unusual manifestations of man's spiritual being which science now takes account of under the name of abnormal psychology. Two centuries ago such phenomena were summarily dismissed, by Catholics and Protestants alike, as witchcraft, sorcery, or, in brief, the work of the devil. But this was before the reality of the hypnotic trance was recognized, and before attention was thus directed to possibilities of which earlier ages had no conception. We are somewhat wiser now, and the delays which have so far held up any pronouncement by the episcopal commissions appointed to report upon the happenings at Limpias or the case of Theresa Neumann, seem to show that, in enlightened ecclesiastical circles, the lesson of caution has been taken to heart. In the pages which follow I propose to confine myself almost entirely to the strange facts recorded in the Life of Miss Mollie Fancher.

Let me begin with a very brief outline of those features in the case which constitute its principal interest. Mollie Fancher was born in 1848. Her life was spent at her aunt's home in Brooklyn, New York, and she died in the same house shortly before the end of the last century. She seems to have been a tuberculous subject from childhood, but as the result of two very serious accidents in 1865 and 1866, not long after leaving school, she became an incurable invalid and never for more than thirty years quitted her room or, practically speaking, her bed. Her lower limbs, being bent under her, became twisted and atrophied, and this was followed by permanent blindness and a complication of nervous disorders which had curious manifestations. For long years she was incapable of swallowing and lived almost completely without food, but in this crippled state she developed remarkable clairvoyant faculties. It was alleged that she often discerned what was happening in distant towns, that she had knowledge of the contents of scaled letters, that she could read books with great rapidity by passing her hand over the printed page, and it seems certain that she executed the most delicate artistic work in a position over her head—the only position which her paralysed arm rendered possible—where even the full use of her eyes could not have served her. Further, many witnesses attest that she could distinguish, with unerring accuracy, by touch alone the colours of the worsteds, the wax sheets, and other materials she employed in her work.

In addition to this there were manifested in her four separate personalities, each with distinctive characteristics and a handwriting which differed from that of her normal state. She never in any proper sense slept, but these personalities revealed themselves during the night—not, apparently, in the daytime—their appearance being ushered in by violent convulsions and a trance condition which was frequently cataleptic.

What lends exceptional importance to Miss Fancher's experiences is the fact that she had no interest in, or sympathy with, anything which bore the name of Spiritualism. She seems to have been a very religiously minded woman, and several of her most trusted friends were ministers—either Presbyterian or Baptist—in whose eyes any attempted communication with the spirits of the dead savoured of devilry. When an account of this extraordinary case was being compiled by Judge Abram H. Dailey in 1893, Miss Fancher's consent was asked, and she was requested to make known all she could concerning her own experiences. In certain communications received from her with this object, she declared:

> It has been charged and stated that this publication is being prepared in the interest of what is commonly known as Spiritualism. Nothing could be further from the fact, in so far as I am concerned. ... I have

been repeatedly asked to undertake to act the part of a medium for spirit communications, and I have invariably refused to attempt anything of the kind.

At the same time she adds a little further on:

It has been said, as the public generally knows, that I frequently speak of having seen my mother and other friends around me who are dead. Then in answer to these questions I frankly and truthfully say that at times, at least in spirit, away from the scenes of this world, I am with friends in most heavenly places. My consciousness of these things is to me as real as the experiences of my life upon this earth. I often see my mother and other friends around me, and in my dreary days of sickness, pain and suffering, and when my spirit is depressed, I can hear her tender voice speaking to me words of cheer, bidding me "bear up, be brave and endure"... Who with body and limbs racked and disjointed by disease, bedridden for upwards of twenty-seven years, will not long to be released from pain and suffering, even though that relief is only to be found in utter annihilation? ... At times I have seen around me, and around my friends who call to see me, the angel forms of those persons who are supposed to be dead. Whether I see what it seems to me I see, and hear what I seem to hear, let others form their own conclusions. I know what I see as well as they know what they see.

Whatever judgment we may pass upon these visions, it seems clear that they were as real to Mollie Fancher as those which Anne Catherine Emmerich or Teresa Higginson believed so confidently to be revelations of God's special favour. Unfortunately, no details are preserved to us of the impressions Mollie received during her sojourns "with friends in most heavenly places." She certainly seems to have convinced other people that there was something in what she saw in the course of these unusual experiences. A certain Professor C. E. West, the head of Brooklyn Heights Seminary, was an intimate and very early friend of hers. A letter of his to the *Buffalo Courier* in 1878, while describing her as a most devout Christian who "shrinks from any public exhibition "herself," mentions that "Spiritualists and curiosity-seekers have sought access to her, but have failed. Her power of discriminating character is so great that she is rarely, if ever, imposed upon. Some fifteen years later the same Professor West records:

She has revealed things to me of which I had no conception mainly while we were talking on religious topics. She is as earnest a Christian as I ever knew. What she sees [he means clairvoyantly only makes her faith the stronger ... I think she has glimpses o the other world, if she has not indeed been there. I cannot tell you that strangely interesting part of her experience. After she is dead it will be known, but it is more of a revelation than that seen by John from the Isle of Patmos.

And here it may be well to say something of the book in which these testimonies are printed, a book which is unfortunately almost the only available source of information regarding Mollie and her strange phenomena. The compiler, as previously mentioned, was a certain, "Judge Abram H. Dailey." This title seems to imply some sort of official legal position, but whether on account of the writer's advanced age or some other reason, it is not the kind of book which one would expect from a man accustomed to marshal evidence and estimate its value. The narrative is confused, ill written, full of repetitions and by no means free from misprints, especially where dates occur. If the volume represented nothing but Judge Dailey's impressions one might be pardoned for thinking the whole record worthless. But the author, partly, perhaps, to save himself trouble or to swell out the volume to a respectable bulk, has thrown together pell-mell a number of testimonies from the friends and acquaintances of the invalid, and there seems no reason to suppose that these have not been printed as they were written, for the contributors of the statements in question were nearly all living when the book was published. Some of them certainly were men of standing and intelligence. For example, the Professor West who has just been quoted, delivered, in 1882, an address entitled "Fifty years of Progress." From a copy of this brochure of 150 pages, which I have been able to consult at the British Museum, one is led to infer that the writer was a man much respected among his fellow ministers of religion, and the essay also gives proof of intelligence, wide reading, and a religious spirit. A letter is included addressed to Dr. West by Padre Secchi, S.J., in 1877, from the Observatory of the Collegio Romano. I may add here that apart from Professor West's positive testimony (to be quoted later) regarding Miss Fancher's gift of clairvoyance, and her inability to retain nourishment, he, like many more of her intimates, expresses a strong conviction as to her truthfulness. He says for example:

> I never knew a more truthful, sincere and intelligent girl than she has proved herself from the very first of our acquaintance. ... I have spent my life in study and I have devoted much of it for the past twelve years to Mollie Fancher's case.

Naturally in such a case it is the medical evidence which is of most importance. One would have liked fuller details than we possess, but Judge Dailey has, at any rate, preserved a statement which was made on July 26, 1893, by Mollie's ordinary medical attendant, Dr. S. Fleet Speir, and taken down from his dictation, at the patient's residence, 160 Gates Avenue, Brooklyn. From this I copy the more salient points: Dr. Speir informs us that he had been in charge of the case since April 6, 1866, a period of twenty-seven years, and also that Dr. Robert Ormiston had been associated with him in consultation during most of that time. It is important to note that Dr. Ormiston was present when the statement was made and that he formally corroborated it, declaring: "I am familiar with nearly all the facts to which Dr. Speir has referred, and in so far as I recall them they are correctly stated by him."

Regarding the general impression that Miss Fancher was paralysed, Dr. Speir raises some demur as to the correctness of the term.

> As a matter of fact [he says] she has never been paralysed in the sense in which that word is usually understood. She has lost the use of her limbs and at times has lost the power of sensation. As nearly as I can recollect, for a period of about nine years her lower limbs were in a three twist. The result to the limbs has been that, instead of being the natural hinge joint, the knee approaches the condition of a ball and socket joint; her limbs are drawn up backwards the ankles bent over, and the bottom of the foot upwards—and remaining in that condition. This is so of both feet. The limbs cannot be straightened out; they are contracted underneath.

> For a period of about nine years, day and night, she was subjcct to trances, spasms and catalepsy. During this time the most constant care and attention were required to prevent personal injury. In these spasmodic conditions she was liable from time to time to be thrown upon the floor, so that barricades were placed around her bed to prevent this happening. Her spasmodic conditions were so violent that she was hurled backwards and forwards with great force and rapidity. There was a back motion which is hard to explain, by which she seemed to

be thrown into the air, rising from her bed. At times her body would become rigid, and upon one occasion one portion of her body was turned to the right, and the other to the left in a distressing manner, and remained so for quite a time, she being in a rigid condition.

These violent convulsive movements are of much interest in connection with those cases in which the sufferer was believed by mediaeval observers to have been assaulted and thrown about by the devil. Not less important are Dr. Speir's comments on Mollie's rejection of all nourishment. He seems evidently to have suspected at first that there was some deception in the matter, as the following passage shows:

> To be certain that Miss Fancher was living without solid food for the long period of time which was stated, I resorted to giving her emetics, and the result was that nothing was thrown from the stomach, showing conclusively that the stomach was empty. During the period of nine years the quantity of food which she took into her stomach was so little that it was a matter of great astonishment how life could be sustained.

We learn from the notes of Miss Crosby, the patient's aunt, that enemas, bathing with oil and other indirect methods of nutrition had been employed, but they were abandoned as useless after more or less prolonged tests. In 1866 at the beginning of this period of inanition we are told that on May 20th she asked for food, ate a small piece of cracker and took a teaspoonful of punch, this being the first food which her stomach had been able to retain since the beginning of April. On June 2nd food was introduced through her contracted throat by the aid of a stomach pump, but "it threw her into convulsions and her throat closed. She could neither take nourishment nor utter a sound." Miss Crosby, who seems to have kept careful notes at this period, records that "the only nourishment she has retained on her stomach from April 4, 1866, to October 27th, has been four teaspoonfuls of milk punch, two of wine, one small piece of banana, and a small piece of cracker." A Mrs. Townsend, a friend who was constantly and out of the house at this early period, confirms this. "It is well known," she writes, "that for the first nine years she could keep nothing solid on her stomach. I am positive that she was unable to keep anything down and in fact could not swallow during the first years I knew her."

What renders this testimony the more convincing is the fact that Mollie in her crippled state was certainly incapable of getting out of bed, and for a long time, on account of the convulsive spasms to which she was subject, could not apparently be left alone during the night. To eat by stealth, for her, must have been impossible. Dr. West, who also visited her frequently, stated in a printed letter to a newspaper (1878):

> Water, the juices of fruits and other liquids have been introduced into her mouth, but scarcely any of them ever make their way into her stomach. So sensitive has this organ become that it will not retain anything. In the earlier part of her illness it collapsed so that, by placing the hand in the cavity, her spinal column could be felt.

When some attention was drawn to the case in 1878, the *New York Herald* on October 20th published an article which seems to have escaped the notice of Judge Dailey. The reporter of the *Herald* had very rightly been refused admittance to the house in which the poor invalid was living, but he managed to discover the names of her medical advisers. Dr. Ormiston, on being interviewed, is stated to have said: "It seems incredible, but from everything I can learn, Mollie Fancher never eats." The doctor went on to declare that the aunt, her constant companion, who testified to this, was a person of the highest character, and he added: "During a dozen visits to the sick chamber I have never detected evidence of the patient's having eaten a morsel." Finding his way thence to Dr. Speir, the reporter put the question: Has she eaten nothing during all these fourteen years? " The reply was in these terms:

> I can safely say she has not. I do not believe that any food— that is, solids has ever passed the woman's lips since her attack of paralysis consequent upon her mishap. As for an occasional teaspoonful of water or milk, I sometimes force her to take it by using an instrument to prize open her mouth. But that is painful to her. The case knocks the bottom out of all existing medical theses, and is, in a word, miraculous.

After referring to the emetics he had administered, Dr. Speir went on:

> I have taken every precaution against deception, sometimes going to the house at eleven or twelve o'clock at night without being announced, but have always found her the same and lying in the same position.

My brethren in the medical profession at first were inclined to laugh at me and call me a fool and a spiritualist when I told them of the long abstinence and keen intellectual powers of my interesting patient. But such as have been admitted to see her are convinced. These are Dr. Ormiston, Dr. Elliott and Dr. Hutchison, some of the best talent in the city, who have seen and believed.

The reporter then went back to Dr. Ormiston, but found him in no way inclined to withdraw from his former declarations. On the contrary, he strengthened them by saying: "Her tenacity of life for fourteen years, without sustenance enough to feed a baby for a week, appeals strongly to my unwilling belief in supernatural visitations."

I cannot find in subsequent issues of the *Herald* that the doctors who were so reported made any attempt to repudiate the language attributed to them.

The nutrition trouble seems to have begun in Mollie Fancher's school days. Her stomach even then "rejected most kinds of food," and the doctors, being persuaded that she suffered from nervous indigestion, recommended her to take up riding as an exercise. This resulted in a very bad fall in which she struck her head against the kerbstone and broke a rib, though her completely crippled condition only followed upon a second accident when in stepping out of a tram-car her crinoline got caught in the vehicle and she was dragged for many yards along the roadway. A curious remark is recorded of her in the early stages of her illness when they were trying to force food upon her which her stomach rejected, and which caused her great distress. Her aunt, Miss Crosby, urging her to make an effort because it was necessary to eat in order to maintain life, she is said to have replied that she received nourishment from a source of which they were all ignorant.

In the presence of the facts just quoted it seems difficult to affirm with confidence that the disinclination for food which we find so constantly recurring in the case of almost all visionaries—Anne Catherine Emmerich, Domenica Lazzari, Louise Lateau, Teresa Higginson, Theresa Neumann, etc., not to speak of many canonized Saints—is necessarily of supernatural origin.

To return, however, to Dr. Speir's statement of 1893, we have still to quote the observations made by him concerning Mollie's very abnormal faculty of sight. He says:

With reference to the condition of Miss Fancher's eyes. When I first attended her it seemed to me that her eyes were in such a state that she could not see by the use of them. On that date her eyes were glaring open, and did not close day or night, and there were no tears or secretion in them. I made the usual test for anaesthesia, even going to the extent of touching the ball of the eye with my finger, without provoking any reaction. During the first part of her troubles, the pupils were considerably dilated and the impression of light effected no change. The pupils are still considerably dilated, though not so much as formerly and still do not change at the approach of light. We have caused a careful and critical examination to be made by a competent expert—an oculist—in whose skill we have great confidence, and agree with him that she cannot see by the use of her eyes—at least as a person ordinarily can see. She has the power of seeing with a great deal of distinctness, but how she does it I am unable to state. The condition has remained substantially unchanged since I first began to attend her. This feature of Miss Fancher's power of sight has attracted a great deal of comment. At one time she did all her work, crocheting, etc., at the back of her head. When she selected worsted or colour she put it behind her head to see it. For nine years her right arm was behind her head, where she did her work by bringing the left hand up to the right hand, which was at the back of her head.

I recall one instance, when, Dr. Ormiston and myself being present, Miss Crosby received a letter from the postman. I took the letter in my hand; it was sealed, and Miss Fancher, at the time being unable to speak, took a slate and pencil and wrote out the contents of the letter, which, on being opened and read, was found to correspond exactly with what she had written. During that time she maintained conversation with her physicians and friends by the use of the slate, she being unable to speak. On another occasion she gave me warning that I was likely to be robbed, and told me to be on my guard. The sequel was that, immediately after, I was robbed of a valuable case of instruments. On another occasion I had invited a number of doctors to call at Miss Fancher's house, and we were waiting for one to arrive, when she said: "He is coming; I see him coming now," and told where he was, which was correct.

During my acquaintance with Miss Fancher and her aunt, Miss Crosby, during her lifetime, the actions and conduct of both entitle them to what they always had—our highest respect and esteem. . . .

Upon one occasion when she had lost the power of speech, I was present when someone made a remark to which she took exception. She took a pencil in her left hand and rapidly wrote a reply, which at first none could read. She had written backward, commencing at the end of a line and end of a word and so to the beginning. By holding a looking glass we readily made it out.

It was a sharp, caustic reply.

One remarkable feature during all these years she has been confined to her bed is that she has never been afflicted with bedsores, although her right hip, from constant pressure, is flattened, and the flesh is gone, so that the bone is merely covered by the integument. She has always explained, when asked how she saw without the use of her eyes, that she saw out of the top of her head.

Miss Fancher experiences quite remarkable conditions from the action of her heart. At times the chest over the heart seems considerably enlarged; it presents something the appearance of oedema, but responds to pressure in a different manner. It seems more elastic, and every day she coughs up about half an ounce of blood, which comes from the mucous membrane of the throat and bronchial tubes.

These are the principal data attested by Miss Fancher s ordinary medical attendant, Dr. Speir, and confirmed by his colleague, Dr. Ormiston. But so far as regards her powers of vision there is abundance of corroborative evidence contained in the statements of other intimate friends of hers. Judge Dailey avers, apparently as the result of what he himself had witnessed, that if one took a sharp knife and made a movement as if to thrust it into her eyes, she would not recoil or exhibit the slightest apprehension of danger.

At the same time in her most sensitive conditions—he admits none the less that the acuteness of her perceptions varied considerably according to the state of her health, the weather, and other causes—"she is able to distinguish colours, even to the most delicate shades, not only when absolutely concealed from her normal sight, but while in the pocket of another and when the experimenters did not know the colour of the article to be described." He also remarks: "that she did see, could and can see, from the top of her head and from her forehead, cannot permit of a reasonable doubt. She reads letters placed upon her forehead, and has done so hundreds of times." Her friend, Mrs. Townsend, referred to above, states: "she used to put sealed letters under her pillow and read them. Sometimes she read by rubbing her hand over them, and I have seen her read books in the same way." Professor West testifies similarly:

When I first saw her she had but one sense, that of touch. With that she could read with many times the rapidity of one by eyesight. This she did by running her fingers over the printed pages with equal facility in light or darkness. With the fingers she could discriminate the photographs of persons, the faces of callers, etc. She never sleeps, her rest being taken in trances. The most delicate work is done in the night. She performs none of the ordinary functions of life except that of breathing.

Some further details which have still to be given concerning Miss Fancher's visions, her power of sight, and her different personalities, must be postponed to another occasion, but there is one final remark I should like to make before concluding this chapter. Whatever we may think of the statements of fact contained in Judge Dailey's book, they certainly were not made with any *arriere pertsee* of discrediting the phenomena of Catholic mysticism. When we are dealing with such writers as Pierre Janet, Charcot, Paul Richer, Binet and others, we may not unreasonably suspect the possibility of some underlying purpose hostile to theories involving belief in the supernatural. But there is not in the American book, so often referred to, the faintest indication of any acquaintance with Catholic hagiology or its phenomena. No, hint emerges of a controversial motive. Certain friends of Miss Fancher, profoundly impressed by what they had seen, thought it desirable that the circumstances should be put on record: that is all. It is quite likely that some of them were guilty of considerable exaggerations. Everyone with a novel discovery to announce is anxious to make his story as impressive as possible and inevitably errs in the direction of overstatement. But I cannot persuade myself that such a book as *Mollie Fancher, the Brooklyn Enigma* could have been compiled and published if the experiences and faculties laid to her credit were not substantially in accord with facts. What is certain is that the oral statement taken down in 1893 from the lips of Drs. Speir and Ormiston, then still in charge of the case, is in full agreement with the account communicated by them fifteen years earlier to the reporter of the *New York Herald*. Anyone who wishes to do so may verify the fact, as I have done, by consulting the file of that journal accessible in the British Museum.

2

Perhaps the most satisfactory evidence preserved to us regarding Mollie Fancher's strange powers of vision and in particular her faculty of reading sealed documents, is contained in certain communications of a Mr. Henry Parkhurst who wrote to the *New York Herald* when the case was being discussed by the American Press in 1878. Mr. Parkhurst was a scientist of some standing, and a little later held an official position in connection with the observatory of Harvard University. He and his wife lived near Miss Fancher at Brooklyn and were welcome visitors in Mollie's sickroom. In the earlier stages of the case—the year, to be precise, was 1867—while the poor paralytic was still unable to speak, Mr. Parkhurst devised a crucial experiment to test her alleged power of reading without the use of the organs of vision. A slip of printed paper, so chosen at random that neither Mr. Parkhurst himself nor any other person knew its contents, was given to the blind girl in a carefully sealed envelope, precautions being taken against fraudulent opening. As Mollie at that time could neither speak nor even write, she communicated laboriously by knocks, spelling out single words letter by letter as the alphabet was called aloud.

"Consequently," says Mr. Parkhurst, "all that was expected or desired of her was so much of an indication of the content of the printed slip as should be absolutely beyond guessing or chance." She first intimated that the slip was about "Court." She next read the word "jurisdiction," stating positively that the word was there. Finally, she notified that the cutting contained the figures 6, 2, 3, 4. This Mr. Parkhurst regarded as sufficient information for his purpose, for, as he explains, "I had no idea that there were any figures on the slip and should have guessed that there were not. The letter was returned to me with the seal intact and was opened in my presence. The word "Court" occurs four times, jurisdiction once, and there are the figures 6, 2, 3, 4, 5, and no other figures." The cutting, he explains, was taken from the printed draft of a bill before the Maryland Constitutional Convention. Mr. Parkhurst had no notion that there were likely to be numbers on the slip he had submitted. "It was not," he writes, "until the envelope was opened and found to contain section 6 with the lines numbered 2, 3, 4, 5, that the idea occurred to me that the line numbers could possibly have been upon the slip." The details furnished by Mr. Parkhurst are somewhat too copious for quotation in full, but he states clearly that the account printed in the *New York Herald* on November 30, 1878, was copied by him from documents drawn up and witnessed at the time, and also that the printed slip used for the test was still in his possession.

An editorial comment was appended to these communications. It seems thoroughly to endorse the trustworthiness of the experiment, and begins as follows:

> Professor Parkhurst's interesting letter detailing an attempt to test the clairvoyant powers of Miss Fancher ... is the most important paper yet called forth by the discussion of the case. It seems hardly probable that a man of scientific bent and methodical business habits, as the writer of the letter is known to be, could have been deceived at any stage of the experiment, the details of which he gives so minutely to the public.

It is noteworthy that the publicity given to Miss Fancher's case by the newspaper discussion of 1878—it was, in fact, carried on in several other journals besides the *New York Herald*—was extremely distasteful to the invalid herself. Mr. Parkhurst, for example, remarks in his letter: "these publications have been thus far made without the consent and against the wishes of Miss Fancher and her friends; and as one of her friends I shall continue to keep silence with reference to the physical aspects of the case." He adds, however, that he had obtained her permission to make known the facts of the test he had carried out, because "it demonstrates, as it seems to me, so far as it is possible for a single experiment to demonstrate a general principle, that there may be a clairvoyance independent of mind-reading." We can feel little doubt that Mollie was greatly harassed by curious would-be investigators, and the *New York Herald*, in its comments, wishes her "good riddance of the swarms of inquirers who beset her without respect for her feeble health." What made her, no doubt, quite resolute in closing her door to all except those whom she recognized as personal friends, was her consciousness of her pitiable impotence and the knowledge that convulsive spasms often came upon her with little or no warning. Of these curious states it will be necessary to speak further on. She seems by nature to have been sensitive and reserved. From the testimony of Professor West and Judge Dailey, one gathers that she was by no means anxious to talk of her visions. This, we must believe, is also the case with Catholic mystics. Teresa Higginson reiterates again and again that only the positive order of her director could induce her to speak of what she had seen in her ecstasies, and whatever we may think of the record of Anne Catherine's revelations made to Brentano, he often complains of the difficulty he found in inducing her to continue her narrative. Mollie Fancher had no confessor to put her under obedience, and when she was questioned about her trances by Judge Dailey she replied only in general terms as follows:

> Well, when I go into my trances, I am usually conscious of being in existence, but they are not like dreams. They are like indistinct wanderings, something like the dreams I used to have when asleep before I was injured. When I come out of my trances, they at times leave quite distinct recollections or impressions upon my mind. Sometimes they are dim and are slowly recalled and then become very distinct. Now, as a usual thing, when I go into a trance, I go out and around and see a great deal. Sometimes I go into a house and view the condition of the rooms, and do not see anyone in the rooms. Sometimes I see persons and nothing more. I very seldom speak of where I have been and who I have seen. At the time when Mr. Sargent was incorporating this company I am connected with, he was at Muskegon, Michigan. I went into a trance and was gone for hours. My friend, Bert Blossom, was present in the room, and when I came out of the trance I found him greatly alarmed thinking I was dead. I told him I had been away to where Mr. Sargent was, and saw him on a stage, and he was singing to an audience of people in a large room. I had seen and heard him. Mr. Blossom said that that was most unlikely; but within the next three days I received from Mr. Sargent a letter, informing me of the fact that a Mr. Chase, at Muskegon, had opened a large piano factory, and that they had celebrated the event by a concert, at which he had taken a part in singing; and he also sent me a newspaper giving an account of the affair, and I subsequently learned from him that I had correctly described the event and scene.

Several similar incidents, in one or two of which he was personally concerned, are recorded by Judge Dailey. But most of Miss Fancher s friends had something of the sort to relate. Mrs. Townsend on one occasion was sitting in the invalid's room with Mrs. Parkhurst, the wife of the Professor whose test experiment has just been described, when suddenly Mollie "went into a rigid trance." When she came to, her two visitors asked her where she had been. She told them that she had been to see "Aunt Susie" (Miss Crosby) then on a visit to Cornwall, a small town about thirty miles off on the Hudson. "She gave a description of the people in the Cornwall house and of what they were doing." Miss Crosby, we are assured, on her return corroborated every detail. This faculty of clairvoyance, if we may so describe it, seems to have varied greatly in intensity, and on the whole to have diminished as Miss Fancher's physical condition improved in the course of years. Answering some questions put to her by Dailey on June 15, 1893, Mollie is stated to have replied:

> Well, as I have said, my vision is not always the same; much depends upon how I am feeling, and the weather conditions. Sometimes the whole top of my head seems on fire with the influx of light; my range of vision is very great, and my sight astonishingly clear. Then again it seems as if I were seeing through a smoked glass, and my vision, or consciousness of things, is dim and indistinct. Sometimes I can see all through the house. When my aunt was alive it was the most common thing for her to mislay her purse, veil or gloves, and not know where to look for them.
>
> She used to come to me to find them, and I would go rummaging through the house and finally tell her where they were lying. I have the same powers now, but not at all times. Were someone to come suddenly and ask me to do such a thing, I might not at the moment be able, but after a little, when not anxious to see, I can see most clearly.

Professor West, who had known her when she was most afflicted, declares:

> She knows who her visitors are long before they are ushered into the hall below, and she allows them to see her, or refuses, just as the whim takes her. I took Kossuth's sister there just before her departure for the Old World. Miss Mollie refused to see her. Afterwards I asked Mollie for an explanation. "Why! I didn't like her looks when she entered the door," was the reply. The door is on the floor below.

At the time when Dailey's book was in preparation (c. 1893) Mr. Sargent formed the impression that Mollie was regaining her natural sight. Judge Dailey did not agree. They were both conversing in the invalid's room, and the last named, as he tells us, took steps to prove to his friend that her vision was still altogether preternormal.

I immediately rose, and securely covered her eyes by placing a double handkerchief over them, and covering the lower part of her face as she lay upon her bed. There was not a movement any of us could make, or a thing which we could do, which she could not distinctly describe to us, with as much readiness as either of us could have done had the same been done before our eyes. . . .

She sees best and reads most readily when the room is so dark that others can scarcely see the print. The most hardened sceptics in these matters have been compelled to succumb when in the presence of Miss Fancher.

I should be the first to admit that such tests as that of the folded handkerchief just described afford a very inadequate guarantee against the practised impostor, but when we are dealing with a sufferer, bedridden for twenty-seven years, whose sincerity, patience, charity, and simple religious faith are commended by all her most intimate friends, the case seems to me to be very different from that of a professional medium who depends for a livelihood upon the impression he produces on his dupes. Ever since girlhood Miss Fancher s condition had been most pitiable, and her own statement regarding the beginning of her illness in 1866 is borne out by the evidence of her aunt and of the doctors.

For two months [she says] after my traduces commenced, fourteen persons were in constant Attendance on me, a relay of seven being required to hold me upon the bed during the spasms. My body and limbs were drawn together until I was almost a ball; then I leaped forward like an arrow, and would have been killed but for the protection of friends and the wadded obstruction placed in the way. These conditions continued until the first week in May of 1866, when I went into a long trance.

Her aunt's contemporary diary corroborates this, stating, for example, in the early part of February 1866: "Her head and feet coming together, she would roll like a hoop, she would also stand on her toes and spin like a top. Several persons were required to prevent her from doing personal injury to herself." These and similar convulsive spasms recurred at frequent intervals down to the time at which Dailey's book was compiled, in all, twenty-seven years. For anything that I have been able to learn to the contrary, they continued until her death, which, from a statement made in *Bulletin* No. XI of the Boston Society for Psychical Research, seems to have occurred not, as I previously supposed, before 1900, but after the beginning of the present century. What is certain is that as late as April 6, 1887, in one of her convulsive seizures, Mollie Fancher fell out of bed and severely injured the back of her neck. Similar falls had occurred many times previously when she had been left unattended. A barricade had been erected all round to prevent her hurting herself in such circumstances, but on this occasion it proved ineffective.

These alarming spasms were particularly liable to recur at night, and were often marked by a dissociation of personality. Besides the normal Mollie Fancher known to those who visited her in the daytime, her very intimate friends, and in particular her aunt, were acquainted with no less than five other Mollie Fanchers, who manifested themselves with varying frequency. One of them persisted for nine years (1866 to 1875), during what she was accustomed to refer to as her "great trance," but when that crisis was over, this personality never came to the surface again. During the nine years' period spoken of, her right arm was rigidly bent in such a position that the hand was fixed over the back of the head. She had some control of the thumb and index finger, and in order to do her work of flower making, sewing, etc., she had to bring up her left arm, of which she retained full use, to meet the right hand at the back of her head. The work which she learned to do in that position, as previously stated, was extraordinarily delicate and minute. When, however, this condition passed, she remembered absolutely nothing of all that had happened to her during those nine years, and the skill which she had acquired in her craftsmanship was as if it had never been. She had to begin to learn her flower work all over again.

This period of nine years, which remained to the end a perfect blank in her memory, began on Sunday, June 3, 1866. Her medical attendant, Dr. Speir, was visiting her that morning and by way of excuse for a rather hurried departure he remarked that his wife was giving him "chicken-pot-pie" for dinner which would be no good if it was allowed to get cold. When, nine years later, after endless trances and more convulsive seizures, the rigidity of the right arm suddenly relaxed, it was in some sense a new Mollie who awoke to consciousness. On the appearance of Dr. Speir, though he had never ceased to visit her in the interval, Mollie asked him, "Well, Doctor, were you in time for your "chicken-pot-pie?" To her aunt she said: "Why, Aunt Susie, what has become of your red cheeks? You look so old and changed." Her brother, who was a lad of thirteen at the time "the great trance" came on, was immediately repelled by her as being too familiar for a stranger. She remembered him a boy; he was now a man wearing a moustache. She had kept a diary and written thousands of letters with her left hand during the interval, but she did not recognize the handwriting, and had some difficulty in recovering the use of pen or pencil.

One of her most intimate friends during this later stage of her suffering life, was a Mr. George Sargent, a manufacturer of invalid furniture, with whom she entered into a sort of business partnership. He used to visit her quite late and relieve her aunt in sitting up with her. In this way he became acquainted with Mollie's different personalities, and, to distinguish them, christened them by such rather absurd names as "Idol," "Rosebud," "Pearl" etc. He has left an account of his personal experiences, dated July 5, 1893, which Judge Dailey has printed and from which I venture to quote. Mr. Sargent tells us, for example:

> My first acquaintance with "Idol " began April 8, 1886. Three days previous to that date, Miss Fancher had accidentally fallen from the bed, striking her head on the floor, which added injury to injury, causing unusual suffering.
>
> On the evening mentioned her aunt Susie (Miss Crosby) and I were sitting by her bedside, when Miss Fancher went into a trance.
>
> While in this condition her aunt left the room. When she came out of the trance I was alone with her, and was startled to see her eyes wide open, since I had never before seen her except with closed eyes. She looked strangely at me and asked "Who arc you? as though it was an impertinence for a stranger to be sitting by her bedside, and at the same time asked, "Where is---------?" naming a person wholly unfamiliar to me, and then asked about a matter of which I was entirely ignorant. ... I was nonplussed, and each moment added to my confusion. ... I was trying to explain my identity when her aunt returned. She was almost as surprised as I, and she said it was three or four years since "that Mollie " had made an appearance.

Mr. Sargent was then formally introduced, "as a friend of the other Mollie," whereupon—

> She made all sorts of inquiries concerning the other Mollie, wanted to know if I would think as much of this Mollie as I did of the other Mollie. She said nobody cared anything for her. They put off her questions and tried to get rid of her. ... After a stay of about three quarters of an hour, she said: "I am very tired," and with the saddest, sweetest expression on her face, and with pleading arms outstretched towards her aunt Susie, she said, with a voice of such pathos that I shall never

forget it, "Hold me close, kiss my eyes down," and in the twinkling of an eye her features became rigid as sculptured marble.

After a lapse of some ten or fifteen minutes she returned to consciousness, and the original Mollie again appeared on the scene and seemed wholly ignorant of what had happened.

From that date, for perhaps a year, the second Mollie came at frequent, though irregular, intervals, and the length of her visits increased. She seemed to have no note of time; there were no yesterday or tomorrow in her calendar. When she came, it was always through a trance condition, and usually accompanied by severe spasms, and her exit was in a similar manner. If she had been talking at the time of her departure on any subject, on her return, whether it happened to be an hour, a day or a week, she would take up the thread of conversation where she dropped it, if the same people were present.

The curious thing was that these personalities, learning in the course of conversation of each other's existence, were apt to be very inquisitive about the character and doings of her whom they were each disposed to regard as a sort of rival. Mr. Sargent came in time to know them all and found them easy to distinguish.

"Pearl " seemed to reproduce the characteristics of Miss Fancher at the age of sixteen, just before her terrible accidents, and her memory covered all that she had experienced up to about 1865.

Her expression and accent were those of a very properly brought up young lady of that period. "Her visits," we are told, "were very brief, sometimes five, at others ten or fifteen minutes, and sometimes only a minute. Then she makes her presence known by the pressure of her fingers and holds no conversation at all." There was nothing evil about any of these personalities, but they were inclined to be jealous of "Sunbeam," the name given to the normal Miss Fancher whom her friends knew in the daytime.

> I soon found [writes Mr. Sargent] that when we told "Idol" of the numerous friends of "Sunbeam," of her beautiful work which we showed her, she seemed to become exceedingly jealous, and was sad that she had no friends, and that she could not do the work that the other Mollie, "Sunbeam," could do. She would get hold of u Sunbeam's "work, and hide it away about the bed, or in other places within her

reach, and to prevent this, "Sunbeam" secretes it, or asks others to put the work away. "Idol " sometimes unravels her crochet work.

Undoubtedly the most attractive of all the personalities is that which Mr. Sargent christened "Rosebud." He gives the following account of his first introduction to Mollie Fancher in that character.

> One year after "Idol " came I first saw "Rosebud." It was the sweetest little child's face, the voice and accent that of a little child. She was apparently frightened, and was asking for her mother. I inquired "Who is this?" Without answering she asked me who I was. I asked her whom she knew. She said she knew Spencer, who, I have since learned, was a friend and a little boy acquaintance of Miss Fancher's childhood. Miss Crosby told me that "Rosebud" came first eight years before, but only at intervals. I began to strike up an acquaintance with her. She asked me if I loved her? I asked how old she was, and she said "Six years old." I asked her if she went to school, and she said "Yes, sir." She told me the names of her playmates. ... She is a great mimic and can imitate animals and fowls very nicely. I asked her to sing for me and she sang "I want to be an angel" and other children's songs.

Let me here remark in passing that the "Rosebud " personality presents a remarkable analogy with the case of Anna Maria Castreca, discussed above. This nun, at the age of twenty-seven, suddenly put on the outward semblance of childhood, completely forgetting all that she had previously learnt. The condition persisted for some months, and then as suddenly disappeared. She had also before this exhibited the phenomena of paralysis, loss of sight, inability to take nourishment, clairvoyance, and innumerable convulsive seizures in which she was violently thrown to the ground. She was subsequently marked with the stigmata and died as Abbess in the odour of sanctity A.D. 1736.

As Mollie's personalities hardly ever emerged except at night, we have, unfortunately, no medical report regarding them, but Mr. Sargent and Miss Crosby are far from being the only witnesses. Such intimate friends as Dailey, the Townsends, Mr. Howard S. Jones and his wife, whose presence at late hours Miss Fancher in no way resented, all give similar descriptions. It is stated that Mollie, like Teresa Higginson, never slept, but Mollie, also like Teresa Higginson, was subject to frequent trances, and she herself was of opinion that the trances served her in place of sleep. What is perhaps most noteworthy in connection with these trances is the passage from what Dailey calls the "rigid trance" through the "relaxed trance" to normal conditions. In these convulsive seizures there must have been much that was painful to look upon.

He writes:

> The rigid trance was followed by a relaxed trance, then by violent spasms of the body, and the shaking of the bed and floor; and then came swinging of the arms, the beating of the breast and the top of the head with her fists, and the efforts to restrain her, and finally a reawakening to consciousness.

Again he describes how he himself witnessed the relaxing of her arms from their rigid condition which was "the first evidence of returning consciousness."

> Then came violent spasms and twitching of the limbs, then the rapid swaying of her head from side to side set in, followed by moans as of distress, then she violently beat her breast over the region of the heart with one fist and with the other hand attempted to tear her hair and beat her head. These acts were restrained as much as possible, but the violence of the spasms perceptibly shook the floor.

Supposing Mollie had been going through this *crise de nerfs* alone behind a locked door, I ask myself what would have been the impressions of some pious companion outside who had inherited all the mediaeval traditions as to the physical interference of the demon with those who led lives of exceptional austerity. Teresa Higginson reported to her director in 1880:

> Sometimes the Devil used to throw me completely out of bed, throw things at me that were in the room, and make awful noises, and I used to be afraid at first that Miss Gallagher or the people of the house would hear.... Whenever our dear good God accepted my poor prayers and little nothings in behalf of poor sinners, he, the Devil, used to be infuriated, and beat and drag and almost choke me.... The Devil used to make me strike myself as I have seen children playing with each other.

So again we read, in connection with other experiences of the same mystic, that, "these strange illnesses were supernatural—Teresa was, in fact, in ecstasy, a condition which became very constant at this time," and Miss Ryland is further quoted as saying "There are two ways in which Teresa was taken. In one the body was supple and she showed either excessive grief or excessive joy. In the other the body was rigid and it was almost impossible to move her.... Twice she was like that in the street." It would certainly be presumptuous to deny that these seizures may have been supernatural," but remembering Teresa's sickly childhood, her fall into a saw-pit and her fall from a tree ("after which she was ill for six or seven weeks"), her persistent insomnia and abstention from food, is it quite safe to affirm that her experiences were specifically different from those of such an invalid as Mollie Fancher? No doubt Teresa was not bedridden as Miss Fancher was, but Miss Fancher was just as busy so far as her mind and hands were concerned, and it is not obvious that the privation of the powers of locomotion would greatly affect the conditions of these inexplicable seizures. The same Miss Ryland who is responsible for the above thus describes Teresa's vision of the Passion:

> She sees Him bound in the garden, stretches out her hands and legs to be bound instead. Blow on the right cheek by the mouth. Blow on left eye. Heavy groans. A blow on mouth. Pulling of beard. Holds her chin. Low cries of pain. Sickness. A blow on the left side of the head. Beard is pulled, etc.

So, after contemplating the first fall under the Cross—

> "Oh Jesus let me raise Thee." A blow on the left cheek. "Stand back." A blow on the right cheek.... Five fearful blows about the head and face, one on the mouth. "Oh, my heart will break... Fearful fall. Galls out in pain. Seven blows about head and face. One on the stomach.

The blows here referred to are, of course, the blows which Teresa in her trance-state struck herself, with her own closed hands. She seems exactly to have reproduced the self-inflicted injuries with which the stigmatica Elizabeth of Herkenrode, in the year 1275, punctuated her visions of the Passion, and there are numerous similar examples. One is impelled to ask whether we have any sufficient guarantee that the noises heard in Miss Higginson's room "as if someone gave her five heavy blows on the side of her head; then as if she was taken and banged violently against the room floor three or four times," were not simply due to some convulsive seizure analogous to Mollie's "spasms?"

Again the whole question of Miss Fancher's five personalities seems to me a matter of considerable interest to the hagiographer. The normal Mollie, "Sunbeam," was absolutely sincere in disavowing all knowledge of anything which had been either said or done by "Idol" or "Pearl." It was the mere accident of her helpless condition, entailing more or less continuous observation, which led to the existence of these dissociated personalities being discovered at all. "Pearl" might have eaten, or drunk, or stolen, or lied, without "Sunbeam" having the least idea that anything of the sort had happened. In the case of Theresa Neumann we know that she who answers questions while the ecstasies of the Passion are in progress exhibits an intelligence of the most rudimentary kind, incapable even of counting numerals or of grappling with any abstract idea. Can we positively say that this is not a new personality—the more so that the history of the case with its spinal injuries, six years immobility with paralysed members, supervening blindness, inability to absorb nourishment, clairvoyant knowledge, and sudden recoveries of faculties in abeyance, exhibits striking analogies with the experiences of Mollie Fancher? When the phenomena of the lady last mentioned were being discussed in the New York papers in 1878, a prominent American neurologist, Dr. W. H. Hammond, in a letter to *The Sun*, remarked: "This girl in Brooklyn is a Protestant; so she confines her vision to seeing heaven and her dead friends. Were she a Catholic, she'd see the Virgin Mary or the Saviour, like that girl at Lourdes." The observation is offensively worded, and the present writer for one, after devoting a good deal of attention to the history of the apparitions at the Grotto, would indignantly reject any attempt to class St. Bernadette with the type of invalid we have here been considering; but where neurotic symptoms are conspicuously in evidence, it does not seem clear that the sarcasm of the New York scientist is altogether devoid of foundation. If the thoughts of such a patient were concentrated upon any particular class of religious mysteries, these impressions would be likely to recur in the visions or dreams appertaining to a state of trance.

3

Among the various articles which were published in the periodical *Etudes Carmilitaines* in April 1933 upon the phenomena of Theresa Neumann, a contribution by Père Lavaud, O.P., commented incidentally upon the *inedia* of Mollie Fancher, which had been not long since discussed in *The Month*. Whether Pdre Lavaud had himself seen what was written in those pages, or whether he was speaking from some second-hand report, I am unable to say; but he reproved Dom Mager, O.S.B., for introducing the name of "the fasting girl of Brooklyn" in such a connexion, and he declared that there is overwhelming evidence that Miss Fancher's fast was far from being absolute. Dom Mager in his Paris conference had made reference to the matter in these terms:

> Konnersreuth remains a problem also from another point of view. What seems more than anything to be established beyond doubt is Theresa's complete fast. In 1927 a watch which was maintained for a fortnight confirmed the belief that she neither eats nor drinks. It is true that at present, specialists are inclined to think that the watch then kept was not sufficiently strict. Moreover in modern times a case of fasting has been heard of which even if it is not so absolute as that of Konnersreuth affords matter for reflection. I refer to the case of Mollie Fancher at Brooklyn in the United States which has been described and appraised in *The Month*, the periodical of the English Jesuits. If we admit the possibility of so prolonged a natural fast it is not inconceivable that Theresa Neumann's fast may find a more or less natural explanation. However this may be, it would seem desirable that Theresa should accept the invitation of the Bavarian bishops to undergo a fresh medical test.

It will be noticed that Dom Mager expressly declares that Miss Fancher's fast was not so absolute as that of Konnersreuth, and this also was made clear in my articles in The Month. I quoted Dr. Speir, her most regular medical attendant, as saying in 1878: "I do not believe that any food—that is solids—has ever passed the woman's lips since her attack of paralysis [in 1866]. As for an occasional teaspoonful of water or milk, I sometimes force her to take it by using an instrument to prize open her mouth. But that is painful to her."

But Père Lavaud appends a footnote to the remark quoted above as to the overwhelming proof that Miss Fancher's fast was not absolute. It runs in these terms:"

With regard to her being without food Dr. George Beard said that he had evidence unsought which showed that not only was she eating but she was living on the fat of the land." This is quoted [in English] by de Hovre. See also the two articles of Dr. Witry, a psychotherapist at Metz, in *Schildwache*, 28 Nov. and 5 Dec., 1931. The author shows how entirely the observation of the case was devoid of any scientific character. If Theresa's fast had not been better controlled and more solidly demonstrated no one would trouble to enter into explanations; everyone would simply refuse to credit it. It is strange to find Catholic writers like Father Thurston, S.J., whom Dom Mager here refers to, taking these marvellous statements on non-Catholic authority at their face value, without criticism, and on the other hand showing a hypercritical rigour when there is question of phenomena duly observed and attested in Catholic surroundings.

It is such a passage as this which makes me wonder whether Pere Lavaud can himself have read the articles of mine which are here criticized. I have never expressed any doubt as to the genuineness of Theresa Neumann's fast, or as to her stigmata. On the contrary, I have on more than one occasion very clearly affirmed my belief in them. For example, in September 1931, wrote: "There can be no thought of disputing the fact that the fortnight s observation of Theresa Neumann has proved to the satisfaction of all unprejudiced persons that she did not during that period take either food or drink. And in *Studies* for March 1929 I said, "for the last two years nothing has passed her lips save the particle received in Holy Communion. There seems absolutely no reason to doubt the fact of this *inedia*." What I have hesitated to accept is not the fast, but the inference that the fast is miraculous. Neither have I denied that it may very well be miraculous; I have only urged that with such cases as those of Mollie Fancher and a number of others before our eyes, we shall do well to suspend our judgment until medical science is in a position to pronounce more positively upon the abnormal faculties of paralytic subjects with complicated neuroses. Père Lavaud objects that the observation of Mollie Fancher's fast was devoid of all scientific character. But so, most assuredly, was the observation of the fast of all the previous stigmatics—of Louise Lateau, of Anne Catherine Emmerich, of Domenica Lazzari, of Marie-Julie Jahenny, not to speak of St. Catherine of Siena and others in the Middle Ages. We have much better evidence for Mollie Fancher's fast, incomplete as it was, than we have for most of those just mentioned.

Let me in proof of this call attention to one or two points which must press themselves upon the notice of anyone who reviews the circumstances of the Fancher case with any care. We know that she was bed-ridden for nearly thirty years. Details are lacking for the period after Judge Dailey's book was published in 1894; and it is not disputed that before this date she had begun to take a little nourishment again and had partly recovered her sight. It is certain, in any case, that for twenty-six years she lived in one room upon the second floor of a house in Brooklyn, that during practically the whole of this period she was attended by two respected medical men (who sometimes brought other doctors to see her) and that they, not only in 1878, after the illness had lasted twelve years, but again in 1893, when she had been a prisoner for twenty-seven years, both affirmed that for at least twelve years together she had lived "without sustenance enough to feed a baby for a week." If it be objected that her doctors only visited her at intervals, we have to remember that a patient who was not only bed-ridden, but who had one arm in a fixed position above her head, and whose legs "were drawn up backwards, the ankles bent over and the bottom of the foot upwards," so that "her limbs could not be straightened out," could not possibly obtain food without assistance. Moreover, the very first point to which a doctor's attention would inevitably be directed would be the question of natural relief. Did anything pass, or could anything possibly pass without those in attendance being aware of it? For some years Mollie Fancher's aunt, Miss Crosby, did everything for her niece, and during a few months she kept a diary from which Judge Dailey quotes, and in this occurs an entry: "Since the 6th day of August (a period of three months) the natural functions for relief have not been exercised at all." If there were any indication that during this early period of her illness Mollie Fancher courted publicity, we might suppose that she had a confederate who had found means of hiding such matters from her aunt and from the doctors. But even apart from the tribute which all who knew her paid to her truthfulness and sincerely religious character, there is not a hint of the likelihood or even the possibility of such confederacy. Moreover, I should find it hard to believe that anyone afflicted, as the reports of her doctors show Miss Fancher to have been, racked and thrown about by nerve storms which gave no warning of their approach, should have been engaged all the time in carrying on an elaborate and apparently motiveless imposture. At the beginning of the trouble, Dr. Speir, as he tells us, perplexed by the nutrition problem, succeeded on one or two occasions in administering an emetic, "with the result that nothing was thrown from the stomach, showing conclusively that the stomach was empty."

But Dr. George Beard declared, so Pdre Lavaud assures us, that he had "evidence that she was living on the fat of the land" Lest anyone should suppose that this piece of information was brought to light by diligent research on the part of himself or Canon de Hovre because they had access to sources of which I knew nothing, let me point out that Dr. Beard's statement is quoted at length and answered in the same book of Judge Dailey to which most of my references were made. Dr. George Beard and Dr. W. H. Hammond were in the 'seventies of the last century prominent neurologists in New York, and entirely identified with the out-and-out scepticism characteristic of the scientists of that period.

Virchow and Huxley and Tyndall and Haeckel had set the fashion, and to all this school the slightest hint of a belief in the preternatural was like a red rag to a bull. Even the mention of the word telepathy " infuriated them. As late as 1914 Sir H. B. Donkin wrote to *The Times* that "all the evidence produced in support of telepathy was valueless, not only to scientists but also to men of ordinary common sense." Similarly Sir Ray Lankester described telepathy as "simply a boldly invented word for a supposed phenomenon which has never been demonstrated," and Mr. Clodd spoke of it "as invoking the unknown to explain the non-existent." No sooner had the case of Mollie Fancher begun to attract some attention in the New York papers than both Dr. Hammond and Dr. Beard plunged into the fray, and, as experts in up-to-date neurology, they sought to overwhelm with ridicule these preposterous assertions about a girl seeing without using her eyes and living almost entirely without food. They neither of them had any personal knowledge of the case, and it is interesting to note that Jr. Hammond denounced the stigmata of Louise Lateau, which had created some sensation throughout Europe a few years before this, as a piece of pure imposture. But even so, I think it desirable to quote the actual words of Dr. Beard. They leave rather a cutierent impression from that given by the contracted statement reproduced by Père Lavaud. What Dr. Beard wrote runs as follows:

> Unsought-for evidence has been brought to me from various quarters—from physicians and from clergymen as honourable and as able as any whose names have appeared in connexion with this case—that Mollie Fancher intentionally deceives; that she lives on the fat of the land, that the fancy articles that she professes to make are made for her; that her reading without eyes is done by trickery; but all this like the evidence on the opposite side is of non-expert character, and can, in science receive no consideration.

Let us note in the first place that Dr. Beard made no attempt to produce the "evidence" which had been brought to him unsought. On the contrary he admits it was of a kind which in science could receive no consideration. Moreover, it is plain that the doctors, etc., who accepted the phenomena of Miss Fancher, and who did know the case from personal observation, were not people who could well be treated with contempt. Dr. Beard says of them in fact—

> We have not in our profession a more honourable or able body of men than some of the Brooklyn physicians who have been, directly or indirectly, connected with the case of Miss Fancher; and yet the instincts of the majority, both of general practitioners and specialists of nervous diseases, reject all their testimony relating to the claims of clairvoyance, mind-reading and prophecy.

One does not quite see why an honourable and able physician in general practice should be less capable of deciding whether a patient did or did not take food, or whether she was able to read letters and distinguish colours without the use of her eyes, than the neuropath specialist. But, of course, to admit the possibility of these marvels would have given the whole materialist case away. Dr. Beard elsewhere writes, "it is a fact, *capable of absolute proof,* that no phenomena of this kind [he is speaking of clairvoyance or seeing at a distance] have ever appeared in the world in any human creature, in the trance or out of the trance." The "proof" no doubt, is Hume's argument against miracles, that the common experience of mankind must outweigh any individual testimony which appears to run counter to it. It was in the same spirit that such rationalists as Dr. Hubert Boens and Professor Virchow and Professor Schwann ridiculed the phenomena of Louise Lateau. Boens called her "an unfortunate Christ-maniac " and an "idiot," speaking also of "the comedy which was played every Friday at Bois d'Haine, and which has been so completely exposed by the disclosures of Prof. Schwann and of myself." Dr. Beard was somewhat less discourteous to his opponents than the Continental rationalist, but he belonged to the same school as Virchow and Boens, and I must own that I do not think his testimony of any value in discrediting preternormal phenomena which he did not even pretend to have studied, much less to have witnessed.

I do not for a moment doubt that Dr. Beard had many letters written to him on the subject. When the case began to be discussed in the newspapers, there are bound to have been indignant sceptics, who, finding themselves excluded, as all strangers were excluded, from Miss

Fancher's sick-room, were keen to accept any back-stairs gossip they could collect to her detriment, and retailed it promptly to Dr. Beard. That is the sort of thing which always happens. It happened in the case of Louise Lateau, it happened in the case of Anne Catherine Emmerich, and what of Doctors Hauche and Blau in Teresa's own case? What is certain is that Dr. Beard did not venture to produce this "evidence." He said himself that it "could receive no consideration." Moreover, he had not before him the multiplied testimonies printed sixteen years later in the Dailey book. Even if they had been at hand, he probably would not have troubled to read them. The whole claim was to him preposterous. But I submit that the evidence supplied in Judge Dailey's volume shows that Dr. Beard, in suggesting that Mollie Fancher "lived on the fat of the land" was simply talking nonsense.

Père Lavaud, as noticed above, further complains that the observation of the Fancher case was devoid of any scientific character. But there is one example of a partial abstinence with regard to which this cannot rightly be said. This was the case of a Bavarian girl, Marie Furtner, who in 1835 after various illnesses came to take a disgust for all solid food and eventually was said to live entirely on cold water. Assuming that she breathed common air and exhaled carbon-dioxide like everybody else, one wonders where the carbon came from. Marie Furtner was a devout Catholic, but it was never pretended that her fast had any religious complexion. It is noteworthy that when an attempt was made to induce Marie to submit to a second period of medical supervision at Munich the self-respect of the modest Catholic peasant 'at once took the alarm. She declared that she would rather die than allow herself to be watched, weighed, pulled about and stared at by a crowd of strange men. Probably Theresa Neumann's alleged dislike of the idea of a period of observation in a Regensburg Klinik is due to some similar feeling.

CHAPTER XIV
MORE SEEING WITHOUT EYES

The case of Mollie Fancher, of which an account has been given in Chapter XIII, is not an isolated one. So far at least as certain features are concerned we can appeal to many parallels, and while some of these may reasonably fail to convince because they are insufficiently attested, others are based upon evidence which offers no loophole for scepticism. At the very time that Mollie Fancher, in Brooklyn, U.S.A., was astonishing the small circle of friends who were admitted to her sick-room by her accurate description of objects and colours which she had no eyes to see, a certain Mrs. Croad in the West of England was causing similar embarrassment to her medical attendants and to quite a number of people acquainted with her history. Like Miss Fancher, Mrs. Croad, also, was a paralytic who had been bedridden for many years. She was born in 1840. Without very much education or any pretensions to gentility, she belonged to respectable people who were in fairly comfortable circumstances and were regular chapel-goers. We learn that in her 'teens she had fits which were possibly epileptic, but which do not seem to have given occasion for any grave anxiety. She married at nineteen, and this union, with a mate or captain in the merchant service, appears to have been a happy one. But not long afterwards she was subjected to a series of mental and physical shocks, which in the end contributed to bring about pathological conditions of a very distressing kind. The trouble began with a very bad fall in which it is said that the spine was injured, and which was followed after a short interval by the recurrence of frequent epileptic seizures. Then she lost her child, who by some accident was scalded to death. Finally, she had a second bad fall down some steps, the mischief being complicated by the effort she made to save an infant whom she happened to be carrying in her arms at the time. These distressing accidents occurred in 1864, and, paralysis supervening, in 1866 she became bed-ridden, remaining m this condition until 1880, when she removed to Bristol and came under the observation of Dr. J. G. Davey. His medical description of the case, published in the *Journal of Psychological Medicine*, runs as follows:

> In 1870, it is stated, Mrs. Croad became totally blind, in the following year deaf, and in 1874 speechless. The paralysis which was limited to the lower extremities, involved, in 1879, the upper limbs; but at this time [he was writing early in 1881] the loss of sensation and motion is limited to the left arm, the fingers and thumb of the left hand being but partially affected. The right hand and arm have recovered their once-lost functions. She is now able to articulate, though with difficulty, from, as it appears to me, a tetanic rigidity of the temporal and masseter muscles, by which the mouth is kept, to a large extent, fixed and closed. It was in October last [*i.e.*, October 1880] that I was asked to see Mrs. Croad. I found her sitting in a semi-recumbent position in a small bedstead, her head and shoulders resting on pillows. The eyelids were fast closed, and the left arm and hand resting by the side. The knees I found then, as they are still, bent at an acute angle, the heels closely pressed to the under part of the thighs.

In this, of course, there was nothing unusual. Similar cases may be found by the score in every hospital for functional nervous disorders. But from Swindon and other places where the patient had resided since her invalid condition had become permanent, strange things were reported of Mrs. Croad's abnormal powers of perception in spite of her blindness and closed eyelids. It was this which had interested Dr. Davey in the case and which led to the publication of this detailed report in a specialist journal of high standing. The reader will, I trust, pardon a somewhat long quotation. Dr. Davey goes on:

> Since October, and through the months of November and December 1880, I have subjected Mrs. Croad to many and various tests with the view of satisfying myself as to the truth or otherwise of the statements

given to the world of her blindness, sense of touch, and marvellous sympathies. To my near neighbours Drs. Andrews and Elliot—I am much indebted. The various tests referred to were witnessed by them in my presence, and with the effect of assuring us that she (Mrs. Croad) was and is enabled to perceive, through the aid only of touch, the various objects, both large and small, on any given card or photograph. After an experience extending over some nine or ten weeks, during which the "tests" were many times repeated, and, now and then, in the presence of several medical and non-medical (ladies and gentlemen) friends, there remained (I believe) not the least doubt of this "transference of sense" from the eyes of Mrs. Croad to her fingers and the palm of her right hand. It need not be supposed that I and others were content to believe in Mrs. Croad's blindness, and to take no specific precautions against any possible trick or deception—far from this. On solicitation, she very kindly assented to be blindfolded, after a very decided fashion; and so blindfolded that neither deception on her part nor prejudice nor false judgment on ours were—either the one or the other—possible. The blindfolding was accomplished thus: a pad of cotton wool being placed on each orbit, the face was then covered by a large and thickly folded neckerchief; this was tied securely at the back part of the head, and—even more than this—more cotton wool was pushed up towards the eyes, on either side of the nose. Not content with this, however, the aid of two fingers of a bystander was requisitioned, and with these a continued pressure was kept up, during the testing, outside and over the neckerchief and wool, and above the closed eyes. At this stage of the proceedings the room was, on two different occasions, very thoroughly darkened. Under such circumstances it was the testing commenced, and continued to the end; the result being, as theretofore, in the highest degree conclusive and satisfactory. The transference of sense from one organ to another as an acquired and spontaneous condition of being must, on the evidence here adduced, be accepted as a demonstrated and certain fact. I would state here, that on receiving a picture card or a photo from a bystander she (Mrs. Croad) places it on and about the chin or mouth, and perhaps draws it across the forehead, but the minute examination of the card is, apparently, the work of the fingers of the right hand. These several acts are, for the most part, followed by a quiet and intense thought, a well-marked concentration of mind on the picture, or whatever it may be, when, after a short time, she writes on a slate kept near her a description— sometimes a full and detailed one—of the card, its colouring, and the several objects thereon. I have seen some forty or fifty picture cards and photographs described by Mrs. Croad at different times with various degrees of accuracy during the whole period I have known her. Occasionally her rapid and precise perception, or, if you prefer the word, conception, of the picture, and of the many but minute and trifling, objects going to form its entirety, is really startling. I have but seldom seen her wholly at fault, though she has met with her failures.

In another passage Dr. Davey reminds his readers of the disabilities which at all times interfered with Mrs. Croad's use of the natural organs of vision.

> Bear in mind [he says] that for a period of many years her eyelids have been persistently closed by, as it would seem, a spasmodic or involuntary action of the muscular structures thereto attached. In her there is no aperture or apertures—unless you make such by your own act, *i.e.*, unless you pull the eyelids apart."

It is also perhaps worthwhile to point out that the writer of this report was not a spiritualist, nor apparently a believer in any sort of supernatural revelation. "If any one here" he writes—the paper was originally read at a meeting of a learned society— "expects me to discourse or speculate on the immaterial, the metaphysical, he will be disappointed: for this single and sufficient reason, I believe in nothing of the kind. As a materialist, I hold, etc.", and he goes on to express views which are hardly consistent with the acceptance of any doctrine of a future life. This certainly adds weight to his testimony as witness to phenomena so abnormal. Moreover, though he does not dwell upon the more psychic aspect of Mrs. Croad's abnormal perceptions, Dr. Davey was evidently not prepared to dismiss unceremoniously the stories current as to that lady's possession of strange knowledge which could hardly have come to her through any "transference of special sense." For example he writes:

> As a further illustration of Mrs. Croad's peculiar and clairvoyant gifts it should be stated that, at my second interview with her and in the presence of Dr. Andrews and others, certain of my own personal and private convictions on a particular subject became, as it would seem, in a strange and exceptional manner, known to Mrs. Croad. She asked

me if I would allow her to tell me a secret of my own life-history, and would I be offended if she wrote it on her slate. I replied, "No." That written on the slate was and is a fact, than which nothing could or can be more truthful and to the point. Dr. Andrews is prepared to verify [corroborate] this; the others present on this occasion were but little known to me.

Although Dr. Davey's statement, supported as it is by his appeal to the personal experience of other medical men who assisted him in his investigation of the case, seems to me thoroughly convincing, it should be pointed out that it does not stand alone. At the time when he was writing, a short biographical sketch of Mrs. Croad was already in print, the work of an acquaintance of hers who was apparently a Nonconformist Minister. This gentleman, a Mr. J. G. Westlake, evidently entertained a deep regard for Mrs. Groad s high religious character and was also impressed by the strange faculties of which he had had ample evidence in the course of his intercourse with her. She had at one time been for some months the guest of himself and his wife, and he had no doubt had special opportunities of learning the facts of her history. He called his little book *A Service of Suffering*, and when the first issue was sold out, he prepared another edition in 1882 in a somewhat enlarged form. When Mr. Westlake mooted the idea of writing some such account, he tells us that the invalid raised objections on the score of the publicity likely to be entailed. "I would ask you," she wrote to him, "not to bring my name before others; not that I am ashamed, but I have a great dislike to be talked about. ... You are quite welcome to tell, far and near, of the great love of my God to me a sinner, only do not give my name." It was inevitable, especially in a small country town— Mrs. Croad was at Swindon at the time—that the strange faculties she possessed should be a good deal talked about locally, but, if we may trust the statements of Mr. Westlake and others, she was a sincerely good woman with a deep sense of the supernatural. One day the well-known writer of religious verse, Miss Frances Havergal, was taken to see Mrs. Croad. The invalid was at that time quite unable to articulate, but in the course of the visit she wrote upon the slate these words: " I think I just begin to see the splendour of Gods will." Some little time afterwards Miss Havergal sent her a poem for which this utterance served as a text. It is much too long to quote entire, but these two stanzas give a fair impression of its drift:

> For her God's will was suffering
> Just waiting, lying still;
> Days passing on in weariness,
> In shadows deep and chill;
> And yet she had begun to see
> The splendour of God's will.
>
> A splendour that is shining
> Upon His children's way,
> That guides the willing footsteps
> That do not want to stray,
> And leads them ever onward
> Unto the perfect day.

It cannot be claimed for Mr. Westlake's booklet that it is in any way critical. It is not written as a scientific discussion of preternormal psychological facts. But it shows plainly enough that Mrs. Croad's remarkable perceptions did make a very profound impression upon those who lived in her company. Besides bearing out Dr. Davey's testimony as to her power of describing pictures and colours without the use of normal sight, he quotes several remarkable instances of her knowledge of what was taking place beyond her room. Some of these were matters of observation; others are based only upon her own statement. The value we attach to them must depend upon our opinion of her truthfulness. Here is one example of the latter class. Mr. Westlake writes:

> Mrs. Croad has frequently told me that she has had communications from departed friends, and also from others still living, at times when they have been in peculiar peril. She tells me that at the time she was living with her grandparents, while her father was at sea, his life was more than once in jeopardy from shipwreck, but on each occasion, though hundreds of miles away, she saw what was transpiring and informed his father and mother; and that when they next heard from him, they found that what she had described to them was substantially true. She also says that soon after they were married she and her husband agreed with each other that the one that died first should communicate the fact in some intelligible way to the other; and that at the moment when he fell senseless on the deck of the vessel, he appeared in the most unmistakable manner to her and said "Goodbye,

Carrie. I am going." She was so certain he was dead that she told her friends at Brading what she had seen, and although they did not place much confidence in her statement, they took note of the exact time, and in a few weeks after, when the news came, they found that, making allowance for the difference of longitude, the time of his death coincided exactly with his appearance to her.

This is, of course, a relatively common type of experience of which countless examples have been collected by Messrs. Gurney and Myers, and by Mrs. Sidgwick, but the familiarity of stories of this kind rather strengthens the case for Mrs. Croad's veracity. All this happened and was in print before the Society for Psychical Research had ever begun its work. Mr. Westlake's own personal observation of Mrs. Croad's powers seems to have been rather vague, but this is the sort of thing he tells us:

> She would frequently, while living with us, ask that her room should be put in order, as she expected visitors to see her shortly, and this, possibly, when she had not had anyone to see her for some days, nor had any apparent reason to expect that anyone was coming; we found her uniformly correct in her impressions.... Recently, when she was living at Swindon, Mr. Harris went from Redland to see her; he had not seen her for five weeks, nor had she any intimation of his intended visit. Early in the morning she asked her daughter to put the room straight, as she expected Mr. Harris would call in the course of the day. When he arrived about mid-day, she wrote on her slate "I have been expecting you."

Dr. Davey himself had some similar experiences when his patient was living near Bristol, for he records in the article previously referred to:

> It is said also by those near and dear to her that such is Mrs. Croad's prevision that she has been known to foretell my own visits to her; what I mean is, that on my approach to the house she occupies and when at a distance from it, and unseen by anyone about her—in fact not within sight—she has said, "Dr. Davey is coming; he will be here directly."

It is curious to find St. Augustine of Hippo fifteen hundred years ago describing a similar case of which apparently he had personal knowledge. He calls his invalid "possessed," and says that he spoke in a kind of a delirium, but the visitor whose arrival the sufferer looked for with so much impatience was a priest, and from his sick bed the man described accurately every stage of the priest's journey from the moment he started until the moment he knocked at the door of the house. It would seem that St. Augustine had no better reason for supposing that this sufferer was the victim of diabolical possession than the simple fact that he had convulsive seizures and possessed an inexplicable knowledge of the movements of the friend upon whom his whole thought centred. A similar strange telepathic bond seems to have existed between Blessed Marie d'Oignies and her devoted "preacher," James de Vitry, afterwards Cardinal. But in the fifth century, as in the thirteenth, all nervous disorders presenting features which seemed to transcend normal experience were apt to be attributed either to diabolical possession or to a supernatural cause.

There seems to be no doubt that Mrs. Croad's helpless condition was attended with much physical suffering which she bore with exemplary patience. Mr. Westlake writes:

> Mrs. Croad is a great sufferer from convulsive fits. As the fit comes on, she is seized with severe shaking, till she becomes rigid and unconscious. My wife with others stayed with her all night in one of these attacks. A fit lasted so long that they thought her dead and were preparing to lay her out; but after waiting a while, and administering a stimulant, they were thankful to see her revive. Since then she has had so many and such severe attacks, that it really seems incredible that any human being could endure so much. I often think that, physically, she is maintained in a miraculous manner, especially when I see how little food she takes. In the month of December last, for three weeks, she did not take nourishment equal to half a pint of milk.

This last statement is peculiarly interesting in view of the rejection of nearly all food which, as I have previously pointed out, characterizes not only the case of Mollie Fancher, but those of Teresa Higginson, Anne Catherine Emmerich, Domenica Lazzari, Louise Lateau, and Theresa Neumann at the present day. Dr. Davey does not seem to have attempted to study this feature of Mrs. Croad's nervous condition, but he was not altogether ignorant of it and does not seem to have discredited it, for in his summary account of the earlier history of the case before it came under his observation, he remarks; "She became at length powerless or paralytic; whilst as a consequence attendant on a chronic gastric affection she is said to have lost all power to partake of or digest solid food."

I have directed attention more than once in these pages to the book of Dr. Haddock, *Somnolism and Psycheism (sic)*, in which he gives an account of the remarkable faculty possessed by his illiterate servant Emma of describing pictures without the use of her eyes. She held them over the top of her head, felt them with her fingers and was then able to tell what they represented and to indicate the colours. The tests applied seem to have been of a very effective kind, and success was attained even when no one present knew anything of the subject of the particular picture submitted to her, thus excluding the possibility of mere telepathy from the mind of a bystander. It is true that Emma, when making these experiments, was first put into a hypnotic trance, but the faculty she possessed in that condition seems to have been the exact counterpart of what is recorded of Mollie Fancher and Mrs. Croad, both of whom were afflicted with complicated neuroses.

But for fear anyone should suppose that such abnormal powers are only heard of in heretical countries, where diabolical influences might be conceived to enjoy an exceptional range of activity, let us take a case from Italy. It is recorded by no less an authority than the late Professor Cesare Lombroso, the famous neuropath and criminologist, as a psychological marvel which had developed under his own eyes. He himself tells us that this experience, which came to him at the age of forty-six, was the first shock to the resolute materialism in which all his early life was passed. It led him in the end to so much belief in the spiritual nature of man as postulates survival after death, though the revelation he accepted was unfortunately that of the séance room, not that of Catholic tradition. Anyway, in the opening sentences of his latest published work, Lombroso remarks:

> If ever there was anyone in this world who by his scientific training and by a sort of instinct was resolutely opposed to Spiritism, I was that man; for out of the principle that all force was merely a property of matter, and that the soul was an emanation of the brain, I had created for myself the line of study which was to be my life's work. To think that I, of all men, who for so many years had laughed at the very idea of spirits, and table-turning and seances, should come to believe what I now believe! But if I have always been enthusiastically loyal to the banner of Science, I have had one passion which is even stronger still—a

veneration for truth, a resolve to be content with nothing short of the evidence of ascertained facts.

Now, in the year 1882, I, who had been so bitter an enemy to Spiritism that for years together I would not touch it, or be present at any experiment of the kind, was, in the course of my professional duties as a neuropathologist, brought into contact with certain remarkable psychic phenomena of which science could give no account except to note the circumstance that the subjects concerned were all either hysterical or hypnotized.

The first experience, which is the most to our purpose, is described by Lombroso as a "transference of sense perceptions," and is recounted as follows:

One morning in 1882 I was sent for to the bedside of the Signorina C.S., aged fourteen, the daughter of one of the most active and capable of our Italian public men. The mother was sane, intelligent and healthy, but her two sons at the age of about twelve or fourteen had shot up in height in an extraordinary way and seemed to show physical symptoms. The girl herself... had just previously grown seven inches within a very short space of time and had developed serious gastric troubles of hysterical origin (vomiting, dyspepsia, etc.),.so much so that for one month she had been able to take nothing but solid food, and then for another month nothing but liquids, while during a third month she had developed attacks of hysterical convulsive spasms with hyperaesthesias so pronounced that if a thread were laid upon her hand she declared it felt as heavy as a bar of iron.

After the occurrence of another monthly period she became blind, while hysterogenic pressure points were noted in the little finger and in the forefinger. When these were touched they produced convulsions. There were also motor pareses [attacks of imperfect paralysis] in the legs, with exaggerated reflexes and spasms, while her muscular energy was enormously increased, so much that, measured by a dynamometer, the force of her handclasp augmented from 32 to 47 kilograms.

And at this point extraordinary phenomena began to present themselves. First there was a somnambulistic condition in which she showed an amazing activity in work about the house, a very affectionate disposition towards the whole family and a conspicuous musical talent; at a later stage there was a change of character; she developed a masculine boldness and a lack of moral principle.

But the most remarkable fact was this, that while she lost the power of seeing with her eyes, she saw, as clearly as before, with the tip of her nose and the lobe of her left ear. By these improvised organs, though I had bandaged her eyes, she read a letter which had just then come to me by post and she was able to distinguish the figures on the dial of a dynamometer.

Very curious was her realization in gesture of the function of these new substitutes which took the place of eyes. If, for example, I put my finger close to her nose or to her ear making pretence to touch them, or still better if I only directed a beam of light upon either, even if it were but for a moment or two, she manifested instant sensibility and irritation. "You want to blind me," she cried out. Then with an instinctive movement as unforeseen as the phenomenon itself, she put her arm in the way to protect the lobe of the ear or the tip of her nose and remained in that position for some minutes.

There was also a transference of the seat of the sense of smell.

While ammonia and asafoetida if they were thrust under her nose provoked not the least reaction, even a slightly odorous substance placed beneath her chin produced a lively impression which manifested itself in expressive gesture. If the scent was an agreeable one, she smiled, her eyelids fluttered and she inhaled rapid breaths.

If the odour was nauseous she put up her hands to that part of the chin which had become sensitive and shook her head violently.

Later on her sense of smell was transferred to the insteps of her feet, and then when any odour was unpleasant to her, she kicked out with her feet to left and right with contortions of her whole body, but when she enjoyed the scent she stood quite still, smiling and drawing her breath quickly.

Deferring any comment upon this statement, I propose to call attention to one final example of the same kind of sense transference, which was reported in 1840 by Professor Carmagnola. It is referred to, along with several others, by Lombroso, but I have been able to consult Carmagnola's own account of the matter which is printed in the *Giornale delle Scienze Mediche* for the year mentioned. Considerations of space must restrain me from going into much detail, but I may note that the Professor's first sentences show him to have been almost as much startled by what he witnessed as Lombroso was by his experiences with the Signorina C.S. He tells his readers that he is going to describe a series of facts which had come under his own observation, but he adds that he himself, if he had merely heard these recounted by someone else, would have dismissed the whole as a cock-and-bull story unworthy of serious attention. While unable to offer any sort of scientific explanation, he protests that he held it his duty to be sternly and strictly truthful in his statement of what he had witnessed.

Like the case last referred to, this also was concerned with a young girl of thirteen or fourteen, and here again the starting point of the subsequent harassing developments must be looked for in the physiological conditions attendant on the approach of womanhood. The trouble began with a nervous cough which came on whenever the child attempted to eat or drink and which was so persistent that for three months she could hardly take nourishment of any kind. Then followed exaggerated hyperaesthesias and all sorts of neurotic troubles. In her normal waking condition she became speechless, but while asleep and dreaming she spoke freely recounting past adventures with great animation, and singing, with perfect accuracy as to words and music, the airs of the operas then in vogue. Upon this supervened a state of constantly recurring somnambulism, alternating with cataleptic trances. The details are curious, but I must content myself with noting that at this stage of her illness, while she was absolutely deaf and blind, so far as concerned the special organs of these two senses, she could hear with her shoulders—or, more strictly, her shoulder-blades (*spalle*)—and see with her hands. In her somnambulisms she dressed herself, moved about and performed all sorts of little domestic tasks in her room, without ever knocking against any obstacles. She conversed freely, and when shown pretty coloured ribbons and other things she would discriminate the colours with perfect accuracy, and yet all the time the pupils of her eyes were completely turned up and only the lower portion of the sclerotic was visible.

She went about holding the palms of her hands open before her, and it soon became clear that these in her somnambulant condition served her as organs of sight. Professor Carmagnola's statement in justification of this conclusion is interesting:

> I took [he says] the first book that I chanced to pick up; it was a copy of *Telemaque*. I opened it at random and put it under her extended hands. They were not in contact with the book but remained at a distance of half an inch or so from the printed page.
>
> In that position she read the text correctly and rapidly. I put the book in a different position and she went on reading as before. It was night time and I held a candle near to see if what she read aloud corresponded accurately with the printed text. The reading, I found, was quite correct. Then I moved the candle away to ascertain if she was dependent upon the light it gave but she went on reading quite evenly and without stumbling. Her mother wrote these words on a scrap of paper *Therese, je vous aime*, and she not only read the words with her hands but she recognized that it was her mother's writing. She wanted to look at herself in the glass and so she spread out her hands in front of the mirror, but she only saw her hands; then she lowered them to see her face but apparently saw nothing at all, then by a sort of instinct she put up her hands once more, and again she saw only her hands; so she put one in front of the other, but with no better success. Finally she lost her temper, stamped on the floor, tore off her cap from her head and hastily beat a retreat.

It is, of course, open to the reader to suggest that the two Italian children last spoken of were the victims of diabolical possession. The contention might seem to be sustained by the fact that Lombroso's patient made uncanny but quite accurate prophecies as to the future course of her illness and recommended strange remedies for the alleviation of her attacks, which in fact were employed with some measure of success. Limits of space preclude me from giving details, though one very curious feature may be mentioned. On June 15th, the Signorina C.S. foretold that on July 2nd a spell of delirium would supervene, to be followed by severe cataleptic seizures "which would be cured by gold." In point of fact the attacks occurred as predicted and the suggested remedy proved efficacious both then and on another occasion. One rubs one's eyes and wonders whether from the year 1880, the epoch of Huxley and Tyndall and Virchow and Haeckel, we have suddenly been transported back into the Middle Ages, for it was no internal administration of the chloride of gold which was thus indicated but a simple surface contact with the raw metal. I say this because Petetin, in his *Electricite Animale* (1808), had spoken of the use of this remedy in the treatment of similar neuroses, and because Professor Garmagnola's patient in 1840 was so immensely relieved by clutching a piece of gold that she went hunting everywhere for more gold, and finding an object of gilt bronze, mistook it for real gold and thought she had discovered a treasure. But while she was sensibly relieved by the genuine metal, the bronze proved of no use at all. Is it conceivable that gold, after all, does generate some form of radio-activity to which peculiarly-conditioned persons are sensitive? What is certain is that many water-diviners, the reality of whose strange gift can hardly now be contested, are also convinced that metals may be detected in a precisely similar way by the influence they exercise, even at a distance, upon the nervous tension of the adequately disposed subject.

So far, however, as regards the question of diabolical possession, the cases of Miss Fancher, Mrs. Croad, and the Italian girls must surely all hang together. We have comparatively full knowledge of the life history of the two former, who were bed-ridden for twenty or thirty years, and in whose case there is not a trace of anything evil, but on the contrary every presumption of a most admirable spirit of Christian resignation. If the neuroses of the two other patients cannot be traced to any such terrible physical accidents as befell Miss Fancher and Mrs. Croad, Professors Lombroso and Carmagnola seem to have been satisfied that there was no sudden invasion of any malign influence from outside.

The morbid condition had developed slowly by well-marked stages and was clearly associated with the physiological changes belonging to the age of puberty. In any case this transference of special sense seems to constitute a serious problem for those who would attempt to draw a clear line of demarcation between the merely abnormal and the miraculous or supernatural.

CHAPTER XV
THE MYSTIC AS HUNGER-STRIKER

1

The question how long a man can live without food has been much debated of late by all sorts of writers and in all sorts of contexts. It is obvious that the answer in every case must depend very largely upon what kind of man we are thinking of. It depends, in other words, upon how he is constituted, not only physically, but also morally and psychically. I may confess that I am not yet quite convinced that in the course of nature everyone must die who deprives himself of both solid and liquid nourishment for more than a few weeks. No doubt, if we are talking of the ordinary course of nature, the rule that a man must eat to live is true enough. But there seem to be exceptions, and it is not quite clear to me that these exceptions can only be explained by assuming the intervention of the supernatural.

Speaking from general impressions, one would be tempted to affirm that all the more conspicuous and protracted cases of abstinence from food (total *inedia*) are to be found among the ranks of the Catholic mystics. Whether this is so exclusively the case as is commonly supposed will appear further on in the next chapter, but there can be no question that the Lives of the Saints, assuming for the moment that their data are reliable, present us with many most astounding examples of unbroken fasts. It is alleged that St. Lidwina (1433) ate nothing for twenty-eight years; the Venerable Domenica dal Paradiso (1553) for twenty years; Blessed Nicholas von Flue (1487) for nineteen years; Blessed Elizabeth von Reute (1420) for fifteen years, and so on; while in modern times a twelve years' abstinence from food (always, of course, excepting the consecrated Host received in Holy Communion) was observed in the case of both Domenica Lazzari (1848) and Louise Lateau (1883).

Of Domenica Lazzari a good deal has already been said in the chapter on stigmatization. Dr. Dei Cloche, whose medical report of the case was there largely quoted from, seems to have had no misgivings as to the fact of Domenica's total abstention from food, and the same is apparently true of the German doctors whom Lord Shrewsbury and Mr. Allies and his friends found to be studying the phenomena at a very much later date. It is noteworthy that Domenica was absolutely bedridden, and any somnambulistic tendencies could hardly have escaped the attention of her sister who lived with her. Of course' it is possible that an hysterical patient who turns away with loathing from all food during the day may prowl about at night in a somnolent state and satisfy unconsciously her dormant physical craving. Such a thing might go on undetected for a month, or even several months, but hardly for thirteen years. Moreover, one cannot but be impressed by the analogous features present in other similar mediaeval cases which it would violate all probability to suppose that Domenica had ever heard of. One of the most remarkable mystical documents of the early thirteenth century is the Life of Blessed Mary of Oignies by Cardinal Jacques de Vitry, an unusually intelligent and conscientious observer, who knew her intimately. In perfect accord with the physical repulsion for food which was so conspicuous in Domenica Lazzari and Louise Lateau, we read of Mary of Oignies:

> On one occasion she went for as long as thirty-five days without any sort of food, passing all the time in a tranquil and happy silence.... She would say nothing for many days but "Give me the Body of our Lord Jesus Christ," and as soon as her request was granted she returned to her former silent converse with her Saviour. ... At length, after five weeks, returning to herself, to the wonder of those who were present, she began to speak and to take food. But for a long time afterwards she could not in any way endure even the smell of meat, or of anything cooked, nor of wine, unless it was an ablution after the Blessed Sacrament, which was sometimes given her, in which case she minded neither the smell nor the taste.

And again, referring to a period at the end of her life when Jacques de Vitry was himself undoubtedly with her:

> During her illness she was able to eat absolutely nothing, nor could she even endure the smell of bread; yet notwithstanding this, she received the Body of our Lord without any difficulty.
>
> And this dissolving Itself, as it were, and passing into her soul, not only comforted her soul, but relieved her bodily weakness immediately. Twice during her illness it happened that on receiving the Sacred Host, her face was illumined with rays of light. We tried once whether she could take an unconsecrated particle, but she instantly turned away, having a horror for the smell of bread.
>
> And the pain and uneasiness she felt at a small portion having touched her teeth, was so great that she began to cry out, to vomit and spit, and to pant and sob, as if her breast would have burst. And thus she continued to cry out a long time, and though she washed her mouth with water over and over again, yet she could hardly rest throughout the greater part of the night. Yet however infirm she was in body, and however light and weak her head was, since for fifty-three days before her death she ate absolutely nothing, yet she could always bear the light of the sun, and never closed her eyes against its brightness and splendour. And what is still more strange, though we often sang loudly in the church [astonishing as the fact may seem to our modern notions, it is to be remembered that Mary was actually lying in the church, in a side chapel where she had had a couch prepared for her at the beginning of her illness in order to die there] and rang the church bells, which made a loud and sharp noise, close at her ears, and that for a good while together; and again, when many masons were striking and knocking with their mallets at an altar which we were having built to be consecrated by the Bishop of Toulouse, yet none of this noise gave her the least disquiet or uneasiness, when once she knew that it was for the service of God or His Church. She herself said, when we were commiserating her, that the sound did not jar upon her nerves, nor ever go near her brain, but that she received it directly in her soul, where it gave her great sweetness.

It is impossible not to be struck by the analogy between Mary's condition and the hyperaesthesia which, as I have already had occasion to remark, was so conspicuous in Domenica Lazzari.

When Dr. Dei Cloche induced the latter to smell some toast, her face, we are told, was contorted with pain, and, after violent spasms, she fainted away. I am by no means saying that these manifestations are in any degree supernatural or divine. Similar symptoms are common in many hysterical disorders. My contention for the moment is confined to this, that in these states of mystical union, the normal functions of the sentient and nutritive processes of the body often seem to be profoundly altered, or at any rate partially inhibited. The psychical element, in fact, appears in some strange way to dominate the physical. Even the hypnotic trance furnishes phenomena of much the same kind. If I am not mistaken, the experiment has more than once been tried with certain peculiarly sensitive subjects, of administering a strong emetic before inducing the hypnotic trance. As long as the trance lasts, even though it be protracted for two or three hours, the subject is not inconvenienced, but when he is restored to normal consciousness, the emetic at once takes effect.

Somewhat earlier than the experience of Mary of Oignies, we have the case of the visionary in the Abbey of Eynsham, near Oxford. During the year's noviceship which he spent in that house it is recorded of him by the sub-prior Adam, an eye-witness, that "his stomach abhorred so greatly meat and drink that sometimes by the space of nine days or more he might receive nothing but a little warm water. And whatsoever thing of leechcraft or physic any man did to him for his comfort or his amendment, nothing helped him, but all turned contrary." Another example, equally remote from Domenica Lazzari and Louise Lateau, is that of St. Catherine of Genoa, at the close of the fifteenth century. As Baron Friedrich von Hugel, summing up the evidence in the case of this remarkable mystic, remarks:

> As to food, it is clear that, however much we may be able or be bound to deduct from the accounts, there remains a solid nucleus of remarkable fact. During some twenty years, she evidently went, for a fairly equal number of days—some thirty in Advent and some forty in Lent, seventy in all annually—with all but no food; and was, during these fasts, at least as vigorous and active as when her nutrition was normal.... Practically the whole of her devoted service (in her hospital at Genoa) fell within these years, of which well-nigh one-fifth was covered by these all but total abstinences from food.

Baron von Hûgel further calls attention to the fact that during these fasts she received Holy Communion daily, and also, as was customary at Genoa, a draught of wine by way of ablution, and occasionally, at other times, a little water rendered unpalatable by an admixture of salt or vinegar. But the fast seems to have been continuous for forty days without any interruption on the Sundays, and her confessor Marabotto leaves us clearly to understand that she *could* not at these times take any solid food or any other form of drink. Under obedience she attempted to do so, but the stomach instantly rejected anything she received in this way. Still more significant is the fact to which Baron von Hugel specially directs attention, "that these two conditions and functions, her fasts and her ecstasies of a definite, lengthy and strength-bringing kind, arise, persist and then fade out of her life together." And from this he deduces the conclusion that, as the ecstasies must have greatly diminished the stress and strain of ordinary existence, "the amount of food required to heal the breach made by life's wear and tear would by these ecstasies be considerably reduced." This is, no doubt, a possible explanation; but it must be remembered that in the case of Domenica Lazzari, at least, there was no apparent ecstasy, though, at the same time, she had not any external duties to perform, but led only the life of a suffering invalid in bed.

Before turning to any similar experiences which are nearer our own times, it seems necessary to say something of the particularly well-attested case of St. Catherine of Siena. No one who has any knowledge of the wonderful personality of the Saint, of the intense sincerity and devotion which breathe in all her letters, and of her strenuous efforts to reform moral abuses and stimulate any work of charity, can for a moment be in doubt of her personal truthfulness.

The only question which could arise would be as to the possibility of some somnambulistic consumption of food of which she herself was unconscious. But under the conditions in which her life was passed this would be almost incredible. She lived with a retinue of maidens, who, out of devotion to her person, watched her in some sense night and day. They detected at once the unreality of her pretences of taking a meal when she sat at a table with them. To appreciate the full weight of the evidence it is necessary to read the whole of chapter xiv in the *Life of St. Catherine*, by Mother Francis Raphael. She is the only biographer who has been able to utilize all the materials, including more particularly the canonization processes, which throw so much light on this more marvellous aspect of her history. It is only possible to quote a paragraph or two here, but it will be understood that the evidence is much fuller than can be thus indicated. Speaking of the period when St. Catherine began to communicate daily, the writer says:

This heavenly food satisfied and supported not only her soul, but her body also; so that ordinary food became no longer necessary to her, and the attempt to swallow it was attended by extraordinary sufferings. This fact seemed to her family and those about her so incredible that they readily enough decided that it was a deceit of the enemy, and her confessor ordered her to take food daily, and give no heed to any visions which might seem to prescribe the contrary. She obeyed, as she invariably did, but the obedience reduced her to such a state that they feared for her life.

Then he examined her and drew from her the fact that the Blessed Sacrament so satisfied her as that she neither desired nor was able to take any other food; nay, that the mere presence of the Blessed Sacrament, or of the priest who was privileged to touch It, in some sort refreshed her and supported her bodily strength. As he still hesitated, in doubt what to think, Catherine said to him with her customary sweetness and respect: "Father, I would ask you to tell me one thing; in case I should kill myself by over-fasting, should I be guilty of my own death?" "Yes," said he. "Again," said she, "I beseech you resolve me in this: which do you take to be the greater sin, to die by over-eating or by over-abstinence?" "By over-eating, of course," he replied. "Then," she continued, "as you see by experience that I am very weak and even at death's door by reason of my eating, why do you not forbid me to eat, as you would forbid me to fast in the like case?" To that he could make no answer; and, therefore, seeing by evident tokens that she was near the point of death, he concluded by saying: cc Daughter, do as God shall put in your mind, follow the guidance of His Holy Spirit, and pray for me; for I see that the things God works in you are not to be measured by the common rule."

Now these facts do not depend upon the statements of historians who, living long after the events described, gathered their information from hearsay and tradition. Our sources here are the notes of her confessors, Father Thomas della Fonte and Blessed Raymund of Capua himself, together with the testimony of intimate friends and disciples such as Father Thomas Caffarini and Francis Malevolti. From September, 1372, until the Lent of the following year, Catherine could only take the smallest quantity of nourishment, and "from Passion Sunday until Ascension Day, a space of fifty-five days, no kind of food passed her lips, yet neither her weakness nor her sufferings seemed to diminish her activity in all good works." She herself says in a letter still extant:

You tell me I ought to pray God that I may be able to eat; I assure you before God that I use every effort to do so, and that once or twice every day I force myself to take food. I have constantly prayed to God, and I do and will pray, that He will grant me to live like other people, if such be His will.

Though this letter speaks of her forcing herself to take food, it is certain from the testimony of those who sat with her and watched her, that what she took in this way was immediately afterwards rejected. In one of her last letters to her confessor, Blessed Raymund, at the very end of her life, she says: "My body remains without any kind of food, not even so much as a drop of water, and its sweet sufferings are so great that I have never felt anything like them, and my life hangs, as it were, by a thread." Such examples as that of St. Catherine are by no means rare in the annals of Christian asceticism. In the case of another daughter of St. Dominic, the famous Mother Agnes of Jesus, in the seventeenth century, we have precisely the same physical repugnance for ordinary food, induced, it would seem, by a similarly intense devotion to the Blessed Sacrament. She did incredible violence to herself to eat what she was bidden to eat, but do what she would, she could not retain it. Pere Boyre, S.J., one of her directors, assures us that at one period she was allowed to give up the attempt and passed seven months without any other food than the Holy Eucharist. She became very weak, but did not look ill. Afterwards she gradually, but with great suffering, recovered the power of taking ordinary food, although always in a very small quantity. Without delaying further over other ancient examples I will only note that this physical repugnance for solid food, or for certain forms of food and drink, is often found in mystics who are not attempting to practise complete abstinence. For example, to take the case of a very modern stigmatic who has already been several times mentioned in previous chapters, when Sister Maria della Passione wished to abstain from food altogether throughout Lent, her director would not permit it, but required that every forty-eight hours, or in other words, on alternate days, she should take a meal consisting of two or three ounces of bread with a little oil.

This she did under obedience, and all went well. If, however, her superior, or any other person, persisted in requiring her to take other food, she obeyed like a good religious, but what she took in this way she immediately brought up again, together with a quantity of blood. The same director further informs us that he allowed her, in the year 1912, to fast from Easter to Pentecost, during which time it appears that she took no other nourishment than a little coffee in the evening. Let me hasten to add here that I am very well aware of the frequent occurrence in hysterical cases of strange perversions of the appetite and also of inexplicable repugnances for certain articles of food, while the vomiting of blood, sometimes pure, sometimes diluted with a watery fluid, is one of the most common symptoms of the same class of disorders. It is impossible, therefore, without much fuller and more minute inquiry than can be attempted here, to regard these phenomena as constituting a presumption of the interference of the supernatural.

But still, they ought to be recorded, if only because they show that a considerable number of these cases of prolonged abstinence offer many points of analogy with the pathology of hysteria.

But let us turn now to the case of Louise Lateau, the well-known stigmatise of the Bois d'Haine, which not only belongs to modern times, but which has probably been more studied and discussed than any other example of the same kind of phenomenon. We have the advantage of being able to use both the voluminous biography of Canon A. Thiery, still incomplete, and also the much more convenient and better ordered abridgment published recently. Louise Lateau was the daughter of simple peasant folk; she was born in 1850 and died in 1883 in the same one storied cottage in which she saw the light. Although from a medical point of view there was no bad family history in the case of either of her parents, still it seems to me that her biographers exaggerate when they imply that in her early life she was healthy and normal. She was a good child who worked hard and devoted herself to help others in every way she could. At the age of thirteen she was knocked down and trodden upon by a cow, and though she said nothing about it, the internal injury seems to have been serious. Abscesses formed and she suffered a great deal of pain. In 1867 there was some serious trouble of the throat which led to her receiving the Last Sacraments, but she was miraculously cured during a novena to Our Lady of La Salette. Three weeks later she became the victim of neuralgic pains of a very intense kind, and these were followed by more abscesses, and also by blood-spitting. As a result, at the beginning of the following year (1868), she was believed to be again at the point of death, but once more she unexpectedly recovered, and at the same time she began to have visions and to hold colloquies with her celestial visitants. Even before this, on the first Friday of 1868, she had felt intense pain in hands, feet and side, though no external marks were as yet perceptible. On the 24th of April blood ran from her side, on the 1st of May the upper surface of the feet was also bleeding, and a few weeks later the hands were similarly affected.

Concurrently with this Louise began to be notably more absorbed in God during the time of these visitations, and on July 17th, 1868, she passed into an ecstasy which lasted for two or three hours, and then returned later in the same evening for a much longer period.

From that time forward both bleeding and ecstasy recurred on the Friday of every week. Meanwhile the distaste for food was steadily growing. Louise had always been a small eater, but after the ecstasies and the stigmata had begun, though she continued to do hard manual work on all days except Friday, when her wounds incapacitated her, still the amount of nourishment she took became less and less in quantity. On Fridays no food of any sort passed her lips, and what she took at other times amounted to no more than an ounce or two of bread, half an apple or a spoonful of vegetables. March 30th, 1871, was the last day when Louise was able to eat and digest any solid food without acute suffering: she did her utmost to obey when her mother or her confessor urged her to take nourishment, but, as in the cases we have previously noticed, if with great difficulty she forced herself to swallow anything, the stomach rejected it almost immediately afterwards. Dr. Warlamont noticed that when milk which had been taken and returned in this way was examined, it showed no signs of curdling, a proof that the gastric secretions were practically non-existent. Many experiments of this kind were made by various members of the commissions appointed to examine the poor girl's condition.

She could not even retain a non-consecrated host, though she received Holy Communion daily, and there was apparently the same difficulty about a spoonful of pure water. After May 1876 she had to take to her bed, and from that time forth the Blessed Sacrament was brought to her daily, but, curiously enough, I have not found any statement as to whether she was able to receive the ablution of water commonly given to the sick after Communion.

At the time when the very acrimonious discussions concerning the reality of Louise Lateau's inedia took place in the Belgian Academy of Medicine, Louise had already, so, at any rate, it was alleged—lived for more than four years without any sort of nourishment but the Blessed Sacrament. This abstinence continued until her death in 1883. It is admitted by practically all the many medical men, some friendly and some hostile, who concerned themselves with the case, that no fragment of positive evidence has ever been produced which can throw doubt upon the statement made by Louise, her sisters and confessors, that during all those years she took no food. No one pretends, even during the years when she still was busy with hard manual work, to have seen her eating anything by stealth. No testimony was ever forthcoming to disprove her statement that the normal excretory processes were entirely suspended. On three or four occasions at least she was solemnly adjured by those whose authority she recognized as holding the place of God, to tell the truth regarding her abstinence and to confirm her statement with an oath. On these occasions she never showed the slightest hesitation. For example, in March 1878 she was very ill, and Dr. Lefebvre, who was vested by the Bishop with full powers, said to her:

> "Louise, since your strength is ebbing fast and you are near death, in the presence of God before whose tribunal you will soon be judged, tell me if you have eaten or drunk anything during the last seven years?"

To which she replied:

> "In the presence of God who is to be my judge, and of the death I am expecting, I assure you that I have neither eaten nor drunk for seven years."

With regard to the poor sufferer's sincerity there can I think be no shadow of doubt. Even among the most rabid of the anti-clericals, those who had any sort of personal acquaintance with Louise did not question her good faith. As Dr. Lefebvre very well argues;

> When one follows the hidden way of life of this humble and brave girl, who lives so poorly, shrinks from all notice, refuses all presents; who works like a slave to help her mother and yet finds time to nurse the sick and bury the dead; who prays with the fervour of an anchorite and the simplicity of a child; who compresses the most solemn practices of piety within narrow limits for fear of encroaching upon her hours of work, there arises from such a life a perfume of truth which in spite of all doubts and suspicions penetrates to the very bottom of one's soul.

If we do not admit that Louise Lateau's abstinence was real, the only possible alternative is to suppose that during her seemingly sleepless nights (she herself declared under cross-examination that she hardly ever slept) she passed into a somnambulistic condition or assumed some secondary personality, so that her normal self was quite unaware of what then took place. There are undoubtedly cases on record of those who, unable to eat in their waking hours, unwittingly satisfied their cravings of hunger in the night-time. Still, while one might easily believe that such unconscious deception might continue for a few weeks or months without discovery, it is hard to believe in the possibility of its going on undetected for three or four, much less a dozen, years. Would nothing be missed in a thrifty household where every fragment of food is counted and treasured up? Would no signs of this somnambulism or this secondary personality ever betray themselves at any other hour than when the whole household was asleep? Would it never happen that in that tiny cottage some unexpected noise would draw attention to the fact that the invalid was astir, the more so that, as already pointed out, from 1876 Louise was practically bed-ridden? It seems to me, then, very difficult to suppose that the stigmatic's alleged total abstinence was not real. But the question whether it was supernatural is another matter, which can hardly be discussed in the present chapter.

2

It used formerly to be urged against the credibility of the Lausiac History of Palladius and other similar chronicles of the monks of the desert, that the feats of abstinence therein so frequently recorded were physiologically impossible. Undoubtedly many of these fasts are very startling to our modern notions. The pilgrim lady, AEtheria, at the end of the fourth century, speaks of a whole confraternity of ascetics, then known as *hebdomadarii*—perhaps we might say, "week-enders"; to call them the "weekly-ones" would certainly sound inappropriate—who throughout Lent took no food from the Sunday evening until the following Saturday afternoon.

To observe such a rule for six weeks consecutively would seem a great feat of endurance, and, as already noted, this was not confined to one or two individuals of exceptional physique, but appears to have been the practice observed by a whole band of fervent worshippers who were not regarded after all as doing anything very extraordinary. The historical evidence in this case is excellent and first-hand, but it is a satisfaction to find that the pathological experiments undertaken during recent years by such investigators as Dr. R. H. Chittenden and Dr. F. G. Benedict fully establish the ability of any ordinarily healthy subject to support such a strain without permanent injury to the system. Dr. Noel Paton, who more than thirty years ago reported on the case of the Frenchman, Alexandre Jacques, states in the latest edition of his *Essentials of Human Physiology* that when a man is kept quiet and warm and supplied with water, a fast of thirty days may in many cases be borne without injury." No doubt can now reasonably be entertained that Stefano Merlatti, who in 1886 went without food for fifty days; Dr. Tanner, who in 1881 accomplished forty; Succi, Jacques, Penny and others, who in modem times have all supported the same deprivation under test conditions for thirty days or more, performed their self-imposed task without any fraud or imposture. Of course, they all drank water, but they abstained from all forms of what is commonly regarded as nourishment.

There is, however, a wide difference between a fast of seven weeks and one of seven months or seven years. Nothing can be plainer from the detailed reports which we possess of all these performances than that the subjects, as they approached the term they had set before themselves, were drawing near the utmost limits of their physical endurance. In the case of Merlatti's fifty days this was particularly noticeable. The doctors watching the sufferer's condition were thoroughly alarmed, and implored of him to desist. All Paris may be said to have breathed again when the fiftieth day was at last safely reached. On the whole, I think we should have to say that the experience of the professional fasters points rather to the conclusion that any long protracted abstinence from food, and especially from food and drink together, puts an almost insupportable strain upon the system. If this be continued for more than a couple of months, and leaves the vitality of the subject to all outward appearance unimpaired, we are led to assume the operation of some influence or force which is apparently not explainable by ordinary natural causes.

And yet before we commit ourselves to any definite conclusion we must take account of the fact that there is a considerable body of evidence, in cases where no supernatural intervention can reasonably be looked for, attesting the continuance of life without either food or drink, for periods, not only of three or four months, but of three or four years. Let us begin with an example from Kincardine in Ross-shire, which was reported to the Royal Society through the intermediary of the Right Hon. James Stewart Mackenzie, Lord Privy Seal of Scotland.

The sufferer in question was one Janet McLeod, a young woman who at the age of fifteen had had an epileptic attack, and at nineteen another of a still more serious nature which confined her to bed for several months and left her without any control of her eyelids, so that, unless she raised the lid with her finger, she was quite unable to see. A third epileptic seizure when she was twenty-eight reduced her to a still more pitiable condition. She became a helpless invalid, and on Whit-Sunday, 1763, her jaw became fast locked. Her father with a knife forced it open enough to introduce a little thin gruel or whey, but it all, or nearly all, ran out again. From this time, for more than four years, it is stated that she took no food and lost all desire for it, except that on two occasions her jaws for a while relaxed and she asked for water. All the normal excretory processes were suspended, except, of course, from the lungs and skin. The doctor who reports the case declares that when he saw her the girl was not at all emaciated. She was confined to bed, the legs bent up under the body, but she slept a good deal, and he adds that "at present (i.e., 1767) no degree of strength can force open her jaws." This report, which is printed in the Philosophical Transactions of the Royal Society, continues as follows:

> In some of the attempts to open her jaws, two of the under fore-teeth were forced out; of which opening they often endeavoured to avail themselves by putting some thin nourishing drink into her mouth; but without effect, for it always returned by the corners; and about a twelve months ago, they thought of thrusting a little dough of oatmeal through this gap of the teeth, which she would retain a few seconds, and then return with something like a straining to vomit, without one particle going down; nor has the family been sensible, through observing of any appearance like that of swallowing, for now four years, of her consuming anything except the small draught of Braemar water and the English pint of common water which she took in July 1765.

We are further told that the details of the case were taken down by the bedside of the sufferer from the lips of the father and mother, "people of great veracity, who are under no temptation to deceive, for they neither ask, nor expect, nor get anything." The statement is further attested by witnesses of standing who lived in the neighbourhood and who spoke highly of the strict religious principles of the family. "Their daughter's state," it is said, "is a very great mortification to them and universally known and regretted by all their neighbours." The same doctor visited the girl again five years later, when he found that she was beginning to swallow a little crumbled oat-cake introduced through the gap in the teeth. Two years afterwards the jaws relaxed and life became more normal.

One would hesitate perhaps to regard this case as very satisfactory, but for the existence of similar instances in other parts of the world, which certainly do not in any way depend on the account just given, and lend it some indirect confirmation. For example, in the *Bibliotheque Britantiique*, a Swiss periodical published at Geneva, we may find the report drafted by certain men of science in that city of a visit paid to an unfortunate sufferer, Josephine Durand, who, they allege, had already lived for four years without either solid or liquid food. The poor girl was quite blind and also paralyzed. The lower limbs could be pinched or punctured without her experiencing any sensation. The jaws were convulsively locked, but this did not prevent her making herself understood, though with some little difficulty of articulation.

What lends the case exceptional interest is the fact that the girl was a Catholic while her scientific visitors were apparently not of that Communion. Normally she could take neither food or drink, the very idea was repugnant, but they tell us:

> We have learned that being devotedly attached to the practices of the Catholic faith she communicates pretty frequently, that is to say about once a month. She then receives a fragment of the Host small enough to pass through the opening where a tooth has been extracted, and the presence of this small particle of solid in the oesophagus does not seem to excite the same convulsions as the action of the liquid normally does.

The visitors were anxious to be convinced as to her difficulty in taking nourishment; and so their account states:

> At our request she made an attempt to swallow half a spoonful of plain water, an experiment which always exhausts and distresses her more or less. We made the liquid to trickle in by the gap in the teeth. The deglutition of it appeared difficult and painful and its presence in the stomach instantly produced a convulsion which cast all the liquid out of the mouth again. This experiment was followed by a sort of paroxysm which lasted a quarter of an hour, but died away by degrees.

The impressions of the visitors, both as regards the girl herself and her home and surroundings, seem to have been highly favourable. They say, for example:

> The moral character of this poor creature inspires deep interest and true admiration. Her patience and resignation are extreme, as also have been her sufferings. Lying for four years on her back in the same attitude, tortured by pain, and at intervals by hunger and thirst, cravings which sometimes last for as much as a month together, uniting in some sort in her own person every form of misery, she still would not allow us to pity her. She was bent on showing us that there might be many people more unfortunate than herself. She turned the conversation from her own troubles, she even tried to amuse us with little jests which were not without point, and one might see now and again a smile flit across the lips usually compressed with the habit of suffering.

The visitors noted that the abdomen was constricted and seemed to lie quite close to the vertebral column. They also declared that the family, while affording every facility for examination, refused all presents and were well known to make this an invariable rule.

Some of them came quite prepared to detect imposture, but the only suspicious point they could find in the case was the fact that the poor sufferer was held in veneration by the peasantry for some miles round as one in repute of sanctity. In truth, the account I quote from, in view of the high character and simple directness of the parents, dismisses these suspicions as unreasonable. The proposal was made that Josephine should be brought to the town and kept for a while under strict medical observation, and to this the girl and her parents at once readily agreed. The political disturbances of the times, however, rendered it impossible to carry this suggestion into effect, and a few years afterwards the girl died without any autopsy being attempted.

A somewhat more recent case, which acquires importance from the fact that it was observed by a doctor acquainted with the pathological theories of the latter half of the last century, is that of Marie Furtner, of Frasdorf, in Upper Bavaria. If, on the one hand, her fast was less remarkable because she continued at all times to drink large quantities of water, still, on the other hand, it is alleged to have lasted for over forty years. The girl, as far back as 1835, after various illnesses, came to take a violent disrelish for all forms of solid food, and by degrees allowed nothing to pass her lips but draughts of cold water from a mountain spring in her native hamlet. A doctor interested in the case made it known to some of his more learned colleagues. Pressure was used to persuade her parents to allow her to be brought to Munich, and the girl was placed in a hospital, where she was committed to the charge of two nursing-sisters, sworn to keep her under observation night and day. The girl's health suffered under the conditions of city life, and she also grew very homesick. Consequently, after an experiment of twenty-two days, she was sent back to her parents, but during her stay she consumed no solid food of any kind and drank nothing but water, neither was anything discovered about her suggestive of fraud. One of the young doctors concerned in the experiment, Dr. Karl von Schafhaukl, afterwards became a University Professor, and upon Marie Furtner's death in 1884 he published a short essay on the subject of her extraordinary abstinence. As he there points out, the girl and her family bore the very highest character in their native village. No profit of any kind, but only trouble, accrued to them from the strangers who, hearing of the phenomenon, occasionally visited the spot. Marie maintained her aversion to solid food down to within a few months of her death. The successive parish priests who ministered to the spiritual wants of the locality all spoke highly of her, and were convinced of the fact that her abstinence was genuine. She in no way courted notice; it was the doctors who in the first instance spread the story of her avoidance of food and who brought her to Munich in 1844. Moreover, although the girl was a devout Catholic, the case was never represented as having any religious complexion. From all these circumstances, and others too complex to detail, Professor von Schafhaukl convinced himself that, incredible as existence in this foodless condition for forty years might appear, the facts of the case could not rationally be disputed.

While no one will for a moment dream of denying that a large number of pretended fasters were simply impostors trading on popular credulity, still a little investigation discloses the existence of a far greater percentage of well attested cases than would be readily believed. When Prosper Lambertini, afterwards famous as Pope Benedict XIV, was engaged upon his great work, *De Beatificatione et Canonizatione Sanctorum*, he addressed a request to the Academy of Sciences at Bologna asking for a scientific opinion upon the supernatural character of the many remarkable examples of abstention from food which were recorded in the lives of candidates for beatification. The Institute in question appointed a commission, and a memorial on the subject was drafted by J. B. Beccari, which, in 1880, a distinguished Italian physician,

Dr. A. Corradi, in the *Annali Universali di Medicina*, which he then edited, characterizes as "bella e severa dissertazione." This dissertation is printed as an appendix to Book IV, Part I, of Lambertini's great work. In it Beccari, while fully recognizing the likelihood of imposture, credulity, mal-observation, etc., in the majority of reported cases, still upholds the genuineness of certain well attested examples of long-protracted abstinence from food, where no supernatural causation can be reasonably supposed. Acting upon this view, Lambertini, practically speaking, lays down the rule that prolonged fasts must never be assumed to be miraculous when they have originated in any form of illness or when the exercise of full bodily activity is not at the same time maintained by the faster.

In spite of the still primitive condition of medical science in the first half of the eighteenth century, it seems to me that Beccari's reasons for putting confidence in the better attested cases of fasting phenomena, even when protracted for three or four years, are fundamentally sound. The question whether an invalid does or does not consume food or drink, and whether the excretory processes are or are not suspended, is after all a simple question of fact. A sharp-eyed child may often in such matters be a better witness than the most learned physician in Europe. Now, as Beccari points out, the medical faculty in the sixteenth and seventeenth centuries were fully alive to the danger of imposture; they did subject their patients to severe tests and provided that they should be rigorously watched. The very fact that after the publication of Wier's book there was a good deal of controversy upon the subject, compelled them to lay stress upon such precautions. Beccari accepts four cases as satisfactorily proved, the first being that of Apollonia Schreier, which has been recounted in detail by the physician Paullus Lentulus. This girl of eighteen, living in the hamlet of Galz, a few miles from Berne, in Switzerland, and suffering from some mysterious disease by which the lower part of the body was half paralyzed, had gradually begun to eat less and less until she refused both food and drink altogether. She was brought to Berne by order of the magistrates and kept for three weeks under strict observation in a public hospital. Her mother was also incarcerated, and rigorous inquiry was made about the conduct and antecedents of the family. Nothing was discovered pointing to imposture of any sort. There were no excretions; the girl's abdomen looked, as Lentulus said, just as if it were that of a corpse from which all the viscera had been removed. Yet the rest of the body was not notably emaciated. Lentulus first saw her at the end of January, 1602. She had at that time, so it was alleged by her parents, taken neither food nor drink for eleven months. On the last occasion when he visited her, i.e., in July 1603, the conditions of her abstinence had not been changed; and she was still living in May 1604, when his booklet on the subject went to press.

Not less remarkable was the case of Margaret Seyfrit, a little girl of twelve, at Rodt, near Speyer. Her illness does not seem to have been of the same serious character as that of the fasters previously mentioned. She suffered pain in her head and in the abdomen, and was covered with boils, but she was not in any way confined to bed. Still, the child gradually gave up eating, and after a year or more, she refused to take any kind of liquid, so that from the month of May onwards, in the year 1540, though the summer was exceptionally hot, she could not be persuaded to swallow so much as a spoonful of water. The Bishop of Speyer intervened. In 1541 he had the child confined and closely watched for ten days, but she resisted all efforts to induce her to take food or drink, and no trace of fraud was discovered. Somewhat later, the commandant of a castle in the neighbourhood brought her there and kept her under observation for five days, but with no better success. In 1542, when the abstinence from both food and drink had already been going on for nearly two years, Ferdinand King of the Romans came to Speyer and heard of this extraordinary case. He ordered his own physician, Gerard Bucoldianus, with others of his suite, to subject the girl to a rigorous investigation. She was again carried away from home, stripped and clothed anew from head to foot, closely watched night and day for twelve days, while tempting delicacies were put in her way. She could be persuaded with much coaxing to put a cup of wine or water to her lips, but if she took the smallest sip she at once spat it all out again. This was the doctor's own account of the matter, and he failed to discover any symptom of imposture.

But there are quite a number of such cases attested by good medical evidence. They belong to many different periods and many different countries, and the circumstances, symptoms, and also the ages of the subjects are extremely varied. There is an example of a Jewish girl in Russia, who lived from September 1724 to June 1726, taking no food and next to no drink, but at the same time showing no signs of extreme emaciation. In another French case a girl is said to have lived eleven years without solid food.

Still better attested is the story of Louise Gussie of Anglefort en Bugey. From January 1770 to August 1773 she took no food at all, and during two years of that time she drank nothing but plain water.

Her doctor, M. de la Chapelie, sent a report of the case to the *Paris Academie des Sciences,* in the course of which he remarks:

> It is impossible to suspect any imposture in this phenomenon. The woman lives with her brothers and sisters in a poor hovel just below the crest of a steep mountain out of reach of all curious visitors, where the art of deception has never penetrated, and where such a trick would not bring in six sous by way of alms in the whole of a twelvemonth.

In Italy, Prof. L. Rolando apparently gave full credence to the case of Anna Garbero, of Raeonigi, who is stated to have lived thirty-two months and eleven days without any sort of food or drink. Rolando himself, after her death, performed the post-mortem and published an account of it in a pamphlet. Similarly, at the seventh congress of Italian scientists, held in Naples (1847), Dr. Borrelli made himself guarantee for the genuineness of a fasting phenomenon observed in a girl in the Abruzzi who, owing to a convulsive stricture of the oesophagus, which came on whenever food was put to her lips, lived, so it was said, for three years without eating or drinking. The latest case which seems to have attracted attention is that of Bourriou, a peasant woman from Perigord.

At forty-five years of age she became an inmate of the Bourdeilles hospital, and remained there under strict observation from March 9th to July 12th, 1896, 125 days in all. During this time she took nothing but an occasional draught of *eau panee* (toast and water), which her stomach rejected at once. Slices of fresh bread and other comestibles, continually renewed, were left in a drawer of her room, but she never touched any of them. The mind was undoubtedly affected, owing to the death a long time before of her husband and four children, but it was stated that for nine years she had not taken food, and the people of her own village believed the story. She lived alone, and no baker, butcher or farmer remembered ever to have sold her anything to eat.

Although we may readily admit the existence of a large number of cases of imposture in this matter, still where detection has followed, as it often has, the motive for the fraud has generally been quite intelligible. Anne Moore, "the fasting woman of Tutbury," who, under rigorous surveillance, broke down on the ninth day of an attempted fast, and made a full confession in 1813, had deposited £400 in the funds the year before, the proceeds of her trickery. Further, her early history was by no means creditable, and she had children who apparently acted as her confederates. Still, in several of the cases we have been considering, even vanity or the craving for notice could hardly have place.

The interest of playing a part soon evaporates when there is no audience to play to, or where it is limited to the members of a small family circle.

But if we admit the reality and the natural character of these prolonged abstinences how can we reconcile the facts with the laws of physiological science? How can the metabolism necessary for the continuance of human life be maintained under such circumstances for three or four years together? Probably no adequate solution can at present be offered. The cases that occur are too rare and are for the most part attended by such pathological conditions in the sufferer as to prevent the possibility of thorough scientific observation. When an attempt was made to induce Marie Furtner to submit herself to a second period of medical examination at Munich, the self-respect of the modest Catholic peasant at once took alarm. She declared she would rather die than allow herself again to be watched, weighed, pulled about and stared at by a crowd of strange men. The same happened in the case of Louise Lateau, when certain doctors of the Belgian Academy of Medicine were very anxious to persuade her to undergo a similar test of her alleged total inedia. In view of the extremely severe surveillance and the publicity entailed, we cannot be surprised that in both instances, and especially in that of Louise Lateau, whose life was then entirely spent in communion with God, the idea of such an ordeal was utterly repugnant. From the refusal to submit to it, it would be quite unreasonable to deduce any presumption of bad faith.

On the other hand, physiologists seem to suggest that in cases of starvation the actual cause of death is not mere inanition. It is hunger, as Bernheim puts it, not lack of food, that kills the man.

At the same time we are meant to understand by hunger, not only the craving for nourishment, which ordinarily ceases to be acute after the first few days, but the mental condition induced by fear, fretfulness, insomnia, and worry. As long as there is flesh upon the bones, the vital organs, and more especially the brain and nervous system, are nourished at the expense of the muscular tissues. For what period of time this can go on is difficult to determine. But so long as the brain is at rest, to which effect a state of trance, ecstasy or certain forms of amentia probably conduce, the transfer of these reserves proceeds unimpeded, though the whole organism is living on its capital. The process of exhaustion is probably very slow, though we know uncommonly little about the conditions of metabolism in such cases. The quasi hibernation of certain Indian fakirs who allow themselves to be buried in the ground for forty days, or even for four months, without air or food, presents an analogous problem, but the fact seems well attested. Everything points to the conclusion that to maintain life under these conditions the fakirs adopt some method of auto-hypnotism. When Professor Luciani, who has made a special study of this subject, tells us that death in cases of starvation is due to the breakdown of the *sistema regolatore*, by which he means the nervous system, he is evidently laying stress upon the same order of ideas. With regard, then, to the wonderful fasts of Catholic mystics, we seem justified, even from the standpoint of modern science, in adopting the conclusions of Benedict XIV. If these long abstinences from food have their origin in a diseased condition of the organism, and if they are attended with a prevalent state of ecstasy and a suspension of the normal activities of life, we cannot safely conclude that we are dealing with a condition of things which is of supernatural origin. If, however, it can be proved that this entire absence of nourishment, as seems to have been the case, for example, for some years with Louise Lateau, is maintained concomitantly with the continual discharge of ordinary duties, then natural causes supply no explanation of the phenomenon, and we are justified in inferring the intervention of miracle.

CHAPTER XVI
LIVING WITHOUT EATING

1

We have a well attested instance of abstention in the five years' unbroken fast of Theresa Neumann, of Konnersreuth (Bavaria), which, so far as I can learn, is still maintained down to this time of writing (1931). Since Christmas 1922 she has, it is stated, eaten nothing solid, and since Christmas 1926 no liquid has been taken by her for the purpose of nourishment. For a time she continued to receive a mouthful of water each day after Holy Communion, but on September 30, 1927, even this was given up. The result is that since the last-mentioned date her strict fast is said to have remained unbroken. With the exception of the Blessed Eucharist Itself nothing digestible seems to have passed her lips. We have also to remember that she is not a helpless invalid confined to bed. She attends Mass and other services in the church, she goes about the village on errands of charity—more especially to comfort the sick and dying—she talks gaily with those who come to consult her, and performs light tasks to help her own family. Moreover, throughout the greater part of the year she renews every Friday her terrible visions of the Passion and loses a by no means inconsiderable quantity of blood from her stigmata. What adds to the marvel is the fact that Theresa Neumann, in making her daily Communion, does not commonly receive even an entire particle such as is used for the laity. It is only when she is in ecstasy that a whole Host can be given her. So long as she is in conscious possession of her faculties it is not possible for her to swallow more than a tiny fragment rather less than the eighth part of an ordinary Communion wafer.

The astounding nature of this prolonged fast, even apart from the other phenomena, has excited so much attention that the facts called for official enquiry. Accordingly in 1927 a commission was appointed by the Bishop of Regensburg to investigate the case under the direction of a physician of high standing, Dr. Seidl. Four nursing Sisters of Mallersdorf were chosen for the purpose, and a very strict code of regulations was drafted, to the observance of which they were required to bind themselves by oath. Relieving each other by pairs, two of the four were to be continually on duty night and day, never allowing the girl during the prescribed fortnight of observation to be out of their sight even for the shortest interval. Her weight, temperature, pulse, etc., were to be frequently taken. All excreta, whether in the process of natural relief, or by the flow of blood from the stigmata, or by vomiting, etc., were to be preserved, weighed and subsequently submitted for analysis. Her room, clothes, bed, etc., were subjected to a thorough search, and she was always to be under close observation in her intercourse with her parents, family and all other persons. It cannot be questioned that these precautions were strictly necessary if any conclusion was to be reached which would be respected by those—mainly non-Catholics—who declared her to be a vulgar impostor. At the same time, when one reads the chapter in which Dr. Gerlich sets out in the plainest terms the medical details of the investigation, a certain misgiving presents itself. After all, one asks, what higher purpose does the demonstration of this inedia serve? The Almighty cannot wish us to conclude that pious Christians, encouraged by Theresa's example, should strive to live without eating. Abstemiousness carried to this excess would not be a virtue, but a vice—a tempting of God. No doubt it impresses the imagination that any holy person should be so far raised above the infirmities of our nature as to draw all vital energy from the Blessed Eucharist alone, but unfortunately when we come to a demonstration of the fact, we find ourselves forced to inquire into a number of physiological data, of which nice-minded people do not ordinarily speak outside a doctor's consulting-room. The very reverence we owe to sanctity seems to deprecate our pursuing such researches or subjecting God's chosen servants to such tests.

On the other hand we know that the convulsive contraction of the oesophagus, the rejection from the stomach of swallowed food, the loss of natural appetite (otherwise called anorexia), etc., are not of themselves characteristic of moral virtue; they are rather the well-understood symptoms of certain hysterical disorders. If Theresa Neumann, as already mentioned, cannot in her normal consciousness swallow an entire Host, but can do so perfectly well when she is in ecstasy, this surely points to the fact that the neuroses which for several years kept her bed-ridden, contracted, paralysed, blind and deaf, have not yet all been completely eliminated. In the case of several other stigmaticas who are alleged to have lived without food, we know that repeated attempts were made to induce them to take nourishment. In obedience to their spiritual directors or religious superiors many of them forced themselves to swallow the food, liquid or solid, which was set before them, with the result that everything was almost immediately returned, the experiment causing great discomfort and pain to the sufferer. In the lives of St. Catherine of Siena, of Louise Lateau, Anne Catherine Emmerich, Domenica Lazzari, and many others, canonized and uncanonized, we find quite harrowing descriptions of such scenes.

But on the other hand we have exactly similar descriptions of the same results in the case of patients who were not religiously minded but were simply suffering from anorexia and other forms of hysteria.

It may be sufficient to appeal to the witnesses who were cited as testifying to the inedia of Mollie Fancher, Mrs. Croad, the Italian children, etc., not to speak of the examples which are quoted in almost every text-book dealing with nervous disorders. Just as I should like to hear of a stigmatica who had no bad family history, and had always herself been a thoroughly healthy subject, free from neuroses of any kind, so in the considerable list of those holy people who are reported to have lived for long periods with no other nourishment but the Blessed Sacrament, one looks, but looks in vain, for the name of one who was free from strange previous inhibitions in the matter of diet and whom the neuropath specialist would have pronounced to be perfectly sound and normal. No competent physician could possibly have said this of Louise Lateau or Teresa Higginson, or Domenica Lazzari, or Anne Catherine Emmerich, or St. Lidwina of Schiedam.

There can be no thought of disputing the fact that the fortnight's observation of Theresa Neumann has proved to the satisfaction of all unprejudiced persons that she did not during that period take either food or drink. What is even more striking, the pronounced loss of weight which occurred during the Friday ecstasies was in each case made good during the two or three days which followed.

On Wednesday, July 13, 1927, the day before the period of observation began, Theresa weighed 55 kilograms (=121 lbs., or 8 stone 9 lbs.); on Saturday, July 16, she weighed 51 kilograms. On Wednesday, July 20, 54 kilograms were recorded, but this again had fallen by the following Saturday to 52 kilograms, though on the Thursday, the final day, it stood once more at 55 kilograms, just as before the experiment.

The extreme range of loss and gain was therefore about 8 lbs. It is curious that on two occasions within the fortnight (the 15th and 22nd) there is record of natural relief to the amount of half a litre.

There was also on the two Fridays some vomiting, not very considerable in amount, which seems to have been due to the blood from the eyes or forehead running into the mouth. No trace of food was discoverable in the matter thus ejected.

The fortnight's observation of Theresa Neumann, which has done much to confirm the belief in her complete abstention from food and drink, brings to mind another similar test carried out in our own country not so many years ago, though this last unfortunately had a much more tragic ending. In a remote part of Carmarthenshire a little girl, described by all as an exceptionally pretty child, was said to have lived for more than eighteen months without either eating or drinking. In February 1867 when the child's extraordinary condition first began to alarm her parents, she was ten years old, emaciated, frail (possibly as the result of a previous attack of scarlet fever), and the victim of strange neurotic seizures. She was the daughter of a small farmer named Evan Jacob, but the family were Welsh and spoke only a little English.

Under the medical treatment of Dr. H. H. Davies, who was called in, she grew somewhat better, but she gradually developed a marked aversion for any form of nourishment. Even the sight of other people eating caused her discomfort. When food was pressed upon her, she went into what her mother called "a fit," though such fits, so far as they came under the observation of others at a later date, consisted of no more than a short period of real or assumed unconsciousness. There was then no pallor or violent contortions. The child simply closed her eyes and seemed to pass into a state of insensibility. But at the beginning the "fits" were more violent and also more protracted. There were also cataleptic symptoms, and a condition of opisthotonos, i.e., the body was arched backwards, so that the head almost touched the feet. The father, who was an ignorant man and apparently possessed of some strange idea that the girl's abstinence was a manifestation of the Divine favour, declared in 1869 that he had taken an oath two years before that he would not offer Sarah any food until she asked for it, since on a particular occasion at that date she fainted when he pressed her to eat. What is certain is that when the parents consented in December 1869 to allow the child to be watched by nurses, the mother expressly stipulated that the watchers were not to eat in Sarah's presence, because "she would faint if there were food in the room." In the summer of 1867 Sarah still openly took a little nourishment, but in October it is stated that she would consume no more than a morsel of apple "the size of a pill" which she took in a teaspoon; and shortly after this she began to refuse everything. It is not surprising that even in a remote country district the news of the strange case of a child living without food should circulate among the neighbours. Nothing, however, at a later date aroused so much prejudice against the Jacob family as the belief that this curious malady had been turned in indirect ways into a source of gain. Nevertheless, even Dr. Fowler, whose letters to the press did more than anything else to direct attention to what he regarded as a scandalous imposture, admits that "we have no evidence during the first sixteen months of Sarah's illness either that the girl was made a public show of, or that any money whatever flowed into the pockets of the parents." Apart from short paragraphs in the Welsh papers, the earliest communication to the press in English seems to have been that of an Anglican clergyman, the Rev. Evan Jones, Vicar of Llanfihangel-ar-Arth, who wrote to *The Welshman*, in a letter published February 19, 1869:

> Allow me to invite the attention of your readers to a most extraordinary case. Sarah Jacob, a little girl, twelve years of age and daughter of Mr. Evan Jacob, Lletherneuadd, in this parish, has not partaken of a single grain of any kind of food whatever during the last sixteen months. She did occasionally swallow a few drops of water during the first few months of this period; but now she does not even do that. Still she looks pretty well in the face and continues in possession of her mental faculties. She is in this and several other respects a wonderful little girl.

The Vicar goes on to suggest that in view of the incredulous attitude of many medical men at a distance an investigation of the case ought to take place. Although the response to this letter was not enthusiastic,

Mr. Jacob, the girl's father, himself pressed for an inquiry. A committee was formed and a certain number of local people, mostly of the peasant class, agreed to act as watchers.

The investigation which followed was, however, of little value. No attempt was made to search the bed and the cupboards, or to exercise any control upon Sarah's intercourse with her parents and her little sister. There were also stories of a notable neglect of duty on the part of some of the watchers. Certain individuals were said to have fallen asleep, or to have had too much to drink, or to have neglected to put in an appearance at all. Nevertheless they professed to have been satisfied that no food had been taken, and made depositions to that effect. For example:

> Watcher, No. 4, James Harris Davies, a medical student, spoke in like manner, and was perfectly positive that nothing had been given to her during the fortnight he had watched there, with the exception of three drops of water, once, to moisten her lips with.

> He was as great a sceptic as any before he commenced watching, but as he saw nothing to confirm his suspicions, he could conscientiously say that nothing had been given her during his watch.

> Watcher, No. 7, Thomas Davies, who had been the greatest sceptic of all, was strongly convinced. He watched Sarah Jacob tor twelve days, and was quite positive that nothing could have been given her during his watch. He watched her with all possible care, and was very cautious to be in a prominent place, where Sarah Jacob s mouth was always in sight.

It has, of course, to be borne in mind that although Sarah was treated as an invalid, and seems for two years to have remained continuously in bed, there is no evidence that she was really paralysed and incapable of movement. The investigation in the spring of 1869 must have helped to advertise the alleged marvel of the child who lived without eating. Remote as the farm was, curious visitors came in considerable numbers. They found a very pretty little girl, reclining on her back, fancifully dressed, crowned with a wreath and decked in all sorts of gay ribbons, who smiled upon them and was very pleased to be admired. She had a little library of pious books which had been given her, and she delighted to show her skill in reading out of them aloud to such as would listen.

But it was not only books which were presented to her. Not a few of those who came felt that it would be the proper thing to leave a shilling or half a crown behind in acknowledgment of the privilege of admission to this charming spectacle. When they offered money to the father, he demurred, but he said at the same time that a gift might be made to his little daughter; and indeed there seems often to have been a receptacle lying on her breast into which silver could be put.

This could not go on long without attracting some attention in scientific circles. The above-mentioned Dr. Robert Fowler, Vice-President of the Hunterian Society, who had friends in South Wales, paid a visit to Sarah Jacob on August 30, 1869, accompanied by his host, a solicitor who was resident not far off. Both gentlemen were convinced that the plump and smiling little person who glanced about her so slyly out of the corners of her eyes could not for two years past have been living upon air. Dr. Fowler accordingly addressed a strong protest to *The Times* giving a detailed account of his visit, and the effect of this letter eventually was that a new committee was appointed to arrange for a really scientific investigation of the alleged phenomenon. It is important to note that the parents, from the first, seem to have raised no sort of difficulty. Considering the extremely limited accommodation of their wretched one-storied dwelling—Dr. Fowler's book provides a photograph and a plan—it would have been easy for them to plead that a fortnight's observation by nurses who were to remain with the girl continually would be impossible. Moreover, it was December, and the place was horribly cold and damp. Four nurses, one of them a Welsh girl speaking Welsh, were procured from Guy's Hospital. A code of instructions was issued to them in which the point more specially insisted upon was that "they were there to see whether food was given to the girl. They were not themselves to offer her food, but to give food if she asked for it." This was also repeated to them orally in the presence of the father. On this occasion the whole room, with its cupboards, etc., was thoroughly turned out, the bed examined and re-made by the nurses, and the child herself was stripped and re-clothed in her nightdress. The four nurses, relieving each other in pairs after eight hours on duty, were supposed to be acting in concert with, and in subordination to, a committee of doctors, one of whom was to visit the house daily. Unfortunately this part of the arrangements had not been fully thought out. One or two doctors were named without their consent having previously been obtained, and the reader gets the impression that these medical visits were very haphazard and were carried out without any individual amongst them assuming full direction and responsibility.

For the first few days all went well. The child herself was in high spirits; she seemed physically well-nourished and was free from bed-sores. Throughout the inquiry there is no suggestion of any effort having been made by the parents to evade the control or to try to lure the nurses away from the post of duty; neither was little Sarah ever seen to attempt to get out of bed. Asked if she was in pain, she invariably said No. On more than one occasion nature was relieved, and the child had to be moved while the bedding was changed. After three or four days, however, conditions changed considerably for the worse. The period of observation had begun on Thursday, December 9, 1869. At 2 p.m. on the following Tuesday she had a pulse of 144, but Dr. Hughes, who then visited her, said that "being a hysterical child, he did not think so badly of it." On the next day, Wednesday, as t e nurses recorded, she had slept little, her eyes were sunken and the nose pinched; she was restless and unable to read. Still, Dr. Lewis who visited her made the following entry in the nurses' diary Dec. 15, Wednesday. Dr. Lewis visited and found Sarah Jaco as usual, pulse 120. Skin warm on right hand. She is not so ushed as on the first day of watching. She says she has no pain and is placid." On Thursday at 11 a.m. the Vicar called. The child s condition alarmed him and he proposed that the test should end and the nurses be dismissed; Dr. Davies, however, local medical man, who had attended her originally and seen her at intervals for the last two years, was of opinion that there was no danger. On that Thursday afternoon both parents were told that in the opinion of the nurses the child was "threatening to sink," but the father averred that he had "seen her as bad or worse than that before," and he was opposed to the suggestion that the watch should be given up. The child herself at no moment during these eight days expressed any desire for food or drink. At ten o'clock on the Thursday evening she became very restless and the nurses thought she was sinking. The next morning, Friday, she seemed to lose the power of speech, and about three p.m. she died.

All through the country the watch maintained in the room of the "Welsh Fasting Girl " had been a conspicuous item on the news placards, and when the pitiful climax was reached there was a violent outburst of feeling. Every leader-writer and every man in the street was certain that somebody was guilty of murder and ought to be criminally prosecuted, but no two persons could agree in deciding with whom the guilt precisely rested. Some said it was the doctors, some said it was the parents, some said it was the nurses or the Governors of Guy's Hospital, some said it was those who had insisted on such an investigation being carried out, some said it was the police or the officials of the Home Office who had not intervened in time to prevent the catastrophe. A post-mortem was made of the poor child's body, and three medical men of high standing found proof, as they believed, that previously to the coming of the nurses little Sarah Jacob must have been taking nourishment by stealth or otherwise. There was no emaciation; on the contrary they reported that "a considerable layer of subcutaneous fat was cut through " in making the section from the throat to the abdomen. There were faeces in the bowel, and the stomach was not notably contracted. On the other hand the principal organs—lungs, heart, kidneys, etc.—were quite healthy, and the autopsy proved that there was nothing which could cause physical obstruction to the passage of food and its waste products.

Already the *Daily News*, on Thursday, December 16th, had protested against features that were "almost grotesque in the proceedings which are taking place at the bedside of a little girl in Wales":

> The latest report is that at the close of the fifth day of the watching, the girl had actually fasted, and was very weak and ill. This would seem to be so natural a result of five days' fasting that the wonder seems to be that the nurses do not at once persuade her to take some nourishment. Suppose the poor girl has hitherto been fed unconsciously to herself and is too weak to desire food, or too languid to express a wish for it, the result of this watching may simply be that she will be starved to death. Martyr of science, or victim of superstition, which will this poor girl be if she should die under the eyes of these nurses, and die of starvation? Probably the persons concerned have already ascertained what their legal position would be in such a case.

On the very morning of Sarah's death *The Lancet* was "able to declare, on good authority, that no confidence can be placed in the statements made regarding the Welsh fasting girl, since the doctors and nurses are bound to divulge nothing until the inquiry has terminated." But the medical journal adds:

"Of course every precaution has been taken in the event of the girl showing symptoms of exhaustion, and the nurses have special instructions to administer stimulants and food, subject to the advice of the daily medical attendant." All the same a fatal termination was reached on that same Friday afternoon, and the jury, at the inquest which followed, brought in a verdict that Sarah Jacob had "died from starvation caused from negligence on the part of the father to induce the child to take food."

The feeling throughout the country was such that the legal advisers of the Grown felt bound to take action. Accordingly five of the medical men who had been connected with the case, as well as Mr. Evan Jacob and his wife, were all charged with manslaughter before the magistrates of Carmarthenshire, the indictment stating that "you did feloniously kill and slay one Sarah Jacob, of Lletherneuadd aforesaid, against the peace of our Lady the Queen, her Crown and dignity, and contrary to the statute in that case made and provided." The proceedings excited immense interest in the Principality, and the Court in which the magistrates met was crowded to suffocation. After a patient hearing and much legal argument, the doctors were discharged, but Jacob and his wife were committed for trial.

At Carmarthen, on July 15, 1870, the trial came on before Mr. Justice Hannen (afterwards Lord Hannen); while Mr. H. C. Giffard, Q.C., who later on was better known as Lord Chancellor Halsbury, conducted the prosecution for the Crown. Without making any reflection upon the perfect good faith of either the prosecuting counsel or the presiding judge, I think it may be said that justice was meted out to Jacob and his wife in rather harsh measure. After a merciless summing up by the judge, strongly adverse to the prisoners, the jury returned a verdict of guilty. The husband was accordingly sentenced to twelve months' hard labour and the wife to six. Evan Jacob was already a ruined man. The costs of the defence had swallowed up every penny he possessed.

The case presents many features which are extremely puzzling. What is most certain of all is that the father and mother, even if they had been utterly inhuman parents—and every scrap of evidence suggests on the contrary that they were devoted to their daughter and humoured all her whims—had the strongest reasons for wishing to preserve the life of the child, if only as a source of income. I cannot doubt that they had really persuaded themselves that she somehow lived without food. Unfortunately, in a short chapter it is impossible to give details, but the oath which, as they declared, they both had taken never again to press her to eat, must have been founded upon the experience they had had at the beginning of her illness two years before, when, as the mother said, the very sight of food brought on an attack, which at that date was of a very alarming nature. On the day of her death, Dr. Davies, the only medical man who had been a witness to those early seizures, decided not to attempt to give her nourishment, though he had the father's permission to do so. He thought, apparently, that she was now too weak, and that the shock of trying to force food upon her would extinguish prematurely the frail spark of life which remained. What is more, it seems to me most probable that Sarah herself in her normal personality was convinced she took no food. She did not show the slightest reluctance to submit to the new and more rigid inquiry. Not one of the nurses was conscious of any trace of resentment in the child s manner. She was not detected in any trick. I am therefore inclined to suggest that she was able to live with extraordinarily little nourishment, and that when she swallowed food, another (undetected) personality had supervened—the four intermittent personalities of Mollie Fancher will perhaps be fresh in the reader's memory—of whose procedure the normal self had no knowledge. Just as Theresa Neumann in ecstasy can swallow the Host which it would be impossible to give her in her normal state, so poor Sarah Jacob, in another personality, may have been able to take food without difficulty. The unwonted conditions created by the constant presence of two nurses, or by the absence of the little sister who usually slept with her, may sufficiently account for the fact that during the period of observation the secondary personality did not emerge.

2

The case of poor little Sarah Jacob recounted above does not by any means stand alone. There have been many child fasters, and though most of them lived two or three centuries ago, some were observed in circumstances which make it difficult to maintain that imposture was always present. One of the most curious examples is that of Jean Godeau, of Vauprofonde near Sens, in France. He was born towards the end of 1602, or early in 1603, and died of pneumonia on April 16, 1616. The case attracted a good deal of attention because it was taken up by M. Simeon de Provancheres, who enjoyed the title of "medecin du roy," and was in touch with many distinguished people. An account of de Provancheres, as an eminent physician and author, will be found in Michaud's *Biographie Universelle*. When the child died, the doctor published a history of the case which went through four editions in a few months. There had evidently been much talk previously about the fasting boy, for he was taken to be shown to the Duke de Montmorenci, Constable of France, sometime before the latter's death in 1614, and shortly afterwards he and his father were similarly summoned to satisfy the curiosity of the Duke de Vendome (son of Henri IV) and a large company. He had also been at Fontainebleau, and had there been inspected by the Queen Mother (Marie de Medici) and her little son, Louis XIII. I do not know that this notoriety affords any guarantee against imposture, but it must have had the effect of making those amongst whom he lived more on the alert to detect any consumption of food by stealth, and de Provancheres must have realized that, if fraud were discovered, his own reputation in endorsing the marvel as genuine was bound to suffer considerably.

In the little treatise which contains this history there is much more space devoted to theorizing, in accord with obsolete medical axioms, than is given to the evidence of facts. At the same time the author clearly manifests his conviction that the boy had lived for more than four years without eating or drinking, and also his sense that this was an astounding marvel which could not be credited without full investigation. He had the child to stay with him in his house at Sens on five different occasions, and during these visits nothing suspicious was discovered; but the time there spent seems to have been relatively brief, and on the only visit of which any detail is given his stay lasted but five days. Jean's behaviour seems at first to have been shy and rather uncouth, but the doctor treated him tactfully, and before long the lad felt at home in his new surroundings. It is stated that he resented the very sight of food and it made him irritable to be questioned about his not eating. There were also curious features in the case. No signs of emaciation were discernible, and, though not very intelligent, Jean was physically active and was interested in any strange things which were shown him. M. de Provancheres avers that for more than four years there were no excreta of any sort, but one wonders how he could make sure of this. On the other hand, during this period the boy fell ill, and for fifteen months was confined to bed, but at the end of this interval, on Low Sunday, 1614, he suddenly got up without the help of anyone. There was no one in the house at the time but his little sister, and she ran off in a fright to tell her mother, who was visiting a neighbour. After that date, however, Jean went about freely and had no relapse. We are even told that in his father's company he made his way from Vauprofonde to Joigny, a distance of "trois petites lieues"—shall we say six or seven miles?—though he was not carried by his father, and had no beast to ride upon.

Little Jean Godeau died, as said above, in April 1616. Just three weeks before, he had been brought by his father to see M. de Provancheres. Though he had grown very little, he was remarkably full of life and vigour, and went about everywhere. On his return home he seems to have caught a chill. In the burning fever of his last illness he would put his lips to a vessel of water to cool them but he drank nothing. M. de Provanchères was unfortunately prevented from being present at the autopsy which was performed after the boy's death. He tells us, however, that it was made by very skilful surgeons, and he quotes in some detail the results communicated to him. According to this account the surgeons discovered that the upper portion of the oesophagus was constricted in such a way that nothing could pass into the stomach.

Strangely enough, they declared that the other extremity of the alimentary canal was similarly compressed so that no waste products of digestion could have found an outlet. Even supposing that these observations were quite accurate, we do not, of course, know how long this condition of things had been in existence, but it can hardly have supervened suddenly at the very end, and its presence would fully account for the child's inability to take any form of nourishment. We have also to remember that however backward medical science may have been in the seventeenth century so far as regards the treatment of disease and the theories formulated, the surgeons of that day were very good anatomists.

Subjects for dissection were easily obtainable, and the very fact that the pathology of the period was so unsatisfactory would have led students to pay more attention to that form of experimental investigation in which there was really something exact to be learned. In any case death does not seem to have come to little Jean Godeau from lack of food, but from a form of inflammation which in our own day still proves fatal to thousands and thousands of well-nourished people in the very prime of life. It may be interesting to print in a footnote the Latin inscription which Dr. de Provanchères composed for a monument, set up apparently at his own expense in the city of Sens. One thing seems certain, both from this inscription and from the whole narrative, viz., that for nearly five years before his death the child was universally believed to take neither food nor drink. The physical compression of the oesophagus which caused this disinclination must already have begun to make itself felt, and even if he did obtain some nourishment by stealth the quantity must have been very small. Nevertheless, just as in the case of little Sarah Jacob, there were no signs of emaciation. M.

de Provanchères seems rightly to lay stress upon this fact as something very surprising. Is it possible that in the course of a century or two the views now prevalent with regard to nutrition and metabolism may be revolutionized by discoveries as far-reaching in their consequences as those of Sir J. J. Thomson, Rutherford, Planck, and Hertz concerning the constitution of matter?

As already stated, examples of children alleged to have lived without eating or drinking are numerous, and in some of these cases there seems to have been really effective observation and control. Of Apollonia Schreier and Margaret Seyfrit an account has already been given above and I have also referred in the same chapter to the memorial drawn up in the eighteenth century at the instance of Prosper Lambertini (Pope Benedict XIV) by the medical faculty of Bologna, in which, while fully recognizing the likelihood of imposture, credulity and mal-observation, the doctor consulted still uphold the genuineness of certain well-attested examples of long abstinence from food though no supernatural causation could be reasonably supposed. This memorial, which Benedict XIV printed as an appendix to his great work on Beatification and Canonization, cannot be regarded as wholly out of date, for Dr. A. Corradi, the editor of an authoritative scientific periodical of Italy, the *Annali Universali di Medicina*, described it in 1880 as *bella e severa dissertazione*. It would, however, be superfluous to cite other instances such as that of Maria Jehnfeli (eighteenth century) or of Catherine of Schmidweiler (sixteenth century), etc., for no fuller information is accessible to me than in the case of those previously dealt with.

Let us rather turn to an example nearer home, though this is not concerned with a child, but with a very old woman. In the book, Tours in Wales, of the famous Welsh antiquary, Thomas Pennant, the author, speaking of Barmouth in Merionethshire, describes how, on July 18th, 1770, he rowed up the estuary to land near Dolgelly, and at a farm called Taddyn Bach:

> Found the object of my excursion, Mary Thomas, who was boarded here, and kept with great humanity and neatness. She was of the age of forty-seven, of good countenance, very pale, thin, but not so much emaciated as might have been expected, ... her eyes weak, her voice low. She is deprived of the use of her lower extremities, and quite bed-ridden; her pulse rather strong, her intellects clear and sensible. On examining her, she informed me that at the age of seven, she had some eruptions like the measles, which grew confluent and universal.... After this she

was seized, at spring and fall, with swellings and inflammations, during which time she was confined to her bed; but in the intervals could walk about, and once went to Holywell, in hopes of cure.

When she was about twenty-seven years of age she was attacked with the same complaint, but in a more violent manner, and during two years and a half remained insensible, and took no manner of nourishment, notwithstanding her friends forced open her mouth with a spoon, to get something down; but the moment the spoon was taken away, her teeth met and closed with vast snapping and violence; during that time she flung up great quantities of blood.

She well remembers the return of her senses, and her knowledge of everybody about her. She thought that she had slept but a night, and asked her mother whether she had given her anything the day before, for she found herself very hungry. Meat was brought to her; but so far from being able to take anything solid, she could scarcely swallow a spoonful of thin whey. From this time, she continued seven years and a half without any food or liquid, excepting sufficient of the latter to moisten her lips. At the end of this period, she again fancied herself hungry and desired an egg, of which she got down the quantity of a nut kernel. About this time she requested to receive the sacrament; which she did by having a crumb of bread steeped in the wine. She now takes for her daily subsistence a bit of bread weighing about two pennyweights seven grains, and drinks a wine-glass of water; sometimes a spoonful of wine, but frequently abstaining whole days from foods and liquid. She sleeps very indifferently: the ordinary functions of nature are very small and very seldom performed. Her attendant told me that her disposition of mind was mild, her temper even; that she was very religious and very fervent in prayer.

The next mention I have been able to find of Mary Thomas belongs to a period thirty-two years later, and occurs in the account of a visit paid to her by an artist of that date, James Ward, a famous animal painter, who was elected an Associate of the Royal Academy in 1807 and R.A. in 1811. He seems to have been making a tour in Wales, and after reading Pennant's book found that the fasting woman there spoken of was still living. With some difficulty he discovered her whereabouts, but in his short interview with her he was considerably hampered by his ignorance of Welsh and by the difficulty of finding a satisfactory interpreter. Still, he satisfied his curiosity, and in the account he subsequently published he wrote as follows:

> At this time Mary Thomas was of the age of seventy-seven [*sic*]: tranquil, collected and resigned. Through the medium of my interpreter, she freely answered the following questions.
>
> "Do you abstain from every kind of food?"
>
> "Yes."
>
> "Are there any evacuations?"
>
> "None at all."
>
> "Do you ever attempt to swallow?"
>
> "Yes, but my stomach throws up whatever I take immediately."
>
> "Have you much pain?"
>
> "For two years I have never been without it, but I am now free from it."

She put my hand upon her chest, which produced the sensation of its being placed on a skeleton. Her legs and thighs were quite useless and doubled under her, her arms were drawn up towards her shoulders at an acute angle ... I was informed that during a period of ten years ... she had been in a state of torpor, unconscious of her own existence, and that during this long interval she took no sustenance of any kind.

Mr. Ward adds further:

> At this time I met at Sir Robert Vaughan's the Rev. Mr. Lloyd, who informed me that he had often administered the sacrament to Mary Thomas, and that on these occasions he always found her religious feelings so exalted, and her mind so uncommon as to raise his admiration and respect. As far, indeed, as I could judge, piety and resignation were the prominent features of her character.

How far we can place confidence in these statements is a matter very difficult to determine. On the one hand it is plain that when we are dealing with a bed-ridden woman in this condition, those who tended her must have known whether she was supplied with nourishment or not, and whether there was anything which gave proof of the passage of food. On the other hand we are bound to suspect a tendency to say that an invalid who took very little, ate nothing at all. Mr. James Ward remained sufficiently long with the sufferer to complete a crayon sketch of her which is reproduced in the thin folio volume he subsequently published. It was probably this personal contact with Mary Thomas which led James Ward a year or two later to take much interest in the case of another alleged fasting woman, Ann Moore, of Tutbury, to whom reference was made above. Like many others among his contemporaries, the Royal Academician, influenced, no doubt, by his previous experience, made no difficulty about accepting this impostor's claim to have lived without nourishment. But before the final exposure of her fraud, he managed in the year 1807 to pay Mary Thomas a second visit. Taking a young friend with him on this occasion, he tells us that at Dolgelly they had considerable difficulty in finding anyone to show them the way to her cottage. Eventually they came across an old man who acted as a guide to visitors who came to climb Cader Idris. He brought them to the house, and there he saw Mary Thomas once more, "little changed, though she was lying in a new position. She declared she could not last long. On asking her if she did not wish to be released by death, she replied with calmness: "'When it is the will of God.'"

Mr. Ward then continues:

> The persons about her, who were not the same under whose care she was at my former visit in 1802, could give me but little satisfactory information respecting her early history. I pressed upon them the circumstances formerly stated to me, all of which they corroborated, particularly the ten years of torpidity, and they were convinced that she received no sustenance during that period. They admitted, however, that she did now make an effort, occasionally, to swallow a bit of bread, and drink a little water. But the quantity taken did not exceed one ounce of bread in a fortnight, and one wine glass of water, taken at intervals in minute quantities; and even this did not remain in her stomach. Every effort to swallow produced sickness, and whatever she took into her stomach, was *generally* rejected immediately, or never remained more than ten minutes.

Mr. Ward also came across an old man, Lewis Evans, who had known Mary Thomas for fifty years. He declared that the circumstances above related were strictly true, explaining, however, that "she had been very long in the state in which I saw her, but that custom had so blinded curiosity that she was little regarded by the neighbours."

The book written by James Ward was on the point of appearing, when news came to him of the rigorous test to which the pretensions of Ann Moore had been subjected. Under close observation she broke down on the ninth day of this surveillance, and made a clean breast of the whole imposture, attempting no disguise as to the money she had gained by it. Mr. Ward, who had coupled her case with that of Mary Thomas, was plainly much disconcerted, and before his book was actually put in circulation he added the following note:

> The case of Mary Thomas which forms the first part of the preceding pages, is, by the confession of Ann Moore, rendered at least doubtful; and, I am sorry to add, that a full and satisfactory development of the particulars is prevented by her [Mary Thomas's] death, which occurred some time in the last year. But it does not follow as a natural consequence that Mary Thomas must be an impostor because the Tutbury woman has confessed her guilt. The whole tenor of her conduct, with the absence of obvious motives for the practice of fraud, do yet give a degree of authenticity to her history. Having, however, been so far deceived by the plausibility and earnest asseveration of Ann Moore, I feel that the evidence in favour of Mary Thomas has been much weakened.

The cases were, in fact, very different. Ann Moore was a woman of loose character, who had a confederate in the daughter who was living with her, and who made a good deal of money by the fraud she practised. Nothing of the sort can be affirmed of Mary Thomas. She dwelt too far away from any centre of population to attract a notable stream of visitors. There is not the slightest hint of any pecuniary advantage which accrued to her, and her age and infirmity precluded her from taking an active part in any trickery. Her story in some respects presents a remarkable parallel to those of Mollie Fancher and Mrs. Croad, which have been discussed earlier in these pages. The reader may remember that both these afflicted neurasthenics, while remaining prisoners in bed for many years, are stated by those in attendance to have eaten practically nothing. When writing of Mollie Fancher, I had not come across the booklet of Dr. W. H. Hammond, *Fasting Girls; their Physiology and Pathology* (New York, 1879), in which the writer, described as "Professor of Diseases of the Mind and Nervous System in the Medical Department of the University of the City of New York, and in the University of Vermont, etc. set out to crush and extinguish by force of ridicule the contention advanced in certain newspapers that Miss Mollie Fancher lived without taking food. This distinguished physician, the author of many works on mental disorders, had devoted a chapter in a previous book of his to the subject of "Fasting Girls." So when the strange case of Mollie Fancher came to be exploited by certain New York journals, Dr. Hammond at once plunged into the fray, and in the superior tone of the scientific expert—this was, it will be remembered, the age of Huxley and Tyndall—denounced the absurdity of those who believed that anyone could live without eating. In his attack upon Drs. Speir, Ormiston, and the others who proclaimed their belief that Miss Fancher actually took no food or next to nothing, he has occasion to cite the reporter of *The Sun*, a New York journal which had obtained an interview with the physicians in question. Through this channel we learn that this newspaper had recorded on November 24, 1878 opinions expressed by Dr. S. Fleet Speir and by Dr. Ormiston in the following terms. To Dr. Speir the question was put: Is it true that she has not partaken of food in all these thirteen years?"

> "No, I cannot say that she has not; I have not been constantly with her for thirteen years; she may have taken food in my absence. Her friends have used every device to make her take nourishment. Food has been forced upon her, and artificial means have been resorted to that it might be carried to her stomach. Nevertheless the amount in the aggregate must have been very small in all these years."

> "You have considered the case of such extraordinary importance as to take many physicians to see it?"

> "I have, and it has excited very much of attention. I have letters about it from far and near, and the medical journals have asked for information."

Similarly we learn from the same journal that Dr. Ormiston, who had been one of Miss Fancher's physicians from the first, and who had visited her in all the phases of her long illness—

Said that he was convinced that there could be no deception. He could find no motive for it, and he did not believe she had attempted it. As to her not partaking of food, he had, with Dr. Speir, made tests that satisfied him that she ate no more than she pretended to, and in the aggregate it had not, in all these years, amounted to more than the quantity eaten at a single meal by a healthy man.

When we remember that in spite of Dr. Hammond's tirade the two physicians here interviewed stood to their guns and fourteen years later, having remained in attendance upon the case during the intervening period, reaffirmed the same conviction, we can hardly doubt that they were thoroughly in earnest. They had been continuously in contact with the afflicted girl, they knew her character, her helpless condition and the integrity of those who waited upon her. Dr. Hammond had never set eyes upon Miss Fancher and was arguing only from principles which led him to proclaim that Louise Lateau and all the other Catholic mystics who were believed to live without food were either mendacious or self-deluded.

The cases of Marie Furtner, Janet McLeod, and Josephine Durand are, to my thinking, exceptionally convincing. Even if we allow for some exaggeration, it seems that we are forced to admit that quite a number of people in whose case no miraculous intervention can be supposed, have lived for years upon a pittance of nourishing food which could be measured only by ounces, and upon this evidence we shall be forced to admit the justness of the conclusion of Pope Benedict XIV that the mere continuation of life, when food and drink are withheld, cannot be safely assumed to be due to supernatural causes.

CHAPTER XVII
MULTIPLICATION OF FOOD

On June 4th, 1933, which was Whit-Sunday, a devoted secular priest of Poitou, who died a century ago, by name Andrew Hubert Foumet, was canonized in St. Peter's with all the usual solemnities. Although he was the founder of a widely spread religious Congregation, "les Filles de la Croix," his life is probably little known to the majority of Catholics in this country. I happened to be in Rome at the time of the canonization and I was greatly impressed by the vast crowds, mainly French pilgrims, who came to attend the ceremony, as well as by the multitudes who thronged the piazza to witness the illumination of the basilica in the evening. St. Andrew Fournet, who lived to the age of eighty-two, had had charge of a parish at the outbreak of the French Revolution. He had been forced to take refuge for a time in Spain, but returned to his flock at the risk of his life, celebrating Mass by stealth in a barn and setting a marvellous example of holiness and zeal. There was no note of extravagance in his piety. Simplicity, straightforwardness and an all-embracing charity were the keynotes of his character; but, as so often happens, God seems to have rewarded his singleness of heart by extraordinary marks of favour. This is not the place to speak of his efforts to revive the faith of the people after the Revolution, of his miracles of healing, or of the fervour which, on certain occasions, when he was preaching or saying Mass, raised him bodily from the ground before the eyes of all; but he is credited also with another form of prodigy not infrequently met with in the lives of those generous givers who divest themselves of all things in order to supply the temporal or spiritual needs of the forsaken and the destitute. Having before me a copy of the official summary of the evidence presented to the Congregation of Sacred Rites in the cause of St. Andrew's beatification, I cannot, perhaps, better introduce this phenomenon of the multiplication of food than by translating part of the depositions of one or two of the witnesses who gave testimony in the process. They were nuns of that Congregation of the Filles de la Croix, which the Saint, in conjunction with their heroic mother, the Venerable Elizabeth Bidder, had founded m dire poverty to instruct the spiritually neglected peasantry of Western France. Let me take first the sworn statement of Sister Bartholomew who, for the first thirteen years of her religious life, had St. Andrew for her confessor and lived continually under his eye at La Puye.

She begins this part of her evidence by saying: "The servant of God, so far as I know, never had ecstasies. He did not like us to talk of such things as visions, and he kept watch, with a certain mistrust, over Sisters who showed any tendency to have revelations or raptures. Then, after touching on other matters, she goes on:

> While I was still at La Puye, there was committed to my charge the care of the granary and of the laundry. It was, so far as I remember m 1824, but I cannot be quite certain of the year. Just before the feast of St. John the Baptist we were looking forward to the annual retreat, which is made by all the Sisters in common, when our good Mother Elizabeth [this was the Venerable foundress, Elizabeth Bichier] told Father Andrew that it was impossible for that year to assemble all the Sisters who were scattered throughout different parishes of the diocese and in other parts of France, because we had not corn enough in the house and there was no money to buy more. The Father answered: "My child, where is your faith? Do you think God's arm is shortened, and that He cannot do here what He did of old when, as we read in the Gospels, multiplied the loaves? Go and write to the Sisters to come to me retreat. Afterwards, the Servant of God climbed up to the granary where I was occupied at the moment with one of the other sisters. As usual he brought his manservant with him, for it was his custom never to come among the Sisters without a companion.

> He walked around the two little heaps of grain, one of which consisted of wheat, and the other of barley. I do not remember whether he

blessed the heaps, nor can I say exactly, not having measured them, how many bushels (moggi) they each might have contained, but the heaps were very small. The Servant of God then told our good Mother a second time to get the Sisters to come for the retreat without delay. Accordingly, they arrived in due course and, when added to those in the mother house and to a score of orphans, they brought up the number that had to be fed to about 200. I went every day to the granary to take the corn that was needed and during two months and a half, in other words, from the beginning of July to the middle of September, I drew my supplies from those two little heaps without their showing any sign of diminution. I cannot say for certain how long the Sisters from the parishes remained at the mother house. As I mentioned before, I had not measured the two heaps. They contained, perhaps, more than twenty bushels, but certainly not as much as forty, and this was the quantity which, for two hundred people, would at the very most, have lasted a week. In the middle of September I quitted La Puye to go to Angles, leaving the two heaps of grain in just the same condition in which they were when the Servant of God came to the granary. I heard it said that the same two heaps continued to serve the needs of the Community until Christmas, but I cannot depose to this as a witness, for, as I have already stated, I left in the middle of September.

This statement, made, of course, on oath, seems good and straightforward evidence. It is only unfortunate that Sister Bartholomew, then seventy-three years old, was speaking of events which had happened some thirty-four years earlier. But let us turn to another witness, Sister Mamertus (mde Marie Henriette Giraud), aged sixty-eight, who, after confirming, along with several others, the universal conviction among the nuns of the truth of the story just recounted, goes on to describe a personal experience of her own which occurred a year or two later. Sister Bartholomew had been succeeded in her office of looking after the granary by a Sister Mary Magdalen, who was no longer living when these depositions were taken, and Sister Mamertus narrates:

Sister Mary Magdalen came to me one morning and said: "I don't know what to do. There are not more than eight or ten bushels of corn left in the granary at the very most." Our good Mother Elizabeth [the foundress] happened to be away from home at the time; she was, I think, in Paris. Sister Mary Magdalen, accordingly, went off to the

Father and told him that the community would soon be without bread. He replied: (My dear child, how little faith you have! God's Providence watches over our needs. Send the corn you have to be ground." Shortly afterwards I noticed that the Servant of God was making his way to the granary, and my curiosity having been aroused by what Sister Mary Magdalen had told me, I followed him. He went into the granary and closed the door behind him, but I was able to watch him through the keyhole. He knelt down beside the little heap that was there, and began to pray very fervently. I don't know that he did anything else, because in my fear that he himself might catch me spying and might reprimand me for my curiosity, I withdrew almost at once. But in due course, after the Father had left, Sister Mary Magdalen came along with the men from the mill, and I heard from her on that same day that she measured the corn and found that there were sixty bushels.

There was much other testimony given to the same effect, but it is of a less satisfactory kind, and consists mainly of statements of what the nuns or the neighbouring clergy and laity had heard from the lips of those who had been in intimate relation with St. Andrew during his lifetime. Let me add that there seems to be no lack of instances of a similar multiplication of food, etc., in such comparatively modern conditions as those which prevailed in the last century. For example, the Blessed Gaspar del Bufalo and his early companions had a hard struggle with poverty in founding the Congregation of the Precious Blood which, from 1815 onwards, did so much to revive religious fervour in the more neglected parishes of rural Italy. Father Blaise Valentini, who was later on Superior General, giving evidence in the process of beatification, records how, when he himself was in charge of the Mother House of San Felice at Giano during Don Gaspar's absence, he wrote to the founder that it was impossible to pay his way. There were, he declared, no other resources but the stones with which the place abounded. He received in reply only the message: "Bless the stones and they will turn into piastres." Though he took this answer for a jest, it happened shortly afterwards that he was pressed for the immediate payment of a debt. He called the young man who acted as bursar and they looked in the money-box together. There they found fifty "bajocchi"—let us say pence— and no more. This sum was hopelessly insufficient for their purpose, so Father Valentini, at his wits' end, bethought him of the message he had received, and in a spirit of faith pronounced a blessing over the coppers before him.

Then they proceeded to count the money once more, and behold they found there five piastres (dollars) and five "paoli " (francs) the exact sum that was needed. The piastres were coins from the mint of Pius VII, and Father Valentini, in his sworn deposition, insists forcibly upon the impossibility of any oversight or trickery which could explain the mystery.

However much we may be disposed to suspect these witnesses of malobservation or of a too ready credulity, the number of such stories, many of them resting on direct and first-hand evidence, is surprisingly great. A good example, which again, in this case, was attested on oath in the beatification process, will be found recorded in most of the Lives of St. Don Bosco. I translate for brevity's sake the account given by Father Lemoyne. The incident occurred in 1860 in one of the Salesian houses, that of Turin, where a large number of young students were in training.

There was no bread in the house and the baker had refused to supply any more until his bill, which had run up to 10,000 lire, had been settled. They informed Don Bosco, who was then in the confessional, that there was nothing for breakfast, he sent word that they were to collect what little bread could be found and that he would himself come and distribute it. A young man, Francis Dalmazzo, who overheard this discussion [he had been making his confession at the time] was the attentive witness of what then happened. "I found a place," he said, "where I could overlook the scene, just behind Don Bosco, who was preparing to distribute the rolls (pagnottelle) to the 300 lads as they came up. I fixed my eyes upon the basket at once, and I saw that it contained fifteen or twenty rolls at the most. Meanwhile, Don Bosco carried out the distribution, and to my great surprise, I saw the same quantity remain which had been there from the first, though no other rolls had been brought and the basket had not been changed." The impression made by this prodigy was so great that the young man in question who had made up his mind to return home that very morning because he found the life too severe, stayed where he was and became a Salesian.

Still more remarkable were two cases of the multiplication of foodstuffs which were accepted as miracles for the beatification of Ste. Germaine Cousin. Though Ste. Germaine had died in 1601, she was not beatified until 1854, and it was while her cause, held up by circumstances of no interest in the present connexion, was again being pushed forward, that the marvels referred to took place at the

Good Shepherd Convent of Bourges, in 1845 and following years. In a chapter like the present it is, unfortunately, difficult to give those full details which are necessary if the reader is to appreciate the strength of the evidence. I must content myself here with a summary statement, such, for example, as that which may be found in the recent English Life of the Blessed Mother Pelletier. We are told that in the Bourges convent during the exceptionally severe winter of 1845, the flour in the granary was running short.

> There were 116 persons to feed; starvation stared them in the face. The Superior bethought herself of the Venerable Germaine Cousin .... Novenas were made in her honour. . . . Daily a portion of her Life was read, and medals in her honour were distributed, one being hung in the bake-house. The Sisters in charge of the bakery were in the habit of kneading twelve bushels of flour every five days, which made twenty large loaves. The Superior told them henceforth only to use eight bushels and Venerable Germaine was begged to make good the rest. They did not obtain the desired result, the bread only lasted three days. Nor were the second and third attempts more successful. Without losing faith, the Superior prayed to the little Saint "Make the quantity of flour suffice for twenty loaves. . . " The miracle took place. The first batch, though made from only eight bushels, produced twenty large loaves weighing from twenty to twenty-two pounds each. The second batch was even more marvellous; in kneading the dough it swelled to such an extent that it overflowed the trough in a few moments. The Sisters filled the oven with this, and then calculated they still had twenty pounds of paste left, without counting the yeast, and yet only four bushels of flour had been used. Five days later the same multiplication took place with two batches.
>
> This was but the commencement of a series of favours received through Venerable Germaine. In the convent granary was a supply of flour which at most would last, with care, for two months.
>
> After a few weeks the Sisters remarked that although the quantity had lessened, the diminution was quite out of proportion to the amount used. "Wishing," as they said, "to surprise the little Saint red-handed in a miracle," at the beginning of February they began to measure the flour. Again at the end of a fortnight they did the same. The flour weighed exactly what it had done a fortnight before, in spite of two

bakings, so without knowing it the Community had been drawing direct from the granaries of Divine Providence. From November 1845 until February 1846 Ste. Germaine had practised every form of multiplication both of bread and flour.

But the fact is that prodigies of this type are of frequent occurrence in our hagiographical records. For some, of course, the evidence is very inadequate, but others are well attested. Prosper Lambertini (Pope Benedict XIV) in his great treatise on the Beatification and Canonization of Saints, devotes a chapter to the subject, and fully recognizes the supernatural character of these multiplications where proper precautions are taken against errors of malobservation, etc. He himself cites a number of cases in which such incidents are expressly described as miraculous in the bulls of canonization of well-known saints. He mentions in particular St. Clare of Assisi, St. Richard of Chichester, St. Teresa of Avila, St. Frances of Rome, St. Mary Magdalen of Pazzi, St. Pius V, etc., and refers to other cases connected with the names of St. Thomas of Villanova, St. Lewis Bertrand, St. Rose of Lima, St. Aloysius Gonzaga, St. Francis Xavier, St. Cunegund, St. Elizabeth, Queen of Portugal, and several more.

Neither can it be said that marvellous phenomena of this kind are restricted to those whose claim to holiness has been ratified by the official sanction of the Church. There are certain mystics who seem, if I may so speak, to specialize in this type of manifestation, and who light-heartedly have not hesitated to put their wonderful powers to the test upon very slight occasion. Perhaps the most remarkable instance I have come across is that of the Carmelite, Father Angiolo Paoli, who was born of a humble family in Tuscany in 1642, and died at Rome in 1720. It is true that the cause of his beatification was introduced, that the depositions of witnesses were duly taken upon oath, and a full Life published in 1756 which is based upon "the Ordinary and Apostolic processes, already approved by the Holy See." Father Angiolo is, therefore, correctly described therein as "the Venerable Servant of God," but though he died more than 200 years ago, no decree of beatification seems ever to have been issued, and the cause has apparently been dropped. But the long chapter which deals with "his gift of multiplying food and drink in the service of the poor and the sick," confirmed, as it seems to be, in each recorded example, by a reference to the evidence given in the processes, tells us some very curious things. Among Angiolo's friends was a certain Father Castelli, then General of the Servites, and on one occasion, after paying him a visit, the good Carmelite remarked as he took his leave:

> "Father General, what will you give me for my poor? " The other answered that he had nothing he could give him. "No," said Father Angiolo, "I only want a few biscuits and sweets for my poor sick people." "You should have them very willingly," said the other, "if I had any, but I have none." To which Father Angiolo rejoined, "Well, I will try this cupboard; I know I shall find something." Thereupon opening a cupboard in the wall where Father General's Socius used to put napkins and other table utensils, he discovered some scraps of bread (*tozzi di pane*) which all together did not amount to the volume of a small loaf (*pagnotta*) and a half, or two at the utmost, and these he stowed away in his left sleeve. Then the General, and Father Master Maggini who was also present, remarked smilingly: "You haven't got much loot after all, Father Angiolo." When they had talked awhile, he set off home, and the General and Father Maggini decided to accompany him. The three had got as far as the Torre de' Conti, when Father Angiolo began giving alms to various persons of both sexes, big and little, who begged from him, distributing the scraps of bread which he had taken from the General's room, but without breaking them up in any way. He continued to do this all the way to S. Pietro in Vincoli; at which Father Maggini was so astounded that he turned to him and said: "Good gracious! Have you a basketful of bread in your sleeve? You have been giving alms to all the beggars in the city with the bread you got from Father General." Father Angiolo made no answer, but the General, who had watched that happened, made a sign to his companion to hold his tongue.

The account goes on to describe how Father Angiolo, during a long walk, gave to everyone who begged of him, and adds that "with these few scraps of bread, hardly enough to give seven or eight people, he satisfied from fifty to sixty poor beggars who all went away contented with the alms they had received." As Father Maggini commented, "he had nothing but the scraps he had taken from the General, and we, who kept our eyes upon him the whole time, knew that he never stopped in the street to receive a fresh supply from anyone whatever."

All this was clearly a work of genuine charity to the poor in which it is easy to believe that God may have co-operated with His servant even by working a surprising miracle. What is less intelligible is the confidence shown by Father Angiolo that he would at any time be seconded in his efforts to provide an agreeable little picnic for the well-to-do friends who helped him in some of his good works.

On a particularly hot day in June, the Father seems to have taken a group of them to a sort of garden party where he provided lettuces and radishes to make a salad, with a tart, as well as a basket of strawberries for dessert, all which, in that season of drought, were practically unprocurable. These things, wherever he obtained them, sufficed, without being exhausted, to afford refreshment for a dozen people, while a single decanter of wine was freely partaken of by all and yet remained half-full. On another similar occasion, a single flask of wine (*un fiasco di vino della misura di un bocale*) was provided for twenty-five people who drank tumblers-full, some one, some two, some of them only a half, but at the end the flask had still been only half emptied, and a Signor Bellotti, whose statement is quoted from the process of beatification, deposed that "three bocali [decanters] of wine at the very least would not have sufficed to provide a drink for them all, and yet with only half a bocale the whole party quenched their thirst and were satisfied."

Still more surprising are some of the innumerable incidents of the same kind which Father Cacciari has recounted, so surprising, in fact, that one asks oneself whether the whole Life is not an audacious fiction. This, however, is impossible. It is a substantial volume printed in Rome in the pontificate of Benedict XIV, dedicated to the Cardinal Archbishop of Ferrara, and furnished with the necessary imprimatur, as well as with a number of highly laudatory approbations. Many people are cited as witnesses who must have been well known in ecclesiastical circles, and there is a series of references to the Sommario of the beatification process, a printed volume which I know to exist, though, unfortunately, I have not had access to a copy. Over and over again we have accounts of the division of some delicacy into portions which it was easy to count, and then of its subsequent distribution to three or four times the number of hospital patients, each receiving one of these portions entire. But perhaps the most curious feature of all is the assured conviction Father Angiolo seems to have possessed that, if he wished to give to the poor, or only to refresh his thirsty friends with a cup of wine or a handful of fruit, supernatural means would always be fortheoming—and, in fact, according to the testimony of many respectable eye-witnesses, always were fortheoming to enable him to gratify his desire, no matter how great the number of recipients.

Even in more modern times we occasionally find mention of miraculous multiplications which could not be attributed to any real necessity. In the process of Blessed Joseph Cottolengo there is a story told of an incident witnessed by a Canon Vogliotti and another priest. Someone had brought Cottolengo a little basket of cherries which he distributed, handful by handful, to the whole crowd of his students. They sufficed for all, but the amount thus distributed was quite out of proportion to anything which the basket could possibly have contained. The Canon and his companion went away astonished, but by no means disedified, to observe how Divine Providence seemed, "to be taking part in a game" (*quasi scherzare*) with the generous-hearted servant of God.

It would be an endless task to try to compile a list of devout people in whose Lives such multiplications of food are recorded. I will content myself, therefore, with a bare reference to the admirably documented Life of the Venerable Gertrude Salandri (1748), to that of the Alcantarine friar, the Blessed Andrew Ibernon (1602), of the Capuchin, Blessed Crispin of Viterbo (1750), who seemed to delight in such miracles, but made things uncomfortable for those who did not give, and of the mystic of Roveredo, the Venerable Giovanna Maria della Croce (1673). There are many more famous examples, such, for instance, as those recorded of St. Veronica Giuliani, St. Paul of the Cross and St. Lidwina of Schiedam, but what has here been said will suffice to show that this alleged multiplication of food, though the evidence may often be inadequate, cannot lightly be dismissed as a phenomenon belonging merely to the domain of legend.

Paperbacks also available from White Crow Books

Elsa Barker—*Letters from a Living Dead Man*
ISBN 978-1-907355-83-7

Elsa Barker—*War Letters from the Living Dead Man*
ISBN 978-1-907355-85-1

Elsa Barker—*Last Letters from the Living Dead Man*
ISBN 978-1-907355-87-5

Richard Maurice Bucke—*Cosmic Consciousness*
ISBN 978-1-907355-10-3

Arthur Conan Doyle—*The Edge of the Unknown*
ISBN 978-1-907355-14-1

Arthur Conan Doyle—*The New Revelation*
ISBN 978-1-907355-12-7

Arthur Conan Doyle—*The Vital Message*
ISBN 978-1-907355-13-4

Arthur Conan Doyle with Simon Parke—*Conversations with Arthur Conan Doyle*
ISBN 978-1-907355-80-6

Meister Eckhart with Simon Parke—*Conversations with Meister Eckhart*
ISBN 978-1-907355-18-9

D. D. Home—*Incidents in my Life Part 1*
ISBN 978-1-907355-15-8

Mme. Dunglas Home; edited, with an Introduction, by Sir Arthur Conan Doyle—*D. D. Home: His Life and Mission*
ISBN 978-1-907355-16-5

Edward C. Randall—*Frontiers of the Afterlife*
ISBN 978-1-907355-30-1

Rebecca Ruter Springer—*Intra Muros: My Dream of Heaven*
ISBN 978-1-907355-11-0

Leo Tolstoy, edited by Simon Parke—*Forbidden Words*
ISBN 978-1-907355-00-4

Leo Tolstoy—*A Confession*
ISBN 978-1-907355-24-0

Leo Tolstoy—*The Gospel in Brief*
ISBN 978-1-907355-22-6

Leo Tolstoy—*The Kingdom of God is Within You*
ISBN 978-1-907355-27-1

Leo Tolstoy—*My Religion: What I Believe*
ISBN 978-1-907355-23-3

Leo Tolstoy—*On Life*
ISBN 978-1-907355-91-2

Leo Tolstoy—*Twenty-three Tales*
ISBN 978-1-907355-29-5

Leo Tolstoy—*What is Religion and other writings*
ISBN 978-1-907355-28-8

Leo Tolstoy—*Work While Ye Have the Light*
ISBN 978-1-907355-26-4

Leo Tolstoy—*The Death of Ivan Ilyich*
ISBN 978-1-907661-10-5

Leo Tolstoy—*Resurrection*
ISBN 978-1-907661-09-9

Leo Tolstoy with Simon Parke—*Conversations with Tolstoy*
ISBN 978-1-907355-25-7

Howard Williams with an Introduction by Leo Tolstoy—*The Ethics of Diet: An Anthology of Vegetarian Thought*
ISBN 978-1-907355-21-9

Vincent Van Gogh with Simon Parke—*Conversations with Van Gogh*
ISBN 978-1-907355-95-0

Wolfgang Amadeus Mozart with Simon Parke—*Conversations with Mozart*
ISBN 978-1-907661-38-9

Jesus of Nazareth with Simon Parke—
Conversations with Jesus of Nazareth
ISBN 978-1-907661-41-9

Thomas à Kempis with Simon
Parke—*The Imitation of Christ*
ISBN 978-1-907661-58-7

Julian of Norwich with Simon
Parke—*Revelations of Divine Love*
ISBN 978-1-907661-88-4

Allan Kardec—*The Spirits Book*
ISBN 978-1-907355-98-1

Allan Kardec—*The Book on Mediums*
ISBN 978-1-907661-75-4

Emanuel Swedenborg—*Heaven and Hell*
ISBN 978-1-907661-55-6

P.D. Ouspensky—*Tertium Organum:
The Third Canon of Thought*
ISBN 978-1-907661-47-1

Dwight Goddard—*A Buddhist Bible*
ISBN 978-1-907661-44-0

Michael Tymn—*The Afterlife Revealed*
ISBN 978-1-970661-90-7

Michael Tymn—*Transcending the
Titanic: Beyond Death's Door*
ISBN 978-1-908733-02-3

Guy L. Playfair—*If This Be Magic*
ISBN 978-1-907661-84-6

Guy L. Playfair—*The Flying Cow*
ISBN 978-1-907661-94-5

Guy L. Playfair —*This House is Haunted*
ISBN 978-1-907661-78-5

Carl Wickland, M.D.—
Thirty Years Among the Dead
ISBN 978-1-907661-72-3

John E. Mack—*Passport to the Cosmos*
ISBN 978-1-907661-81-5

Peter & Elizabeth Fenwick—
The Truth in the Light
ISBN 978-1-908733-08-5

Erlendur Haraldsson—
Modern Miracles
ISBN 978-1-908733-25-2

Erlendur Haraldsson—
At the Hour of Death
ISBN 978-1-908733-27-6

Erlendur Haraldsson—
The Departed Among the Living
ISBN 978-1-908733-29-0

Brian Inglis—*Science and Parascience*
ISBN 978-1-908733-18-4

Brian Inglis—*Natural and Supernatural:
A History of the Paranormal*
ISBN 978-1-908733-20-7

Ernest Holmes—*The Science of Mind*
ISBN 978-1-908733-10-8

Victor & Wendy Zammit —*A Lawyer
Presents the Evidence For the Afterlife*
ISBN 978-1-908733-22-1

Casper S. Yost—*Patience
Worth: A Psychic Mystery*
ISBN 978-1-908733-06-1

William Usborne Moore—
Glimpses of the Next State
ISBN 978-1-907661-01-3

William Usborne Moore—
The Voices
ISBN 978-1-908733-04-7

John W. White—
The Highest State of Consciousness
ISBN 978-1-908733-31-3

Stafford Betty—
The Imprisoned Splendor
ISBN 978-1-907661-98-3

Paul Pearsall, Ph.D. —
Super Joy
ISBN 978-1-908733-16-0

All titles available as eBooks, and selected titles available in Hardback and Audiobook formats from www.whitecrowbooks.com

www.ingramcontent.com/pod-product-compliance
Lightning Source LLC
Chambersburg PA
CBHW022112080426
42734CB00006B/105